Lecture Notes in Computer Science   14593

Founding Editors

Gerhard Goos
Juris Hartmanis

Editorial Board Members

The series Lecture Notes in Computer Science (LNCS), including its subseries Lecture Notes in Artificial Intelligence (LNAI) and Lecture Notes in Bioinformatics (LNBI), has established itself as a medium for the publication of new developments in computer science and information technology research, teaching, and education.

LNCS enjoys close cooperation with the computer science R & D community, the series counts many renowned academics among its volume editors and paper authors, and collaborates with prestigious societies. Its mission is to serve this international community by providing an invaluable service, mainly focused on the publication of conference and workshop proceedings and postproceedings. LNCS commenced publication in 1973.

Fang-Lue Zhang · Andrei Sharf
Editors

Computational Visual Media

12th International Conference, CVM 2024
Wellington, New Zealand, April 10–12, 2024
Proceedings, Part II

 Springer

Editors
Fang-Lue Zhang 🆔
Victoria University of Wellington
Wellington, New Zealand

Andrei Sharf 🆔
Ben-Gurion University
Be'er Sheva, Israel

ISSN 0302-9743　　　　　　　ISSN 1611-3349　(electronic)
Lecture Notes in Computer Science
ISBN 978-981-97-2091-0　　　ISBN 978-981-97-2092-7　(eBook)
https://doi.org/10.1007/978-981-97-2092-7

This Springer imprint is published by the registered company Springer Nature Singapore Pte Ltd.
The registered company address is: 152 Beach Road, #21-01/04 Gateway East, Singapore 189721, Singapore

Paper in this product is recyclable.

Preface

The 12th International Conference on Computational Visual Media (CVM 2024) was held on April 10–12, 2024, in Wellington, New Zealand. The Computational Visual Media Conference series aims to provide a major international forum for exchanging novel research ideas and significant practical results that both underpin and apply Visual Media. With the rapid progress of Internet technology, large-scale visual data can be found on the Internet, bringing significant opportunities for novel processing of visual information, as well as commercial applications. The primary rationale for this conference series is to target cross-disciplinary research that amalgamates aspects of computer graphics, computer vision, machine learning, image processing, video processing, visualization, and geometric computing. Original research is sought in areas concerning the classification, composition, retrieval, synthesis, and understanding of visual media.

CVM 2024 received 212 valid paper submissions. With the help of 181 international experts in our Program Committee, we were able to evaluate each submission in a rigorous review process. By matching the paper's research topics with the expertise and preferences of committee members, the program co-chairs assigned three reviewers from the Program Committee to each paper. After receiving a sufficient number of reviews, the program co-chairs made decisions on whether a paper was conditionally accepted as a journal paper, conditionally accepted as a poster paper, or rejected. The program co-chairs shepherded conditionally accepted poster papers to incorporate the required revisions. In cases where a program chair or committee member is a co-author, we assigned the paper to other program chairs or committee members to ensure an unbiased reviewing and decision-making process.

Out of 212 submissions, 29 papers were accepted as journal track papers and 34 papers were published in the proceedings (acceptance rate: 29.7%). The journal track papers were conditionally accepted for publication in several journals in the field of computer graphics and visual media.

We would like to thank all the people who generously offered their time and energy to contribute to the review process and the successful technical program of CVM 2024, including the authors of all submitted papers, the members of the CVM 2024 Program Committees, and all the external reviewers. We also thank Shi-Min Hu for his support and help regarding conference management and communication with the journals, Taijiang Mu for his handling and setup of the submission system, and Springer Nature for their support in publishing the CVM 2024 proceedings in LNCS. Finally, we would like to thank the CVM Steering Committee for their great support.

February 2024

Fang-Lue Zhang
Andrei Sharf

Organization

General Chairs

Neil A. Dodgson   Victoria University of Wellington, New Zealand
Wenping Wang   Texas A&M University, USA

Program Committee Chairs

Fang-Lue Zhang   Victoria University of Wellington, New Zealand
Andrei Sharf   Ben-Gurion University, Israel

Program Committee

Amit Bermano	Tel-Aviv University, Israel
Mikhail Bessmeltsev	University of Montreal, Canada
Jun-Xiong Cai	Huawei Technologies Co., Ltd, China
Mingwei Cao	Anhui University, China
Yanpei Cao	Tencent, China
Andrew Chalmers	Victoria University of Wellington, New Zealand
Kang Chen	Netease, China
Shuyu Chen	Institute of Computing Technology, CAS, China
Weikai Chen	Tencent US, USA
Xuejin Chen	University of Science and Technology of China, China
Xuelin Chen	Tencent AI Lab, China
Mingming Cheng	Nankai University, China
Zhanglin Cheng	University of Chinese Academy of Sciences, China
Ming-Te Chi	Chengchi University, Taiwan
Hung-Kuo Chu	Tsing Hua University, Hsinchu, Taiwan
Yoshinori Dobashi	Hokkaido University, Japan
Tianyang Dong	Zhejiang University of Technology, China
Weiming Dong	Institute of Automation, CAS, China
Zhengjun Du	Qinghai University, China
Jihad El-Sana	Ben-Gurion University of the Negev, Israel
Dengping Fan	ETH Zurich, Switzerland
Hui Fang	Loughborough University, UK

Xiaonan Fang	Macau University of Science and Technology, China
Bin Feng	Huazhong University of Science and Technology, China
Hongbo Fu	City University of Hong Kong, China
Lin Gao	Institute of Computing Technology, CAS, China
Jie Guo	Nanjing University, China
Xiaohu Guo	University of Texas at Dallas, USA
Yulan Guo	Sun Yat-sen University, China
Peter Hall	Bath University, UK
Junhui Hou	City University of Hong Kong, China
Qibin Hou	Nankai University, China
Ruizhen Hu	Shenzhen University, China
Shi-Min Hu	Tsinghua University, China
Haibin Huang	Kuaishou Technology, China
Jiahui Huang	Nvidia, USA
Shi-Sheng Huang	Beijing Normal University, China
Sharon X. Huang	Penn State University, USA
Xiaogang Jin	Zhejiang University, China
Jiri Kosinka	University of Groningen, Netherlands
Yu-Kun Lai	Cardiff University, UK
Yoonsang Lee	Dartmouth College, USA
Chenhui Li	East China Normal University, China
Chengfeng Li	Swansea University, UK
Chongyi Li	Nankai University, China
Haodong Li	Shenzhen University, China
Jinjiang Li	Shandong Institute of Business and Technology, China
Manyi Li	Shandong University, China
Zhen Li	The Chinese University of Hong Kong, China
Zhouhui Lian	Peking University, China
I-Chen Lin	Chiao Tung University, Taiwan
Juncheng Liu	Victoria University of Wellington, New Zealand
Juncong Lin	Xiamen University, China
Hantao Liu	Cardiff University, UK
Libin Liu	Peking University, China
Ligang Liu	University of Science and Technology of China, China
Shuaicheng Liu	University of Electronic Science and Technology of China, China
Tiantian Liu	Taichi Graphics, China
Mengyuan Liu	Peking University, China

Xialei Liu	Nankai University, China
Cewu Lu	Shanghai Jiao Tong University, China
Chongyang Ma	Kuaishou Technology, China
Kwan-Liu Ma	University of California at Davis, USA
Lizhuang Ma	Shanghai Jiao Tong University, China
Rui Ma	Jilin University, China
Weiyin Ma	City University of Hong Kong, China
Tianlei Ma	Zhengzhou University, China
Tai-Jiang Mu	Tsinghua University, China
Yongwei Nie	South China University of Technology, China
Kai Niu	Northwest University of Technology, China
Marta Ortin	DIVE Medical, Spain
Fabio Pellacini	Sapienza University of Rome, Italy
Yifan Peng	The University of Hong Kong, China
Yipeng Qin	Cardiff University, UK
Weize Quan	Institute of Automation, CAS, China
Bo Ren	Nankai University, China
Paul Rosin	Cardiff University, UK
Eston Schweickart	Weta Digital, New Zealand
Tianjia Shao	Zhejiang University, China
Bin Sheng	Shanghai Jiaotong University, China
Gurprit Singh	Max Planck Institute, Germany
Peng Song	Singapore University of Technology and Design, Singapore
Ran Song	Shandong University, China
Hang Su	Tsinghua University, China
Jianchao Tan	Kuaishou Technology, China
Shunquan Tan	Shenzhen University, China
Min Tang	Zhejiang University, China
Ruofeng Tong	Zhejiang University, China
Yu-Ting Tsai	Yuan Ze University, Taiwan
Beibei Wang	Nanjing University of Science and Technology, China
Charlie Wang	The University of Manchester, UK
He Wang	University of Leeds, UK
Lizhi Wang	Beijing Institute of Technology, China
Miao Wang	Beihang University, China
Peng-Shuai Wang	Peking University, China
Rui Wang	Zhejiang University, China
Xin Wang	Tsinghua University, China
Xu Wang	Shenzhen University, China
Yunhai Wang	Shandong University, China

Tien-Tsin Wong	The Chinese University of Hong Kong, China
Chenyun Wu	Waymo, USA
Hongzhi Wu	Zhejiang University, China
Jun Wu	Delft University of Technology, Netherlands
Burkhard Wuensche	University of Auckland, New Zealand
Jiazhi Xia	Central South University, China
Guanyu Xing	Sichuan University, China
Kai Xu	National University of Defense Technology, China
Kun Xu	Tsinghua University, China
Pengfei Xu	Shenzhen University, China
Qunce Xu	Tsinghua University, China
Senzhe Xu	Tsinghua University, China
Wei-Wei Xu	Zhejiang University, China
Dongming Yan	Institute of Automation, CAS, China
Lingqi Yan	University of California, Santa Barbara, USA
Jufeng Yang	Nankai University, China
Yin Yang	Clemson University, USA
Yong-Liang Yang	University of Bath, UK
Hantao Yao	Institute of Automation, CAS, China
Ran Yi	Shanghai Jiaotong, China
Renjiao Yi	National University of Defense Technology, China
Ming Zeng	Xiamen University, China
Haotian Zhang	Nvidia, USA
Jessica Zhang	Carnegie Mellon University, USA
Lei Zhang	Beijing Institute of Technology, China
Qi Zhang	Shenzhen University, China
Songhai Zhang	Tsinghua University, China
Xiaoyan Zhang	Shenzhen University, China
Yun Zhang	Communication University of Zhejiang, China
Junhong Zhao	Victoria University of Wellington, New Zealand
Xi Zhao	Xi'an Jiaotong University, China
Jianmin Zheng	Nanyang Technological University, Singapore
Wei-Shi Zheng	Sun Yat-sen University, China
Zichun Zhong	Wayne State University, USA
Xiaowei Zhou	Zhejiang University, China
Yang Zhou	Shenzhen University, China
Yu Zhou	Shenzhen University, China
Yuanfeng Zhou	Shandong University, China
Zhe Zhu	Purdue University, USA
Qiang Zou	Zhejiang University, China

Contents – Part II

Contents – Part I

Rendering and Animation

User Interactions

Facial Images

Zero-Shot Real Facial Attribute Separation and Transfer at Novel Views

Dingyun Zhang[1], Heyuan Li[2], and Juyong Zhang[1(✉)]

[1] University of Science and Technology of China, Hefei, Anhui, China
minnie_vantrin@mail.ustc.edu.cn
[2] The Chinese University of Hong Kong, Shenzhen, Guangdong, China

Abstract. Real-time and zero-shot attribute separation of a given real-face image, allowing attribute transfer and rendering at novel views without the aid of multi-view information, has been demonstrated to be beneficial in real-world scenarios. In this work, we propose an alternating optimization framework and train it on attribute-blending (*i.e.*, unstructured) monocular images. Our framework leverages a pre-trained facial attribute encoder and a 3D-representation face synthesis decoder (*e.g.*, HeadNeRF) to reinforce and guide each other mutually. This allows the facial attribute encoder to better express and separate facial attributes and the face synthesis decoder to render faces with better image similarity and attribute consistency.

Keywords: neural rendering · alternating training · novel view synthesis · facial attribute transfer

1 Introduction

Real-time and zero-shot attribute separation of a given real face, along with attribute transfer and rendering at novel views without the aid of multi-view information, opens the door to a wide range of creative applications, such as talking face animation, face cloning and editing, training feature classifiers and generating synthetic images. In other words, it is desirable that a face avatar model could achieve a good balance in (1) **Zero-shot**, *i.e.*, for a test image, the model does not require optimization of network parameters or conditioned latent codes; (2) **Attribute transfer**, *i.e.*, for a test image, the model is capable of separating the attributes of the face into orthogonal spaces as much as possible and transferring a specific attribute, such as facial identity shape, expression, texture, illumination, hairstyle, and head pose, to another test face, without affecting the other facial attributes of the latter; (3) **Real-time**, *i.e.*, for a test image, the model completes the facial attribute separation and novel-view synthesis via an end-to-end forward pass; (4) **Realistic**, *i.e.*, the model can render facial appearance and expression details as rich as possible, rather than just rendering areas excluding hair, mouth interior and ears.

We investigate the research on neural face avatars and summarize previous works in Table 1. Explicit face models constructed from registered meshes have been widely

F.-L. Zhang and A. Sharf (Eds.): CVM 2024, LNCS 14593, pp. 3–26, 2024.
https://doi.org/10.1007/978-981-97-2092-7_1

Table 1. A summary of current face avatar methods. Δ_1 denotes that the facial attribute transfer could not guarantee a good attribute separation. Δ_2 denotes that the facial attribute transfer can only be performed on expression or head pose. Δ_3 denotes that the facial attribute transfer requires inputting a 3D scan, including the mesh. Δ_4 denotes that the model conducts novel-view synthesis of a real image via an end-to-end forward pass but is unable to separate the facial attributes.

Scheme	Methods	Zero-shot	Transfer	Real-time	Realistic
Explicit 3D Models	[4,24,43,74,86]		✓		
	[12,18,21]	✓	✓	✓	
3D-aware GANs	[10,11,17,28,52]				✓
	[15]	✓		Δ_4	✓
	[16,63,69,71,77]		Δ_1		✓
Personalized Avatars	[2,22,27,54,87]		Δ_2		✓
Talking Head	[19,35,45,60,64]		Δ_2		✓
Implicit Face Models	[32,89]		✓		✓
	[23]		✓		
	[76,81]		Δ_3		✓
	Ours	✓	✓	✓	✓

used in modeling face avatars. However, due to the limitations of the overly simplistic principal component analysis method and the difficulty in obtaining real scans, most of these methods can only model and render the facial region, excluding the hair, mouth interior, and ears. Recent 3D-aware GANs [26] using implicit representations or StyleGAN-based methods can synthesize realistic faces. However, most of these methods require time-consuming GAN inversion for a real face image. For their synthesized fake face images, some models [10,11,17,28,52] are unable to separate and transfer facial attributes, while most of others [16,63,69,71,77] exhibit visible incompleteness in separating certain attributes (Fig. 1). Personalized avatars and talking head methods are often trained in a person-specific manner and can only separate facial expressions and head pose attributes. Recent models using implicit representations either require optimizing latent attribute codes during testing [23,32,89] or rely on mesh input for model fitting [76,81], thereby limiting their generalization ability to unseen identities and expressions.

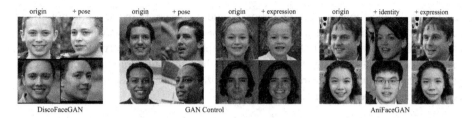

Fig. 1. Recent controllable 3D-aware GAN methods have shown limitations over their synthesized fake faces in separating a certain facial attribute from others. 'origin' refers to the face image synthesized from a random code by the corresponding model. '+' means changing a specific attribute code from the original random code. DiscoFaceGAN [16], for instance, does not achieve thorough separation, as controlling for head pose noticeably impacts the expression. GAN Control [63], when manipulating head pose or expression over the original image, significantly affects other facial attributes. AniFaceGAN [77] exhibits a significant influence of identity (*i.e.*, facial identity shape and texture) attribute on the expression attribute, whereas controlling for expression sometimes affects identity.

In this paper, inspired by the face reconstruction works [20,42], the learning of the facial attribute encoder to separately parameterize the attributes from a real image and the adaptation of the 3D-representation face synthesis decoder to render better a face image based on the conditioned codes is solved jointly using an expectation-maximization-like [13] procedure, where we train the two networks in an alternating manner. The motivation for doing so is based on the observation that during the adaptation of the face synthesis decoder, it optimizes the attribute labels of the face, which could guide the facial attribute encoder to promote the semantic expressiveness of attribute parameter prediction. Conversely, attribute parameter representation of a face with better expressiveness and separation can, in turn, serve as better initialized conditioned codes for the 3D-aware decoder to render a face image that has image similarity and attribute consistency with the ground truth image. Thus, both aspects can be considered as mutually dependent, similar to a chicken-and-egg relationship.

In our task, we construct the facial attribute encoder based on a face recognition network, face reconstruction networks, and a hairstyle encoding network and pre-train them. HeadNeRF [32], a 3D-aware face model based on neural implicit representation, is chosen as the face synthesis decoder. We use these models as an example of our alternating training approach in enhancing the facial attribute representation and separation capability of the encoder and the rendering quality of the face synthesis decoder. The alternating training in each round consists of two steps. In the first step, we update the network parameters and conditioned attribute labels of the face synthesis decoder, while in the second step, we update the parameters of the facial attribute encoder. We only train our model on attribute-blending (*i.e.*, unstructured) and non-multi-view 2D in-the-wild datasets. Considering that lacking the aid of multi-view information for a single identity can significantly degrade the high-frequency rendering quality of neural radiance field (NeRF) [34], we incorporate a pre-trained blind face restoration network, Difface [84], as a refinement network during the inference stage. This addition aims to enhance the rendering quality of the face synthesis decoder, making the rendering results for the face images more realistic. In order to ensure fairness, we do not utilize refined images during experimental testing. Instead, we qualitatively showcase them as references. Inspired by [16,19,63,71], we employ both self-supervised disentanglement loss and cycle-consistency loss as part of the alternating training. Through relevant experiments, we demonstrate the results of the proposed method. In summary, our contributions can be summarized as follows:

– We extend the alternating training algorithm to the focus that to enhance the ability of the facial attribute encoder in representing and separating attributes, and to improve the rendering quality of the 3D-aware face model.
– We present a model that could realize real-time and zero-shot attribute separation of a given real face, allowing attribute transfer and rendering at novel views without the aid of multi-view information.
– We demonstrate the proposed method through relevant experiments.

2   Related Works

2.1   Explicit Face Morphable Models

Explicit representation is widely used for 3D face modeling. It is typically built by performing Principal Component Analysis (PCA) on numerous registered 3D facial scans and represents a 3D face as the linear combination of a set of orthogonal bases. Blanz and Vetter [4] first introduced the concept of a 3D Morphable Face Model (3DMM). Since then, many efforts [1,5,6,9,24,86] have been devoted to improving the performance of 3DMM by either improving the quality of captured face scans or the structure of 3D face model. However, acquiring registered 3D data is laborious, and most of the existing methods [4–6,9,24,43,58] can only render the texture of the facial region, excluding the hair, mouth interior, and ears. Meanwhile, the rendered faces produced by these methods often exhibit visible differences in identity or expression compared to the original faces, resulting in the sense of artificiality. In addition, most models are optimization-based for fitting a real image, requiring solving the inverse rendering equation and, therefore, not real-time.

Recent state-of-the-art regression-based methods [12,18,21] typically render face images with estimated illumination, texture, and geometry of the face model using a differentiable renderer [44,59] and compare the synthetic images with the inputs. Such an analysis-by-synthesis strategy facilitates the demand for in-the-wild images and help to recover geometric details. However, their separation of attributes is visibly incomplete, as changing the parameter of one attribute would significantly affect other facial attributes of the rendered face.

2.2   3D-Aware Implicit Models

3D-aware methods aim to learn a model that can explicitly control the camera viewpoints of the synthesized content. Neural implicit functions have been used in numerous works [46,47,51,53,67,68] to represent 3D scenes or faces. In contrast to explicit representations (*e.g.*, meshes or voxel grids), neural implicit representation is well-suited to model complex surfaces and realistic textures. Recent advances in 3D-aware GANs [26] have enabled the synthesis of realistic multi-view fake faces. Some of these approaches [10,11,17,28,50,52] utilize neural implicit representations but do not focus on separating facial attributes. Additionally, rendering novel views of real images requires time-consuming GAN inversion [61,82] to optimize the input codes. Very recently, some work [15] trained an encoder for the GAN [17] to map a real image to the corresponding latent code. However, it does not address the limitation of real-time separation of facial attributes and attribute transfer. Some implicit [41,62,69,72,77] or 2D-based [8,16,25,38,49,55,63,71] 3D-aware controllable GANs incorporate 3DMM priors to achieve attribute separation control of generated fake faces. However, as shown in Fig. 1, these models often exhibit visible deficiencies in attribute separation control.

Recent works focused on rendering animatable personalized avatars [2,3,22,27,54, 87,88,90] or talking head animation [19,30,35,45,60,64,65,79] often need to train a specific model for one or two persons from monocular videos and can only separate facial expressions and head pose attributes. Other works [57,75] could render static personalized avatars from multi-view images with high fidelity but could not separate facial attributes.

[32] propose the first 3D-aware NeRF-based [34] parametric face model, which controls the facial identity shape, expression, texture, illumination, and head pose of the rendered face by corresponding latent codes. [23,89] propose a model in a similar way. [89] is unable to render the hair region and control the illumination. [23] is incapable of rendering the hair, mouth interior, and ear regions, and it does not further divide the identity attribute into facial identity shape and texture attributes. Although these models enable identity and expression editing by adjusting the associated 3DMM parameters, the limited representation ability of latent parameters bound their ability to recover some facial details in the original frames and their generalization ability to unseen identities, expressions, and head poses. Moreover, to fit a real face image, these methods require time-consuming optimization for the initialized latent attribute codes. [81] propose i3DMM, a deep implicit 3D morphable model that can be animated by learned latent codes. [76] define the deformation filed by standard linear blend skinning (LBS), which allows the avatars to be directly animated by FLAME parameters. However, to fit a real face image, both methods require the simultaneous acquisition of the face image and its corresponding mesh to perform latent attribute code optimization and render the face.

2.3 Disentanglement Representation Learning

Disentangled representation learning (DRL) for face images has been vividly studied in the past. Compared to the real-time attribute separation of a real face, most 3D-aware controllable GANs emphasize seeking an interpretable and highly disentangled latent space of the generator, allowing for explicit control over the facial attributes of the synthesized fake faces. A common tactic is to hallucinate or render synthetic images varying in different attributes and then jointly learn the attribute differences from these images. [49] disentangles head pose and identity with unsupervised learning using 3D convolutions and rigid feature transformations. [16] proposes imitative-contrastive learning to mimic the 3DMM rendering process by the generative model. A similar strategy has also been adopted with concurrent and follow-up works [8, 25, 55, 70, 71]. [38] uses a custom 3D image rendering pipeline to generate an annotated synthetic dataset. This dataset is later used to acquire controls matching the synthetic ground truth, allowing [38] to add controls. [63] utilizes a pairwise contrastive loss to understand the positive and negative relationships between synthetic training pairs for different attribute spaces. One-shot talking head model [19] employs a similar contrastive learning strategy to separate expression and head pose from other facial attributes.

Following [16], the implicit representation [69, 77] mimics mesh deformation to achieve direct control of the identity, expression, and head pose. [72] explicitly models the deformation fields to enforce the disentanglement between geometry (*i.e.*, identity shape and expression) and appearance (*i.e.*, texture and illumination). [23, 32, 76, 80, 89] rely on attribute-disentangled multi-view annotated datasets to learn the attribute separation of the latent space, with the training data for the first five models being collected professionally in a laboratory setting. For a real face image, some regression-based face reconstruction methods [18, 21] predict the parameters of facial attributes through end-to-end unsupervised training or further incorporating the designed consistency losses.

3   Method

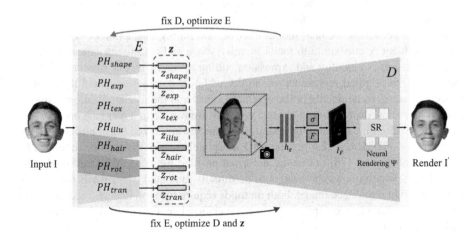

Fig. 2. Method overview. Our model consists of a facial attribute encoder, E, composed of seven facial attribute prediction heads (PH), and a face synthesis decoder, D. E takes in a given face image I and projects it into the latent space divided into separate attribute sub-spaces, generating 1-D feature vector **z**. The conditioned attribute codes **z** are fed to the volumetric-representation face synthesis decoder D to render a reconstruction I'. We alternately trained the decoder D and encoder E using an EM-like heuristic algorithm, enabling them to synergize and provide each other with informative guides or priors. See text in Sect. 3 for details.

First, in Sect. 3.1, we present the model architecture that can perform zero-shot facial attribute separation and transfer at novel views from a real face image after training. Then, in Sect. 3.2, we introduce how to train our model using an EM-like heuristic training algorithm. In Sect. 3.3, we show the model parameters initialization of the EM-like alternating training procedure. Finally, in Sect. 3.4, we demonstrate how to refine the rendered face image using an additional pre-trained face restoration network and clarify its role in our paper.

3.1   Model Architecture

As illustrated in Fig. 2, our model consists of a facial attribute encoder E that takes in a face image I and projects it into the latent space divided into separate attribute sub-spaces, generating a 1-D feature vector $\mathbf{z} = [\mathbf{z}_{shape}, \mathbf{z}_{exp}, \mathbf{z}_{tex}, \mathbf{z}_{illu}, \mathbf{z}_{hair}, \mathbf{z}_{rot}, \mathbf{z}_{tran}]$ about attribute facial identity shape, expression, texture, illumination (lighting) under the Spherical Harmonics illumination model [56], hairstyle (hair shape), face pose rotation and translation under the standard perspective camera model for projecting a point in 3D space onto the image plane, respectively. The feature vector $\mathbf{z}$ is fed as a condition code to a volumetric-representation face synthesis decoder D to render a reconstruction I'.

Facial Attribute Encoder. As illustrated in Fig. 2, the facial attribute encoder E comprises seven prediction heads: PH_{shape} for identity shape, PH_{exp} for expression, PH_{tex} for texture, PH_{illu} for illumination, PH_{hair} for hairstyle, PH_{rot} for face pose rotation, and PH_{tran} for face pose translation. The PH_{shape} utilizes Adaface [36], a face recognition network with ResNet50 [31] as its backbone. The prediction heads PH_{exp}, PH_{tex}, PH_{illu}, PH_{rot}, and PH_{tran} all employ single image reconstruction network, R-Net, from Deep3DFace [18]. Many previous methods [12,18,21,23,32,89] for parameterizing and rendering a real face image at novel views did not consider a specific representation and rendering of the hairstyle. Recently, there have been methods [76,81] that collect or utilize full photogrammetric attribute-disentangled head scans, including mesh, for training purposes, enabling the inclusion of the hair component during rendering. However, GANHead [76] is unable to parameterize hairstyle through latent attribute code, and the hairstyle latent code of i3DMM [81] can only take discrete values - short, long, cap1, or cap2, which to some extent restricts the expressiveness of hairstyle latent code in rendering the real face hairstyle. We adopt the shape encoding network of the 2D hair editing GAN CtrlHair [29] as the predicting head PH_{hair} for hairstyle, which allows us to avoid using professional handcrafted 3D face scan data and instead train on a large number of easily accessible unstructured 2D face images. Although CtrlHair's shape encoding network cannot attribute separate the hairstyle and head pose, meaning that the feature vector obtained from the network for the same hairstyle under different head poses often has significant differences, our experiments demonstrate that after training the entire model, this entanglement can be canceled out. The dimensions of the latent attribute codes are as follows: $\mathbf{z}_{shape} \in \mathbb{R}^{512}$, $\mathbf{z}_{exp} \in \mathbb{R}^{64}$, $\mathbf{z}_{tex} \in \mathbb{R}^{80}$, $\mathbf{z}_{illu} \in \mathbb{R}^{27}$, $\mathbf{z}_{hair} \in \mathbb{R}^{16}$, $\mathbf{z}_{rot} \in \mathbb{R}^{3}$, and $\mathbf{z}_{tran} \in \mathbb{R}^{3}$, where rotation is defined using Euler angles.

Face Synthesis Decoder. The face synthesis decoder D utilized is HeadNeRF [32], a model that integrates 3DMM with the NeRF representation and is capable of synthesizing 3D-aware faces conditioned on 3DMM attributes - identity shape, expression, texture, illumination, and head pose. The modification we made was to adjust the dimensions of the conditioned attribute code to match the output dimensions of the facial attribute encoder E instead of using the previous dimension of HeadNeRF, which was set to facilitate initializing the latent codes with the solution obtained by solving inverse rendering optimization based on [74]. We additionally include the hairstyle attribute code z_{hair} into the conditioned latent codes of HeadNeRF.

Next, we briefly introduce the architecture of the face synthesis decoder D that we have employed. D is a NeRF-based parametric model, which can render an image I' with specified attributes for the given condition codes. It is formulated as: $I' = D(z_{shape}, z_{exp}, z_{tex}, z_{illu}, z_{hair}, z_{rot}, z_{tran})$, where z_{rot} is then transformed to a rotation matrix $\mathbf{R} \in \mathbb{R}^{3 \times 3}$. The MLP-based implicit neural function h_ϵ of NeRF is formulated as:

$$h_\epsilon : (\gamma(\mathbf{x}), z_{shape}, z_{exp}, z_{tex}, z_{illu}, z_{hair}) \mapsto (\sigma, F), \tag{1}$$

where ϵ represents the network parameters, $\gamma(\cdot)$ is the positional encoding in NeRF [34], and $\mathbf{x} \in \mathbb{R}^3$ is a 3D point sampled from one casted camera ray. h_ϵ outputs the density value σ at $\mathbf{x}$ and an intermediate feature vector $F(\mathbf{x}) \in \mathbb{R}^{256}$. Then the 2D feature map $I_F \in \mathbb{R}^{256 \times 32 \times 32}$ is obtained by performing the volume rendering:

$$I_F(r) = \int_0^\infty w(t) \cdot F(r(t)) dt, \tag{2}$$

where $w(t) = exp(-\int_0^t \sigma(r(s)) ds) \cdot \sigma(r(t))$ and $r(t)$ is a ray emitted from the camera center. I_F then passes through a 2D neural rendering network Ψ whose design concept is inspired by StyleNeRF [28], progressively increasing its resolution, and eventually be transformed into the rendered image $I' \in \mathbb{R}^{3 \times 1024 \times 1024}$.

3.2   EM-Like Alternating Training Procedure

Due to the mutual dependencies between the facial attribute encoder E and face synthesis decoder D, we employ an EM-like heuristic training strategy, where we train the two networks in an alternating manner. Similar to other EM-like training strategies, our training process starts from a rough initialization of the model parameters (as described in Sect. 3.3). We then alternately optimize the face synthesis decoder D and facial attribute encoder E, as described in the following.

Training the Face Synthesis Decoder. When training the face synthesis decoder D, the parameters of the facial attribute encoder E are fixed, and only D and the conditioned attribute codes z are optimized. At this step, we assume that the facial attribute encoder E is already good enough, meaning it can separate and parameterize the facial attribute of a real image into the latent space orthogonally as much as possible, and the resulting latent attribute code z exhibits sufficient expressiveness for facial characteristics.

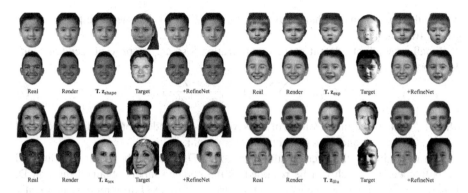

Fig. 3. Zero-shot attribute separation from a real image. 'Real' and 'Target' respectively represent the source and target ground truth real-face images. 'Render' represents the rendering result on the source image. 'T. z_*' denotes replacing the corresponding attribute code of the source image with that of the target image. '+RefineNet' means the results for the rendered images refined by the adopted face restoration network. Our model is capable of real-time attribute-separated representation and rendering a real-face image. The facial attribute encoder E separates various attributes of the face into an orthogonal latent space as much as possible and accurately represents them using latent codes. This allows the face synthesis decoder D to render a face that resembles the attributes of the real face image. During attribute transfer, the rendered face maintains similarity to the target face in the transferred attributes, while the unmodified attributes are preserved well. In this figure, we present examples of transferring identity shape, expression, texture, and illumination. See text in Sect. 4.2 for details.

The overall objective function of this step is:

$$\mathcal{L}_D = \mathcal{L}_{pix} + \mathcal{L}_{perc} + \mathcal{L}_{id} + \mathcal{L}_{reg}. \tag{3}$$

The photometric consistency term $\mathcal{L}_{pix}$ is a pixel-wise L1 distance measured between the synthesized image I' and the ground truth image I, which is formulated as:

$$\mathcal{L}_{pix} = \frac{1}{|M \odot I|} \|M \odot (I' - I)\|_1. \tag{4}$$

M is the head region mask of I and $\odot$ stands for a pixel-wise Hadamard product operator.

The perception-level loss $\mathcal{L}_{perc}$ measures perceptual and semantic differences between two images with an image classification network ϕ:

$$\mathcal{L}_{perc} = \sum_{i=1}^{5} \frac{1}{|\phi_i(I)|} \|\phi_i(I) - \phi_i(I')\|_1, \tag{5}$$

where i denotes the i-th layer of VGG19 [66] network pre-trained on ImageNet [39].

The face identity loss $\mathcal{L}_{id}$ is the cosine distance between the embeddings of a pre-trained face recognition network f [14]:

$$\mathcal{L}_{id} = 1 - \frac{f(I) \cdot f(I')}{\|f(I)\|_2 \|f(I')\|_2}. \tag{6}$$

We use this loss to ensure that the rendered image I' looks like the same person as the ground truth subject.

Finally, we adopt a latent space regularization loss $\mathcal{L}_{\text{reg}}$ to prevent facial attribute degeneration:

$$\mathcal{L}_{\text{reg}} = \sum_* \omega_* (1 - \frac{\mathbf{z}_* \cdot \mathbf{z}_*^0}{\|\mathbf{z}_*\|_2 \|\mathbf{z}_*^0\|_2}), \qquad (7)$$

where $\mathbf{z}_*^0$ denotes the initial values of the seven attribute codes obtained from the facial attribute encoder E, and ω_* represents the loss weight.

During training, the face synthesis decoder D updates the seven conditioned attribute codes $\mathbf{z}$, which can be regarded as the updated labels obtained through D. This step of training aims to encourage the attribute codes to fall in more semantically meaningful and attribute expressive location in the latent space while improving the consistency between the rendered face I' synthesized by face synthesis decoder and real face I, thereby enhancing the decoder's ability to represent a real face based on conditioned attribute codes.

Training the Facial Attribute Encoder. In the second step, we continue to optimize the parameters of the facial attribute encoder E while keeping the face synthesis decoder D fixed. At this step, we assume that the face synthesis decoder D and the updated latent attribute codes $\mathbf{z}^D$ obtained from the previous step are already good enough, meaning that D's latent space is smooth and meaningful, and the updated attribute codes have enough expressiveness for the ground truth face image, thereby could serve as labels for guiding the optimization of the facial attribute encoder E. The overall objective function of this step is:

$$\mathcal{L}_E = \lambda_{\text{cod}} \mathcal{L}_{\text{cod}} + \lambda_{\text{cyc}} \mathcal{L}_{\text{cyc}} + \lambda_{\text{dis}} \mathcal{L}_{\text{dis}} \qquad (8)$$

Real   Render   T. $\mathbf{z}_{hair}$ Target   +RefineNet   Real   Render   Novel-View Synthesis   +RefineNet

Fig. 4. Zero-shot attribute separation from a real image and novel-view synthesis. On the left side of this figure, we present examples of transferring the hairstyle. On the right side of this figure, we illustrate examples of synthesizing novel views of the rendered image from a single image by changing the pose. See text in Sect. 4.2 for details.

Code Consistency Loss. The code consistency loss $\mathcal{L}_{\text{cod}}$ is defined as the separate cosine distance between the parameterized attribute codes obtained by the encoder E for the ground truth image I and the seven updated conditioned attribute codes $\mathbf{z}_*^D$ obtained after the previous training step:

$$\mathcal{L}_{\text{cod}} = \sum_* \overline{\omega}_* \left(1 - \frac{\text{PH}_*(I) \cdot \mathbf{z}_*^D}{\|\text{PH}_*(I)\|_2 \|\mathbf{z}_*^D\|_2}\right). \qquad (9)$$

$\overline{\omega}_*$ represents the loss weight. We use the updated condition codes as labels to encourage the facial attribute encoder E in separating the attributes of real image I to more meaningful and expressive locations in the latent space.

Cycle-consistency Loss. The cycle-consistency loss computes the separate difference between the attribute codes of the ground truth image I predicted by the encoder E and those of the rendered image I':

$$\mathcal{L}_{\text{cyc}} = \sum_* \overline{\omega}_* \left(1 - \frac{\text{PH}_*(\text{I}) \cdot \text{PH}_*(\text{I}')}{\|\text{PH}_*(\text{I})\|_2 \|\text{PH}_*(\text{I}')\|_2} \right). \tag{10}$$

We use this loss to encourage the encoder E to predict more stable latent codes for facial attributes, and the rendered face I' conditioned on these latent codes should convey the corresponding attribute content of the input image I.

Disentanglement Loss. Following the concept in [16,70,71], given two latent attribute codes $\mathbf{z}_i = [\mathbf{z}_{a1}^i, ..., \mathbf{z}_{an}^i]$, $\mathbf{z}_j = [\mathbf{z}_{a1}^j, ..., \mathbf{z}_{an}^j]$ predicted by the attribute encoder E from the corresponding image I^i, I^j in a training batch, we randomly vary one attribute code of $\mathbf{z}_j$ while keeping others unchanged. By replacing $\mathbf{z}_{ak}^j$ with $\mathbf{z}_{ak}^i$, we obtain a new attribute code $\hat{\mathbf{z}}_j$. $\mathbf{z}_j$ and $\hat{\mathbf{z}}_j$ differ only at sub-code for attribute ak, and share the same sub-codes for attribute $al, \forall l \neq k$. For example, ak can represent facial identity shape. In an ideal situation, $\hat{\mathbf{z}}_j$ should retain the expression, texture, scene illumination, hairstyle, and head pose of $\mathbf{z}_j$, but should perform the identity shape specified in $\mathbf{z}_i$. $\hat{\text{I}^j} = \text{D}(\hat{\mathbf{z}}_j)$ corresponding to the image I^j should be modified according to the sub-code of $\mathbf{z}_i$.

Since we do not have ground truth for such a variation, *i.e.*, the image $\hat{\text{I}^j}$ is unknown, we employ supervision based on the disentanglement loss $\mathcal{L}_{\text{dis}}$. The decoded image $\hat{\text{I}^j}$ is again passed through the attribute encoder E to generate $E(\hat{\text{I}^j})$. The disentanglement loss $\mathcal{L}_{\text{dis}}$ enforces that $E(\hat{\text{I}^j})$ should have the same identity shape code as $\mathbf{z}_i$ and enforces consistency of the parameters that should not be changed by the performed edit operation. In the case of modifying identity shape values, the parameters that should not change are expression, texture, illumination, hairstyle, and head pose parameters. This leads to the disentanglement loss function:

$$\mathcal{L}_{\text{dis}} = \overline{\omega}_{ak} \left(1 - \frac{\mathbf{z}_{ak}^i \cdot \text{PH}_{ak}(\hat{\text{I}^j})}{\|\mathbf{z}_{ak}^i\|_2 \|\text{PH}_{ak}(\hat{\text{I}^j})\|_2} \right) \\ + \sum_{l \neq k} \overline{\omega}_{al} \left(1 - \frac{\mathbf{z}_{al}^j \cdot \text{PH}_{al}(\hat{\text{I}^j})}{\|\mathbf{z}_{al}^j\|_2 \|\text{PH}_{al}(\hat{\text{I}^j})\|_2} \right). \tag{11}$$

We perform the same operations in reverse order, *i.e.*, in addition to replacing $\mathbf{z}_{ak}^j$ of $\mathbf{z}_j$ with $\mathbf{z}_{ak}^i$, we also replace $\mathbf{z}_{ak}^i$ of $\mathbf{z}_i$ with $\mathbf{z}_{ak}^j$ and obtain a new attribute code $\hat{\mathbf{z}}_i$. The corresponding disentanglement loss will be calculated in the same way.

3.3 Model Parameters Initialization

As with every other EM-like training strategy, our training needs a proper initialization of the model parameters. To provide an initialization for the prediction heads of the facial attribute encoder E, we individually pre-trained the adopted prediction heads based on their official implementations, ensuring that they can provide certain semantic priors and attribute separability. After initializing the facial attribute encoder E, we trained the face synthesis decoder D for 10 epochs on the training set of the FFHQ dataset [33] using the method described in Sect. 3.2. This step was taken to allow decoder D to initially learn to understand the semantic information conveyed by conditioned attribute codes and acquire the ability to synthesize face images. Initially, the optimization of decoder D and conditioned latent codes will bring significant changes to the latter. Therefore, we then train the facial attribute encoder E using only the code consistency loss $\mathcal{L}_{cod}$ for 5 epochs to synchronize the semantics between E and D, ensuring the stability of subsequent formal training. Initializing the decoder's parameters only on the FFHQ training set may lead to instability during formal training on the complete mixed training set due to domain differences between datasets. However, since we pre-aligned the training data, such instability only appeared in a small number of images, and we excluded these images.

3.4   Rendering Refinement with Blind Face Restoration

In our paper, we use HeadNeRF [32] as an instance of the face synthesis decoder D, which mitigates the high computational cost of NeRF by first rendering low-resolution feature maps and then applying 2D CNNs for super-resolution. However, this structure suffers from a common issue of losing image details, possibly due to the black-box rendering of CNNs. Another major issue is that the NeRF architecture is suitable for novel-view rendering from multi-view images, but we use single-view attribute-blending training data, which is easier to obtain. Therefore, although HeadNeRF renders rich details on the multi-view data used in its work, the rendering effect on single-view images lacks high-frequency details, such as the texture of hair and fur, due to the lack of auxiliary multi-view information, resulting in overly smoothed rendered heads. On the other hand, it's common to apply refinement networks on top of the rendered images to generate more realistic texture details [78,89]. From the visual performance standpoint, we alleviate this limitation by employing a pre-trained real-time blind face restoration network called DifFace [84]. We feed the face I' rendered by our model into DifFace, which outputs refined image I'-refine of the same resolution. In order to ensure fairness, we do not utilize the refined images during experimental testing. Instead, we qualitatively showcase them as references.

4   Experiment

4.1   Implementation Details

Datasets and Data Pre-processing. **FFHQ** [33] and **CelebAMask-HQ** [40] datasets contain 70,000 and 30,000 in-the-wild single-view face images respectively, with rich identity and age diversity, and high image resolution (1024×1024 for the former and 512×512 resolution for the latter). **AffectNet** [48] is a large-scale emotion dataset with face images acquired from the Internet, covering seven emotional states (*i.e.*, anger, disgust, fear, happiness, neutral, sadness, and surprise). To maintain consistency, we resize all the images to 1024×1024. To stabilize the training, we align each image to a similar center before training. We use an off-the-shelf semantic segmentation network [83] to obtain the segmentation labels of each image and remove images that contain hats, earrings, and necklaces. Additionally, we employed these segmentation labels to replace the background region (*i.e.*, without a head) of the images with a white backdrop and generate the head region masks for the images. We randomly take approximately 320,000 images from these datasets as the training set and evaluate the model on the randomly selected images that were not included in the training set.

Training Details. We use PyTorch to implement our model. For the face synthesis decoder D, 1024 rays are sampled in an iteration, each with 64 sampled points in the coarse volume. Similar to [32], we remove the hierarchical volume sampling of NeRF to speed up training and inference. In the formal EM-like training, We first train decoder D for 5 epochs, then train encoder E for 5 epochs, and repeat this process alternately. In order to ensure consistency with the optimizers used during the model parameters initialization, seven Adam optimizers [37] are used for training the face synthesis decoder D and the prediction heads excluding PH_{shape} respectively, while a SGD optimizer [7] is used to optimize PH_{shape}. The initial learning rate of the Adam optimizer was set to 5×10^{-4}, and that of the SGD optimizer was set to 0.1. When training the facial attribute encoder, the gradient of each attribute component of the objective terms in $\mathcal{L}_E$ is summed and backpropagated to the corresponding prediction head, and the weights of the prediction heads are adjusted based on the propagated gradient, respectively. The whole training is conducted on 5 NVIDIA RTX3090 GPUs for 150 epochs.

4.2   Zero-Shot Attribute Separation from Single Image

We validate whether our facial attribute encoder E can zero-shot separate facial attributes from a real face image as orthogonally as possible to the latent space of the face synthesis decoder D. We verify this through facial attribute transfer experiments.

As shown in Fig. 3, we use encoder E to predict facial attribute codes z for both the source ('Real') and target ('Target') real face images. We replace one specific attribute code z_* of the source image with the counterpart from the target image. The original and modified conditioned attribute codes are fed into the face synthesis decoder D for rendering, denoted as 'Render' and '**T. z_***' respectively for the rendered results, where '**T.**' means 'Transfer'. The desired outcome is that the rendered face 'Render' should also strive to be as similar as possible to the source real image 'Real' across various facial attributes. Simultaneously, '**T. z_***' should exhibit sufficient consistency to the target face in terms of the modified attribute z_* while the remaining unmodified attributes should be well preserved. Similarity reflects the expressive capacity of attribute encoder E in predicting latent codes for real facial attributes, while invariance demonstrates the good separation between the latent codes corresponding to different attributes. The results in Fig. 3 thus reveal that our model demonstrates good expressive and attribute separation capacity for facial identity shape, expression, texture, and illumination from a real image without the assistance of multi-view information in both training and testing.

Real   Ours   Ours-refine   HeadNeRF MoFaNeRF-fine Deep3DFace   DECA

Fig. 5. Visual comparison of representation ability. 'Ours-refine' means the results of our rendered images refined by the adopted face restoration network. 'MoFaNeRF-fine' means its refined results. For a real image, we show the regressed prediction [18,21] or fitted prediction [32,73] of the baseline models. The better attribute consistency between the rendered face image and the ground truth real image could indicate a better representation ability of the latent attribute codes. See text in Sect. 4.3 for details.

As mentioned in Sect. 3.1, it is difficult to continuously parameterize the hairstyle attribute, especially without the aid of a professional multi-view 3D scan training dataset that includes hair. The examples on the left side of Fig. 4 demonstrate that the facial attribute encoder E's prediction head for hairstyle PH_{hair} can express and separate this attribute effectively. The hairstyle transfer results from a different head pose of the target image also demonstrate that the predicted hairstyle code z_{hair} and head pose (z_{rot} and z_{tran}) are well separated from each other.

Finally, we anticipate an ideal model that can synthesize novel-view images for the rendered result 'Render' of a real face image 'Real'. If the model can achieve this, then naturally, it can also do the same thing to the attribute transfer result 'T. z_*'. As shown in the right side of Fig. 4, by changing the pose inputted into the face synthesis decoder D, we can achieve novel-view synthesis for the rendered result of a real image with 3D-aware view consistency. The above results demonstrate that our model can perform real-time and zero-shot attribute separation of a given real-face image, allowing attribute transfer and rendering at novel views without the aid of multi-view information, *i.e.*, achieving a good balance in 'zero-shot', 'attribute transfer', 'real-time' and 'realistic', as defined in Sect. 1. In Fig. 3 and Fig. 4, in order to overcome the well-known high-frequency details loss caused by training NeRF without multi-view data, we added the pre-trained DifFace as a RefineNet and demonstrated the refined results (*i.e.*, '+ RefineNet') of the rendered images after passing through the RefineNet (best viewed with zoom-in). It could be observed that the texture details of the rendered face images, such as teeth and hair, become clearer and more realistic, making our model more visually appealing while not compromising real-time performance.

Table 2. Metric comparison of representation ability. See the text in Sect. 4.3 for details.

Model	Image Similarity				Attribute Consistency			
	LPIPS↓	L1↓	SSIM↑	IC↑	AED↓	ATD↓	AID↓	APD↓
Deep3DFace [18]	0.3868	0.1888	0.7231	0.5779	0.0729	0.0409	0.0431	0.022
DECA [21]	0.3098	0.0948	0.5753	0.2047	0.3168	0.1636	0.2861	0.078
MoFaNeRF-fine [89]	0.3255	0.1217	0.4532	0.2118	0.6036	0.2682	0.6129	0.044
HeadNeRF [32]	0.3187	0.1260	0.7553	0.5439	0.1307	0.1137	0.3143	0.032
Ours	**0.2713**	**0.0610**	**0.8112**	**0.7151**	**0.0699**	**0.0318**	**0.0344**	**0.020**

4.3 Comparisons

Baselines. We adopt the following criteria to select baseline methods. First, the model should have the ability to perform attribute separation and novel-view rendering from a real face image, either zero-shot or by optimizing the latent codes. Second, the model and its code for obtaining the attribute parameters from real-face images should be available. The selected models include the classic regression-based explicit 3D face models Deep3DFace [18] and DECA [21], and the advanced fitting-based implicit 3D-aware face models HeadNeRF [32] and MoFaNeRF [89].

Comparison of Representation Ability. For a single-view face image, we use the facial attribute encoders of Deep3DFace, DECA, and our model to directly predict the latent attribute codes, respectively, and use the respective models to render the corresponding face image based on the obtained codes. For HeadNeRF and MoFaNeRF, we first initialize the latent attribute codes of the test image according to the methods they provide, then perform image-base fitting to obtain the optimized attribute codes, input them into the model, and render the corresponding face image, respectively. The better similarity and attribute consistency between the rendered face image and the ground truth real image could indicate a better representation ability of the latent attribute codes and a better render performance of the model.

Figure 5 shows the prediction or fitting results for the same images ('Real'). Our results are represented by 'Ours'. MoFaNeRF also incorporates an additional pre-trained refine network to enhance the realistic texture details of the rendered face. Therefore, for a more fair comparison, we use its fitting results after refinement.

Deep3DFace is unable to represent facial areas such as hair. In some cases, there will be noticeable attribute inconsistencies in facial identity shape (row 4) and expression (rows 1–4) when compared to ground truth images. Additionally, it does not perform well in the expressiveness of some facial texture details such as beard. The face image predicted by DECA also performs poorly in terms of attribute consistency with ground truth images in terms of facial expression (rows 1–4) and texture. For example, DECA does not effectively express the texture color of the lips. In some cases, MoFaNeRF appears to completely fail to recreate a human face. It represents the facial attributes of the region excluding the hair area. HeadNeRF achieves to fit more realistic faces with better attribute consistency in expression and texture than the above three models. However, it does not perform well in maintaining consistency in identity shape in some cases (rows 1,4), and it is unable to represent hairstyles. The face images rendered by our model demonstrate good consistency with ground truth face images in terms of facial identity shape, expression, texture, illumination, and hairstyle. This indicates that the latent attribute codes parameterized by our facial attribute encoder possess a better expressive ability for the facial attributes. We also demonstrated the refined results ('Ours-refine') of our rendered images using the refinement network DifFace as a reference, which improves the facial texture details.

Table 3. Evaluation of attribute separation ability using Disentanglement Score (DS). α, β, γ, η and θ stand for facial identity shape, expression, texture, illumination and head pose, respectively. See text in Sect. 4.3 for details.

Model	DS_α ↑	DS_β ↑	DS_γ ↑	DS_η ↑	DS_θ ↑
Deep3DFace [18]	5.76	39.6	38.3	386	**42.5**
DECA [21]	4.46	**54.8**	28.8	367	36.9
MoFaNeRF-fine [89]	3.12	21.6	21.3	–	37.8
HeadNeRF [32]	7.91	52.1	36.7	471	41.5
Ours	**8.74**	<u>54.5</u>	**39.1**	**476**	<u>42.0</u>

In Table 2, inspired by [23,32,89], we measure the average similarity and attribute consistency between the rendered face image and the ground truth real image with the image similarity comparison metrics: Learned Perceptual Image Patch Similarity (LPIPS) [85], L1-distance, Structural Similarity Index (SSIM), Identity Consistency (IC) and attribute consistency comparison metrics: Average Expression Distance (AED), Average Texture Distance (ATD), Average Illumination Distance (AID), and Average Pose Distance (APD). To evaluate the identity consistency (IC) between the ground truth image and the rendered face image, we compute the cosine distance of their embeddings of a pre-

Table 4. Comparison of the prediction efficiency using Frames per Second (FPS). ∗: Test on an NVIDIA RTX3090 GPU with a batch size of 1.

Model	FPS*↑
Deep3DFace [18]	55
DECA [21]	17
MoFaNeRF [89]	0.002
HeadNeRF [32]	0.031
Ours	15

trained face recognition network [14]. The Average Expression Distance (AED) calculates the average 3DMM expression cosine distance between the real image and the rendered result, and the remaining three metrics of the same type, ATD, AID, and APD, are also calculated in the same manner. [18] is used to extracted the 3DMM attribute parameters. During the metric evaluation, we utilized the refined results of face images rendered by MoFaNeRF, while our model used the results without refinement.

The experimental results show that our model is capable of rendering clearer face images and performs better in terms of identity preservation. It also exhibits a good facial attribute preservation of the ground truth image in expression, texture, illumination, and head pose attributes. This indicates that our facial attribute encoder is capable of parameterizing the facial attributes of a real face to a more expressive position in latent space. Additionally, our face synthesis decoder can accurately understand the semantics of the obtained attribute codes and render the corresponding face image.

Comparison of Attribute Separation. In Table 3, we use the Disentanglement Score (DS) [16] to compare the models' parameterized ability in separating facial attributes from a face image. α, β, γ, η, and θ stand for facial identity shape, expression, texture, illumination, and head pose, respectively. Ideally, when we only vary the latent code for one attribute, other facial attributes of the original rendered face image should be preserved on the re-rendered image, which was synthesized by the decoder conditioned on the modified attribute codes. We estimate the 3DMM parameters from the re-rendered image and calculate the variance of the estimated parameters (α, β, γ, η, θ). The DS_i is calculated as: $DS_i = \prod_{j \neq i} \frac{var(i)}{var(j)}, i, j \in \{\alpha, \beta, \gamma, \eta, \theta\}$. A higher value of DS indicates a better separation between the specific attribute code and the remaining facial attribute codes. MoFaNeRF does not have a specific parameterization for the illumination attribute, so we did not calculate this DS_η for it. Table 3 shows that our model can separate facial attributes into comparatively orthogonal latent space, reducing the influence of a certain attribute code on the remaining facial attributes of the re-rendered face image.

Table 5. Comparison of representation ability with ablated baselines. See text in Sec. 4.4 for details.

Models	Image Similarity				Attribute Consistency			
	LPIPS↓	L1↓	SSIM↑	IC↑	AED↓	ATD↓	AID↓	APD↓
w/o $\mathcal{L}_{dis}$	0.2719	0.0641	0.8106	0.7065	0.0710	0.0330	0.0353	0.020
w/o $\mathcal{L}_{cyc}$	0.2854	0.0743	0.7793	0.6884	0.0750	0.0599	0.0443	0.023
w/o $\mathbf{z}_{hair}$	0.2798	0.0715	0.7854	0.6954	0.0724	0.0597	0.0431	0.021
Ours	**0.2713**	**0.0610**	**0.8112**	**0.7151**	**0.0699**	**0.0318**	**0.0344**	**0.020**

Comparison of Real-Time Performance. The average Frames per Second (FPS) of the different models are reported in Table 4. The models were tested for conducting regression-based or fitting-based prediction from a real face image on an NVIDIA RTX3090 GPU with a batch size of 1. Both MoFaNeRF and our results do not include refinement of the rendered image. The fitting-based methods, HeadNeRF and MoFaNeRF, take an average of 32 and 411 s, respectively, to fit and render a single image. In contrast, our regression-based model demonstrates a real-time performance that is comparable to two other regression-based models, Deep3DFace and DECA.

4.4   Ablation Study

In this section, we first attempt to verify the facial attribute encoder, the disentanglement loss, $\mathcal{L}_{\text{dis}}$ (Eq. 11), and the cycle-consistency loss, $\mathcal{L}_{\text{cyc}}$ (Eq. 10). In Table 5, we compare the representation ability of ablated pipelines which excludes cycle-consistency loss or disentanglement loss on the test set. The results of the complete model are comparatively better than the ablated models in the image similarity and attribute consistency between the rendered face image and the ground truth image, which implies that the face image is separated to a more expressive position in the latent space with the complete model. Table 5 also provides a comparison between the complete model and the ablate pipeline which excludes the hairstyle prediction head PH_{hair} and the hairstyle attribute code $\mathbf{z}_{\text{hair}}$. It shows that parameterizing facial hairstyle and projecting it into the latent space can enhance the model's ability to express facial attributes, particularly in terms of identity similarity and texture consistency.

Table 6 shows the intermediate results during the formal EM-like heuristic training introduced in Sect. 3.2. The 3D-aware face model has better render quality when provided with more expressive conditioned codes from the facial attribute encoder, which may be attributed to the synergy effect of the facial attribute encoder and the face synthesis decoder.

Table 6. Comparison of representation ability during the EM-like heuristic training.

Epoch	Image Similarity				Attribute Consistency			
	LPIPS↓	L1↓	SSIM↑	IC↑	AED↓	ATD↓	AID↓	APD↓
10	0.3244	0.1504	0.7411	0.5248	0.1801	0.1330	0.1937	0.037
50	0.2945	0.1165	0.7843	0.6063	0.1341	0.0914	0.1135	0.028
100	0.2814	0.0843	0.7994	0.6833	0.0958	0.0531	0.0704	0.023
150	0.2713	0.0610	0.8112	0.7151	0.0699	0.0318	0.0344	0.020

5   Conclusion

In this paper, we present a model that enables real-time and zero-shot attribute separation of a given real face, allowing attribute transfer and rendering at novel views without the aid of multi-view information. We achieve this by extending the alternating training algorithm to the focus that to enhance the ability of the facial attribute encoder in representing and separating attributes, and to improve the rendering quality of the 3D-aware face model. In addition, we continuously parameterize the hairstyle attribute without relying on a professional multi-view 3D scan training dataset that incorporates hair.

5.1   Limitation

Similar to [23, 32, 89], our model doesn't explicitly generate 3D shapes and only focuses on rendering performance. Though 3D shapes can be extracted from the neural radiance field by some means, the 3D accuracy is unwarranted. Similar to these parametric models, our model sometimes exhibits inadequate generalization in its rendering results for images that deviate significantly from the training data distribution. Besides, the training set we used does not include a dedicated multi-illumination dataset, which is inadequate for covering various types of illumination. This problem may be alleviated by searching for facial datasets that are specifically designed to capture diverse lighting conditions.

References

1. Abrevaya, V.F., Wuhrer, S., Boyer, E.: Multilinear autoencoder for 3D face model learning. In: 2018 IEEE Winter Conference on Applications of Computer Vision (WACV), pp. 1–9. IEEE (2018)
2. Athar, S., Xu, Z., Sunkavalli, K., Shechtman, E., Shu, Z.: Rignerf: fully controllable neural 3D portraits. In: Proceedings of the IEEE/CVF Conference on Computer Vision and Pattern Recognition, pp. 20364–20373 (2022)
3. Bai, Y., et al.: High-fidelity facial avatar reconstruction from monocular video with generative priors. In: Proceedings of the IEEE/CVF Conference on Computer Vision and Pattern Recognition, pp. 4541–4551 (2023)
4. Blanz, V., Vetter, T.: A morphable model for the synthesis of 3D faces. In: Proceedings of the 26th Annual Conference on Computer Graphics and Interactive Techniques, pp. 187–194 (1999)
5. Booth, J., Roussos, A., Ponniah, A., Dunaway, D., Zafeiriou, S.: Large scale 3D morphable models. Int. J. Comput. Vision **126**(2), 233–254 (2018)
6. Booth, J., Roussos, A., Zafeiriou, S., Ponniah, A., Dunaway, D.: A 3D morphable model learnt from 10,000 faces. In: Proceedings of the IEEE Conference on Computer Vision and Pattern Recognition, pp. 5543–5552 (2016)
7. Bottou, L.: Stochastic gradient descent tricks. In: Neural Networks: Tricks of the Trade, 2nd edn., pp. 421–436 (2012)
8. Bühler, M.C., Meka, A., Li, G., Beeler, T., Hilliges, O.: Varitex: variational neural face textures. In: Proceedings of the IEEE/CVF International Conference on Computer Vision, pp. 13890–13899 (2021)
9. Cao, C., Weng, Y., Zhou, S., Tong, Y., Zhou, K.: Facewarehouse: a 3D facial expression database for visual computing. IEEE Trans. Visual Comput. Graphics **20**(3), 413–425 (2013)
10. Chan, E.R., et al.: Efficient geometry-aware 3D generative adversarial networks. In: Proceedings of the IEEE/CVF Conference on Computer Vision and Pattern Recognition, pp. 16123–16133 (2022)
11. Chan, E.R., Monteiro, M., Kellnhofer, P., Wu, J., Wetzstein, G.: pi-gan: periodic implicit generative adversarial networks for 3D-aware image synthesis. In: Proceedings of the IEEE/CVF Conference on Computer Vision and Pattern Recognition, pp. 5799–5809 (2021)
12. Daněček, R., Black, M.J., Bolkart, T.: Emoca: emotion driven monocular face capture and animation. In: Proceedings of the IEEE/CVF Conference on Computer Vision and Pattern Recognition, pp. 20311–20322 (2022)
13. Dempster, A.P., Laird, N.M., Rubin, D.B.: Maximum likelihood from incomplete data via the EM algorithm. J. Roy. Stat. Soc.: Ser. B (Methodol.) **39**(1), 1–22 (1977)
14. Deng, J., Guo, J., Xue, N., Zafeiriou, S.: Arcface: additive angular margin loss for deep face recognition. In: Proceedings of the IEEE Conference on Computer Vision and Pattern Recognition, pp. 4690–4699 (2019)
15. Deng, Y., Wang, B., Shum, H.Y.: Learning detailed radiance manifolds for high-fidelity and 3d-consistent portrait synthesis from monocular image. In: Proceedings of the IEEE/CVF Conference on Computer Vision and Pattern Recognition, pp. 4423–4433 (2023)
16. Deng, Y., Yang, J., Chen, D., Wen, F., Tong, X.: Disentangled and controllable face image generation via 3D imitative-contrastive learning. In: Proceedings of the IEEE/CVF Conference on Computer Vision and Pattern Recognition, pp. 5154–5163 (2020)
17. Deng, Y., Yang, J., Xiang, J., Tong, X.: Gram: generative radiance manifolds for 3D-aware image generation. In: Proceedings of the IEEE/CVF Conference on Computer Vision and Pattern Recognition, pp. 10673–10683 (2022)

18. Deng, Y., Yang, J., Xu, S., Chen, D., Jia, Y., Tong, X.: Accurate 3D face reconstruction with weakly-supervised learning: from single image to image set. In: Proceedings of the IEEE/CVF Conference on Computer Vision and Pattern Recognition Workshops (2019)
19. Drobyshev, N., Chelishev, J., Khakhulin, T., Ivakhnenko, A., Lempitsky, V., Zakharov, E.: Megaportraits: one-shot megapixel neural head avatars. In: Proceedings of the 30th ACM International Conference on Multimedia, pp. 2663–2671 (2022)
20. Egger, B., et al.: Occlusion-aware 3d morphable models and an illumination prior for face image analysis. Int. J. Comput. Vision **126**, 1269–1287 (2018)
21. Feng, Y., Feng, H., Black, M.J., Bolkart, T.: Learning an animatable detailed 3D face model from in-the-wild images, vol. 40 (2021). https://doi.org/10.1145/3450626.3459936
22. Gafni, G., Thies, J., Zollhofer, M., Nießner, M.: Dynamic neural radiance fields for monocular 4D facial avatar reconstruction. In: Proceedings of the IEEE/CVF Conference on Computer Vision and Pattern Recognition, pp. 8649–8658 (2021)
23. Galanakis, S., Gecer, B., Lattas, A., Zafeiriou, S.: 3DMM-RF: convolutional radiance fields for 3d face modeling. In: Proceedings of the IEEE/CVF Winter Conference on Applications of Computer Vision, pp. 3536–3547 (2023)
24. Gerig, T., et al.: Morphable face models-an open framework. In: 2018 13th IEEE International Conference on Automatic Face & Gesture Recognition (FG 2018), pp. 75–82. IEEE (2018)
25. Ghosh, P., Gupta, P.S., Uziel, R., Ranjan, A., Black, M.J., Bolkart, T.: Gif: generative interpretable faces. In: 2020 International Conference on 3D Vision (3DV), pp. 868–878. IEEE (2020)
26. Goodfellow, I., et al.: Generative adversarial networks. Commun. ACM **63**(11), 139–144 (2020)
27. Grassal, P.W., Prinzler, M., Leistner, T., Rother, C., Nießner, M., Thies, J.: Neural head avatars from monocular RGB videos. In: Proceedings of the IEEE/CVF Conference on Computer Vision and Pattern Recognition, pp. 18653–18664 (2022)
28. Gu, J., Liu, L., Wang, P., Theobalt, C.: Stylenerf: a style-based 3D-aware generator for high-resolution image synthesis. arXiv preprint arXiv:2110.08985 (2021)
29. Guo, X., Kan, M., Chen, T., Shan, S.: Gan with multivariate disentangling for controllable hair editing. In: Avidan, S., Brostow, G., Cisse, M., Farinella, G.M., Hassner, T. (eds.) ECCV 2022, vol. 13675, pp. 655–670. Springer, Heidelberg (2022). https://doi.org/10.1007/978-3-031-19784-0_38
30. Guo, Y., Chen, K., Liang, S., Liu, Y.J., Bao, H., Zhang, J.: Ad-nerf: audio driven neural radiance fields for talking head synthesis. In: Proceedings of the IEEE/CVF International Conference on Computer Vision, pp. 5784–5794 (2021)
31. He, K., Zhang, X., Ren, S., Sun, J.: Deep residual learning for image recognition. In: Proceedings of the IEEE Conference on Computer Vision and Pattern Recognition, pp. 770–778 (2016)
32. Hong, Y., Peng, B., Xiao, H., Liu, L., Zhang, J.: Headnerf: a real-time nerf-based parametric head model. In: Proceedings of the IEEE/CVF Conference on Computer Vision and Pattern Recognition, pp. 20374–20384 (2022)
33. Karras, T., Laine, S., Aila, T.: A style-based generator architecture for generative adversarial networks. In: Proceedings of the IEEE/CVF Conference on Computer Vision and Pattern Recognition, pp. 4401–4410 (2019)
34. Kellnhofer, P., Jebe, L.C., Jones, A., Spicer, R., Pulli, K., Wetzstein, G.: Neural lumigraph rendering. In: Proceedings of the IEEE/CVF Conference on Computer Vision and Pattern Recognition, pp. 4287–4297 (2021)

35. Khakhulin, T., Sklyarova, V., Lempitsky, V., Zakharov, E.: Realistic one-shot mesh-based head avatars. In: Avidan, S., Brostow, G., Cisse, M., Farinella, G.M., Hassner, T. (eds.) ECCV 2022, vol. 13662, pp. 345–362. Springer, Heidelberg (2022). https://doi.org/10.1007/978-3-031-20086-1_20

36. Kim, M., Jain, A.K., Liu, X.: Adaface: quality adaptive margin for face recognition. In: Proceedings of the IEEE/CVF Conference on Computer Vision and Pattern Recognition, pp. 18750–18759 (2022)

37. Kingma, D.P., Ba, J.: Adam: a method for stochastic optimization. arXiv preprint arXiv:1412.6980 (2014)

38. Kowalski, M., Garbin, S.J., Estellers, V., Baltrušaitis, T., Johnson, M., Shotton, J.: CONFIG: controllable neural face image generation. In: Vedaldi, A., Bischof, H., Brox, T., Frahm, J.-M. (eds.) ECCV 2020. LNCS, vol. 12356, pp. 299–315. Springer, Cham (2020). https://doi.org/10.1007/978-3-030-58621-8_18

39. Krizhevsky, A., Sutskever, I., Hinton, G.E.: Imagenet classification with deep convolutional neural networks. Adv. Neural Inf. Process. Syst. **25** (2012)

40. Lee, C.H., Liu, Z., Wu, L., Luo, P.: Maskgan: towards diverse and interactive facial image manipulation. In: Proceedings of the IEEE/CVF Conference on Computer Vision and Pattern Recognition, pp. 5549–5558 (2020)

41. Lee, Y., Choi, T., Go, H., Lee, H., Cho, S., Kim, J.: Exp-gan: 3D-aware facial image generation with expression control. In: Proceedings of the Asian Conference on Computer Vision, pp. 3812–3827 (2022)

42. Li, C., Morel-Forster, A., Vetter, T., Egger, B., Kortylewski, A.: Robust model-based face reconstruction through weakly-supervised outlier segmentation. In: Proceedings of the IEEE/CVF Conference on Computer Vision and Pattern Recognition, pp. 372–381 (2023)

43. Li, T., Bolkart, T., Black, M.J., Li, H., Romero, J.: Learning a model of facial shape and expression from 4d scans. ACM Trans. Graph. **36**(6), 194–1 (2017)

44. Loper, M.M., Black, M.J.: OpenDR: an approximate differentiable renderer. In: Fleet, D., Pajdla, T., Schiele, B., Tuytelaars, T. (eds.) ECCV 2014. LNCS, vol. 8695, pp. 154–169. Springer, Cham (2014). https://doi.org/10.1007/978-3-319-10584-0_11

45. Ma, Z., Zhu, X., Qi, G.J., Lei, Z., Zhang, L.: Otavatar: one-shot talking face avatar with controllable tri-plane rendering. In: Proceedings of the IEEE/CVF Conference on Computer Vision and Pattern Recognition, pp. 16901–16910 (2023)

46. Mescheder, L., Oechsle, M., Niemeyer, M., Nowozin, S., Geiger, A.: Occupancy networks: learning 3D reconstruction in function space. In: Proceedings of the IEEE/CVF Conference on Computer Vision and Pattern Recognition, pp. 4460–4470 (2019)

47. Mildenhall, B., Srinivasan, P.P., Tancik, M., Barron, J.T., Ramamoorthi, R., Ng, R.: Nerf: representing scenes as neural radiance fields for view synthesis. Commun. ACM **65**(1), 99–106 (2021)

48. Mollahosseini, A., Hasani, B., Mahoor, M.H.: Affectnet: a database for facial expression, valence, and arousal computing in the wild. IEEE Trans. Affect. Comput. **10**(1), 18–31 (2017)

49. Nguyen-Phuoc, T., Li, C., Theis, L., Richardt, C., Yang, Y.L.: Hologan: unsupervised learning of 3D representations from natural images. In: Proceedings of the IEEE/CVF International Conference on Computer Vision, pp. 7588–7597 (2019)

50. Niemeyer, M., Geiger, A.: Giraffe: representing scenes as compositional generative neural feature fields. In: Proceedings of IEEE Conference on Computer Vision and Pattern Recognition (CVPR) (2021)

51. Niemeyer, M., Mescheder, L., Oechsle, M., Geiger, A.: Differentiable volumetric rendering: learning implicit 3D representations without 3D supervision. In: Proceedings of the IEEE/CVF Conference on Computer Vision and Pattern Recognition, pp. 3504–3515 (2020)

52. Or-El, R., Luo, X., Shan, M., Shechtman, E., Park, J.J., Kemelmacher-Shlizerman, I.: Stylesdf: high-resolution 3D-consistent image and geometry generation. In: Proceedings of the IEEE/CVF Conference on Computer Vision and Pattern Recognition, pp. 13503–13513 (2022)

53. Park, J.J., Florence, P., Straub, J., Newcombe, R., Lovegrove, S.: Deepsdf: learning continuous signed distance functions for shape representation. In: Proceedings of the IEEE/CVF Conference on Computer Vision and Pattern Recognition, pp. 165–174 (2019)

54. Park, K., et al.: Nerfies: deformable neural radiance fields. In: Proceedings of the IEEE/CVF International Conference on Computer Vision, pp. 5865–5874 (2021)

55. Piao, J., Sun, K., Wang, Q., Lin, K.Y., Li, H.: Inverting generative adversarial renderer for face reconstruction. In: Proceedings of the IEEE/CVF Conference on Computer Vision and Pattern Recognition, pp. 15619–15628 (2021)

56. Ramamoorthi, R., Hanrahan, P.: An efficient representation for irradiance environment maps. In: Proceedings of the 28th Annual Conference on Computer Graphics and Interactive Techniques, pp. 497–500 (2001)

57. Ramon, E., et al.: H3d-net: few-shot high-fidelity 3D head reconstruction. In: Proceedings of the IEEE/CVF International Conference on Computer Vision, pp. 5620–5629 (2021)

58. Ranjan, A., Bolkart, T., Sanyal, S., Black, M.J.: Generating 3D faces using convolutional mesh autoencoders. In: Proceedings of the European Conference on Computer Vision (ECCV), pp. 704–720 (2018)

59. Ravi, N., et al.: Accelerating 3D deep learning with pytorch3d. arXiv preprint arXiv:2007.08501 (2020)

60. Ren, Y., Li, G., Chen, Y., Li, T.H., Liu, S.: Pirenderer: controllable portrait image generation via semantic neural rendering. In: Proceedings of the IEEE/CVF International Conference on Computer Vision, pp. 13759–13768 (2021)

61. Roich, D., Mokady, R., Bermano, A.H., Cohen-Or, D.: Pivotal tuning for latent-based editing of real images. ACM Trans. Graph. (TOG) **42**(1), 1–13 (2022)

62. Schwarz, K., Liao, Y., Niemeyer, M., Geiger, A.: Graf: generative radiance fields for 3d-aware image synthesis. Adv. Neural. Inf. Process. Syst. **33**, 20154–20166 (2020)

63. Shoshan, A., Bhonker, N., Kviatkovsky, I., Medioni, G.: Gan-control: explicitly controllable gans. In: Proceedings of the IEEE/CVF International Conference on Computer Vision, pp. 14083–14093 (2021)

64. Siarohin, A., Lathuilière, S., Tulyakov, S., Ricci, E., Sebe, N.: First order motion model for image animation. Adv. Neural Inf. Process. Syst. **32** (2019)

65. Siarohin, A., et al.: Unsupervised volumetric animation. In: Proceedings of the IEEE/CVF Conference on Computer Vision and Pattern Recognition, pp. 4658–4669 (2023)

66. Simonyan, K., Zisserman, A.: Very deep convolutional networks for large-scale image recognition. arXiv preprint arXiv:1409.1556 (2014)

67. Sitzmann, V., Martel, J., Bergman, A., Lindell, D., Wetzstein, G.: Implicit neural representations with periodic activation functions. Adv. Neural. Inf. Process. Syst. **33**, 7462–7473 (2020)

68. Sitzmann, V., Zollhöfer, M., Wetzstein, G.: Scene representation networks: continuous 3D-structure-aware neural scene representations. Adv. Neural Inf. Process. Syst. **32** (2019)

69. Sun, K., Wu, S., Huang, Z., Zhang, N., Wang, Q., Li, H.: Controllable 3d face synthesis with conditional generative occupancy fields. arXiv preprint arXiv:2206.08361 (2022)

70. Tewari, A., et al.: Pie: portrait image embedding for semantic control. ACM Trans. Graph. (TOG) **39**(6), 1–14 (2020)

71. Tewari, A., et al.: Stylerig: rigging stylegan for 3d control over portrait images. In: Proceedings of the IEEE/CVF Conference on Computer Vision and Pattern Recognition, pp. 6142–6151 (2020)
72. Tewari, A., Pan, X., Fried, O., Agrawala, M., Theobalt, C., et al.: Disentangled3d: learning a 3d generative model with disentangled geometry and appearance from monocular images. In: Proceedings of the IEEE/CVF Conference on Computer Vision and Pattern Recognition, pp. 1516–1525 (2022)
73. Tewari, A., et al.: Mofa: model-based deep convolutional face autoencoder for unsupervised monocular reconstruction. In: Proceedings of the IEEE International Conference on Computer Vision Workshops, pp. 1274–1283 (2017)
74. Tran, L., Liu, X.: Nonlinear 3D face morphable model. In: Proceedings of the IEEE Conference on Computer Vision and Pattern Recognition, pp. 7346–7355 (2018)
75. Wang, X., Guo, Y., Yang, Z., Zhang, J.: Prior-guided multi-view 3D head reconstruction. IEEE Trans. Multimedia **24**, 4028–4040 (2021)
76. Wu, S., et al.: Ganhead: towards generative animatable neural head avatars. In: Proceedings of the IEEE/CVF Conference on Computer Vision and Pattern Recognition, pp. 437–447 (2023)
77. Wu, Y., Deng, Y., Yang, J., Wei, F., Chen, Q., Tong, X.: Anifacegan: animatable 3D-aware face image generation for video avatars. arXiv preprint arXiv:2210.06465 (2022)
78. Xu, S., et al.: Deep 3D portrait from a single image. In: Proceedings of the IEEE/CVF Conference on Computer Vision and Pattern Recognition, pp. 7710–7720 (2020)
79. Yao, S., Zhong, R., Yan, Y., Zhai, G., Yang, X.: DFA-NERF: personalized talking head generation via disentangled face attributes neural rendering. arXiv preprint arXiv:2201.00791 (2022)
80. Yenamandra, T., et al.: i3dmm: deep implicit 3D morphable model of human heads. In: Proceedings of the IEEE/CVF Conference on Computer Vision and Pattern Recognition (CVPR) (2021)
81. Yenamandra, T., et al.: i3dmm: deep implicit 3D morphable model of human heads. In: Proceedings of the IEEE/CVF Conference on Computer Vision and Pattern Recognition, pp. 12803–12813 (2021)
82. Yin, Y., Ghasedi, K., Wu, H., Yang, J., Tong, X., Fu, Y.: Nerfinvertor: high fidelity nerf-gan inversion for single-shot real image animation. In: Proceedings of the IEEE/CVF Conference on Computer Vision and Pattern Recognition, pp. 8539–8548 (2023)
83. Yu, C., Wang, J., Peng, C., Gao, C., Yu, G., Sang, N.: Bisenet: bilateral segmentation network for real-time semantic segmentation. In: Proceedings of the European Conference on Computer Vision (ECCV), pp. 325–341 (2018)
84. Yue, Z., Loy, C.C.: Difface: blind face restoration with diffused error contraction. arXiv preprint arXiv:2212.06512 (2022)
85. Zhang, R., Isola, P., Efros, A.A., Shechtman, E., Wang, O.: The unreasonable effectiveness of deep features as a perceptual metric. In: Proceedings of the IEEE Conference on Computer Vision and Pattern Recognition, pp. 586–595 (2018)
86. Zheng, M., Yang, H., Huang, D., Chen, L.: Imface: a nonlinear 3D morphable face model with implicit neural representations. In: Proceedings of the IEEE/CVF Conference on Computer Vision and Pattern Recognition, pp. 20343–20352 (2022)
87. Zheng, Y., Abrevaya, V.F., Bühler, M.C., Chen, X., Black, M.J., Hilliges, O.: Im avatar: implicit morphable head avatars from videos. In: Proceedings of the IEEE/CVF Conference on Computer Vision and Pattern Recognition, pp. 13545–13555 (2022)

88. Zheng, Y., Yifan, W., Wetzstein, G., Black, M.J., Hilliges, O.: Pointavatar: deformable point-based head avatars from videos. In: Proceedings of the IEEE/CVF Conference on Computer Vision and Pattern Recognition, pp. 21057–21067 (2023)
89. Zhuang, Y., Zhu, H., Sun, X., Cao, X.: Mofanerf: morphable facial neural radiance field. In: Avidan, S., Brostow, G., Cisse, M., Farinella, G.M., Hassner, T. (eds.) ECCV 2022, vol. 13663, pp. 268–285. Springer, Heidelberg (2022)
90. Zielonka, W., Bolkart, T., Thies, J.: Instant volumetric head avatars. In: Proceedings of the IEEE/CVF Conference on Computer Vision and Pattern Recognition, pp. 4574–4584 (2023)

Explore and Enhance the Generalization of Anomaly DeepFake Detection

Yiting Wang[1,2], Shen Chen[2], Taiping Yao[2], Lizhuang Ma[1(✉)],
Zhizhong Zhang[1], and Xin Tan[1]

[1] East China Normal University, Shanghai, China
51215901088@stu.ecnu.edu.cn, {lzma,xtan,zzzhang}@cs.ecnu.edu.cn
[2] Tencent YouTu Lab, Shenzhen, China
{kobeschen,taipingyao}@tencent.com

Abstract. In recent years, Anomaly DeepFake Detection (ADFD) has made significant breakthroughs in terms of generalization when meeting various unknown tampers. These detection methods primarily enhance generalization by constructing pseudo-fake samples, which involve three main steps: mask generation, source-target preprocessing, and blending. In this paper, we conducted a systematic analysis of some core factors in these steps. Based on the aforementioned observations at the mask generation step, we find that previous ADFD methods have limitations as they only consider specific tampering types, which is not representative of real-world scenarios, and generate noise samples that closely resemble real samples, causing confusion and hindering generalization. To alleviate these issues, we propose our new method, which consists of the Boundary Blur Mask Generator (BBMG) and the Noise Refinement Strategy (NRS) modules. BBMG leverages the inherent characteristics of boundary blur to simulate a comprehensive range of tampering techniques, enabling a more realistic representation of real-world scenarios. In conjunction with BBMG, the NRS module effectively mitigates the influence of noise samples. Extensive ablation experiments and comparative evaluations demonstrate the effectiveness of our method.

Keywords: Anormaly DeepFake Detection · Pseudo-fake · Noise Strategy · DeepFake Detection

1 Introduction

With the rapid advancements in artificial intelligence and deep learning, the creation of fake facial content has become efficient. However, the misuse of such technology can lead to harmful consequences, including the spread of false information, social engineering attacks, political manipulation, reputation damage, and financial fraud. Therefore, the emergence of deepfake detection technology is crucial in order to discern between genuine and artificially generated fake faces, thereby safeguarding societal security and order.

Y. Wang and S. Chen—Equal Contribution. This work was done when Yiting Wang was a research intern at Tencent Youtu Lab.

© The Author(s), under exclusive license to Springer Nature Singapore Pte Ltd. 2024
F.-L. Zhang and A. Sharf (Eds.): CVM 2024, LNCS 14593, pp. 27–47, 2024.
https://doi.org/10.1007/978-981-97-2092-7_2

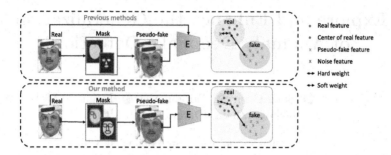

Fig. 1. Comparison of the previous method and our method. Previous methods focused on either local or global tampering. In contrast, our method considers both local and global tampering and employs a noise refinement strategy to mitigate the impact of noisy samples.

Prior arts, such as Face X-ray [17], SBI [29], SLADD [2] have greatly enhanced the generalization capability of deepfake detection. These methods primarily generate pseudo-fake faces through three typical steps: mask generation, source-target preprocessing, and blending. As shown in the top left part of Fig. 1, most of them are primarily trained using only real face data, hence we refer to this kind of approach as Anomaly DeepFake Detection (ADFD). Building upon the break-through generalization capability of ADFD methods, we investigate several key factors that influence the performance of these methods. Through experiments, we make the following observations: *1) Local tampering based on facial features, which involves making subtle changes to facial features (mouth, nose, eyes, etc.), is less effective compared to global tampering, and simple fusion of both does not improve generalization. 2) The generalization of the model is sensitive to the choice of boundary blur processing methods.*

During our exploration, we found that previous methods in ADFD have focused on specific tampering techniques, neglecting the importance of simulating a comprehensive range of tampering scenarios. However, tampering can occur in both local manipulations (e.g., subtle changes in facial features) and global manipulations (e.g., complete face replacement) specifically related to facial images. Therefore, it is crucial to develop a solution that can effectively handle both types of tampering challenges related to facial manipulation to ensure robust detection of deepfake anomalies. Another key challenge is that previous research has neglected the impact of noise samples introduced during the source-target preprocessing step on the quality of generated facial images. As depicted in the upper-right portion of Fig. 1, these noise samples closely resemble real facial images and can significantly affect the model's performance. The similarity between noise samples and genuine facial images can introduce confusion and hinder the model's ability to generalize and make reliable predictions.

In light of the aforementioned challenges, we propose a new method, including Boundary Blur Mask Generator (BBMG) and Noise Refinement Strategy (NRS), as shown in Fig. 1. BBMG introduces boundary blur tampering traces at both global and local levels to simulate attacks that are more closely aligned with real-world scenarios. However, the randomness in the data augmentation process of BBMG can still produce pseudo-fake samples that resemble real samples and introduce noise. To alleviate this, we propose the NRS method, where we construct a real feature memory to find the center of the real distribution and select noise samples based on feature similarity. We assign lower weights to the noise samples to suppress their interference with the model's generalization capability. We systematically validate the feasibility of these two methods, demonstrating that our proposed approaches significantly improve the generalization of detection models, achieving state-of-the-art results. The main contributions of our work are summarized as follows:

- We systematically explore a series of Anomaly DeepFake Detection (ADFD) methods, analyzing core factors in the generation of pseudo-fake samples. We find that the design of mask region size and the boundary blurring operation have significant impacts on the generalization capability.
- Based on the above explorations, we propose a new method, which consists of two parts: Boundary Blur Mask Generator and Noise Refinement Strategy. Boundary Blur Mask Generator effectively simulates both local and global tampering techniques, thereby improving model generalization. Besides, Noise Refinement Strategy mitigates the impact of noise samples in ADFD methods.
- Through extensive ablation experiments, we demonstrate that our proposed methods for deepfake detection achieve state-of-the-art performance. These contributions significantly advance the field of deepfake detection and provide valuable insights into improving the generalization capability of ADFD.

2 Related Work

2.1 Conventional DeepFake Detection

In the early stages, deepfake detection algorithms relied on manual prior knowledge. With the introduction of deep learning, algorithms started focusing on spatial information and neural network design. For instance, compact network Mesonet [1], capsule network [24], autoencoder [8], recurrent convolutional networks [12,27], and attentional networks [34]. Some methods have also investigated the utilization of frequency domain information [10,16,21,22,25,28,32], leveraging the characteristics of frequency domain to effectively capture forgery traces. Additionally, other methods have utilized temporal information to enhance the model's ability to discriminate forgeries, such as local mouth motion [13,35], Facial Action [30] and temporal consistency [11,20,33]. While these methods have shown good performance in detecting known tempering, many of them struggle to generalize well to detect deepfakes created by unknown temperings, resulting in poor generalization.

2.2 Anomaly DeepFake Detection

To improve the generalization of deepfake detection, several researches have proposed Anomaly DeepFake Detection(ADFD) [2, 17, 29, 36] that mainly use real training data to improve model's discriminative ability towards unknown tampering methods. OC-FakeDect [14] proposed a one-class anomaly detection approach using a one-class Variational Autoencoder (VAE) trained solely on real face images to detect Deepfakes. Some other methods tried to synthesize pseudo-fake data, encouraging models to learn generalizable features for deepfake detection. Face-Xray [17] introduced blending the altered face into an existing background image to simulate forgery traces and generate synthetic training data. PCL [36] proposed using an inconsistency image generator (I2G) to synthesize forgery data and detect whether an image is forged based on patch consistency. SLADD [2] focused on local feature tampering using facial landmarks and employs adversarial learning to generate more sophisticated and novel forgery configurations, thereby improving detector performance. SBI [29] generated fake faces by blending pseudo source and target images from single pristine images, achieving higher generalization compared to previous methods.

3 Approach

3.1 Overview

In this section, we review previous Anomaly DeepFake Detection (ADFD) methods and explore influencing factors on pseudo-fake sample generation. Based on these insights, we introduce our innovative methods, including the Boundary Blur Mask Generator (BBMG) and Noise Refinement Strategy (NRS), as depicted in Fig. 3.

3.2 Review and Exploration of ADFD

Previous ADFD methods [2, 17, 29, 36] generate pseudo-fake faces D_{pf} from real faces D_r typically through blending, and then learn to distinguish real and fake samples through feature extractor $E(I; \Theta)$ and classifier $\mathscr{F}(I; \omega)$. The generating process can be mainly divided into the following three steps, as shown in Fig. 2:

1. **Mask Generation.** To obtain the tampered regions, it is necessary to generate corresponding masks M as the areas of manipulation. SBI, Face X-ray, and SLADD propose a variety of mask generation methods, among which Face X-ray and SBI are based on the global mask, and SLADD is based on the local mask of the facial features, such as left eye, right eye, nose, and mouth. Typically, various augmentations such as boundary-blurring are employed to obtain the processed mask M^b. This approach helps to make the mask softer, resulting in a more realistic simulation of tampering.

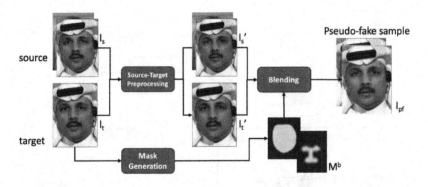

Fig. 2. The Pipeline of pseudo-fake face generation in ADFD.

2. **Source-Target Preprocessing.** This part primarily involves preprocessing the source images I_s and target images I_t before tampering. For Methods blending two different faces, such as Face X-ray, SLADD, alignment adjustment, and color correction operations are typically performed to make the source face better fit the target. In the case of methods like SBI, where I_t and I_s are derived from the same image, color transform, and frequency transform are applied to accentuate the differences between I_t and I_s in this step. After the preprocessing step, the processed versions of I_s and I_t are obtained, denoted as I'_t and I'_s, respectively.

3. **Blending.** This part generally blends the processed source image I'_s and the processed target image I'_t to generate a pseudo-fake sample I_{pf} based on the generated mask M^b. The fusion formula for getting I_{pf} is as follows:

$$I_{pf} = M^b \cdot I'_s + (1 - M^b) \cdot I'_t. \tag{1}$$

Different ADFD methods offer various parameters for these three steps, which may affect the generalization capability of the model on unseen tampering scenarios. Therefore, we conducted experiments to explore the impact of these parameters and identify key factors that contribute to the improvement of model generalization. Comparative experiments are conducted based on a common baseline (SBI), and the specific experimental procedures and results can be found in Sect. 4.2.

Based on our exploration of mask generation, we draw the following conclusions: *1) Local tampering based on facial features is less effective compared to global tampering, and simple fusion of both does not improve generalization. 2) The model's generalization is susceptible to the influence of boundary blur processing methods.*

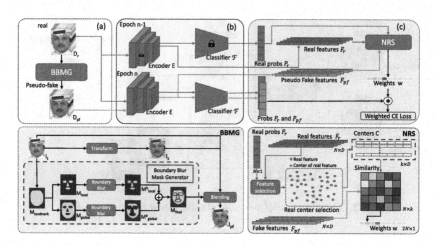

Fig. 3. Overview of our method. The overall process can be divided into three steps. (a) We generate pseudo-fake training data using our proposed Boundary Blur Mask Generator. (b) The real face image D_r and the pseudo-fake face image D_{pf} are fed into the encoder and classifier, obtaining the features and scores for each image. (c) We calculate the weighted CE loss using the Noise Refinement Strategy, which is used to update the network.

3.3   Boundary Blur Mask Generator

In this part, we propose a Boundary Blur Mask Generator (BBMG), corresponding to Fig. 3. According to our previous exploration, existing methods have difficulty in covering all types of tampering. Moreover, we observed that random fusion methods did not improve generalization, possibly due to the limited effectiveness of local masks in generating tampering traces. To cover a wider range of tampering types and increase the visibility of tampering traces, we propose to design a method that can simultaneously simulate both local and global tampering. Our exploration revealed the significant impact of the boundary-blurring operation on model generalization. Therefore, we propose our Boundary Blurring Mask Generator (BBMG), which allows for simple modification of the mask to learn both local and global tampering. This approach enhances tampering traces and improves the generalization of the model.

First, we select the facial region of the input image as the mask ($M_{landmark}$) based on landmarks. Then, we further localize the facial features, i.e. left eye, right eye, nose, and mouth, and randomly select some of these features. After that, selected features are extracted from the global mask, resulting in two masks: a local mask (M_{local}) containing only the selected features and a global mask (M_{global}) with some features removed. The calculation of M_{global} is as follows:

$$M_{global}(i,j) = M_{landmark}(i,j) - M_{local}(i,j), \qquad (2)$$

where (i, j) represents the pixel position in the mask. Next, we apply Boundary Blur to both M_{local} and M_{global}. Considering the widespread use of Gaussian Blur, we also employ Gaussian Blur to blur the boundaries. After applying Gaussian Boundary Blur, we obtain blurred masks M_{local}^b and M_{global}^b. Finally, we merge the two blurred masks by taking the maximum value at each pixel position, resulting in a final mask M_{final} with both local and global Boundary Blur characteristics. Calculations are as follows:

$$M_{final}(i,j) = max(M_{global}^b(i,j), M_{local}^b(i,j)). \tag{3}$$

Through these steps, we successfully generate a mask with both local and global Boundary Blur characteristics. Following SBI, we initialize source image I_s and target image I_t by copying input image I, then randomly apply image transformations to either of them to get a processed source image I_s' and a processed target image I_t'. We then blend the processed source and target images based on the generated mask M_{final} using the blending operation, resulting in a pseudo-fake face image. This pseudo-fake image is treated as a fake sample in the training set and used to train the model. The calculation of the pseudo-fake face image is as follows:

$$I_{pf} = M_{final} \cdot I_s' + (1 - M_{final}) \cdot I_t'. \tag{4}$$

Our proposed BBMG method generates a mask that incorporates both local and global tampering traces, and experimental results have shown that this mask-generation method can further improve the model's generalization.

3.4   Noise Refinement Strategy

Since the use of random data augmentation to generate corresponding source or target images introduces noise and makes the pseudo-fake samples too similar to real samples in BBMG method, we propose Noise Refinement Strategy to reduce the impact of noise samples on the model's generalization, corresponding to Fig. 3. We measure the distance between N pseudo-fake sample features $F_{pf} = E(I_{pf}, \Theta) \in \mathbb{R}^{N \times D}$ and the centers $C \in \mathbb{R}^{k \times D}$ of real sample features $F_r = E(I_r, \Theta) \in \mathbb{R}^{N \times D}$ to identify pseudo-fake samples that are too close to the center of the real sample distribution. These samples are considered noise samples and assigned lower loss weights to reduce their influence on the model's learning, thereby improving the model's generalization.

First, we need to determine the centers of the real sample distribution. Considering that real samples will dynamically change during training, in order to obtain the latest distribution of features for real samples, we use the encoder trained in the last epoch to get the real features $F_r = E(I_r, \Theta) \in \mathbb{R}^{N \times D}$. To obtain a more accurate center of the real feature distribution, we select the top k_s correctly predicted real features, i.e. features with the highest probability value $P_r \in \mathbb{R}^{N \times 1}$, as the memory of real features. These features in memory are then clustered using k-means clustering to obtain k center features $C = \{c_1, c_2, ..., c_k\} \in \mathbb{R}^{k \times D}$, which serve as the clustering centers of the real samples and are used as references for selecting noise samples in the current epoch.

Once we have obtained the distribution centers $C \in \mathbb{R}^{k \times D}$ of the real features, we can filter out noise samples by measuring the feature distances. For the pseudo-fake samples features $F_{pf} = E(I_{pf}, \Theta) \in \mathbb{R}^{N \times D}$, we calculate the cosine distance between the pseudo-fake features and each center point to determine the distance, selecting the minimum distance as the final noise distance score $Dist(F_{pf}, C)$. Samples with noise distance scores below a threshold value λ are considered noise samples. As the discriminative ability of the model is relatively poor in the early stages, we introduce the epoch parameter β when calculating weights of loss $w(F, C)$ to gradually reduce the importance of the noise samples as the epoch increases. The weights of loss can be calculated as:

$$w(F,C) = \begin{cases} \alpha_{pf}(F,C) \, , \, Dist(F,C) < \lambda \wedge F \in F_{pf} \\ 1 \, , \, Dist(F,C) \geq \lambda \vee F \in F_r, \end{cases} \tag{5}$$

$$\alpha_{pf}(F_{pf},C) = Dist(F_{pf},C) * (epoch/\beta) + 1 * (1 - epoch/\beta), \tag{6}$$

The cross-entropy loss is represented as:

$$p(I) = \mathscr{F}(E(I,\Theta),\omega), \tag{7}$$

$$L_{ce}(I,y) = -(y\log(p(I)) + (1-y)\log(1-p(I))), \tag{8}$$

where y represents the label of the image I. Combining Eq. 5 and Eq. 8, we obtain the final loss function as follow:

$$L = 1/N * \sum_{I \in D_r, D_{pf}} (w(E(I,\Theta),C) * L_{ce}(I,y)), \tag{9}$$

where N represents the number of training samples.

3.5 Algorithm

The training pipeline of the proposed algorithm can be roughly divided into two stages. In the early stage, before the T_kth epoch, we focus on learning the differences between real and generated samples. For each step, we first generate fake samples using the Boundary Blur Mask Generator. Then, we feed the generated fake samples and real samples from the training set into the Encoder $E(I;\Theta)$ and the Classifier $\mathscr{F}(F;\omega)$, updating the weights using a simple Cross-Entropy (CE) loss to learn the distribution of real and fake samples. After reaching the T_kth epoch, the model has acquired some discriminative ability between real and fake samples. At this stage, we introduce the Weighted Loss Noise Refinement Strategy. This strategy assigns lower loss weights to noise samples to reduce their impact on learning real-face features. The specific training strategy is shown in Algorithm 1.

Algorithm 1. Algorithm of our proposed method

Input: Real Training Images D_r

Parameter: Encoder E with Θ, Classifier $\mathscr{F}$ with ω, epoch T_k and T_{max}, fixed λ,β,k, k_s, batch size B

Output: the model parameter $W = \{\Theta, \omega\}$

1: **for** t=1,2,...,T_{max} **do**
2:      shuffle training set D_r.
3:      **for** n=1,...,$|D_r|/B$ **do**
4:          Fetch n-th mini-batch D_r^n from D_r.
5:          Read preprocessed landmark L_r^n.
6:          Obtain pseudo-fake data D_{pf}^n by BBMG using D_r^n and L_r^n.
7:          $p_r^n = \mathscr{F}(E(I_r, \Theta), \omega), \forall I_r \in D_r^n$.
8:          $p_{pf}^n = \mathscr{F}(E(I_{pf}, \Theta), \omega), \forall I_{pf} \in D_{pf}^n$.
9:          $F_r^n = E(I_r, \Theta), \forall I_r \in D_r^n$.
10:         $F_{pf}^n = E(I_{pf}, \Theta), \forall I_{pf} \in D_{pf}^n$.
11:         **if** $t >= T_k$ **then**
12:             Calculate loss L by NRS using λ,β,C and F_{pf}^n.
13:         **else**
14:             Calculate cross-entropy loss L.
15:         **end if**
16:         Update $\{\Theta, \omega\}$;
17:      **end for**
18:      **if** $t >= T_k - 1$ **then**
19:          select k_s real features F_{rm} from $F_r = \{F_r^1, F_r^2, ..., F_r^{|D_r|/B}\}$ according to $P_r = \{p_r^1, p_r^2, ..., p_r^{|D_r|/B}\}$.
20:          Get k centers $C = c_1, c_2, ...c_k$ using Kmeans by F_{rm}
21:      **end if**
22: **end for**
23: **return** $\{\Theta, \omega\}$

---

4 Experiments

4.1 Experiments Setting

Dataset. We trained our model on the widely used FaceForensics++ (FF++) dataset [26], and evaluated its generalization performance on the Celeb-DF-v2 (CDF) [19], DeepFake Detection Challenged Preview (DFDCP) [7], DeepFake Detection Challenge (DFDC) [6], and FFIW-10K (FFIW) [38] datasets.

Comparison. We compare our method with previous methods includes DSP-FWA [18], Face X-ray+BI [17], LRL [3], FRDM [22], PCL+I2G [36], SBI [29] and SLADD [2]. At the video-level, we compare our method with previous approaches using the receiver operating characteristic curve (AUC). Frame-level predictions are typically averaged over video frames.

Data Preprocessing. Following the preprocessing method in SBI, during the testing phase, we used the 81 facial landmarks shape predictor from Dlib [15] and RetinaFace [5] to extract facial landmarks and bounding boxes for each frame.

Table 1. Implementation details of the three steps of pseudo-fake face generation in the ADFD approach.

Step	Part	Parameters
Mask Generation	Local and global mask regions	Local(SLADD), Global(SBI, landmark augmentation library)
	Parameter settings of mask	Mask LineType(LINE_88, LINE_AA), Mask DataType(Uint8, Float32), Mask Value(1, 255)
	Boundary-blurring operations	Blurring Operation(Gaussian, Average, Median), Blurring Degree(Gaussian Blur Kernel Size)
Source-Target Preprocessing	Transform methods	RGBShift, HueSaturation, RandomBrightnessContrast, etc.
	Transform Objects	Source Transform, Target Transform
Blending	Blending types	Dynamic Blending, Alpha Blending

The facial region was randomly cropped with margins ranging from 4% to 20%. During inference, we only use RetinaFace to detect the facial region and fixed the cropping margin at 12.5%.

Implementation Details. We used the EfficientNet-b4 [31] pre-trained on ImageNet [4] as the encoder and trained it for 100 epochs using the SAM [9] optimizer. The learning rate was set to 0.001, and the batch size was 32, including 16 real faces and corresponding 16 generated pseudo-fake faces. During training, we only used the real samples from the FF++ and extracted 8 frames from each video as the training set. It is worth noting that our BBMG and NRS modules are training strategies applied during the training phase. During inference, we only utilize the forward propagation of the EfficientNet model to obtain the prediction results. Therefore, our proposed method does not introduce any additional parameters or increase the inference FLOPs. For data augmentation, we applied techniques including ImageCompression, RGBShift, HueSaturationValue, and RandomBrightnessContrast. The hyperparameters used in our algorithm, as shown in Algorithm 1, are $\lambda = 0.5, \beta = 200, k = 5, k_s = 500$. During testing, we extracted 32 frames from each video and selected the maximum predicted value among all the faces in each frame as the prediction score for that frame. The average of all frame prediction values was taken as the confidence score for the video. To ensure fairness, for videos where no faces were detected, we set the confidence score to 0.5.

4.2   Exploration Experiments of ADFD Methods

In this section, we provide an experimental exploration of Anomaly DeepFake Detection methods, with a focus on the Mask Generation, Source-Target Preprocessing, and Blending step, as details in Table 1.

Exploration of Mask Generation Exploration of Local and Global Mask Regions. We summarize the mask generation strategies into three types,

Table 2. AUC comparison of different mask generation strategies based on SBI.

Name	Test Set AUC(%)						
	FF++	CDF	DFDC	DFDCP	FFIW	Avg.	Avg. w/o FF++
SBI w/ global mask	99.01	80.31	70.40	82.37	79.58	82.33	78.17
SBI w/ LAL	**99.56**	**91.23**	**72.10**	**86.25**	83.68	**86.56**	**83.32**
SBI w/ local mask	95.89	73.99	61.70	60.89	72.08	72.91	67.17
SBI w/ LAL and local mask	99.29	88.73	71.70	81.55	**84.49**	85.15	81.62

Table 3. AUC comparison of different parameter settings of the mask.

Parameters				Test Set AUC (%)						
LineType	DataType	Value	Size	FF++	CDF	DFDC	DFDCP	FFIW	Avg.	Avg. w/o FF++
LINE_8	uint8	1	facehull	99.01	80.31	70.40	82.37	79.58	82.33	78.17
LINE_8	uint8	255	facehull	99.01	80.31	70.40	82.37	79.58	82.33	78.17
LINE_AA	uint8	1	facehull	99.05	79.67	70.37	83.19	79.88	82.43	78.28
LINE_8	float32	1	facehull	99.36	89.74	71.52	84.05	85.76	86.09	82.77
LINE_AA	float32	255	facehull	99.36	88.23	71.46	84.54	85.41	85.80	82.41
LINE_AA	float32	255	LAL	99.56	91.23	72.10	86.25	83.68	86.56	83.32

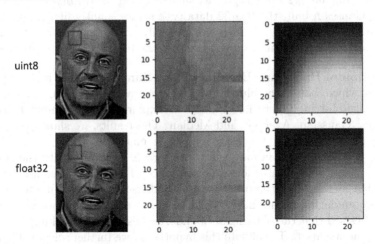

Fig. 4. Comparison of the mask with different data types. We visualize the blurred mask with uint8 and float32 data types respectively. Mask with float32 data type shows slightly higher blurring at the boundaries.

i.e. global mask used in the source code of SBI[1], the global landmark augmentation library (LAL) from Face X-ray[2], and the local mask proposed by the SLADD. We conducted ablation experiments on these strategies and the corresponding combinations, the results are shown in Table 2. From Table 2, we can observe several interesting phenomena: 1) Despite both being based on

---

[1] https://github.com/mapooon/SelfBlendedImages.
[2] https://github.com/AlgoHunt/Face-Xray.

landmark-based global masks, the mask generation method based on SBI performs much worse in terms of generalization compared to the method based on LAL. 2) The local mask generation method based on SLADD ignores the global tampering patterns and produces images that are too close to the real images, resulting in low generalization performance. 3) By randomly selecting between the LAL and local masks, the results are still lower than those obtained using the global LAL tampering. The above experiments illustrate that different mask strategies have a significant impact on generalisability.

Exploration of Parameter Settings of Mask. To further explore the factors at the heart of the performance differences between the global mask and LAL, we identify four main areas of distinction: line drawing method (LineType), mask data type (DataType), mask value range (Value), and mask size selection(Size). We conduct experiments by adjusting these parameters, and the results are shown in Table 3. Through this exploration, we find that the core influencing parameter causing this difference lies in the mask DataType. Simply changing the mask DataType from uint8 to float32 leads to a 4.6% improvement in average generalization performance (Avg w/o FF++). Then, we visualize the masks with uint8 and float32 data types, as shown in Fig. 4. We observe that after applying Gaussian blur, the float32 data type shows slightly higher blurring at the boundaries. Therefore, we can preliminarily conclude that the boundary-blurring approach has a significant impact on the model's generalization.

Exploration of Boundary-Blurring Operation. We further investigate the extent to which boundary blurring affects generalization in the Exploration of Boundary-blurring Operation. Firstly, we explored three different boundary operations: Gaussian, Average, and Median. The results are shown in Table 4. The experiment revealed that there was not much difference in the results between the Gaussian method and the Average method, while the Median method yielded significantly lower performance. The main difference between the Median method and the other two methods is that Gaussian and Average blur the boundaries of the mask, while the Median method does not. Hence, we hypothesized that the blurring of boundaries has a substantial impact on the model's generalization. To validate this hypothesis, we further selected Gaussian blur and fixed the regions in the mask without any blurring, i.e. regions with a mask value of 1, to solely examine the effect of boundary-blurring degree on the model's generalization, which is shown in Fig. 5. The experiment confirmed that different boundary blurring degrees, i.e., different sizes of the Gaussian blur kernel, have a significant difference in the model's generalization. Therefore, we further prove that the generalization of ADFD methods is sensitive to boundary-blurring operations. The maximum difference in average generalization can reach up to 9.64% (from 62.39% to 72.03%).

Exploration of Source-Target Preprocessing Exploration of Transform Methods. In the Source-Target Preprocessing step, most methods employ augmentation techniques such as transformations to help generate pseudo-fake

Table 4. AUC comparison of different boundary-blurring operations.

Name	Test Set AUC (%)						
	FF++	CDF	DFDC	DFDCP	FFIW	Avg.	Avg. w/o FF++
Gaussion	99.37	88.45	71.57	84.79	83.19	85.47	82.00
Average	99.31	89.41	71.80	84.67	87.02	86.44	83.23
Median	96.16	83.08	63.52	83.63	73.95	80.07	76.05

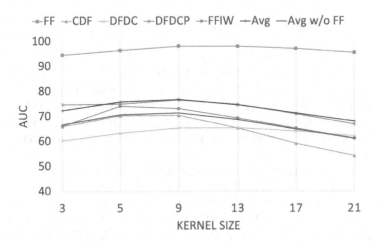

Fig. 5. AUC comparison of different boundary-blurring degrees. We visualize the experiments with different Gaussian kernel sizes with fixed regions in the mask.

samples that facilitate model learning. Taking SBI as an example, we categorize different transformation methods into three types: color transform, frequency transform, and affine transform. For color transformation, we select data augmentation techniques related to image color, including RGBShift, HueSaturationValue, and RandomBrightnessContrast. Frequency transform primarily involves random downscaling or sharpening. Affine transform mainly involves random translation, scaling, and elastic deformation. According to the results shown in Table 5, we observed a significant improvement in model generalization with affine transform, achieving an average generalization improvement of 10.15%. This indicates the importance of affine transformations in enhancing model generalization. On the other hand, the effectiveness of frequency transforms varied across different datasets, which could be attributed to the variations in the types of forgery present in each dataset. Overall, combining all three transformation methods yielded the best results in terms of average improvement.

Exploration of Transform Objects. The Source-Target Preprocessing step primarily involves applying various transform operations to two objects, i.e. source images and target images. We explored different combinations of transform objects to investigate their impact on model generalization, as shown in

Table 5. AUC comparison of different transform methods.

Transform Method			Test Set AUC (%)						
Color	Frequency	Affine	FF++	CDF	DFDC	DFDCP	FFIW	Avg.	Avg. w/o FF++
✓	✓	✓	99.56	**91.23**	**72.10**	86.25	83.68	**86.56**	**83.32**
–	✓	✓	99.54	90.81	69.70	82.05	82.71	84.96	81.32
✓	–	✓	91.19	71.79	66.99	**86.72**	**89.81**	81.30	78.83
✓	✓	–	**99.62**	80.50	61.47	78.26	73.66	78.70	73.47

Table 6. AUC comparison of different transform objects.

Name	Test Set AUC (%)						
	FF++	CDF	DFDC	DFDCP	FFIW	Avg.	Avg. w/o FF++
source transform	99.19	74.09	65.73	84.82	**86.06**	81.98	77.68
target transform	98.10	90.76	66.16	77.65	64.90	79.51	74.87
target and source transform	98.89	89.19	71.95	**89.57**	80.83	86.09	82.89
target/source transform	**99.56**	**91.23**	**72.10**	86.25	83.68	**86.56**	**83.32**

Table 7. AUC comparison of different blending types.

Name	Test Set AUC(%)						
	FF++	CDF	DFDC	DFDCP	FFIW	Avg.	Avg. w/o FF++
dynamic blend	99.56	91.23	72.10	86.25	83.68	86.56	83.32
alpha blend	98.61	87.02	67.83	80.80	81.25	83.10	79.23

Table 6. We observed that performing transforms on both the source and target simultaneously ("target and source transform") or randomly selecting one with a probability of 0.5 ("target/source transform") allows for a greater variety of tampering simulations. Consequently, these approaches exhibit stronger generalization compared to solely applying transforms to either the source or target image.

Exploration of Blending Exploration of Blending Types. We experimented with two blending types: dynamic blend and alpha blend. Dynamic blend refers to a blending method where the blending ratio μ between two images is dynamically adjusted, i.e. we sample μ from $\{0.25, 0.5, 0.75, 1, 1, 1\}$ following SBI. On the other hand, alpha blend is a traditional blending technique that uses a fixed blending ratio $\mu = 1$. The experimental results for these two blending types are shown in Table 7. Compared to alpha blend, dynamic blend provides more variations and can simulate a wider range of tampering scenarios. Besides, the dynamic blend enables a seamless and natural transition between the source and target images, making it more closely resemble real-world attack scenarios. Therefore, dynamic blend exhibits superior generalization compared to alpha blend.

Table 8. Cross-dataset evaluation on CDF, DFDC, DFDCP, and FFIW. The results of prior methods are directly cited from SBI and the original paper, and their subsequences for fair comparisons. Bold and underline represent the first and second highest results, respectively. * denotes results reproduced by our own.

Method	Training Set		Test Set AUC (%)				
	Real	Fake	CDF	DFDC	DFDCP	FFIW	Avg.
DSP-FWA [18]	✓	✓	69.30	–	–	–	69.30
Face X-ray + BI [17]	✓		–	–	71.15	–	71.15
Face X-ray + BI [17]	✓	✓	–	–	80.92	–	80.92
Two-branch [23]	✓	✓	76.65	–	–	–	76.65
DAM [38]	✓	✓	75.30	–	72.80	–	74.05
LipForensics [13]	✓	✓	82.40	–	–	–	82.40
FTCN [37]	✓	✓	86.90	71.00	74.00	74.47	76.59
LRL [3]	✓	✓	78.26	–	76.53	–	77.40
FRDM [22]	✓	✓	79.40	–	79.70	–	79.55
PCL+I2G [36]	✓		90.03	67.52	74.37		77.31
SBI [29]	✓		<u>91.23*</u>	<u>72.10*</u>	**86.25***	<u>83.68*</u>	<u>83.32*</u>
SLADD [2]	✓	✓	79.70	–	76.00	–	77.85
Ours	✓		**91.37**	**72.98**	<u>85.89</u>	**87.77**	**84.50**

Table 9. Cross-manipulation validation on FF++.

Method	Test Set AUC (%)				
	DF	F2F	FS	NT	FF++
Face X-ray + BI [17]	99.17	98.57	98.21	98.13	98.52
PCL+I2G [36]	**100.00**	98.93	99.86	97.63	99.11
SLADD [2]	–	–	–	–	98.40
SBI [29]	<u>99.99*</u>	99.77*	**99.90***	**98.57***	**99.56***
Ours	99.98	**99.83**	<u>99.89</u>	<u>98.38</u>	<u>99.52</u>

4.3 Comparison Experiments

Cross-Dataset Evaluation. We conducted Cross-Dataset Evaluation to demonstrate the generalization of our method. The model was trained on FF++ and evaluated on other datasets, *i.e.* CDF, DFDC, DFDCP, and FFIW. From Table 8, our method basically outperformed all methods, with an average AUC of 84.50%. Furthermore, it shows improvements over the SBI on other datasets such as CDF, DFDC, and FFIW. Particularly on the FFIW dataset, our method achieves a significant improvement of 4.09% (from 83.6% to 87.77%) compared to the second-ranked method SBI, surpassing other methods by a large margin.

Cross-Manipulation Evaluation. Following the evaluation protocol used in previous methods, we tested our method on the FF+ with different tampering techniques, *i.e.* DeepFake (DF), Face2Face (F2F), FaceSwap (FS), and NeturalTextures (NT) to validate its generalization across various manipulations, as

Fig. 6. Qualitative Analysis. We compare our method (second row) with the baseline (first row) by showing a cross-section of visual examples of real (Green) and fake (Red) faces with different anomaly scores. (Color figure online)

shown in Table 9. The experimental results demonstrate that our method performs on par with the SOTA for each manipulation method. Therefore, our method not only improves cross-dataset generalization but also maintains accuracy on the FF++ (cross-manipulation).

Qualitative Analysis. We compare our method with the baseline by showing a cross-section of visual examples of real and fake samples with different anomaly scores. This analysis helps us understand the strengths and limitations of our method. According to Fig. 6, it can be observed that our method has improved the generalization of the model in distinguishing real faces, particularly in real facial images with noticeable contrast (corresponding to the second column in the figure) and color deviations (third column). This demonstrates the effectiveness of our NRS method in suppressing noise and enhancing generalization. In addition to the improvement in generalization for real faces, our method also exhibits significant enhancements in the accuracy of detecting fake faces, both in cases of full-face tampering (fourth column) and localized tampering (mouth area of figures in the fifth column). These results provide further evidence of the effectiveness of BBMG method. However, admittedly, there is still room for improvement when dealing with highly realistic fake face images (corresponding to the sixth column in the figure).

Robustness Study. To evaluate the robustness of our method, we applied different image distortion methods to raw images from all test datasets. Our robustness testing is conducted using weights trained on raw images without any fine-tuning. The result is shown in Table 10. The distortion types we considered include 1) "Resize": the process of downsampling the original image to an $s \times s$ size and then upsampling it back to the original image size, simulating the compression process during image transmission, 2) Gaussian blurring with a kernel size of k, and 3) JPEG compression with a quality factor q. The experimental results demonstrated that our method consistently outperformed the baseline in terms of generalization, regardless of the distortion method applied. Moreover, in most cases, our method exhibited superior performance on the FF++ dataset

Table 10. Robustness analysis of the proposed method.

Operations	Baseline		Ours	
	FF++	Avg.	FF++	Avg.
Raw	99.56	83.32	99.52	84.50
Resize (s = 128)	98.00	81.17	98.16	82.26
Resize (s = 256)	99.29	83.20	99.29	84.34
GaussianBlur (k = 3)	99.35	80.34	99.32	82.09
GaussianBlur (k = 5)	98.81	79.50	98.90	81.33
JPEGCompress (q = 50)	92.48	81.95	93.35	83.04
JPEGCompress (q = 100)	99.48	81.71	99.51	82.53

Table 11. Ablation study of the proposed method.

Methods		Test Set AUC (%)				
BBMG	NRS	CDF	DFDC	DFDCP	FFIW	Avg.
–	–	91.23	72.10	86.25	83.68	83.32
✓	–	91.37	72.57	85.66	86.31	83.98
–	✓	**91.38**	72.80	**86.50**	86.18	84.22
✓	✓	91.37	**72.98**	85.89	**87.77**	**84.50**

Table 12. Ablation study of Boundary Blur Mask Generator with different types of masks. We experimented with three forms of masks, which are visualized in Fig. 7.

Method	Test Set AUC (%)						
	FF++	CDF	DFDC	DFDCP	FFIW	Avg.	Avg. w/o FF++
1	**99.64**	91.30	71.96	84.40	83.79	86.22	82.86
2	99.60	90.90	72.04	84.37	85.76	86.53	83.27
3	99.55	**91.37**	**72.57**	**85.66**	**86.31**	**87.09**	**83.98**

compared to the baseline. These findings confirm the robustness of our proposed method in handling various image distortions.

Ablation Study of the Proposed Method. In Table 11, we conducted an ablation study on the Boundary Blur Mask Generator (BBMG) and the Noise Refinement Strategy (NRS). From the experimental results, we observed that the inclusion of both methods improved performance on most datasets and the average AUC. Furthermore, the fusion of these two methods resulted in a further improvement in the average AUC. This confirms that both Boundary Blur Mask Generator and Noise Refinement Strategy contribute significantly to enhancing the model's generalization capabilities.

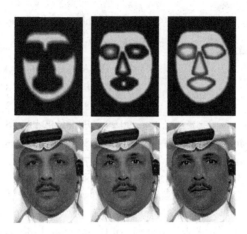

Fig. 7. Different masks in BBMG. We experimented with three forms of masks: using only the result of M_{global}^b (first column), the result of scaling M_{local}^b (second column), and the method mentioned in our method (third column).

Table 13. Ablation study of Noise Refinement Strategy.

Parameters		Test Set AUC (%)						
Filter	Distance	FF++	CDF	DFDC	DFDCP	FFIW	Avg.	Avg. w/o FF++
random	cosine	99.51	90.91	72.38	85.24	86.96	87.00	83.87
random	L2	99.52	90.85	72.39	85.37	87.12	87.05	83.93
predicts	cosine	99.52	91.37	72.98	85.89	87.77	87.51	84.50
predicts	L2	99.52	91.40	73.06	85.90	87.00	87.38	84.34

Ablation Study of Boundary Blur Mask Generator. To provide a clearer representation of the mask effects, we excluded the Weighted Loss Noise Refinement Strategy in this experiment and solely utilized our Boundary Blur Mask Generator. We experimented with three types of masks generated by the Boundary Blur Mask Generator. These three masks are 1) Using only the result of M_{global}^b (first column); 2)Narrowing M_{local}^b; and 3)The method mentioned in our method. The visual results are shown in Fig. 7. The experimental results in Table 12 indicate that the first type of mask achieved the best performance on the FF++ [26], exhibiting the highest accuracy. On the other hand, the third method (as mentioned in our approach) showed the most pronounced local tampering artifacts in the visual results and demonstrated the highest generalization performance across different datasets.

Ablation Study of Noise Refinement Strategy. We conducted various experiments with different Noise Refinement Strategies, as shown in Table 13. The "Filter" column refers to the method used to filter real face samples. In this part, we selected 500 samples from the training set as input for k-means clustering to calculate the cluster centers representing the distribution of real faces. The "random" strategy involved randomly sampling 500 real samples, while the "predicts" strategy involved selecting the 500 real samples with the highest predicted probabilities based on the model's predictions from the previous epoch. The "Distance" column indicates the distance metric used to measure the distance between generated fake samples and real samples. Specifically, we compared the cosine distance and L2 distance. The experimental results revealed that the cosine distance metric outperformed the L2 distance metric. Additionally, the strategy of selecting samples based on predicted probabilities showed improvement when using either the L2 or cosine distance metric.

5   Conclusion

In this paper, we first systematically analyze a range of existing anomalous deep forgery detection methods and identify the core factors that have a relatively large impact on generalisability, such as mask selection as well as boundary processing. In addition, we point out that previous work generates some pseudo-noise samples. To address these issues, we propose a new framework that contains Boundary Blur Mask Generator and Noise Refinement Strategy. Extensive experiments have fully demonstrated the excellent generalization capability of our approach, achieving state-of-the-art performance in deep forgery detection.

Acknowledgments. This work was supported in part by the National Natural Science Foundation of China under Grants 62222602, 62302167, 62176224, 62106075, 61972157 and U23A20343, in part by Science and Technology Commission under Grant 21511100700, in part by CCF-Tencent Rhino-Bird Young Faculty Open Research Fund under Grant RAGR20230121.

References

1. Afchar, D., Nozick, V., Yamagishi, J., Echizen, I.: Mesonet: a compact facial video forgery detection network. In: 2018 IEEE International Workshop on Information Forensics and Security (WIFS), pp. 1–7. IEEE (2018)
2. Chen, L., Zhang, Y., Song, Y., Liu, L., Wang, J.: Self-supervised learning of adversarial example: towards good generalizations for deepfake detection. In: Proceedings of the IEEE/CVF Conference on Computer Vision and Pattern Recognition, pp. 18710–18719 (2022)
3. Chen, S., Yao, T., Chen, Y., Ding, S., Li, J., Ji, R.: Local relation learning for face forgery detection. In: Proceedings of the AAAI Conference on Artificial Intelligence, vol. 35, pp. 1081–1088 (2021)
4. Deng, J., Dong, W., Socher, R., Li, L.J., Li, K., Fei-Fei, L.: Imagenet: a large-scale hierarchical image database. In: 2009 IEEE Conference on Computer Vision and Pattern Recognition, pp. 248–255. IEEE (2009)
5. Deng, J., Guo, J., Zhou, Y., Yu, J., Kotsia, I., Zafeiriou, S.: Retinaface: single-stage dense face localisation in the wild. arXiv preprint arXiv:1905.00641 (2019)
6. Dolhansky, B., et al.: The deepfake detection challenge (DFDC) dataset. arXiv preprint arXiv:2006.07397 (2020)

7. Dolhansky, B., Howes, R., Pflaum, B., Baram, N., Ferrer, C.C.: The deepfake detection challenge (DFDC) preview dataset. arXiv preprint arXiv:1910.08854 (2019)
8. Du, M., Pentyala, S., Li, Y., Hu, X.: Towards generalizable deepfake detection with locality-aware autoencoder. In: Proceedings of the 29th ACM International Conference on Information & Knowledge Management, pp. 325–334 (2020)
9. Foret, P., Kleiner, A., Mobahi, H., Neyshabur, B.: Sharpness-aware minimization for efficiently improving generalization. arXiv preprint arXiv:2010.01412 (2020)
10. Frank, J., Eisenhofer, T., Schönherr, L., Fischer, A., Kolossa, D., Holz, T.: Leveraging frequency analysis for deep fake image recognition. In: International Conference on Machine Learning, pp. 3247–3258. PMLR (2020)
11. Guan, J., et al.: Delving into sequential patches for deepfake detection. Adv. Neural. Inf. Process. Syst. **35**, 4517–4530 (2022)
12. Güera, D., Delp, E.J.: Deepfake video detection using recurrent neural networks. In: 2018 15th IEEE International Conference on Advanced Video and Signal Based Surveillance (AVSS), pp. 1–6. IEEE (2018)
13. Haliassos, A., Vougioukas, K., Petridis, S., Pantic, M.: Lips don't lie: a generalisable and robust approach to face forgery detection. In: Proceedings of the IEEE/CVF Conference on Computer Vision and Pattern Recognition, pp. 5039–5049 (2021)
14. Khalid, H., Woo, S.S.: Oc-fakedect: classifying deepfakes using one-class variational autoencoder. In: Proceedings of the IEEE/CVF Conference on Computer Vision and Pattern Recognition Workshops, pp. 656–657 (2020)
15. King, D.E.: Dlib-ml: a machine learning toolkit. J. Mach. Learn. Res. **10**, 1755–1758 (2009)
16. Li, J., Xie, H., Li, J., Wang, Z., Zhang, Y.: Frequency-aware discriminative feature learning supervised by single-center loss for face forgery detection. In: Proceedings of the IEEE/CVF Conference on Computer Vision and Pattern Recognition, pp. 6458–6467 (2021)
17. Li, L., et al.: Face x-ray for more general face forgery detection. In: Proceedings of the IEEE/CVF Conference on Computer Vision and Pattern Recognition, pp. 5001–5010 (2020)
18. Li, Y., Lyu, S.: Exposing deepfake videos by detecting face warping artifacts. arXiv preprint arXiv:1811.00656 (2018)
19. Li, Y., Yang, X., Sun, P., Qi, H., Lyu, S.: Celeb-df: a large-scale challenging dataset for deepfake forensics. In: Proceedings of the IEEE/CVF Conference on Computer Vision and Pattern Recognition, pp. 3207–3216 (2020)
20. Liu, B., Liu, B., Ding, M., Zhu, T., Yu, X.: Ti2net: temporal identity inconsistency network for deepfake detection. In: Proceedings of the IEEE/CVF Winter Conference on Applications of Computer Vision, pp. 4691–4700 (2023)
21. Liu, H., et al.: Spatial-phase shallow learning: rethinking face forgery detection in frequency domain. In: Proceedings of the IEEE/CVF Conference on Computer Vision and Pattern Recognition, pp. 772–781 (2021)
22. Luo, Y., Zhang, Y., Yan, J., Liu, W.: Generalizing face forgery detection with high-frequency features. In: Proceedings of the IEEE/CVF Conference on Computer Vision and Pattern Recognition, pp. 16317–16326 (2021)
23. Masi, I., Killekar, A., Mascarenhas, R.M., Gurudatt, S.P., AbdAlmageed, W.: Two-branch recurrent network for isolating deepfakes in videos. In: Vedaldi, A., Bischof, H., Brox, T., Frahm, J.-M. (eds.) ECCV 2020. LNCS, vol. 12352, pp. 667–684. Springer, Cham (2020). https://doi.org/10.1007/978-3-030-58571-6_39
24. Nguyen, H., Yamagishi, J., Echizen, I.: Use of a capsule network to detect fake images and videos. arXiv preprint arXiv:1910.12467 (2019)

25. Qian, Y., Yin, G., Sheng, L., Chen, Z., Shao, J.: Thinking in frequency: face forgery detection by mining frequency-aware clues. In: Vedaldi, A., Bischof, H., Brox, T., Frahm, J.-M. (eds.) ECCV 2020. LNCS, vol. 12357, pp. 86–103. Springer, Cham (2020). https://doi.org/10.1007/978-3-030-58610-2_6

26. Rossler, A., Cozzolino, D., Verdoliva, L., Riess, C., Thies, J., Nießner, M.: Faceforensics++: learning to detect manipulated facial images. In: Proceedings of the IEEE/CVF International Conference on Computer Vision, pp. 1–11 (2019)

27. Sabir, E., Cheng, J., Jaiswal, A., AbdAlmageed, W., Masi, I., Natarajan, P.: Recurrent convolutional strategies for face manipulation detection in videos. Interfaces (GUI) 3(1), 80–87 (2019)

28. Shao, R., Wu, T., Liu, Z.: Detecting and recovering sequential deepfake manipulation. In: Avidan, S., Brostow, G., Cisse, M., Farinella, G.M., Hassner, T. (eds.) ECCV 2022, vol. 13673, pp. 712–728. Springer, Heidelberg (2022). https://doi.org/10.1007/978-3-031-19778-9_41

29. Shiohara, K., Yamasaki, T.: Detecting deepfakes with self-blended images. In: Proceedings of the IEEE/CVF Conference on Computer Vision and Pattern Recognition, pp. 18720–18729 (2022)

30. Tan, L., Wang, Y., Wang, J., Yang, L., Chen, X., Guo, Y.: Deepfake video detection via facial action dependencies estimation. In: Proceedings of the AAAI Conference on Artificial Intelligence, vol. 37, pp. 5276–5284 (2023)

31. Tan, M., Le, Q.: Efficientnet: rethinking model scaling for convolutional neural networks. In: International Conference on Machine Learning, pp. 6105–6114. PMLR (2019)

32. Wei, J., Wang, S., Huang, Q.: F^3net: fusion, feedback and focus for salient object detection. In: Proceedings of the AAAI Conference on Artificial Intelligence, vol. 34, pp. 12321–12328 (2020)

33. Yu, Y., Zhao, X., Ni, R., Yang, S., Zhao, Y., Kot, A.C.: Augmented multi-scale spatiotemporal inconsistency magnifier for generalized deepfake detection. IEEE Trans. Multimedia 99, 1–13 (2023)

34. Zhao, H., et al.: Multi-attentional deepfake detection. In: Proceedings of the IEEE/CVF Conference on Computer Vision and Pattern Recognition, pp. 2185–2194 (2021)

35. Zhao, H., Zhou, W., Chen, D., Zhang, W., Yu, N.: Self-supervised transformer for deepfake detection. arXiv preprint arXiv:2203.01265 (2022)

36. Zhao, T., Xu, X., Xu, M., Ding, H., Xiong, Y., Xia, W.: Learning self-consistency for deepfake detection. In: Proceedings of the IEEE/CVF International Conference on Computer Vision, pp. 15023–15033 (2021)

37. Zheng, Y., Bao, J., Chen, D., Zeng, M., Wen, F.: Exploring temporal coherence for more general video face forgery detection. In: Proceedings of the IEEE/CVF International Conference on Computer Vision, pp. 15044–15054 (2021)

38. Zhou, T., Wang, W., Liang, Z., Shen, J.: Face forensics in the wild. In: Proceedings of the IEEE/CVF Conference on Computer Vision and Pattern Recognition, pp. 5778–5788 (2021)

Deep Tiny Network for Recognition-Oriented Face Image Quality Assessment

Baoyun Peng[1] , Min Liu[1,2(✉)] , Zhaoning Zhang[3] , Kai Xu[3] , and Dongsheng Li[3]

[1] Academy of Military Science, Beijing 100097, People's Republic of China
pengbaoyun13@alumni.nudt.edu.cn
[2] Intelligent Game and Decision Laboratory, Beijing 100071, People's Republic of China
gfsliumin@gmail.com
[3] National University of Defense Technology, Changsha 410073, People's Republic of China
{zhangzhaoning,kevin.kai.xu,dsli}@nudt.edu.cn

Abstract. Face recognition has made significant progress in recent years due to deep convolutional neural networks (CNN). In many face recognition (FR) scenarios, face images are acquired from a sequence with huge intra-variations. These intra-variations, which are mainly affected by low-quality face images, cause instability of recognition performance. Previous works have focused on ad-hoc methods to select frames from a video or use face image quality assessment (FIQA) methods, which consider only a particular or combination of several distortions. In this work, we present an efficient non-reference image quality assessment for FR that directly links image quality assessment (IQA) and FR. More specifically, we propose a new measurement to evaluate image quality without any reference. Based on the proposed quality measurement, we propose a deep Tiny Face Quality network (tinyFQnet) to learn a quality prediction function from data. We evaluate the proposed method for different powerful FR models on two classical video-based (or template-based) benchmarks IJB-B and YTF. Extensive experiments show that, although the tinyFQnet is much smaller than the others, the proposed method outperforms state-of-the-art quality assessment methods in terms of effectiveness and efficiency.

Keywords: Face image quality assessment · Lightweight network · Face recognition

1 Introduction

The performance of face recognition (FR) has been considerably improved in recent years, mainly owing to the combination of deep neural networks and

Supported by NSFC 62302517, 62325211, 62132021.

large-scale labeled face images. On the representative academic benchmarks IJB-C [32] and IQIYI-VID [31], several FR methods [2,9,22] have even surpassed humans in terms of face verification. However, in many real scenarios where face images are captured as a sequence with high uncertainty, the FR performance degrades sharply due to the sequence's low-quality face images. Figure 1 shows such a typical scenario in which the input of the FR model is a sequence of images. In such a sequence, the difficulty of recognizing the person in various face images is different. Usually, images with a high-resolution, neural head pose, and little distortions (occlusion, blur, or noises), are easier to recognize. For the sake of throughput capacity, the FR system may only sample one or a few images from a sequence to recognize. Without a good selection method, the FR system may fail to recognize when selecting a low-quality image that is hard to recognize. Face image quality assessment (FIQA) can correctly assess face images' quality to improve an FR system's performance.

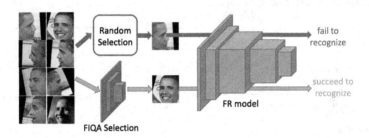

Fig. 1. A typical selection process. Random selection may select a low-quality image that is hard for the FR model to recognize. A good FIQA selection method can improve the performance of recognition.

Evaluating the influence of face image quality on an FR system's performance is non-trivial since the performance is affected by many underlying variations, and there is no unified definition or standard metric on face image quality. Several efforts have been made to develop common standards [15,38]. In these standards, the factors that influence the face image quality can be categorized into perceptual variations and biometric variations. Many prior works have contributed to automatic FIQA methods [1,4,53], and these works are similar to general image quality assessment that relies on either the difference among several known properties of the human visual system between target and reference images [13] or the degradation in structural information of face images [45]. However, considering one or several particular factors may result in unsuitable face image selection since the face image quality is influenced by many potential factors.

Several new learning-based FIQA methods have been proposed in recent years that attempt to address the limitations of earlier techniques through automatically learning how to assess face image quality from amounts of data [5,19,33,42]. For instance, [44] uses the matching score between a face image and a reference image as a quality score based on hand-crafted features, while [19] and [33] are based on features extracted from a well-performed FR model. Both of them need to select an image as a reference for each class to evaluate quality scores before training their models. For non-reference FIQA, [23] proposes pixel-level face image quality assessment that measures face recognition performance changes when inserting or deleting pixels based on their predicted quality. [7] uses knowledge distillation on difficult samples to train an efficient lightweight FIQA network focused on the quality classification boundary. Besides, there are also several non-reference IQA methods [3,5] that use GAN or CNN to assess face image quality based on noise exploration or sample relative classifiability (Fig. 2).

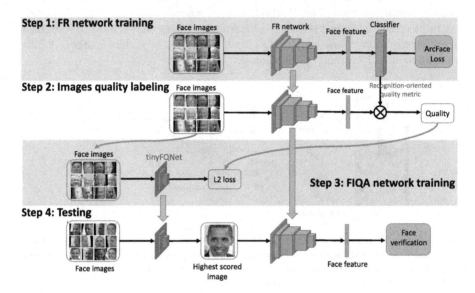

Fig. 2. The pipeline for video-based FR. The base set contains multiple identities, and each identity is with several images. In common, the frames are captured under significant variations, such as large head pose, illumination, motion blur, and occlusion. Our method consists of four steps. In Step 1, we train the FR network. Then, the trained FR network is used to label face images with quality. We use L2 regression loss in Step 3 to train a FIQA network. For testing in Step 4, we first use our trained FIQA network to select high-quality face images and feed them to our trained FR network to extract features, then the extracted feature will be used for face verification.

Unlike the above FIQA methods, we propose an efficient deep image quality assessment method for face recognition in this paper. More specifically, we propose a novel non-reference quality measurement for face image quality scoring that directly links Face IQA with FR without a reference. The details of the proposed quality metric are presented in Sect. 3.1. Using the proposed quality measurement, we can generate amounts of training data with quality labels in a fully automatic way. Besides, previous methods are usually based on complicated networks (e.g., ResNet-50 in [54] and VGG-16 in [19]) while training them on a relatively small dataset. They may ignore that computation and memory costs are important when applying face IQA to a real FR system. However, the computation or memory cost of FIQA is truly a key factor when designing a resource-limited FR system, such as face unlock on mobile phones and other embedded devices. Based on this consideration, we propose a tiny but effective FIQA network with only **21.8k** parameters, and the average time of processing an image is only 4ms on Samsung S10.

To verify the effectiveness of the proposed method, the performance evaluation of the FR model when combined with face IQA as a plug-in is carried out. We provide extensive analysis of the impact on the performance of the FR model in terms of different network sizes and show that even a tiny network can achieve comparable performance with much more complicated networks on face image quality assessment. To evaluate the influence of different factors on the FR model's performance, we provide extensive experiments on three perceptual factors: head pose, blurriness, and JPEG compression rate. We also provide a comprehensive comparison among perceptual-based and learning-based FIQA methods and compare the proposed method with several other FIQA methods.

The proposed method can also be used to generate video representation by quality-weighted averages like [39,49], but this is not our scope in this work. We evaluate the proposed method on three common datasets, including the IARPA Janus Benchmark-B (IJB-B) [46], IARPA Janus Benchmark-C (IJB-C) [32], and Youtube Faces Database (YTF) [47]. The results show that our proposed method can improve the baseline FR performance significantly and is also superior to other FIQA methods. The contributions of this paper are summarized as follows:

- We propose a new quality measurement that directly targets face recognition for face image quality assessment (FIQA), and no reference is required. Using the proposed quality measurement, we can automatically generate amounts of data with quality labels to train the IQA model;
- We propose an efficient and effective deep network based on the proposed quality measurement as a face IQA model and demonstrate the effectiveness of the proposed method on the unconstrained IJB-B dataset and YTF dataset;
- We provide extensive analysis on the influence of several perceptual factors on FR's performance and a comprehensive comparison between perceptual-based and learning-based FIQA methods;
- We provide extensive analysis on the influence of FIQA network size on FR's performance, and show that even a tiny network with only 21.8K parameters can achieve comparable performance with a much more complicated network with 23M parameters;
- We provide extensive analysis on the influence of data size and quality score distribution of the training dataset on FR's performance, and provide an effective sampling method to make the training dataset more balanced, which is proved that it can further improve FR's performance;

The rest of this paper is organized as follows. In Sect. 2, we review related works on FR and FIQA. In Sect. 3, we present the details of the proposed FIQA method, including a novel recognition-oriented quality metric in Sect. 3.1, a tiny network for FIQA in Sect. 3.2, and an easy and efficient method that can quickly generate amounts of labeled data in Sect. 3.3. In Sect. 4, evaluations on IJB-B and YTF datasets are presented. Finally, the concluding remarks are presented in Sect. 5.

2 Related Work

This work mainly focuses on face image quality assessment (FIQA) for face recognition. Many of the previous works are extended from general image quality assessment (IQA). Therefore, we first discuss the related works of general IQA, then face recognition and FIQA.

2.1 Image Quality Assessment

Image quality assessment methods are mainly categorized into full-reference methods and non-reference (or blind) methods. The former needs full access to the reference images [11, 24, 41]. Several full-reference IQA methods are based on human visual systems [11, 26], which predict quality scores from visible image differences. Changes of structure in a distorted image are also taken to measure the quality in [37, 45]. Non-reference IQA methods require no or limited information about the reference image. These methods try to detect a particular or several distortions, such as blurriness [14, 17], JPEG compression [40, 51], noise [8], and combination of several distortions [12, 34]. Recently, several methods [27, 28, 52] have adopted a deep convolutional neural network (CNN) to predict image quality on training datasets with quality labels. Note that the ultimate goal of these quality assessment measurements is for human perceptual cognition rather than face recognition.

2.2 Face Image Quality Assessment

Existing methods for face image quality assessment are mainly based on the similarity to a reference (ideal) image, and these methods measure the face image quality by comparing several known properties between target images and reference images. Specifically, perceptual image quality (such as contrast, resolution, sharpness, and noise) and biometric quality (such as pose, illumination, and occlusion) have been used to evaluate face image quality [1, 50]. Prior works [35] proposed a weighted quality fusion approach that merged the weights of factors (rotation, sharpness, brightness, and resolution) into a quality score. Wong et al. [48] predicted a face image quality score by determining its probabilistic similarity to an ideal face image via local patch-based analysis for FR in a video.

Another way for FIQA is to leverage learning-based approaches [4, 6, 44]. Unlike conventional approaches that measure the quality by analyzing pre-defined biometric and perceptual image characteristics, learning-based methods learn a prediction function from amounts of face images with quality scores. Hence, the learning process is highly dependent on the training dataset. To assess a face image's quality, [21,25] used a discrete value to indicate matching results. Best-Rowden et al. [4] obtained a training dataset through pairwise comparisons performed by workers from Amazon Mechanical Turk. They used a support vector machine to predict the quality score using features extracted from a face image. Chen et al. [6] learned a ranking function for quality scores by dividing datasets according to quality. These methods aim to establish a function from image features to quality scores. Besides, these learning-based methods use either hand-crafted features or features extracted from pre-trained recognition models as inputs to learn the prediction function and train the FIQA model on small datasets collected in laboratories (e.g., FRGC [36]). In [42], deep CNN is used to determine the category and degree of degradation in a face image by considering five perceptual image characteristics (resolution, blurriness, additive white Gaussian noise, salt-and-pepper noise, and Poisson noise). In [54] and [19], the face recognition model is also used to generate quality labels, and the deep CNN model is learned from labeled data to predict quality scores. FaceQAN [3] links face image quality with adversarial examples learned by gradient descent information from the FR model. Recently, [5] proposes CR-FIQA that estimates the face image quality by predicting its relative classifiability using the sample feature representation concerning its class center and the nearest negative class center.

3   Method

In this section, we describe the details of our proposed FIQA method, including a recognition-oriented non-reference quality metric, a tiny but efficient deep network (tinyFQnet), a simple technique to quickly generate amounts of quality-labeled data that can be used to train the tinyFQnet, and a data sampling method to make the distribution of scores in the training dataset more balanced.

3.1   Recognition-Oriented Non-reference Quality Measurement

Empirically, focusing on one particular or a combination of several factors (blurriness, head pose, noise, etc.) may not be effective since FR is affected by amounts of variations, and some of these variations are not quantifiable or hand-crafted. Besides, it is hard to determine the relative importance of each factor. We argue that the QA model should be linked with the face recognition process directly.

Inspired by [19], of which the quality score of a given image is defined as the normalized Euclidean distance between it and a reference image of the same subject, we propose a recognition-oriented non-reference quality measurement that directly links quality assessment with face recognition. More specifically, given an image x and its label y, the quality score of x is defined as the cosine similarity between x and the distribution center of the same class with x in angular space, as follows:

$$quality(x) = cosine(\boldsymbol{f}_x, \boldsymbol{u}_y) = \frac{\boldsymbol{f}_x \cdot \boldsymbol{u}_y}{\|\boldsymbol{f}_x\| \, \|\boldsymbol{u}_y\|} \tag{1}$$

where $\boldsymbol{f_x}$ is the feature vector of image $\boldsymbol{x}$ extracted by the FR model, $\boldsymbol{u_y}$ is the center feature vector of y class. Compared with using a hand-selected image [54] or the highest-quality image selected by a commercial system [19] as the reference to compute image quality, the proposed method in Eq. 1 is more reasonable in the following aspect: $cosine(\boldsymbol{f_x}, \boldsymbol{u_y})$ directly reflects how difficult for the FR model to recognize the image $\boldsymbol{x}$ correctly. The lower the $cosine(\boldsymbol{f_x}, \boldsymbol{u_y})$ is, the more difficult the FR model is to recognize $\boldsymbol{x}$ correctly.

Although the center $\boldsymbol{u_y}$ is hard to obtain due to the ground-truth distribution of a given class being unknown for a particular FR model, we can regard the last fully connected layer output of an FR model as the class center in the angular space as in [29,30].

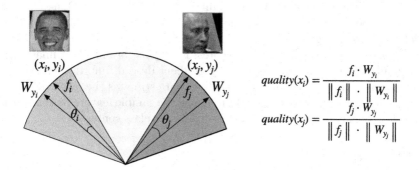

Fig. 3. Geometry interpretation of recognition-oriented quality metric in a 2D feature embedding space. $\boldsymbol{W_{y_i}}$ and $\boldsymbol{W_{y_j}}$ are the centers of y_i and y_j class, $\boldsymbol{f_i}$ and $\boldsymbol{f_j}$ is the feature vector of $\boldsymbol{x_i}$ and $\boldsymbol{x_j}$, θ_i and θ_j is the angle between $\boldsymbol{f_i}$ & $\boldsymbol{W_{y_i}}$ and $\boldsymbol{f_j}$ & $\boldsymbol{W_{y_j}}$, respectively.

Figure 3 shows the geometry interpretation of the 2D feature and two samples $(\boldsymbol{x_i}, y_i)$ and $(\boldsymbol{x_j}, y_j)$ with different difficulties to recognize. θ_j is bigger than θ_i, which means that $\boldsymbol{x_j}$ is harder to recognize compared to $\boldsymbol{x_i}$. Consequently, the quality score of $\boldsymbol{x_j}$ is smaller than $\boldsymbol{x_i}$.

3.2   Tiny Face Quality Network

The primary purpose of learning-based FIQA is to provide a prediction function for the face image quality score. Unlike previous learning-based methods that access quality scores via deep or hand-crafted features, we adopt an end-to-end method to directly predict the quality score of a raw image through deep CNN. The reason is that a deep CNN can learn more relative features from raw images compared with features extracted from pre-trained models.

We noticed a few works that adopt an end-to-end deep CNN [19,54] to predict face image quality. The core difference is that the proposed method in this work doesn't need to pick an image as a reference using other methods before generating quality scores, while [19] needs to use ICAO compliance software to pick an image with the highest score and [54] needs to select an image as a reference through human perceptual vision. Given this point, both [19] and [54] are more like reference-based methods, while our method is more similar to non-reference methods. Besides, these works didn't take the memory and computation costs into account and used very complex networks (ResNet-50 in [54] and VGG-16 in [19]) as face quality networks. However, both computation and memory costs are key factors when one needs to apply FIQA to real FR scenarios.

Table 1. Our tinyFQnet architecture. Each conv layer is followed by a batch norm layer and a ReLU layer. Block1 and Block2 are shown in Fig. 4.

layer name	output size	tinyFQnet
input	$64 \times 64 \times 3$	
conv	$32 \times 32 \times 11$	$3 \times 3 \times 11$, stride $= 2$
Block1	$32 \times 32 \times 2$	$[1 \times 1, 8\ 3 \times 3, 8\ 1 \times 1, 2] \times 1$, stride $= 1$
Block2	$16 \times 16 \times 5$	$[1 \times 1, 8\ 3 \times 3, 8\ 1 \times 1, 5] \times 1$, stride $= 2$
Block1	$16 \times 16 \times 5$	$[1 \times 1, 20\ 3 \times 3, 20\ 1 \times 1, 5] \times 1$, stride $= 1$
Block2	$8 \times 8 \times 11$	$[1 \times 1, 20\ 3 \times 3, 20\ 1 \times 1, 11] \times 1$, stride $= 2$
Block1	$8 \times 8 \times 11$	$[1 \times 1, 44\ 3 \times 3, 44\ 1 \times 1, 11] \times 2$, stride $= 1$
Block1	$8 \times 8 \times 22$	$[1 \times 1 \times 44\ 3 \times 3 \times 44\ 1 \times 1 \times 22] \times 1$, stride $= 1$
conv	$8 \times 8 \times 256$	$1 \times 1 \times 256$, stride $= 1$
avgpool	256	
fc	1	1×256

In this study, we introduce the Tiny Face Quality Assessment Network (tinyFQnet), a compact yet efficient network designed specifically for FIQA. The architectural design of tinyFQnet is inspired by and follows the modular principles of MobileNetV2, as detailed in [20]. As depicted in Fig. 4, tinyFQnet incorporates two distinct types of blocks. While these blocks share a common topology, they differ in the presence or absence of a residual connection. Each block within tinyFQnet comprises three convolutional layers. Following each convolutional layer, there is a batch normalization layer and a ReLU layer. Despite sharing identical hyper-parameters, e.g. filter sizes, padding, and bias, the two types of blocks are differentiated by their respective input and output channel dimensions.

Table 1 shows the details of the architecture of tinyFQnet, noted as Q. There are 7 blocks in Q, including 5 non-residual blocks and 2 residual blocks in Q. The output of Q will be normalized to $(0, 1)$ by a sigmoid layer. Q only has 2.356 Mflops and 21.806k parameters, while ResNet-50 has 3.898 Gflops and 22.421M parameters, and VGG-16 has 14.528 Gflops and 128.041M parameters. Compared with ResNet-50 and VGG-16 used in previous methods, our tinyFQnet has a significant advantage in memory and computation costs. Thanks to the low computation cost, our tinyFQnet can significantly speed up FR systems.

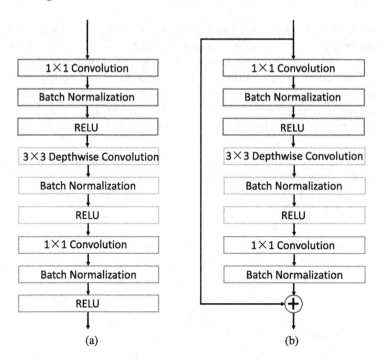

Fig. 4. The details of two basic blocks in tinyFQNet. (a): non-residual block; (b): residual block.

To cooperate with the FR network, we use RetinaFace [10] to detect and align images. Then, the aligned images are resized to 64×64 which is the same as tinyFQnet's input size. L2 regression loss in Eq. 2 is adopted to train the tinyFQnet as follows:

$$L = \frac{1}{N} \sum_{i=1}^{N} \|\phi(x_i, \theta) - q_i\|_2,\tag{2}$$

where $\phi(x, \theta)$ denotes the prediction model with parameter θ. Stochastic gradient descent is used to train the network. The learning rate is initialized to 0.01 and degrades by 0.1 at every 5 epochs. The training batch size is set as 1024, and the weight decay is set as 0.0001. The training takes 17 epochs in total.

3.3   Generating Training Dataset with Quality Labels

Usually, learning-based methods require amounts of labeled data to learn the desired function. Previous learning-based FIQA methods tried to train a prediction model from small lab-collected datasets (e.g., SCFace, FRGC, GBU, and Multi-PIE) due to the lack of a large number of face images that are labeled with quality scores. The lack of training data limits the capability of deep learning models. Similar to [54] and [19], we adopt a feasible but fast method to generate a large number of labeled data. More specifically, since the proposed quality metric only involves a well-trained FR model and a training dataset, we can automatically generate amounts of data with quality labels and use labeled data to train our tinyFQnet.

The whole process of generating the labeled dataset for training the tinyFQnet is shown as follows:

Algorithm 1. Quality label generating process

Train model Q on $\mathcal{D}$;
Extract weights $\mathcal{W}$ of the classifier layer in Q;
Extract features $\mathcal{F}$ of training data $\mathcal{D}$ using Q;
Compute quality scores of $\mathcal{D}$ using Eq. 1;

The first step is to train the FR model Q. Usually, we can use an existing well-trained FR model and its training dataset. Then, we extract the weights $\mathcal{W}$ of the classifier and all training data features from the FR model. Finally, the quality of the image can be computed with Eq. 1.

3.4 Data Sampling and Augmentation Strategy for Balancing the Distribution of Scores

While the aforementioned method enables the generation of substantial data accompanied by quality scores, it has been observed that the distribution of these scores is notably unbalanced. The left subfigure in Fig. 5 illustrates the histogram representation of the quality score distribution as produced in Sect. 3.3. A majority of the images cluster within a limited score range. This concentration can be attributed to the proposed quality metric's direct correlation with the cosine similarity between the image and its class centers in the embedding space. Essentially, as the training loss of the face recognition (FR) model decreases, the features within each class become more closely aligned. As a result, a highly effective FR model inadvertently leads to an unbalanced distribution of quality scores. This imbalance, in turn, can skew the optimized results obtained from the tinyFQnet.

To address this issue, we implemented a data sampling strategy that considers both identity and quality scores. Specifically, we initially filtered out identities associated with fewer than a predetermined number of images (in our experiments with the Ms-Celeb-1M dataset, this threshold was set at 100 images). This process resulted in approximately 7,900 identities and 860,000 images. Subsequently, we categorized these images into 100 bins based on their quality scores, ranging from 0 to 1.0, with each bin representing an equal interval. In this stratification, we purposefully oversampled images with quality scores in the lowest 10% and the highest 5%. Conversely, we downscaled the number of images from the remaining 85% of bins, adjusting the sampling rate according to the volume of images in each bin. The application of this dual strategy of identity filtering and score-based sampling yielded a more balanced distribution of quality scores

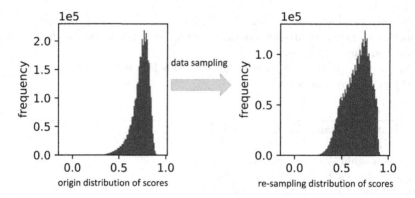

Fig. 5. Distribution of quality scores under different data sizes, including large size (left column), middle size (middle column), and small size (right column). The dataset is Ms-Celeb-1M [16], and the FR model is R50. The top row shows the results of a random sampling strategy, and the bottom row shows the results of a smooth sampling strategy.

within our training dataset. The effectiveness of this approach is evidenced in the right subfigure of Fig. 5, which contrasts starkly with the initial distribution.

4   Experimental Results

4.1   Experimental Setup

To evaluate the effectiveness of our FIQA on real FR systems, we consider the tiny recognition-oriented quality network (tinyRQNet) as a component independent of FR. We only use tinyRQNet to select the appropriate frames from a video. More specifically, we use the tinyRQNet to predict all the images in a video or a template (a template consists of several images and videos belonging to the same subject in the IJB-B dataset) and select the image with the highest quality score. Then, we evaluate those selected images using the FR model.

We compare the proposed method with three learning-based methods, including SVM [4], RQS [6], and FaceQnet [19]. RQS learns to predict and rank the quality scores from hand-crafted features. SVM [4] uses a support vector machine to predict the quality scores with features extracted by a deep FR model. Similar to our method, FaceQnet adopts deep CNN to predict quality scores from raw images. Beyond these comparisons, we also present the results of the most common perceptual factors, including blurriness, JPEG compression, head pose, and their combination. All the quality scores predicted by each method are rescaled to a range from 0 to 100, of which a higher score means higher quality.

We use two classical networks, including a complicated network ResNet-50 [18] and a lightweight network EfficientNet-b0 [43], to train the FR model on

MS-Celeb-1M [16] separately. ResNet-50 is widely used in many tasks as a baseline model due to its powerful capacity, while EfficientNet-b0 achieves considerably better accuracy compared to classical MobileNet-V2 [20] while using fewer parameters and flops. All the images are aligned using 5 landmarks provided by RetinaFace [10] and cropped to 112×112 resolution. For all learning-based methods, we keep the same settings as the original papers. All the training is carried out on 8 TiTANX GPUs. Note that we focus on face image quality assessment in this work, rather than learning video-level representations for face recognition. One can apply the proposed method to video-level face recognition, but this is beyond the scope of our work.

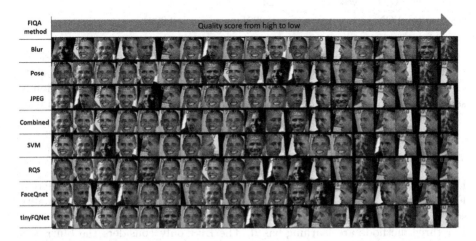

Fig. 6. Some face images were randomly selected from one subject in the IJB-B dataset. We rank them with quality scores predicted by several FIQA methods.

4.2   Datasets and Protocols

Three popular video-based (or template-based) datasets are used for evaluation: IJB-B [46], IJB-C [32], and YTF [47]. The IJB-B dataset consists of 21,798 images and 7,011 videos from 1,845 subjects captured under unconstrained conditions. Instead of image-to-image or video-to-video recognition and verification, the IJB-B challenge protocol aims to evaluate the FR model on templates. Due to large variations existing in different templates, this protocol is more difficult for the FR model than other benchmarks. We follow the template-based 1:1 verification task to evaluate the proposed method against other methods on the IJB-B dataset. The IJB-C dataset adds an extra 1,686 subjects based on IJB-B and contains 31,334 images and 11,779 videos. To improve the representation of the global population, the IJB-C emphasizes occlusion and diversity of subjects. By increasing the size and variability of the dataset, the IJB-C is more challenging than the IJB-B and other datasets in unconstrained face recognition.

The YTF dataset is a video-based dataset with 3,425 videos belonging to 1,595 different subjects. Each subject has 2.15 videos on average. All videos are

Table 2. The memory and computation costs of different methods. Since several methods are based on aligned images while the others are not, we also present whether it is necessary to align images.

method	need aligning?	parameters (MB)	computation (Gflops)
Blur	no	few	low
Pose	yes	0	low
JPEG	no	0	low
SVM	yes	few	low
RQS	yes	few	low
FaceQNet	yes	23	3.9
tinyFQNet	yes	0.022	0.0024

collected in unconstrained conditions with large variations in poses, expressions, illuminations, etc. Like the IJB-A verification task, the YTF protocol splits the dataset into ten-fold cross-validation sets. Each set contains 500 randomly selected video pairs, of which 250 pairs are positive and the other 250 pairs are negative.

4.3 Visualization of Different FIQA Methods

Figure 6 shows the images and corresponding quality scores predicted by different FIQA methods in the IJB-B dataset. We rank the face images by the quality scores from high to low. The first four methods are perceptual-based, and the last three methods are learning-based. The Blur only considers the blurriness of face images, and it chooses those with high resolution while ignoring other factors, such as head pose. The Pose only considers the head pose of a face. Although it can choose images under neural head poses, these images may be too blurry to recognize. The JPEG only considers the jpeg compression rate of face images, and the less compressed images have higher quality scores. The combination consists of Blur, Pose, and JPEG. The learning-based methods learn quality prediction functions from labeled datasets. It shows that an image with a higher quality score contains relatively more information about the identity and is easier to recognize in most situations.

4.4 Memory and Computation Costs

The memory cost and computation cost are the key factors when applying FIQA to a real FR system. Fewer parameters and less computation cost can improve the throughput of a real FR system.

Table 2 delineates the memory and computation costs associated with various methods. Typically, perceptual-based methods require fewer parameters, whereas learning-based approaches entail greater memory and computational demands. The SVM, despite its minimal parameter count and low computational expense, is reliant on features extracted from the FR model. This necessitates processing all images through the FR model, potentially reducing throughput due to the discarding of some images. The RQS method employs hand-crafted features such as HoG, Gabor, Gist, LBP, and features from a face alignment network. While it boasts lower memory usage and computational costs, the RQS faces challenges in GPU deployment due to its design. In comparison, FaceQnet requires approximately 23M parameters and 3.9 Gflops for its operation. In contrast, our tinyFQnet is significantly more efficient, needing only about 21.8k parameters and approximately 0.0024 Gflops. This efficiency makes tinyFQnet an ideal candidate for integration as a plug-in within the FR model framework, offering substantial benefits without imposing considerable additional computation or memory overhead.

Table 3. The overall results on the 1:1 verification task of the IJB-B dataset. Two different recognition models ResNet-50 [18] and EfficientNet-b0 [43] are chosen as recognition models. The true accept rates (TAR) vs. false positive rates(FAR) are used as the evaluation metric.

FR model	method	tpr				
		fpr = e-1	fpr = e-2	fpr = e-3	fpr = e-4	fpr = e-5
ResNet-50	random	92.09	87.64	83.08	77.22	64.02
	Blur	93.62	89.96	86.71	82.05	65.25
	Pose	93.45	90.34	86.91	82.39	75.57
	JPEG	95.27	93.14	90.87	88.46	81.93
	Combination	95.55	93.75	91.37	88.56	83.23
	SVM	94.75	91.44	88.51	84.13	75.29
	RQS	96.06	93.78	91.82	89.42	83.13
	FaceQnet	95.15	92.76	90.36	87.29	79.63
	tinyFQNet	**95.99**	**94.32**	**92.73**	**90.78**	**85.21**
EfficientNet-b0	random	92.65	87.81	82.72	75.34	53.74
	Blur	93.98	90.04	86.39	79.71	48.04
	Pose	93.99	90.31	86.64	81.65	70.29
	JPEG	95.7	93.15	90.99	87.85	79.06
	Combination	96.11	93.73	91.55	88.42	80.84
	SVM	95.11	91.56	87.61	82.71	61.54
	RQS	96.14	94.12	91.85	88.89	81.8
	FaceQnet	95.47	92.74	90.22	86.61	76.36
	tinyFQNet	**96.31**	**94.41**	**92.65**	**90.16**	**84.06**

4.5   Quantitative Evaluation on IJB-B and IJB-C Datasets

Table 3 summarizes the overall results of the 1:1 verification task on the IJB-B dataset. We use true positive rates (TPR) under $10^i (i = -1, -2, -3, -4, -5)$ and false positive rates (FPR) as the evaluation metric. We choose the random selection as the baseline. We evaluate two different recognition models, including ResNet-50 [18] and EfficientNet-b0 [43]. We compare the tinyFQnet with three learning-based methods, including SVM [4], RQS [6], FaceQnet [19]. All these methods showed higher performance compared with perceptual-based methods. Since both the [6] and [19] have released their code, we use the released code to compute the quality scores. For SVM [4], we implement their method and replace the training dataset with the MS1M used in this paper. We also report the results of perceptual-based methods, including Blur, Pose, JPEG, and their combination.

Table 3 shows that the learning-based methods outperform the perceptual-based methods, and both of them are superior to random selection. Among all these methods, our tinyFQnet achieves 85.21 tpr@fpr = e-5 when using the ResNet-50 network as the FR model (84.06 tpr@fpr = e-5 for EfficientNet-b0), which is the best performance. The SVM performs the worst among learning-based methods. A possible explanation for the results of SVM is that the goal of the FR model is to learn feature representation invariant to perceptual or other potential factors, and the feature of an image extracted from the FR model contains little information on image quality. SVM, which tries to learn a quality prediction function from the feature of a face image, may not learn an effective prediction function about the image quality.

Table 4. The overall results on the 1:1 verification task of the IJB-C dataset. The true accept rates (TAR) vs. false positive rates (FAR) are used as the evaluation metric.

FR model	method	tpr				
		fpr = e-1	fpr = e-2	fpr = e-3	fpr = e-4	fpr = e-5
ResNet-50	random	92.24	87.88	83.11	76.75	68.42
	Blur	94.33	90.69	87.32	83.28	74.65
	Pose	93.8	90.95	87.45	83.06	75.22
	JPEG	96	94.04	91.88	89.27	84.64
	Combination	95.97	93.79	91.41	88.81	83.77
	SVM	94.94	91.98	88.92	84.67	77.21
	RQS	96.17	94.21	92.13	89.72	85.36
	FaceQnet	95.37	93.12	90.8	87.34	82.3
	tinyFQNet	**96.29**	**94.77**	**93.05**	**91.12**	**87.68**
EfficientNet-b0	random	92.31	87.66	82.97	75.51	51.6
	Blur	94.25	90.66	87.41	81.3	57.88
	Pose	94.45	91.09	87.16	82.13	69.76
	JPEG	96.17	93.73	91.84	88.67	81.02
	Combination	96.21	93.61	91.31	88.23	80.23
	SVM	95.29	91.92	88.1	82.97	68.78
	RQS	96.46	94.35	92.21	89.37	84.54
	FaceQnet	95.49	93.13	90.61	86.8	80.12
	tinyFQNet	**96.53**	**94.83**	**93.05**	**90.73**	**86.06**

We also conduct experiments on a more recent and challenging benchmark IJB-C dataset [32]. Table 4 summarizes the overall results of the 1:1 verification task on the IJB-C dataset. Similar to the results on IJB-B, the learning-based methods outperform the perceptual-based methods, and the random selection strategy performs the worst.

Table 5. Performance evaluation for two recognition models with different FIQA methods on the YTF dataset. We adopt 10-folder cross-validation to calculate the verification accuracy.

method		accuracy with ResNet-50	accuracy with Efficientnet-b0
perceptual-based	random	96.34 ± 0.11	96.53 ± 0.09
	blur	96.39 ± 0.07	96.53 ± 0.04
	pose	96.58 ± 0.05	96.55 ± 0.04
	JPEG	96.72 ± 0.03	96.72 ± 0.02
	combined	96.11 ± 0.06	96.54 ± 0.05
learning-based	SVM	95.57 ± 0.08	96.01 ± 0.04
	RQS	96.89 ± 0.06	**97.02 ± 0.05**
	FaceQnet	96.35 ± 0.03	96.64 ± 0.04
	tinyFQNet	**97.02 ± 0.03**	97.00 ± 0.04

4.6 Quantitative Evaluation on YTF Dataset

Table 5 shows the results on the YTF dataset. Similar to the results shown in Table 3, our tinyFQnet achieves the best performance among all methods. We find that learning-based methods slightly outperform perceptual-based methods. Unlike the results on the IJB-B dataset, the random selection achieves a comparable performance with the others on the YTF dataset. This is probably due to the fewer variations in a YTF video compared to an IJB-B template. Among all the methods, SVM performs the worst, as explained in Sect. 4.5. An interesting phenomenon in Table 5 is that the combination of Blur, Pose, and JPEG performs even worse than each separate method.

4.7 Ablation Studies

The Impact of the FIQA Network's Size. In this part, we delve into the crucial aspect of memory and computation costs, which are pivotal when integrating Face Image Quality Assessment (FIQA) into a real-world Face Recognition (FR) system. To comprehensively evaluate the influence of network size on performance, we employed two distinct network architectures: MobileNetV2 and ResNet-50. Within the MobileNetV2 framework, we experimented with four different architectural variations: mbn_t4_w0.35_64, mbn_t6_w1_64, mbn_t4_w0.35_112, and mbn_t6_w1_112. Here, the parameter t signifies the channel expansion factor, while w denotes the width multiplier for the basic block in MobileNetV2. The postfix number in each architecture's name corresponds to the network's input size.

Table 6 shows the results of different networks on IJB-B. As illustrated in the table, for a particular FR model, the size of the FIQA network makes little difference on FR's performance. On the IJB-B dataset, the largest network ResNet-50 with 23M parameters achieves 86.93 tpr@fpr = e-5, only 1.7 higher than the smallest network mbn_t4_w0.35_64 with 21.8k parameters. On the YTF

Table 6. Results of different networks on the IJB-B dataset. Five architectures, including mbn_t4_w0.35_64, mbn_t6_w1_64, mbn_t4_w0.35_112, mbn_t6_w1_112, and ResNet-50 are explored.

network	input size	parameters	(Mflops)	tpr@fpr = e-5
mobilenet_t4_w0.35	64 × 64	0.013M	1.43	85.21
mobilenet_t6_w1	64 × 64	0.02M	2.5	85.81
mobilenet_t4_w0.35	112 × 112	0.5M	44.4	85.19
mobilenet_t6_w1	112 × 112	2.1M	206.9	86.38
ResNet-50	112 × 112	22.4M	3907	86.93

dataset, the size of the FIQA network almost makes no difference in the FR's performance.

The Impact of the Sampling Strategy Under Different Data Sizes. To evaluate the impact of the data sampling strategy, we evaluate the tinyFQNet on FR performance when using different data sampling strategies to generate a training dataset. Two different sampling strategies are chosen for comparison, including the random strategy and the smooth strategy, as mentioned in Sect. 3.4. Figure 7 shows the histogram distribution of quality scores when applying two different strategies, the top row for the random strategy and the bottom row for the smooth strategy.

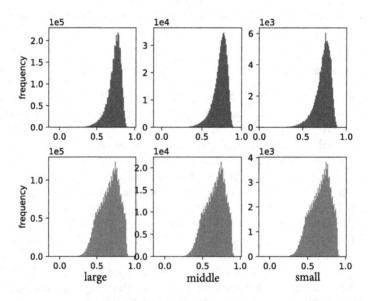

Fig. 7. The distribution of quality scores under different data sizes, including large, middle, and small. The top row shows the results of the random sampling strategy, and the bottom row shows the results of a smooth sampling strategy.

Table 7 shows the results of tinyFQNet on the IJB-B data set when using different sampling strategies to generate a training dataset for training tinyFQNet. For a fair comparison, we keep the same number of training images for both two sampling strategies. It can be observed that the number of identities of the smooth strategy is much lower than the random strategy due to applying identity filtering. In all three different data sizes, the smooth strategy is better than the random strategy.

Table 7. Results on IJB-B dataset when using two different sampling strategies for generating training datasets to train tinyFQNet. To make the results more convincing, we conduct this experiment on three datasets with different sizes.

sampling	data size	number (images, ids)	IJBB tpr@fpr = e-5
random	large	3.5M, 92.9K	83.95
random	middle	0.61M, 87.4K	84.73
random	small	0.11M, 57.0K	84.78
smooth	large	3.5M, 34K	85.85
smooth	middle	0.61M, 5.3K	85.64
smooth	small	0.11M, 0.9K	85.45

The Influence of the Labeling Model. Since the FR model generates quality scores, a natural thought is how the labeling model (we denote the model used to generate quality scores as the labeling model.) would influence the overall performance of an FR model.

Table 8. Results of different quality labeling models on the IJB-B dataset.

FR model	labeling model	IJBB tpr@fpr = e-5	YTF 10-fold accuracy
ResNet-50	ResNet-50	85.21	97.0
ResNet-50	EfficientNet-b0	85.15	97.0
EfficientNet-b0	EfficientNet-b0	83.71	96.9
EfficientNet-b0	ResNet-50	84.06	97.0

Table 8 shows the results of two different labeling models (used to generate quality labels for face images to train tinyFQnet) on the performance of two different FR models. It shows that both FR models perform better when using ResNet-50 as a labeling model to generate quality scores, but there is no significant difference between them. It can be concluded that with a better labeling model, the FIQA model can improve the performance of an FR system.

5   Conclusion

In this paper, we present a novel deep FIQA method, in which a novel and effective recognition-oriented metric is proposed that directly links face image quality assessment with the performance of the face recognition model. We design a tiny but efficient face quality network (tinyFQnet) and use it to train a FIQA model. We provide analysis by many experiments about the influences of network size on FR's performance and show that even a tiny network with only 21.8K parameters can achieve comparable performance to a much more complicated network with 23M parameters. We show that learning-based methods are superior to perceptual-based methods, and the proposed method outperforms other learning-based methods on two classical benchmarks.

However, limitations exist. The quality metric relies only on cosine similarity comparisons and could explore alternatives and needs to test on more diverse datasets to confirm generalizability. Further efforts on more diverse datasets, alternate metrics, and model optimizations can build on this initial exploration of linking quality directly to recognition accuracy.

References

1. Abaza, A., Harrison, M.A.F., Bourlai, T., Ross, A.: Design and evaluation of photometric image quality measures for effective face recognition. IET Biometrics **3**(4), 314–324 (2014)
2. An, X., et al.: Partial FC: training 10 million identities on a single machine. In: Proceedings of the IEEE/CVF International Conference on Computer Vision, pp. 1445–1449 (2021)
3. Babnik, Ž., Peer, P., Štruc, V.: FaceQAN: face image quality assessment through adversarial noise exploration. In: 2022 26th International Conference on Pattern Recognition (ICPR), pp. 748–754. IEEE (2022)
4. Best-Rowden, L., Jain, A.K.: Learning face image quality from human assessments. IEEE Trans. Inf. Forensics Secur. **13**(12), 3064–3077 (2018)
5. Boutros, F., Fang, M., Klemt, M., Fu, B., Damer, N.: CR-FIQA: face image quality assessment by learning sample relative classifiability. In: Proceedings of the IEEE/CVF Conference on Computer Vision and Pattern Recognition, pp. 5836–5845 (2023)
6. Chen, J., Deng, Y., Bai, G., Su, G.: Face image quality assessment based on learning to rank. IEEE Sig. Process. Lett. **22**(1), 90–94 (2015)
7. Chen, K., Yi, T., Lv, Q.: LightQNet: lightweight deep face quality assessment for risk-controlled face recognition. IEEE Sig. Process. Lett. **28**, 1878–1882 (2021)
8. Corner, B.R., Narayanan, R.M., Reichenbach, S.E.: Noise estimation in remote sensing imagery using data masking. Int. J. Remote Sens. **24**(4), 689–702 (2003)
9. Deng, J., Guo, J., Xue, N., Zafeiriou, S.: ArcFace: additive angular margin loss for deep face recognition. In: Proceedings of the IEEE Conference on Computer Vision and Pattern Recognition, pp. 4690–4699 (2019)
10. Deng, J., Guo, J., Zhou, Y., Yu, J., Kotsia, I., Zafeiriou, S.: RetinaFace: single-stage dense face localisation in the wild. arXiv preprint arXiv:1905.00641 (2019)
11. Eckert, M.P., Bradley, A.P.: Perceptual quality metrics applied to still image compression. Sig. Process. **70**(3), 177–200 (1998)

12. Cohen, E., Yitzhaky, Y.: No-reference assessment of blur and noise impacts on image quality. Sig. Image Video Process. **4**, 289–302 (2010). https://doi.org/10.1007/s11760-009-0117-4
13. Eskicioglu, A.M., Fisher, P.S.: Image quality measures and their performance. IEEE Trans. Commun. **43**(12), 2959–2965 (1995)
14. Ferzli, R., Karam, L.J.: A no-reference objective image sharpness metric based on the notion of just noticeable blur (JNB). IEEE Trans. Image Process. **18**(4), 717–728 (2009)
15. Gao, X., Li, S.Z., Liu, R., Zhang, P.: Standardization of face image sample quality. In: Lee, S.-W., Li, S.Z. (eds.) ICB 2007. LNCS, vol. 4642, pp. 242–251. Springer, Heidelberg (2007). https://doi.org/10.1007/978-3-540-74549-5_26
16. Guo, Y., Zhang, L., Hu, Y., He, X., Gao, J.: MS-Celeb-1M: a dataset and benchmark for large-scale face recognition. In: Leibe, B., Matas, J., Sebe, N., Welling, M. (eds.) Computer Vision – ECCV 2016. LNCS, vol. 9907. Springer, Cham (2016). https://doi.org/10.1007/978-3-319-46487-9_6
17. Hassen, R., Wang, Z., Salama, M.: No-reference image sharpness assessment based on local phase coherence measurement. In: 2010 IEEE International Conference on Acoustics, Speech and Signal Processing, pp. 2434–2437 (2010)
18. He, K., Zhang, X., Ren, S., Sun, J.: Deep residual learning for image recognition. In: Proceedings of the IEEE Conference on Computer Vision and Pattern Recognition, pp. 770–778 (2016)
19. Hernandez-Ortega, J., Galbally, J., Fierrez, J., Haraksim, R., Beslay, L.: FaceQnet: quality assessment for face recognition based on deep learning. In: 2019 International Conference on Biometrics (ICB), pp. 1–8. IEEE (2019)
20. Howard, A.G., et al.: MobileNets: efficient convolutional neural networks for mobile vision applications (2017)
21. Hsu, R.L.V., Shah, J., Martin, B.: Quality assessment of facial images. In: 2006 Biometrics Symposium: Special Session on Research at the Biometric Consortium Conference, pp. 1–6 (2006)
22. Huang, Y., et al.: CurricularFace: adaptive curriculum learning loss for deep face recognition. In: Proceedings of the IEEE/CVF Conference on Computer Vision and Pattern Recognition, pp. 5901–5910 (2020)
23. Huber, M., Terhöst, P., Kirchbuchner, F., Damer, N., Kuijper, A.: On evaluating pixel-level face image quality assessment. In: 2022 30th European Signal Processing Conference (EUSIPCO), pp. 1052–1056. IEEE (2022)
24. Ke, G., Wang, S., Zhai, G., Lin, W., Yang, X., Zhang, W.: Analysis of distortion distribution for pooling in image quality prediction. IEEE Trans. Broadcast. **62**(2), 446–456 (2016)
25. Kim, H.I., Lee, S.H., Ro, Y.M.: Face image assessment learned with objective and relative face image qualities for improved face recognition. In: 2015 IEEE International Conference on Image Processing (ICIP), pp. 4027–4031. IEEE (2015)
26. Larson, E.C., Chandler, D.M.: Most apparent distortion: full-reference image quality assessment and the role of strategy. J. Electron. Imaging **19**(1), 011006 (2010)
27. Li, Y., Po, L.M., Feng, L., Fang, Y.: No-reference image quality assessment with deep convolutional neural networks. In: 2016 IEEE International Conference on Digital Signal Processing (DSP) (2016)
28. Liu, J., Zhou, W., Li, X., Xu, J., Chen, Z.: LIQA: lifelong blind image quality assessment. IEEE Trans. Multimedia **25**, 5358–5373 (2022)
29. Liu, W., Wen, Y., Yu, Z., Li, M., Raj, B., Song, L.: SphereFace: deep hypersphere embedding for face recognition. In: IEEE Conference on Computer Vision and Pattern Recognition, pp. 6738–6746 (2017)

30. Liu, W., Wen, Y., Yu, Z., Yang, M.: Large-margin softmax loss for convolutional neural networks. In: Proceedings of the 33rd International Conference on Machine Learning (2016)
31. Liu, Y., et al.: iQIYI-VID: a large dataset for multi-modal person identification. arXiv preprint arXiv:1811.07548 (2018)
32. Maze, B., et al.: IARPA Janus Benchmark-C: face dataset and protocol. In: 2018 International Conference on Biometrics (ICB), pp. 158–165. IEEE (2018)
33. Meng, Q., Zhao, S., Huang, Z., Zhou, F.: MagFace: a universal representation for face recognition and quality assessment. In: Proceedings of the IEEE/CVF Conference on Computer Vision and Pattern Recognition (CVPR), June 2021, pp. 14225–14234 (2021)
34. Moorthy, A.K., Bovik, A.C.: Blind image quality assessment: from natural scene statistics to perceptual quality. IEEE Trans. Image Process. **20**(12), 3350–3364 (2011)
35. Nasrollahi, K., Moeslund, T.B.: Face quality assessment system in video sequences. In: Schouten, B., Juul, N.C., Drygajlo, A., Tistarelli, M. (eds.) BioID 2008. LNCS, vol. 5372, pp. 10–18. Springer, Heidelberg (2008). https://doi.org/10.1007/978-3-540-89991-4_2
36. Phillips, P.J., Moon, H., Rizvi, S.A., Rauss, P.J.: The FERET evaluation methodology for face-recognition algorithms. IEEE Trans. Pattern Anal. Mach. Intell. **22**(10), 1090–1104 (2000)
37. Sampat, M., Wang, Z., Gupta, S., Bovik, A., Markey, M.: Complex wavelet structural similarity: a new image similarity index. IEEE Trans. Image Process. **18**(11), 2385–2401 (2009)
38. Sang, J., Lei, Z., Li, S.Z.: Face image quality evaluation for ISO/IEC standards 19794-5 and 29794-5. In: Tistarelli, M., Nixon, M.S. (eds.) ICB 2009. LNCS, vol. 5558, pp. 229–238. Springer, Heidelberg (2009). https://doi.org/10.1007/978-3-642-01793-3_24
39. Sankaran, N., Tulyakov, S., Setlur, S., Govindaraju, V.: Metadata-based feature aggregation network for face recognition. In: ICB, February 2018, pp. 118–123 (2018)
40. Shan, S.: No-reference visually significant blocking artifact metric for natural scene images. Sig. Process. **89**(8), 1647–1652 (2009)
41. Sheikh, H.R., Bovik, A.C.: An information fidelity criterion for image quality assessment using natural scene statistics. IEEE Trans. Image Process. **14**(12), 2117–2128 (2006)
42. Sun, K., Gao, F., Zhu, S., et al.: Face biometric quality assessment via light CNN. Pattern Recogn. Lett. **107**, 25–32 (2017)
43. Tan, M., Le, Q.V.: EfficientNet: rethinking model scaling for convolutional neural networks. arXiv preprint arXiv:1905.11946 (2019)
44. Vignesh, S., Priya, K.M., Channappayya, S.S.: Face image quality assessment for face selection in surveillance video using convolutional neural networks. In: 2015 IEEE Global Conference on Signal and Information Processing (GlobalSIP), pp. 577–581. IEEE (2015)
45. Wang, Z., Bovik, A.C., Sheikh, H.R., Simoncelli, E.P.: Image quality assessment: from error visibility to structural similarity. IEEE Trans. Image Process. **13**(4), 600–612 (2004)
46. Whitelam, C., et al.: IARPA Janus Benchmark-B face dataset, pp. 592–600 (2017)
47. Wolf, L., Hassner, T., Maoz, I.: Face recognition in unconstrained videos with matched background similarity. In: Computer Vision and Pattern Recognition, pp. 529–534 (2011)

48. Wong, Y., Chen, S., Mau, S., Sanderson, C., Lovell, B.C.: Patch-based proba-
    bilistic image quality assessment for face selection and improved video-based face
    recognition. In: 2011 IEEE Computer Society Conference on Computer Vision and
    Pattern Recognition Workshops (CVPRW), pp. 74–81. IEEE (2011)
49. Yang, J., Ren, P., Chen, D., Wen, F., Li, H., Hua, G.: Neural aggregation network
    for video face recognition. In: CVPR, pp. 1–8. IEEE (2017)
50. Zhang, G., Wang, Y.: Asymmetry-based quality assessment of face images. In:
    Bebis, G., et al. (eds.) ISVC 2009. LNCS, vol. 5876, pp. 499–508. Springer, Hei-
    delberg (2009). https://doi.org/10.1007/978-3-642-10520-3_47
51. Zhang, J., Ong, S.H., Le, T.M.: Kurtosis-based no-reference quality assessment of
    JPEG2000 images. Sig. Process. Image Commun. **26**(1), 13–23 (2011)
52. Zhang, W., Ma, K., Yan, J., Deng, D., Wang, Z.: Blind image quality assessment
    using a deep bilinear convolutional neural network. IEEE Trans. Circ. Syst. Video
    Technol. **30**(1), 36–47 (2020)
53. Zhu, J., Fang, Y., Ji, P., Abdl, M.E., Wang, D.: RRAR: a novel reduced-reference
    IQA algorithm for facial images. In: IEEE International Conference on Image Pro-
    cessing (2011)
54. Zhuang, N., et al.: Recognition oriented facial image quality assessment via deep
    convolutional neural network. Neurocomputing **358**, 109–118 (2019)

Face Expression Recognition via Product-Cross Dual Attention and Neutral-Aware Anchor Loss

Yongwei Nie[1] , Rong Pan[1], Qing Zhang[2], Xuemiao Xu[1], Guiqing Li[1], and Hongmin Cai[1(✉)]

[1] South University of Technology, Guangzhou 510006, China
hmcai@scut.edu.cn
[2] Sun Yat-sen University, Guangzhou 510006, China

Abstract. Face expression recognition is an important task whose aim is to classify a face image to a kind of expression such as happy, sad, or surprise, etc. This task is challenging due to the ambiguities in expressions and also in the diverse poses and occlusions of the head. To handle this challenging task, recent approaches usually rely on attention mechanism to make the network focus on the most critical regions of a face, or apply a consistency loss that enforces extracting similar features from the same expressions. This paper proposes a new attention mechanism that combines the advantages of dot-product attention and feature cross-attention. The proposed new product-cross dual attention mechanism can better leverage the landmarks to extract more discriminative features from an input image. Second, although previous approaches can enforce similarity between features of the same expressions, they do not consider the arousal degree of an expression. We propose a neutral-expression-aware expression feature similarity loss based on the traditional anchor loss, which can further guide the network to learn better features from an input image. Extensive experiments demonstrate the advantages of our method over previous approaches.

Keywords: Face expression recognition · attention mechanism · expression arousal degree · face landmark

1 Introduction

Facial expressions are one of the most powerful, natural, and universal signals that humans use to convey emotional states and intentions [8]. Psychologists Ekman and Friesen [13] proposed that human emotions can be expressed through six basic expressions: surprise, sadness, disgust, happiness, fear, and anger (neutral expressions have also been included in recent years). As a fundamental task in computer vision, facial expression recognition, i.e., recognizing the kind of expression in a face image, has great applications in many image and video analysis tasks [6,7,23,28,33,34,36,49,54].

F.-L. Zhang and A. Sharf (Eds.): CVM 2024, LNCS 14593, pp. 70–90, 2024.
https://doi.org/10.1007/978-981-97-2092-7_4

Traditional FER methods typically rely on manual feature extraction or shallow learning techniques such as Local Binary Pattern (LBP) [41], Non-negative Matrix Factorization (NMF) [58], and Sparse Learning [59]. Shan introduced Local Binary Pattern to describe local texture features in images, David proposed the Scale-Invariant Feature Transform (SIFT) [26] to enhance tolerance to noise, lighting, and other interferences. In 2008, Bashyal [2] presented a method for extracting expression features based on Gabor wavelet transform. In recent years, an increasing number of approaches have shifted towards deep learning techniques, including convolutional neural networks (CNNs) [20], generative adversarial networks (GANs) [15], transformers [44], for the extraction and classification of facial expression features. These methods have achieved state-of-the-art recognition accuracy, significantly surpassing results obtained by traditional machine learning methods.

Despite the increasing number of methods aimed at improving the accuracy of facial expression recognition, they continue to grapple with the inherent challenges of this task: 1) Intra-class Variability: the same emotion can manifest with significant variations in facial shape and intensity across different faces. 2) Inter-class Similarity: different individuals may share similar features even among distinct facial expressions (e.g., in regions like the forehead and cheeks).

To address the aforementioned issues, many different approaches have been developed. Some studies leverage auxiliary tasks related to facial expression recognition to enhance accuracy. For example, Chang et al. [4] summarized AU labeling rules from FACS, then designed facial partitioning schemes to extract local facial region features using a backbone, and finally used the correlations between features from different regions to guide the training of the feature learning framework. Li et al. [25] employed AU recognition as an auxiliary task, facilitating mutual improvement between the two tasks by summarizing the distribution relationship between expressions and AUs. Recently, Xue et al. [50] introduced a Transformer-based approach called TransFER. After extracting feature maps using a backbone CNN, they designed local CNN blocks to pinpoint different local patches, and subsequently, used a Transformer encoder equipped with multi-head self-attention modules to compute global relationships among these local patches. Zheng et al. [57] proposed POSTER, which utilizes a pyramid cross-fusion Transformer to explore the correlation between image features and landmark features, aiming to address issues related to inter-class similarity, intra-class variation, and scale sensitivity in facial expression recognition.

Summarizing the advantages of all the above approaches, we find that, to achieve higher accuracy, the network needs to focus on the most critical facial regions, and to our best knowledge, the above recent advances [50, 57] achieve this by using attention mechanism such as that in Transformer [44]. Inspired by the POSTER approach [57], this paper proposes a combined dot-product and feature-cross dual attention mechanism. Specifically, we follow POSTER to employ a landmark detector to extract landmark position features and utilize these features to calculate an attention map. Our dot-product attention is then implemented as the multiplication between the attention map and the image features extracted by the backbone, which guides the network to filter irrelevant features away from the crucial facial areas. After that, we further feed the attended features to a cross-attention module, which uses the landmark feature as the query, and the image feature as the key and value to update the image features. The sequentially applied two kinds of attention mechanisms constrain the network to focus on specific facial regions, reducing the importance of irrelevant areas and minimizing their impact on facial expression recognition.

Besides the network's own capability in identifying discriminative features by attention mechanism, many researchers also explicitly address issues related to intra-class variation and inter-class similarity by applying loss functions such as center loss [48], anchor loss [40], and locality-preserving loss [24] etc. These losses aim to increase inter-class distances or decrease intra-class distances, thereby mitigating intra-class variation and inter-class similarity problems in facial expressions. However, these losses treat all expressions equally and overlook the differences in intensity that exist among different expressions. For example, within happy expressions, there can be significant dynamic differences between a smile and a hearty laugh, whereas neutral expressions typically lack such dynamic variations. Additionally, if an expression's intensity is relatively weak, the network may easily misclassify it as a neutral expression. Consequently, neutral expressions require distinct treatment. The second contribution of this work is that we enhance the anchor loss to accommodate the characteristics of neutral expressions and propose the so-called neutral-expression-aware anchor loss. It strengthens the ability to distinguish between neutral expressions and other expressions by constraining the features of neutral expressions.

In summary, the contributions of this paper are

- We propose a product-cross dual attention mechanism. On one hand, we incorporate landmarks into the computation by taking their product with facial expression features to adjust the weights of facial regions. On the other hand, within the ViT [11] architecture, we calculate cross-attention between landmark features and image features to reinforce the network's focus on crucial areas.
- We propose a neutral-expression-aware anchor loss, which improves the original anchor loss with the characteristics of neutral expressions to strengthen the network's ability to distinguish between neutral expressions and other expressions.
- Experimental results on several datasets demonstrate that our approach yields superior performance compared to other methods.

2   Related Work

2.1   Landmark

The auxiliary tasks of facial expression recognition typically include facial attribute prediction, facial landmark detection, facial recognition, and facial action unit detection, among others. Many approaches [19, 25, 30, 37, 53] improve facial expression recognition accuracy by jointly training multiple auxiliary tasks.

Among these auxiliary tasks, facial landmark detection has matured significantly. For expression recognition, facial landmark detection provides valuable facial geometry information, and when combined with spatial image features, it effectively enhances the accuracy of expression recognition. Additionally, facial landmarks accurately locate key facial regions such as eyes, mouth, eyebrows, which are crucial for expressing emotions. By pinpointing these locations, the network can narrow down its focus on these areas when selecting facial features. Jung and colleagues [18] employed two deep networks: the first one extracts temporal appearance features from images, while the second one extracts temporal ensemble features from facial landmarks. They used a novel fusion method to combine these two models, resulting in improved performance in expression recognition. In the case of POSTER [57], they utilized a pre-trained facial landmark detection model, MobileFaceNet [5], to extract landmark features. They designed a pyramid structure and a dual-stream structure, and calculated cross-attention between the features extracted from the backbone and the landmarks. In this study, pre-trained landmark detectors were used to extract geometric features and compute attention maps, guiding the network's focus towards crucial facial areas and reducing the weight assigned to irrelevant regions.

2.2 Transformer in FER

The powerful attention mechanism within the Transformer architecture [44] has led to leading results in various computer vision domains. In the field of facial expression recognition, it is common to cascade Convolutional Neural Networks (CNNs) with Transformers, feeding the features extracted by CNNs into Transformers for attention computation. Ma et al. [27] were among the first to introduce Transformers into facial expression recognition. They extracted features from RGB and LBP images and used an Attention Selective Fusion module (ASF) to merge global and local features. These merged features were then transformed into visual tokens and fed into a Multi-layer Transformer for encoding. Xue et al. [50] incorporated a multi-attention dropping module within the Transformer, enabling the model to extract comprehensive local information from every part of the face, rather than just the most discriminative parts. Additionally, they designed a pooling module within the Transformer to progressively reduce the number of tokens in the blocks, eliminating information irrelevant to expression recognition. Zheng et al. [57] employed cross-attention within the Transformer, exchanging Query matrices between the image stream and landmark stream, facilitating the fusion of features from both streams.

2.3 Losses Used in FER

Due to the characteristics of expressions having intra-class variations and inter-class similarities, various loss functions have been applied in networks to increase inter-class distances and reduce intra-class distances. Ruan et al. [39] employed a compactness loss to learn class centers, aiming to ensure that features from different images of the same expression are close to the respective class centers.

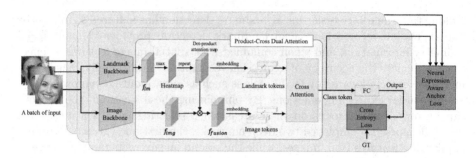

Fig. 1. Overview of our method. Given a face image, our method first extracts landmark features and image appearance features by existing backbone networks. After that, we propose a product-cross dual attention module to fuse the two kinds of features. After the attention module, we obtain a vector of class token, which is finally input to a fully-connected (FC) classifier head to output the expression type of the input face. To optimize the above model, besides the cross-entropy loss, we also propose a neutral expression aware anchor loss applied to the class tokens of all of the samples in a training batch.

Zhang et al. [55] utilized annotator information to calculate triplet loss, introducing a hierarchical structure to construct more refined triplets based on existing triplets, which were used for fine-tuning the network. Cai et al. [3] proposed a island loss function to extract discriminative features. Li et al. [24] introduced a locality-preserving loss to minimize the distances between samples and their surrounding K samples, preserving the local structure of each sample while maintaining compactness among samples of the same expression. Furthermore, Li et al. [22] proposed an AdaReg loss, which adaptively adjusts expression weights based on the number of different expressions within each batch. This approach addresses class imbalance issues and enhances the discriminative capability of expression representations.

3   Our Method

Figure 1 shows the overview of our method. Given an input face image $\mathbf{I} \in \mathbb{R}^{H \times W \times 3}$, we use a landmark backbone to extract the landmark feature map $f_{lm} \in \mathbb{R}^{h \times w \times c_{lm}}$, where h and w are the height and width of the feature map which has c_{lm} channels, respectively. In this paper, $h = w = 14$, and $c_{lm} = 128$. At the same time, we use an image backbone to extract the image feature map $f_{img} \in \mathbb{R}^{h \times w \times c_{img}}$ ($c_{img} = 256$). The landmark backbone used in this paper is the MobileFaceNet [5], and the image backbone adopted is IR50 [10].

We extract both landmark features and image features because we would like to use the landmark features to guide the learning of the image features, i.e., using the landmark information to enforce the network to focus on the image features around the most prominent landmark regions.

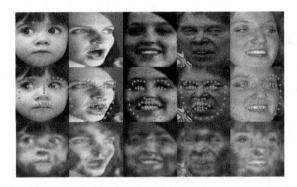

Fig. 2. The visualization of original images (top), images with landmarks (middle) and images with heatmaps (bottom). The facial landmarks are detected by [5]. As we can observe, guided by the heatmap generated for landmark features, the network pays closer attention to crucial facial features such as the eyes, nose, and mouth.

To achieve the above goal, we send both the landmark and image features into the proposed product-cross dual attention module, by which we achieve the fusion of the two kinds of information. After the attention module, we obtain a class token of size c_t (e.g., 768). The class token is then fed into a FC (fully-connected) layer to output the expression class scores of the input image. Each sample in a training batch undergoes the same feature extraction process to output a class token. We compute neutral expression aware anchor loss over all the class tokens of the training batch.

In the following, we elaborate the attention module and the anchor loss (and other losses used to train our model) in detail.

3.1 Product-Cross Dual Attention Module

The proposed product-cross dual attention mechanism in this paper aims at leveraging the positional information provided by facial landmarks. The landmarks can help assign larger weight to important facial regions (such as eyes and mouth) while smaller weight to the unimportant regions (such as hair and background). To achieve this, our product-cross dual attention module uses the landmark features as Query for calculating cross attention. In contrast to traditional self-attention mechanisms, cross attention focuses more on the relationship between the input landmark features and facial features, enabling the model to capture more semantic information about crucial areas. The product-cross dual attention module combines two kinds of attentions: one is the dot-product attention, and the other is the cross-feature attention, which are elaborated in detail as following.

Dot-Product Attention. By the dot-product attention, our aim is to enhance the image features around the landmarks. To this end, we first compute a heatmap $\mathbf{H} \in \mathbb{R}^{h \times w \times 1}$ by applying the max pooling operation to the landmark feature f_{lm}

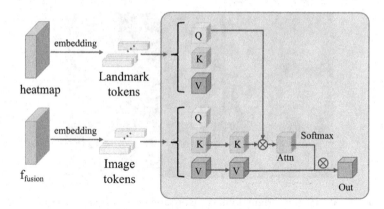

Fig. 3. Illustration of the cross-attention mechanism. We compute both the query, key, and value embeddings for the landmark and fusion tokens. However, we use the queries of landmark, and keys and values of fusion tokens to perform the cross-attention.

along the channel dimension. As shown in Fig. 2, the values of heatmap around the face landmarks are larger than other places. Than the heatmap is repeated c_{img} times along the channel dimension to obtain $\mathbf{H}' \in \mathbb{R}^{h \times w \times c_{img}}$. Finally, we multiply the heatmap attention map and the image feature map f_{img} in an element-wise manner to obtain the result of the dot-product attention mechanism, i.e.,

$$f_{fusion} = \mathbf{H}' \otimes f_{img}, \tag{1}$$

where $f_{fusion} \in \mathbb{R}^{h \times w \times c_{img}}$, and $\otimes$ represents the element-wise multiplication. After the dot-product attention, the image features around the landmarks are enhanced (such as eye and mouth regions), while the features at other places are weakened (such as hair regions and background).

Cross-Feature Attention. After obtaining the landmark feature and fusion feature, we proceed to embed them into landmark tokens $t_{lm} \in \mathbb{R}^{(hw) \times c_t}$ and fusion tokens $t_{fusion} \in \mathbb{R}^{(hw) \times c_t}$. Additionally, we introduce a learnable class token in $\mathbb{R}^{1 \times c_t}$ to represent global features (this class token is ultimately fed into a fully connected layer for expression classification), resulting in full landmark tokens $t_{lm} \in \mathbb{R}^{(hw+1) \times c_t}$ and fusion tokens $t_{fusion} \in \mathbb{R}^{(hw+1) \times c_t}$.

$$\begin{aligned} t_{lm} &= Cat(Embedding(f_{lm}), t_{lm\_class}), \\ t_{fuison} &= Cat(Embedding(f_{fuison}), t_{fusion\_class}), \end{aligned} \tag{2}$$

where t_{lm_class} and $t_{fuison\_class} \in \mathbb{R}^{1 \times c_t}$ are landmark class token and fusion class token, respectively. t_{lm} and t_{fuison} are landmark tokens and fusion tokens, respectively, which are inputted into the subsequent transformer blocks.

We employ a transformer to compute relationships between tokens. The process of cross-feature attention is illustrated in Fig. 3. To begin with, the landmark features and fusion features are mapped into three matrices each: a fusion query matrix Q_{fusion}, a fusion key matrix K_{fusion}, and a fusion value matrix V_{fusion}, as well as a landmark query matrix Q_{lm}. The expressions for this mapping are as follows:

$$Q_{fusion} = t_{fusion} \times W_{q\_fusion},$$
$$K_{fusion} = t_{fusion} \times W_{k\_fusion},$$
$$V_{fusion} = t_{fusion} \times W_{v\_fusion}, \qquad (3)$$
$$Q_{lm} = t_{lm} \times W_{q\_lm},$$

where $W_{q\_fusion}, W_{k\_fusion}, W_{v\_fusion}, W_{q\_lm} \in \mathbb{R}^{c_t \times c_t}$ are the mapping matrices.

Then, we calculate the cross-attention between the landmark query matrix Q_{lm} and the fusion key matrix K_{fusion}, along with the fusion value matrix V_{fusion}. This process can be mathematically described as follows:

$$CrossAttention(Q_{lm}, K_{fusion}, V_{fusion}) = Softmax(\frac{Q_{lm}K_{fusion}^T}{\sqrt{d}})V_{fusion}, \quad (4)$$

where $Softmax(\cdot)$ is softmax activation function and $\sqrt{d}$ is the scaling factor for normalization.

Using the landmark query matrix Q_{lm} instead of the fusion query matrix Q_{fusion}, is done to make better use of the spatial positional information contained within the landmark feature. This helps guide and focus on the regions within the fusion feature that are more relevant to the expression being conveyed. Subsequently, we calculate the output of a transformer block t_{fusion_out}. The t_{fusion_out} is of the same size as t_{fusion}.

$$t'_{fusion} = CrossAttention(Q_{lm}, K_{fusion}, V_{fusion}) + t_{fusion},$$
$$t_{fusion\_out} = MLP(Norm(t'_{fusion}) + t'_{fusion}, \qquad (5)$$

where $MLP(\cdot)$ is multi-layer perceptron, $Norm(\cdot)$ is normalization function.

After passing through several transformer blocks, the class token is putted into the FC to calculate the final classification prediction.

3.2 Neutral Expression Aware Anchor Loss

Due to the inherent challenge of facial expressions characterized by intra-class variation and inter-class similarity, several loss functions, such as center loss, triplet loss, anchor loss, and others, have been proposed to minimize the feature distances among samples of the same class while increasing distances between samples of different classes. These loss functions treat all expressions uniformly. However, in practice, neutral expressions differ from other expressions.

In a continuous expression representation space like arousal-valence model (as shown in Fig. 4), neutral expressions exhibit no distinction on arousal or valence, meaning that the extracted features for neutral expressions should be very close in the feature space, with minimal variance. In contrast, other expressions such

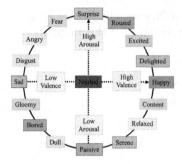
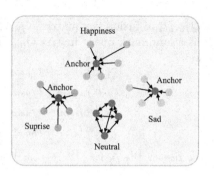

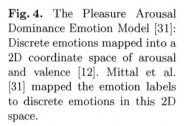

Fig. 4. The Pleasure Arousal Dominance Emotion Model [31]: Discrete emotions mapped into a 2D coordinate space of arousal and valence [12]. Mittal et al. [31] mapped the emotion labels to discrete emotions in this 2D space.

Fig. 5. Illustration of neutral-expression-aware anchor loss. For expressions other than "neutral", we find an anchor and reduce the distance between the training samples to the anchor. For neutral expression, we directly minimize the distance between any pair of neutral samples, as we argue that all the neutral expressions own the same degree of expressiveness without arousal-valence variance.

as happy, sad, etc., exhibit different degrees, i.e., there are very happy or just a little happy expressions.

The above insight inspires that we need to handle neutral and non-neutral expressions differently. Therefore, we propose an improvement to the anchor loss, introducing the Neutral-Expression-Aware Anchor Loss (see Fig. 5).

Firstly, let us define the traditional anchor loss. For a batch of samples, the anchor loss function first identifies an anchor sample for each class of expressions:

$$anchor\_c = \arg\min_{i \in N_c} \text{Confidence}(f_i), \qquad (6)$$

where $anchor\_c$ represents the index of the anchor sample of the cth expression class, $i \in N_c$ indexes all the samples in the training batch with expression class c, and Confidence($\cdot$) is the formula used for calculating sample confidence which is computed as the entropy of the predicted expression classification scores by the FC classification layer. f_i is the final feature of the sample output by the attention module, i.e., the class token. In total, Eq. 6 finds for each class the most confident sample and returns the index of the sample.

With the anchors for different expression class, the anchor loss function calculates the loss as the distance between other samples of the same class and the anchor sample, as shown in the following formula:

$$L_{anchor} = \frac{1}{N_c} \sum_{c=0}^{C} \sum_{i=0}^{N_c-1} \text{Dist}(f_i, f_{anchor\_c}) \qquad (7)$$

where C is the number of all the expression classes, N_c represents the number of samples from the c-th expression class in the batch, f_i is i-th sample in c-th class, f_{anchor_c} is the anchor sample in this class. Dist($\cdot$) is the formula used for distance calculation, and in this paper, we employ the mean square error function.

Now we define our proposed neutral-aware anchor loss. It composes of two parts. The first part computes the above anchor loss but excludes the neutral expression class.

$$L_{non-neutral} = \frac{1}{N_c} \sum_{c=0}^{C'} \sum_{i=0}^{N_c-1} \text{Dist}(f_i, f_{anchor\_c}) \tag{8}$$

where C' is the set of all the expression classes except the neutral class. As for neutral expressions in the training batch, we impose a stricter constraint by requiring all sample features to be equal. Through this more rigorous constraint, we aim to make their distribution in the feature space converge towards a single point. The complete description of the loss of the neutral class is as follows:

$$L_{neutral} = \frac{1}{(N_n - 1)^2} \sum_{i=0}^{N_n-1} \sum_{j=0,j\neq i}^{N_n-1} \text{Dist}(f_i, f_j), \tag{9}$$

where N_n represents the number of samples from the neutral expression class in the batch.

Finally, the Neutral-Aware Anchor (NeAA) loss is defined as:

$$L_{NeAA} = L_{non-neutral} + L_{neutral}. \tag{10}$$

3.3   Total Loss Function

In the proposed model, the image backbone, the landmark backbone, and the cross-attention module are jointly trained in an end-to-end fashion. We calculate the cross-entropy loss L_{cls} for the final classification results. Overall, the total loss in the training of the entire network is as follows:

$$L = L_{cls} + \lambda L_{NeAA}, \tag{11}$$

where the hyper-parameter $\lambda = 0.01$ is used to balance the loss function.

4   Experiments

4.1   Datasets

RAF-DB: The Real-world Affective Face Database (RAF-DB) [24] is a large-scale database, which includes 29,672 real-world facial images collected by searching on Flickr. The images are with great variability in age, ethnicity, lighting conditions, etc. With manually crowd-sourced annotation and reliable estimation, RAF-DB provides 7 basic expression classes (happiness, surprise, sadness, anger, disgust, fear, and neutral). For facial expression recognition task, there are 15,339 facial expression images utilized (12,271 images are used for training and 3,068 images are used for testing).

FERPlus: The FERPlus dataset [1] is extended from FER2013 [16] used in the ICML 2013 Challenge. FER2013 is a large-scale dataset collected by APIs in the Google search, which includes images resized to 48×48 pixels. It contains 28709 training images, 3589 validation images and 3589 test images. It is relabeled in 2016 by Microsoft with each image labeled by 10 individuals to consist 8 classes (7 basic expressions and contempt expression), thus has more reliable annotations.

AffectNet: AffectNet [32] is one of the largest datasets in the wild, containing over a million images collected from the Internet by querying various search engines. It provides two facial expression models (categorical model and dimensional model). For the FER task, there are a total of 420K images manually annotated into eight classes of expressions. Following the setup in [54], we used 280K training images and 3500 validation images (500 images per category) with 7 expression categories.

4.2   Implementation Details

All images are resized to 112×112 pixels before feeding into the model. We initialize the image backbone with IR50 [10], pretrained on the Ms-Celeb-1M dataset [17], and use MobileFaceNet [5] as the landmark backbone. During training, we keep the landmark backbone parameters fixed to ensure the accuracy of landmark information. For the cross-attention module, we employ a ViT with 2 transformer blocks. The MLP ratio is set to 4, and the drop ratio is 0.5. Our model is trained for 200 epochs using the Adam optimizer, with a batch size of 144. For the RAF-DB and FERPlus datasets, the learning rate is set to $3.5e-5$, while for the AffectNet dataset, it is set to $1e-6$. To augment the training data, we apply random horizontal flips and random erasing, while for the testing data, we only perform resize operation. Our model is implemented using PyTorch [35] and trained on two NVIDIA RTX 3090 GPUs.

4.3   Ablation Study

We conducted ablation study on the RAF-DB dataset to investigate the impact of the model's architecture, various proposed modules, and loss functions.

Effectiveness of Dot-Product Attention and Cross-Feature Attention. To evaluate the impact of the modules proposed in this paper, we conducted an ablation study on the RAF-DB dataset to investigate the effects of Dot-Product Attention and Cross-feature Attention on the final classification results. As shown in Table 1, it is evident that the addition of these modules leads to an overall improvement in accuracy on the validation set. After incorporating the Dot-Product Attention module into the model, the accuracy increased from 91.67% (row 6) to 92.31% (row 8), marking a 0.64% improvement. Similarly,

Table 1. Evaluation (%) of Dot-Product Attention, Cross-Feature Attention and NeAA Loss on RAF-DB.

	Dot_attn	Cross_attn	NeAA Loss	RAF-DB
1				91.30
2	✓			91.42
3		✓		91.49
4			✓	91.65
5	✓	✓		91.79
6		✓	✓	91.67
7	✓		✓	91.95
8	✓	✓	✓	**92.31**

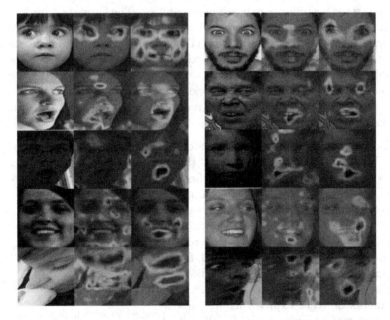

Fig. 6. The visualization of original images (left column), features without (middle column) and with Product-Cross Dual Attention Module (right column). The results show that the model emphasizes regions that significantly represent facial expressions.

with the inclusion of the Cross-feature Attention module, the accuracy on the test set also increased by 0.36% (from row 7 to row 8). With the use of both Attention modules, the accuracy increased from 91.65% (row 4) to 92.31% (row 8). We employed Grad-CAM to visualize the features after the application of the Product-Cross Dual Attention Module. Figure 6 shows that the model emphasizes regions that significantly represent facial expressions, such as the mouth in surprised expressions (row 2 and row 3 on the left half) and happy expressions (row 4), and the eyes in surprised expressions (row 1 and row 5 on the right

Table 2. Evaluation (%) of pre-trained ViT model on RAF-DB.

Pre-trained ViT	#Param	#FLOPs	RAF-DB
✓	67.3M	17.9G	91.88
	34.2M	9.3G	**92.31**

half). Furthermore, due to the implicit inclusion of head pose information in landmark features, the model can better extend to facial expression recognition in real-world scenarios with various head poses. As illustrated in the last row of Fig. 6, even under substantial head pose variations, the model remains capable of accurately identifying the positions of important areas in facial images.

We also experimentally explore whether the pre-trained large ViT model can help improve the accuracy of expression recognition. The Cross-feature Attention network is initialized with the parameters of ViT pre-trained on ImageNet [9]. As shown in Table 2, the pre-trained ViT model did not yield improvement in accuracy. The possible reason is that existing expression recognition datasets are small, and deeper networks increase the risk of overfitting. Therefore, a simplified ViT model with only 2 blocks is deemed sufficient. This not only ensures recognition accuracy but also reduces the consumption of computing resources and time.

Effectiveness of Neutral Expression Aware Loss. To validate the impact of the proposed Neutral Expression Aware Loss (NeAA Loss), we compared the accuracy of models trained with and without NeAA Loss on the RAF-DB test set. As shown in Table 1, the first row and the fourth row indicate that NeAA Loss is beneficial for improving model accuracy. The confusion matrix in Fig. 7(a) also reveals that only a few instances of other expressions are misclassified as neutral expressions. The Recall and F1-score for neutral expressions with and without the use of NeAA Loss is shown in Table 3. It is evident that the model's ability to recognize neutral expressions improves when the NeAA Loss is applied. Additionally, it enhances the discriminative ability between neutral expressions and other expressions with low arousal level. As shown

Table 3. Recall and F1-score for neutral expressions with and without the use of NeAA Loss on RAF-DB.

NeAA Loss	Recall	F1-score
✓	0.8971	0.9050
	0.9397	**0.9116**

Table 4. Evaluation (%) of different methods that generate the dot-product attention that is multiplied with the image feature f_{img}, on RAF-DB.

	Method	RAF-DB
1	Conv	91.46
2	Sum+Repeat	91.72
3	Abs+Sum+Repeat	91.59
4	Max+Repeat	**92.31**

in Fig. 8, many neutral expressions and other expressions with low arousal are incorrectly predicted (red labels) when there is no NeAA loss, while with the application of NeAA Loss, these predictions are corrected (black labels).

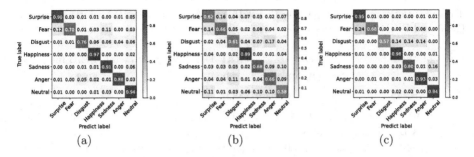

(a)   (b)   (c)

Fig. 7. Confusion matrices of our model on RAF-DB (subfigure (a)), AffectNet (7cls) (subfigure (b)) and FERPlus datasets (subfigure (c)). Our method exhibits clear and strong performance in terms of class-wise accuracy (diagonals of each confusion matrix) across all three datasets.

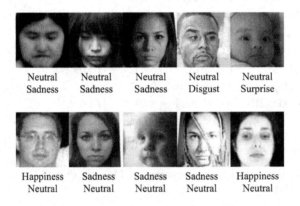

| Neutral | Neutral | Neutral | Neutral | Neutral |
| Sadness | Sadness | Sadness | Disgust | Surprise |

| Happiness | Sadness | Sadness | Sadness | Happiness |
| Neutral | Neutral | Neutral | Neutral | Neutral |

Fig. 8. Misidentified expressions in low arousal levels (top) and neutral expressions (bottom). The wrong predictions without NeAA are highlighted in red. With the application of the NeAA Loss, these predictions are corrected (black labels). (Color figure online)

Effectiveness of Different Dot-Product Attention Map Generation Methods. There are various methods for generating the dot-product attention map (see Fig. 1) that is multiplied with the image feature map. We conducted an ablation study on these methods using the RAF-DB dataset to assess their impact on the final results. As shown in Table 4, we generated the attention map from landmark features using Conv (a convolutional layer that directly maps the landmark feature f_{lm} in space $\mathbb{R}^{14 \times 14 \times 128}$ to the dot-product attention map in space $\mathbb{R}^{14 \times 14 \times 256}$), Sum+Repeat (sum the f_{lm} along the channel dimension to obtain a feature map in space $\mathbb{R}^{14 \times 14 \times 1}$ and then repeat it 256 times along the channel dimension to obtain the attention map), Abs+Sum+Repeat (compute $abs(f_{lm})$ at first, then sum it along the channel dimension, and finally repeat 256 times), and Max+Repeat (compute max pooling of f_{lm} along the channel dimension and then repeat) methods. Among these, the Max+Repeat method

Table 5. Performance comparison (%) with SOTA methods on RAF-DB, AffectNet (7cls) and FERPlus datasets.

Method	Year	RAF-DB	AffectNet (7cls)	FERPlus
SCN [46]	CVPR 2020	87.03	-	89.39
PSR [45]	CVPR 2020	88.98	63.77	-
RAN [47]	TIP 2020	86.90	-	89.16
DACL [14]	WACV 2021	87.78	65.20	-
KTN [22]	TIP 2021	88.07	63.97	90.49
DMUE [42]	CVPR 2021	89.42	63.11	-
FDRL [39]	CVPR 2021	89.47	-	-
ARM [43]	arXiv 2021	90.42	65.20	-
TransFER [50]	ICCV 2021	90.91	66.23	90.83
APViT [51]	CVPR 2022	91.98	66.91	90.86
Meta-Face2Exp [52]	CVPR 2022	88.54	64.23	-
EAC [56]	ECCV 2022	89.99	65.32	89.64
RANet [29]	FG 2023	89.57	65.09	-
SwinFace [38]	TCSVT 2023	90.97	-	-
Latent-OFER [21]	ICCV 2023	89.6	63.9	-
POSTER [57]	ICCV 2023	92.05	**67.31**	91.62
Ours	-	**92.31**	67.14	**92.97**

Table 6. Per-class performance comparison (%) with POSTER on RAF-DB and AffectNet (7cls) datasets.

Dataset	Method	Neutral	Happy	Sad	Surprise	Fear	Disgust	Anger	mean Acc
RAF-DB	POSTER	92.35	**96.96**	**91.21**	**90.27**	67.57	75.00	**88.89**	86.04
RAF-DB	Ours	**93.97**	**96.96**	91.00	89.67	**70.27**	**75.62**	87.65	**86.45**
AffectNet (7cls)	POSTER	**67.20**	**89.00**	67.00	**64.00**	64.80	56.00	62.60	**67.23**
AffectNet (7cls)	Ours	58.20	88.60	**68.40**	62.40	**66.00**	**60.80**	**65.60**	67.14

achieved the best result (92.31%). The convolution method performed worse than all the other operators, possibly due to significant alterations in the original landmark information caused by convolution operations, leading to a change in the network's focus area.

4.4 Comparison with the State-of-the-Art Methods

We compared the proposed method in this paper with some state-of-the-art (SOTA) methods on the RAF-DB, FERPlus, and AffectNet datasets, and the results are presented in Table 5.

Results on RAF-DB. The results of the comparison with the SOTA methods on the RAF-DB dataset are shown in Table 5, in the 3-th column. Our proposed method outperforms all the compared methods in terms of accuracy (accuracy across all samples), achieving an accuracy of 92.31%, which is 0.26% higher than the second-best method, POSTER. We conducted an analysis in Table 6 comparing the accuracies of our method and POSTER on each class in the RAF-DB dataset. It is evident that our method achieved a higher accuracy on the neutral, fear, disgust expression compared to POSTER, but had a relatively lower accuracy on the Anger expression.

Results on AffectNet. Since the test set of the AffectNet dataset is not publicly available, we conducted our comparison on the validation set following SOTA methods. Due to the extreme class imbalance in the AffectNet data, we applied oversampling techniques similar to RAN, POSTER, and APViT. We compared the accuracy of different methods on the 7-class emotion recognition task in the AffectNet dataset. From the 4-th column of Table 5, it can be seen that our method achieved an accuracy of 67.14%. While not the highest, it secured the second position. Our result is 0.17% lower than POSTER's results, probably because we do not process the feature in a multi-resolution manner, while POSTER performs that by employing a pyramid network structure. However, in terms of running time per image, POSTER takes 3 ms (see Table 7), while our model only takes 1.3 ms. Our model achieves more efficient expression recognition with a small loss of accuracy. We conducted a detailed analysis comparing our method and POSTER's accuracy on each emotion class in Table 6. Our method achieved the best results on the sad, fear, disgust and anger emotions, outperforming POSTER a lot. However, the recognition accuracy on the neutral emotion was relatively lower. It is also worth noting that the confusion matrix for AffectNet (see Fig. 7(b)) indicates an improved ability of our model to differentiate between neutral and other emotions.

Results on FERPlus. The results of the comparison with the SOTA methods on the FERPlus dataset are displayed in Table 5, in the 5-th column. Our method achieved an accuracy of 92.97%, surpassing the second-best method, POSTER, by 1.35%. The confusion matrix for FERPlus is illustrated in Fig. 7(c), which reveals that we have less error in neutral expression and other expressions.

4.5 Comparison on Number of Parameters and Running Performance

In Table 7, we compare our method with the SOTA approaches on the number of parameters and the FLOPs. As can be seen, our method not only outperforms other methods in terms of recognition accuracy, but also uses less network parameters and runs faster than the SOTA approaches. Compared to models with similar structures such as APViT and POSTER, our model incorporates MobileFaceNet, a lightweight and efficient landmark detector, into the network. Moreover, we reduce the Cross-Attention Module to only 2 blocks, aiming to simplify the model while maintaining effectiveness. This design choice facilitates better scalability in real-time or resource-constrained environments. Table 8 reveals the number of parameters and FLOPs for each module in our model, showing

Table 7. Comparison on Parameter Number and FLOPs. The image backbone (IR50) and facial landmark detector (MobileFaceNet) are taken into account when computing Params and FLOPs.

Methods	#Param	#FLOPs	RAF-DB	AffectNet	Running time
DMUE [42]	78.4M	13.4G	89.42	63.11	-
TransFER [50]	65.2M	15.3G	90.91	66.23	-
APViT [51]	-	12.7G	91.98	66.91	3.9 ms
POSTER [57]	71.8M	15.7G	92.05	**67.31**	3.0 ms
Ours	**34.2M**	**9.3G**	**92.31**	67.14	**1.3 ms**

Table 8. Parameter Number and FLOPs of each module in our method.

Module	#Param	#FLOPs
Image Backbone	17.6M	5.5G
Landmark Backbone	1.0M	0.2G
Cross Attention Module	15.6M	3.6G

that the added Landmark Backbone has minimal impact on model complexity and the number of parameters. We conducted test on a single GPU, and the average running time taken for each method per image is shown in Table 7. Our model demonstrates shorter inference time compared to APViT and POSTER, being only 1/3 of APViT and 2/5 of POSTER. This indicates that we can use more concise network architecture to fulfill the FER task if more effective data processing modules are designed and adopted such as the proposed product-cross dual attention method and the neutral-expression-aware anchor loss function.

5   Conclusion

This paper proposes a simple yet effective face expression recognition method. The two main contributions of this paper are that we propose a product-cross dual attention mechanism and a neutral-expression-aware anchor loss. With the dual attention module, we combine the features extracted by the landmark back-bone and image backbone. The features around the position of landmarks are successfully enhanced, while reducing the influence of features at other places. This indicates that making the network focus on important regions is useful and can indeed improve recognition accuracy. The neutral-aware loss takes the special characteristic of neutral expressions into consideration, i.e., all the neutral features should be similar to each other. With this constraint, we further improve the recognition accuracy by constraining the learning space of the network meaningfully. We have conducted comparison and ablation experiments which validate the effectiveness of our method. In particular, our method outperforms the latest method POSTER while running faster.

Acknowledgements. The work is supported by Guangdong International Technology Coopertation Project (No. 2022A0505050009), and National Science Foundation of China (No. 62072191, 61972160).

References

1. Barsoum, E., Zhang, C., Ferrer, C.C., Zhang, Z.: Training deep networks for facial expression recognition with crowd-sourced label distribution. In: Proceedings of the 18th ACM International Conference on Multimodal Interaction, pp. 279–283 (2016)
2. Bashyal, S., Venayagamoorthy, G.K.: Recognition of facial expressions using Gabor wavelets and learning vector quantization. Eng. Appl. Artif. Intell. **21**(7), 1056–1064 (2008)
3. Cai, J., Meng, Z., Khan, A.S., Li, Z., O'Reilly, J., Tong, Y.: Island loss for learning discriminative features in facial expression recognition. In: 2018 13th IEEE International Conference on Automatic Face & Gesture Recognition, FG 2018, pp. 302–309. IEEE (2018)
4. Chang, Y., Wang, S.: Knowledge-driven self-supervised representation learning for facial action unit recognition. In: Proceedings of the IEEE/CVF Conference on Computer Vision and Pattern Recognition, pp. 20417–20426 (2022)
5. Chen, C.: PyTorch face landmark: a fast and accurate facial landmark detector (2021). https://github.com/cunjian/pytorch_face_landmark
6. Chen, J., Gao, C., Sun, L., Sang, N.: CCSD: cross-camera self-distillation for unsupervised person re-identification. Vis. Intell. **1**(1), 27 (2023)
7. Cheng, R., Wang, X., Sohel, F., Lei, H.: Topology-aware universal adversarial attack on 3D object tracking. Vis. Intell. **1**(1), 1–12 (2023)
8. Darwin, C., Prodger, P.: The Expression of the Emotions in Man and Animals. Oxford University Press, USA (1998)
9. Deng, J., Dong, W., Socher, R., Li, L.J., Li, K., Fei-Fei, L.: ImageNet: a large-scale hierarchical image database. In: 2009 IEEE Conference on Computer Vision and Pattern Recognition, pp. 248–255. IEEE (2009)
10. Deng, J., Guo, J., Zafeiriou, S.: ArcFace: additive angular margin loss for deep face recognition (2018)
11. Dosovitskiy, A., et al.: An image is worth 16 × 16 words: transformers for image recognition at scale. arXiv preprint arXiv:2010.11929 (2020)
12. Ekman, P., Friesen, W.V.: Head and body cues in the judgment of emotion: a reformulation. Percept. Mot. Skills **24**(3), 711–724 (1967)
13. Ekman, P., Friesen, W.V.: Constants across cultures in the face and emotion. J. Pers. Soc. Psychol. **17**(2), 124 (1971)
14. Farzaneh, A.H., Qi, X.: Facial expression recognition in the wild via deep attentive center loss. In: Proceedings of the IEEE/CVF Winter Conference on Applications of Computer Vision, pp. 2402–2411 (2021)
15. Ganin, Y., et al.: Domain-adversarial training of neural networks. J. Mach. Learn. Res. **17**(1), 1–35 (2016)
16. Goodfellow, I.J., et al.: Challenges in representation learning: a report on three machine learning contests. In: Lee, M., Hirose, A., Hou, Z.-G., Kil, R.M. (eds.) ICONIP 2013. LNCS, vol. 8228, pp. 117–124. Springer, Heidelberg (2013). https://doi.org/10.1007/978-3-642-42051-1_16

17. Guo, Y., Zhang, L., Hu, Y., He, X., Gao, J.: MS-Celeb-1M: a dataset and benchmark for large-scale face recognition. In: Leibe, B., Matas, J., Sebe, N., Welling, M. (eds.) ECCV 2016, Part III. LNCS, vol. 9907, pp. 87–102. Springer, Cham (2016). https://doi.org/10.1007/978-3-319-46487-9_6

18. Jung, H., Lee, S., Yim, J., Park, S., Kim, J.: Joint fine-tuning in deep neural networks for facial expression recognition. In: Proceedings of the IEEE International Conference on Computer Vision, pp. 2983–2991 (2015)

19. Kollias, D.: Multi-label compound expression recognition: C-expr database & network. In: Proceedings of the IEEE/CVF Conference on Computer Vision and Pattern Recognition, pp. 5589–5598 (2023)

20. LeCun, Y., Bottou, L., Bengio, Y., Haffner, P.: Gradient-based learning applied to document recognition. Proc. IEEE **86**(11), 2278–2324 (1998)

21. Lee, I., Lee, E., Yoo, S.B.: Latent-OFER: detect, mask, and reconstruct with latent vectors for occluded facial expression recognition. In: Proceedings of the IEEE/CVF International Conference on Computer Vision, pp. 1536–1546 (2023)

22. Li, H., Wang, N., Ding, X., Yang, X., Gao, X.: Adaptively learning facial expression representation via CF labels and distillation. IEEE Trans. Image Process. **30**, 2016–2028 (2021)

23. Li, P., Sun, H., Huang, C., Shen, J., Nie, Y.: Interactive image/video retexturing using GPU parallelism. Comput. Graph. **36**(8), 1048–1059 (2012)

24. Li, S., Deng, W., Du, J.: Reliable crowdsourcing and deep locality-preserving learning for expression recognition in the wild. In: Proceedings of the IEEE Conference on Computer Vision and Pattern Recognition, pp. 2852–2861 (2017)

25. Li, X., Deng, W., Li, S., Li, Y.: Compound expression recognition in-the-wild with au-assisted meta multi-task learning. In: Proceedings of the IEEE/CVF Conference on Computer Vision and Pattern Recognition, pp. 5734–5743 (2023)

26. Lowe, D.G.: Object recognition from local scale-invariant features. In: Proceedings of the Seventh IEEE International Conference on Computer Vision, vol. 2, pp. 1150–1157. IEEE (1999)

27. Ma, F., Sun, B., Li, S.: Facial expression recognition with visual transformers and attentional selective fusion. IEEE Trans. Affect. Comput. **14**, 1236–1248 (2021)

28. Ma, T., Nie, Y., Zhang, Q., Zhang, Z., Sun, H., Li, G.: Effective video stabilization via joint trajectory smoothing and frame warping. IEEE Trans. Vis. Comput. Graph. **26**(11), 3163–3176 (2019)

29. Ma, X., Ma, Y.: Relation-aware network for facial expression recognition. In: 2023 IEEE 17th International Conference on Automatic Face and Gesture Recognition (FG), pp. 1–7. IEEE (2023)

30. Meng, Z., Liu, P., Cai, J., Han, S., Tong, Y.: Identity-aware convolutional neural network for facial expression recognition. In: 2017 12th IEEE International Conference on Automatic Face & Gesture Recognition, FG 2017, pp. 558–565. IEEE (2017)

31. Mittal, T., Bhattacharya, U., Chandra, R., Bera, A., Manocha, D.: M3ER: multiplicative multimodal emotion recognition using facial, textual, and speech cues. In: Proceedings of the AAAI Conference on Artificial Intelligence, vol. 34, pp. 1359–1367 (2020)

32. Mollahosseini, A., Hasani, B., Mahoor, M.H.: AffectNet: a database for facial expression, valence, and arousal computing in the wild. IEEE Trans. Affect. Comput. **10**(1), 18–31 (2017)

33. Nie, Y., Zhang, Q., Wang, R., Xiao, C.: Video retargeting combining warping and summarizing optimization. Vis. Comput. **29**, 785–794 (2013)

34. Pan, Y., Niu, Z., Wu, J., Zhang, J.: InSocialNet: interactive visual analytics for role-event videos. Comput. Vis. Media **5**, 375–390 (2019)
35. Paszke, A., et al.: Automatic differentiation in PyTorch (2017)
36. Peng, Z., Jiang, B., Xu, H., Feng, W., Zhang, J.: Facial optical flow estimation via neural non-rigid registration. Comput. Vis. Media **9**(1), 109–122 (2023)
37. Pons, G., Masip, D.: Multi-task, multi-label and multi-domain learning with residual convolutional networks for emotion recognition. arXiv preprint arXiv:1802.06664 (2018)
38. Qin, L., et al.: SwinFace: a multi-task transformer for face recognition, expression recognition, age estimation and attribute estimation. IEEE Trans. Circ. Syst. Video Technol. (2023)
39. Ruan, D., Yan, Y., Lai, S., Chai, Z., Shen, C., Wang, H.: Feature decomposition and reconstruction learning for effective facial expression recognition. In: Proceedings of the IEEE/CVF Conference on Computer Vision and Pattern Recognition, pp. 7660–7669 (2021)
40. Ryou, S., Jeong, S.G., Perona, P.: Anchor loss: modulating loss scale based on prediction difficulty. In: Proceedings of the IEEE/CVF International Conference on Computer Vision, pp. 5992–6001 (2019)
41. Shan, C., Gong, S., McOwan, P.W.: Facial expression recognition based on local binary patterns: a comprehensive study. Image Vis. Comput. **27**(6), 803–816 (2009)
42. She, J., Hu, Y., Shi, H., Wang, J., Shen, Q., Mei, T.: Dive into ambiguity: latent distribution mining and pairwise uncertainty estimation for facial expression recognition. In: Proceedings of the IEEE/CVF Conference on Computer Vision and Pattern Recognition, pp. 6248–6257 (2021)
43. Shi, J., Zhu, S., Liang, Z.: Learning to amend facial expression representation via de-albino and affinity. arXiv preprint arXiv:2103.10189 (2021)
44. Vaswani, A., et al.: Attention is all you need. In: Advances in Neural Information Processing Systems, vol. 30 (2017)
45. Vo, T.H., Lee, G.S., Yang, H.J., Kim, S.H.: Pyramid with super resolution for in-the-wild facial expression recognition. IEEE Access **8**, 131988–132001 (2020)
46. Wang, K., Peng, X., Yang, J., Lu, S., Qiao, Y.: Suppressing uncertainties for large-scale facial expression recognition. In: Proceedings of the IEEE/CVF Conference on Computer Vision and Pattern Recognition, pp. 6897–6906 (2020)
47. Wang, K., Peng, X., Yang, J., Meng, D., Qiao, Y.: Region attention networks for pose and occlusion robust facial expression recognition. IEEE Trans. Image Process. **29**, 4057–4069 (2020)
48. Wen, Y., Zhang, K., Li, Z., Qiao, Yu.: A discriminative feature learning approach for deep face recognition. In: Leibe, B., Matas, J., Sebe, N., Welling, M. (eds.) ECCV 2016, Part VII 14. LNCS, vol. 9911, pp. 499–515. Springer, Cham (2016). https://doi.org/10.1007/978-3-319-46478-7_31
49. Xiao, C., Nie, Y., Hua, W., Zheng, W.: Fast multi-scale joint bilateral texture upsampling. Vis. Comput. **26**, 263–275 (2010)
50. Xue, F., Wang, Q., Guo, G.: Transfer: learning relation-aware facial expression representations with transformers. In: Proceedings of the IEEE/CVF International Conference on Computer Vision, pp. 3601–3610 (2021)
51. Xue, F., Wang, Q., Tan, Z., Ma, Z., Guo, G.: Vision transformer with attentive pooling for robust facial expression recognition. IEEE Trans. Affect. Comput. **14**, 3244–3256 (2022)
52. Zeng, D., Lin, Z., Yan, X., Liu, Y., Wang, F., Tang, B.: Face2Exp: combating data biases for facial expression recognition. In: Proceedings of the IEEE/CVF Conference on Computer Vision and Pattern Recognition, pp. 20291–20300 (2022)

53. Zhang, K., Huang, Y., Du, Y., Wang, L.: Facial expression recognition based on deep evolutional spatial-temporal networks. IEEE Trans. Image Process. **26**(9), 4193–4203 (2017)
54. Zhang, Q., Nie, Y., Zhu, L., Xiao, C., Zheng, W.S.: A blind color separation model for faithful palette-based image recoloring. IEEE Trans. Multimedia **24**, 1545–1557 (2021)
55. Zhang, W., Ji, X., Chen, K., Ding, Y., Fan, C.: Learning a facial expression embedding disentangled from identity. In: Proceedings of the IEEE/CVF Conference on Computer Vision and Pattern Recognition, pp. 6759–6768 (2021)
56. Zhang, Y., Wang, C., Ling, X., Deng, W.: Learn from all: erasing attention consistency for noisy label facial expression recognition. In: Avidan, S., Brostow, G., Cissé, M., Farinella, G.M., Hassner, T. (eds.) Computer Vision, ECCV 2022. LNCS, vol. 13686, pp. 418–434. Springer, Cham (2022). https://doi.org/10.1007/978-3-031-19809-0_24
57. Zheng, C., Mendieta, M., Chen, C.: POSTER: a pyramid cross-fusion transformer network for facial expression recognition. In: Proceedings of the IEEE/CVF International Conference on Computer Vision, pp. 3146–3155 (2023)
58. Zhi, R., Flierl, M., Ruan, Q., Kleijn, W.B.: Graph-preserving sparse nonnegative matrix factorization with application to facial expression recognition. IEEE Trans. Syst. Man Cybern. Part B (Cybern.) **41**(1), 38–52 (2010)
59. Zhong, L., Liu, Q., Yang, P., Liu, B., Huang, J., Metaxas, D.N.: Learning active facial patches for expression analysis. In: 2012 IEEE Conference on Computer Vision and Pattern Recognition, pp. 2562–2569. IEEE (2012)

Image Generation and Enhancement

Deformable CNN with Position Encoding for Arbitrary-Scale Super-Resolution

Yuanbin Ding[1], Kehan Zhu[1], Ping Wei[1], Yu Lin[2(✉)], and Ruxin Wang[3(✉)]

[1] National Pilot School of Software, Engineering Research Center of Cyberspace,
Yunnan University, Kunming, China
weip@ynu.edu.cn
[2] Kunming Institute of Physics, Kunming, China
lwlinyu@163.com
[3] Alibaba Group, Beijing, China
rosinwang@gmail.com

Abstract. Implicit neural representation (INR) has been widely used to learn continuous representation of images, as it enables arbitrary-scale super-resolution (SR). However, most existing INR-based arbitrary-scale SR methods simply concatenate neighboring features and directly stack the position information with the image features, without fully exploiting the correlations among the input information. This processing method may produce artifacts and erroneous texture in the SR image. To address this problem, we propose a deformable CNN with position encoding (DCPE). Our method consists of three main components: (1) Deformable Feature Unfolding (DFU) module, which selectively concatenates the image features to ensure accurate recovery of texture; (2) Fusion With Learned Position Encoding (FPE) module, which generates position encoding that can be better fused with image features, thereby enhancing the correlation between them; and (3) Deep ResMLP module, which enhances the representation capability of the local implicit image function to focus more on learning the high-frequency information of the image, thus reducing the generation of artifacts in SR image. We conduct extensive experiments and demonstrate that our method outperforms previous methods in both qualitative and quantitative evaluations.

Keywords: arbitrary-scale super-resolution · implicit neural representation · deformable CNN · position encoding

1 Introduction

Single-image super-resolution is a fundamental computer vision task that aims to recover a low-resolution (LR) image into a corresponding high-resolution (HR) image. Most SR methods use convolutional neural networks to extract features and append an upsampling module at the end, which can reconstruct the LR image and generate a high-quality HR image. However, these traditional SR methods often have limitations: they can only perform SR on a fixed scale. In practical scenarios, the limitations of single-scale SR methods become apparent as they inadequately cater to the multifaceted demands of real-life applications, and training a dedicated model for each scale

© The Author(s), under exclusive license to Springer Nature Singapore Pte Ltd. 2024
F.-L. Zhang and A. Sharf (Eds.): CVM 2024, LNCS 14593, pp. 93–108, 2024.
https://doi.org/10.1007/978-981-97-2092-7_5

is impractical. Hence, the proposal of arbitrary-scale SR methods is necessary, as they can achieve SR at arbitrary scales with only one model.

Most of the existing arbitrary-scale SR methods achieve their goals by preserving the backbone network of traditional SR models while substituting the original standard up-sampling module with one capable of arbitrary-scale up-sampling. This is a simple and effective way to transform the SISR method into an arbitrary-scale SR method and improve the SR performance of the original network. In Meta-SR [13], the Meta-Upscale Module is proposed to replace the traditional up-sampling module and achieve SR at arbitrary scales. However, Meta-SR exhibits limited generalization ability when confronted with large-scale SR scenarios beyond its training scope. To overcome the limitation of Meta-SR, implicit neural representation is introduced by LIIF for arbitrary-scale super-resolution, which parameterizes the signal as a continuous function and maps the coordinates to the corresponding signals. Based on this idea, LIIF proposes a local implicit image function that replaces the traditional up-sampling module. The local implicit image function employs a multi-layer perceptron (MLP) to map the 2D coordinates and the local features to the RGB values. Since the coordinates are continuous values, it can naturally achieve arbitrary-scale SR, even for scales not seen during training.

It is noteworthy that the input to the local implicit image function consists exclusively of the position information of the target pixel and its corresponding feature vector. Consequently, the processing method of position information and feature vectors is crucial for restoring high-quality SR images. However, LIIF [6] simply stacks them together, resulting in a limited correlation between the stacked components, which may lead to the distortion of image texture. UltraSR [38] and IPE [24] enrich the position information by combining it with periodic encoding, but the periodic encoding is fixed and may not be optimal for different scales. As for the processing method of feature vectors, some previous methods [6, 20] concatenate all the features within a 3×3 neighborhood. However, this approach may aggregate some irrelevant or redundant features that could negatively impact texture recovery.

In order to address these problems, we propose a deformable CNN with position encoding, named DCPE. Unlike previous methods [6, 20], we exploit the available information more effectively, concatenate the extracted LR feature information correctly, and fuse the processed feature information with the learned position encoding deeply to enhance the correlation between different types of information. We also use a residual-structured MLP to enhance the representation capability of the local implicit image function, thereby improving the quality of the SR image.

Our principal contributions can be summarized as follows:

- We propose a deformable CNN with position encoding (DCPE) for arbitrary-scale SR, which can concatenate feature vectors that are useful for recovering texture, while deeply fusing the learned position encoding with the image features to obtain SR images with correct texture.
- We propose Deep ResMLP, which optimizes the MLP structure by combining local and global residual connections. This approach enables the network to learn the high-frequency information of the image more effectively, thus reducing the artifacts in the output.

– We conduct extensive experiments on DIV2K and four other benchmark datasets, demonstrating that DCPE outperforms previous methods in most cases.

2   Related Work

2.1   Implicit Neural Representation

Many natural signals (e.g. images, shapes of objects, etc.) are continuous, but computers can only use discrete storage and representation methods. To overcome the physical limitations of computers and to connect with the continuous representation of the real world, implicit neural representation has attracted increasing attention and research [8,26,27] due to its excellent ability to represent continuous signals. Implicit neural representation is a method that approximates a continuous function with a neural network, typically using an MLP to map 2D/3D coordinates to the signals at that location. When an object is modeled as an implicit neural function, the memory required to parameterize the signal depends only on the complexity of the underlying signal, not on the spatial resolution, which greatly enhances the usability of implicit neural representation. Implicit neural representation was initially applied to 3D scenes, such as 3D shape modeling [2,7,12], 3D scene modeling [15,32], and 3D structure rendering [3,23,27,28]. Recently, implicit neural representation has also emerged in 2D applications, such as image SR [6,20,24,38], which can naturally achieve infinite resolution with implicit neural representation, and is of great significance for arbitrary-scale SR.

2.2   Single Image Super-Resolution (SISR)

SISR is the task of transforming LR image into HR image. SR methods can be classified into three categories: interpolation-based, reconstruction-based, and learning-based. Presently, the most effective and influential methods are learning-based methods. Convolutional neural network (CNN) has been widely used in SR reconstruction studies due to their excellent detail characterization ability. CNN can implicitly learn the prior knowledge of the image and use it to generate superior SR outputs. SRCNN [10] was the first CNN-based SR method, which consisted of three convolutional layers. It used bicubic interpolation to upscale the LR image to the target resolution size as input, and then obtained the SR image by applying the SRCNN. Later, ESPCN [31] introduced an efficient sub-pixel convolution layer at the end of the network, which learned a set of upsampling filters to map the LR features to the HR output. This approach avoided using bicubic interpolation to upscale the LR image before feeding the image into the network, which reduced the computational complexity and improved the model performance.

After that, most CNN-based SR methods adopted a similar structure: a backbone network to extract LR image features, followed by an upsampling module to generate SR images. Various new network designs were also proposed for the backbone network, such as VDSR [16], EDSR [22], IRCNN [41] using residual learning; RDN [43] using a combination of dense and residual connections; DRCN [17], DRRN [33] using recurrent networks; SRGAN [19], ESRGAN [36] using generative adversarial networks to obtain perceptually pleasing texture; RCAN [42], SAN [9] using different attention mechanisms; and IPT [5], SwinIR [21], SwinFIR [40] using transformer structures. While these advancements continue to improve SR performance, most of these methods remain confined to single-scale SR applications, limiting their practical utility in diverse real-world scenarios.

2.3 Arbitrary-Scale Super-Resolution

Arbitrary-scale SR is the task of transforming LR image into HR image at arbitrary scales. Due to the limitations of single-scale SR, arbitrary-scale SR has attracted more attention recently, and the first method to propose it was Meta-SR [13], which used a Meta-SR upsampling module instead of the traditional single-scale upsampling module. This approach enabled the existing SISR methods to adapt to arbitrary-scale SR easily. The Meta-SR upsampling module could dynamically predict the weights of the upsampling filters for any scale factor, and then use them to generate HR images. Inspired by Meta-SR, RSAN [11] and Arb-SR [35] were proposed, which could perform asymmetric SR. Later, Chen et al. [6] proposed the LIIF, which replaced the traditional single-scale upsampling module with a local implicit image function. LIIF took the position information of the target resolution image and the nearest LR feature vector as inputs, and predicted the RGB values at that position. LIIF had better generalization ability for large-scale factors and bridged the gap between 2D discrete and continuous representations.

After LIIF was proposed, many researchers improved it. For example, Xu et al. [38] proposed UltraSR, which deeply integrated spatial coordinates and periodic encoding with the implicit neural representation; Lee et al. [20] proposed a Local Texture Estimator (LTE), which characterized the image texture in 2D Fourier space and enabled the implicit function to reconstruct the image continuously while capturing details; Liu et al. [24] proposed Integrated Position Encoding (IPE), which extended traditional position encoding by aggregating frequency information over pixel regions to enhance the expressiveness of implicit neural networks.

3 Methods

In this section, we present a comprehensive introduction to the novel method called DCPE, which is designed for arbitrary-scale SR. Our method begins by estimating the sampling offsets for each feature reference point using a dedicated offset estimation network. These offsets determine the precise location of sampling points. Bilinear interpolation is subsequently employed to sample features at these specified locations. The sampled features are then concatenated to enrich the feature information of the corresponding reference point. Next, we combine the position information with scale, and obtain the position encoding with the same dimension as the concatenated image features through an MLP. We deeply fuse position encoding with the concatenated feature information. Finally, to improve the expressiveness of the local implicit image function, we increase the depth of the implicit neural network by using global and local residual connections. The overall structure is shown in Fig. 1 (a).

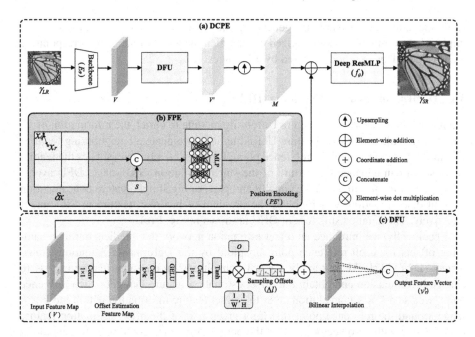

Fig. 1. The overall structure of our proposed deformable CNN with position encoding (DCPE) is illustrated in sub-figure (a). First, the backbone network extracts the LR image features and obtains V. Then, the DFU module (sub-figure (c) shows the detailed structure) selectively samples the features from V to get information-rich features V', and upsample V' to obtain M using nearest-neighborhood interpolation. Next, the FPE module (sub-figure (b)) generates the position encoding and fuses it deeply with M, and finally, the SR image is obtained by the Deep ResMLP module.

The feature extraction process of LR images can be defined as follows:

$$V = E_\varphi(\gamma_{LR}), \tag{1}$$

where $\gamma_{LR} \in \mathbb{R}^{H \times W \times 3}$ represents the LR image, and E_φ is the backbone network used by the model. Extracting the features of γ_{LR} through the backbone network, we obtain $V \in \mathbb{R}^{H \times W \times C}$.

We can define our method as follows:

$$\gamma_{SR} = f_\theta \left(\emptyset_{DFU}(V)_\uparrow, \emptyset_{FPE}(\delta x, s) \right)$$
$$\delta x \propto x_q - x_r, \tag{2}$$

where x_q is the coordinate of the query point in the HR image domain, and x_r is the coordinate of the nearest reference point to x_q in the LR image domain. Both x_r and x_q have the value range of $[-1, 1]$, δx signifies the relative distance between x_q and x_r, while s represents the scale factor. $\uparrow$ stands for the nearest-neighborhood interpolation, and $\gamma_{SR} \in \mathbb{R}^{sH \times sW \times 3}$ denotes the final SR image. $\emptyset_{DFU}(\bullet)$ and $\emptyset_{FPE}(\bullet)$ are both trainable functions. The former serves to enrich the information contained in $v_r \in V$, while the latter is responsible for generating the position encoding. f_θ denotes a local implicit image function parameterized by θ, which maps coordinates to corresponding RGB values. This function is shared by all images.

3.1 Deformable Feature Unfolding (DFU)

We propose the Deformable Feature Unfolding module to enrich the information of V. Unlike LIIF [6], which uses Feature Unfolding to concatenate all neighboring features within a 3×3 range around the reference point, DFU selectively concatenates the feature vectors that can enhance the texture of the super-resolution (SR) image. DFU avoids treating each feature in the range equally and performing simple feature concatenation without discrimination, which solves the problem of incorrect texture in SR images effectively. The detailed structure of DFU is shown in Fig. 1 (c).

Specifically, we introduce an offset estimation network that predicts multiple sampling offsets for each reference point, inspired by the Deformable Attention Transformer (DAT) [37]. We first apply a 1×1 convolution on the input feature map V to change its dimension and obtain the offset estimation feature map. For each reference point, we use a $k \times k$ convolution layer to extract feature information within the $k \times k$ range around the reference point (the light green part of the offset estimation feature map, padded with zero vectors outside the boundary), which contributes to generating the final sampling offsets. Then, we use a GELU activation layer and a 1×1 convolution to get the sampling offsets $\Delta L \in \mathbb{R}^{P \times 2}$, P stands for the number of sampling points, which can be defined as follows:

$$\Delta L = \{(\Delta x_p, \Delta y_p)\}_{p \in \{1,2,3,...,P\}}, \tag{3}$$

where Δx_p and Δy_p represent the offsets of the p-th sampling point along the x-axis and y-axis, respectively. To maintain training stability and avoid excessively large offsets, we employ the Tanh activation function to constrain sampling offsets within the range of $[-1, 1]$. Subsequently, the Δx and Δy components of all sampling offsets are normalized by the width (W) and height (H) of the input feature maps, respectively. We also multiply them by an offset range factor o to control the range of the offsets, and finally obtain a reasonable range of the sampling offsets $\Delta l \in \mathbb{R}^{P \times 2}$. It is defined as follows:

$$\Delta l = o \cdot \tanh(\frac{\Delta L}{(W, H)}). \tag{4}$$

Subsequently, we determine each location of sampling points according to the sampling offsets and the location of the reference point, and use bilinear interpolation to obtain the feature vectors at locations of sampling points. We concatenate P sampled feature vectors to get new feature vectors. This process is defined as follows:

$$v'_r = \text{Concat}(\{V_{lr+\Delta l_{rp}}\}_{p \in \{1,2,3,...,P\}}), \tag{5}$$

where l_r denotes the coordinate of a feature reference point in the LR image domain, and Δl_{rp} denotes one of its sampling offsets. Then $l_r + \Delta l_{rp}$ is one of its sampling coordinates, and $V_{lr+\Delta l_{rp}}$ is a feature vector obtained by bilinear interpolation at that position. A new feature vector v'_r is obtained after applying Eq. 5, and we perform this operation for each feature reference point in the LR image domain to obtain $V' \in \mathbb{R}^{H \times W \times PC}$. V' enlarges the receptive field, selectively concatenates the information around V_{l_r}, discards useless or even harmful information, enhances the content within each feature vector, and facilitates the restoration of texture. Finally, we upsample the latent representation V' using nearest-neighbor interpolation to obtain $M \in \mathbb{R}^{sH \times sW \times PC}$.

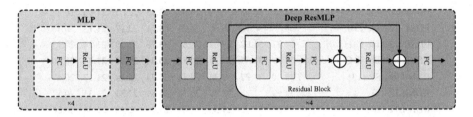

Fig. 2. The figure shows the original MLP in LIIF [6] (left) and our proposed Deep ResMLP (right) structure.

3.2   Fusion with Learned Position Encoding (FPE)

The core idea of implicit neural representation is to map position information to RGB values, so the representation of position information is crucial. Previous work [6,30] simply stacked the position information with the feature vectors, which resulted in low correlation and unequal information amount between them. This uneven information distribution makes it challenging for the local implicit image function to exploit the relationship between them effectively. Meanwhile, to solve the problem that the fixed encoding method is difficult to optimize, we introduce an approach that seamlessly integrates learned position encoding with image features inspired by the Transformer [34].

Figure 1 (b) illustrates our method. The position information we use is δx, which represents the relative distance between x_q and x_r. This is similar to previous work [6, 30,38], but we employ distinct encoding and combination methods for the δx. We input δx into a three-layer MLP to obtain a position encoding $PE \in \mathbb{R}^{sH \times sW \times PC}$ with the same dimension as M. Then we add PE to M. This method balances the information amount of the position and the image features, and enhances their association.

However, the position information can only inform the network about the orientation and distance of the target pixel with respect to the LR feature reference points, failing to convey how much space the pixel should occupy within the entire SR image. This deficiency may affect the overall structure of the SR image. Therefore, we introduce a scale factor, and stack it with δx before feeding them into MLP to obtain $PE' \in \mathbb{R}^{sH \times sW \times PC}$. Finally, we add PE' to M and feed it into $f_\theta(\cdot)$.

Table 1. Quantitative results on the DIV2K validation set (PSNR (dB)). The table compares the performance of several arbitrary-scale SR methods. EDSR-baseline [22] uses models trained at specific scales, and other methods use the same model at all scales (×2–×30). † indicates that the method is implemented by [20]. Bold indicates the best performance.

Method	In-scale			Out-of-scale				
	×2	×3	×4	×6	×12	18	×24	×30
Bicubic [22]	31.01	28.22	26.66	24.82	22.27	21.00	20.19	19.59
EDSR-baseline [22]	34.55	30.90	28.94	–	–	–	–	–
EDSR-baseline-Meta-SR [13]	34.64	30.93	28.92	26.61	23.55	22.03	21.06	20.37
EDSR-baseline-LIIF [6]	34.66	30.96	29.00	26.75	23.71	22.17	21.18	20.48
EDSR-baseline-LTE [20]	34.72	31.02	29.04	26.81	23.78	22.23	21.24	20.53
EDSR-baseline-DCPE (ours)	**34.78**	**31.07**	**29.11**	**26.87**	**23.84**	**22.33**	**21.34**	**20.66**
RDN-Meta-SR [13]	35.00	31.27	29.25	26.88	23.73	22.18	21.17	20.47
RDN-LIIF [6]	34.99	31.26	29.27	26.99	23.89	22.34	21.31	20.59
RDN-LTE [20]	35.04	31.32	29.33	27.04	23.95	22.40	21.36	20.64
RDN-DCPE (ours)	**35.06**	**31.33**	**29.34**	**27.07**	**24.00**	**22.47**	**21.45**	**20.76**
SwinIR-Meta-SR† [13]	35.15	31.40	29.33	26.94	23.80	22.26	21.26	20.54
SwinIR-LIIF† [6]	35.17	31.46	29.46	27.15	24.02	22.43	21.40	20.67
SwinIR-LTE [20]	**35.24**	**31.50**	**29.51**	**27.20**	24.09	22.50	21.47	20.73
SwinIR-DCPE (ours)	35.23	31.49	29.50	**27.20**	**24.11**	**22.55**	**21.54**	**20.82**

Table 2. Quantitative results on benchmark datasets (PSNR (dB)). The table compares the performance of several arbitrary-scale SR methods. Each method uses the same model at all scales (×2–×10). All arbitrary-scale SR methods use EDSR-baseline as backbone. Bold indicates the best performance.

Dataset	Method	In-scale			Out-of-scale		
		×2	×3	×4	×6	×8	×10
Set5	EDSR-baseline-Meta-SR [13]	37.99	34.38	32.05	28.69	26.72	25.42
	EDSR-baseline-LIIF [6]	37.99	34.40	32.18	28.95	26.98	25.61
	EDSR-baseline-LTE [20]	**38.04**	34.43	32.24	28.97	27.04	25.69
	EDSR-baseline-DCPE (ours)	38.03	**34.48**	**32.27**	**29.03**	**27.05**	**25.72**
Set14	EDSR-baseline-Meta-SR [13]	33.61	30.27	28.51	26.31	24.79	23.69
	EDSR-baseline-LIIF [6]	33.57	30.33	28.63	26.45	24.92	23.83
	EDSR-baseline-LTE [20]	**33.72**	30.37	28.65	26.50	**24.99**	23.88
	EDSR-baseline-DCPE (ours)	33.71	**30.37**	**28.68**	**26.53**	24.98	**23.90**
B100	EDSR-baseline-Meta-SR [13]	32.17	29.09	27.54	25.74	24.69	23.95
	EDSR-baseline-LIIF [6]	32.16	29.11	27.59	25.84	24.80	24.06
	EDSR-baseline-LTE [20]	32.21	29.14	27.62	25.87	24.82	**24.08**
	EDSR-baseline-DCPE (ours)	**32.22**	**29.15**	**27.64**	**25.88**	**24.83**	24.08
Urban100	EDSR-baseline-Meta-SR [13]	32.05	28.10	25.94	23.58	22.28	21.40
	EDSR-baseline-LIIF [6]	32.09	28.17	26.12	23.75	22.44	21.54
	EDSR-baseline-LTE [20]	32.29	28.32	26.24	23.85	22.53	21.64
	EDSR-baseline-DCPE (ours)	**32.33**	**28.36**	**26.28**	**23.88**	**22.56**	**21.65**

3.3   Deep ResMLP

We found that an MLP formed by simple concatenation of fully connected layers and activation functions has limited expressive power and struggles to effectively map coordinates to RGB values, as illustrated in the left side of Fig. 2. Therefore, we introduce the Deep ResMLP network, which adds residual connections to increase the network depth and allows the network to focus more on learning high-frequency information. Deep ResMLP contains multiple residual blocks, each with two fully connected layers, two activation layers and a short residual connection, as shown by the gray boxes on the right side of Fig. 2. In addition, within the entire Deep ResMLP network, a long residual connection spans all residual blocks, with fully connected layers positioned before and after it. The overall structure is shown on the right side of Fig. 2. The experimental results show that our Deep ResMLP can effectively enhance the expressive power of the local implicit image function, achieve superior SR performance, and reduce the generation of artifacts in SR images.

4   Experiments

4.1   Datasets and Metrics

The DIV2K dataset [1] contains 1000 images with 2K resolution, divided into 800 for training, 100 for testing, and 100 for validation. We trained all models on the training set of the DIV2K dataset. To evaluate the model performance, we used the validation set of DIV2K, as well as four benchmark datasets: Set5 [4], Set14 [39], B100 [25], and Urban100 [14]. We used peak signal-to-noise ratio (PSNR) as our evaluation metric. Following previous methods [6,13,20,24,35,38], we calculated PSNR values for the three RGB channels of the DIV2K validation set, and for the Y channel of the YCbCr format of the benchmark datasets.

4.2   Implementation Detail

Most of our implementation settings are the same as LTE [20]. The training scale factors s are uniformly distributed in $\mathcal{U}(1,4)$, which we call In-scale, and the scale factors larger than $\times 4$ are called Out-of-scale. To obtain the training image pairs, we randomly crop the HR image in DIV2K to a size of $48\,s \times 48\,s$ and then use the bilinear interpolation of PyTorch [29] to downscale the cropped image to 48×48. We use the obtained 48×48 LR image as the input to the model. In the training stage, to ensure that the shape of ground-truths in a batch is the same as that of LR images, and to reduce the memory consumption and accelerate the training speed, we randomly sample $48 \times 48 = 2304$ pixels in the cropped HR image, and record coordinates of each sampled pixel in HR image domain. During training, we only upsample the feature information on the sampled coordinates, and then perform backpropagation. We choose Adam [18] as the optimizer with betas of 0.9 and 0.999, respectively, and L1 loss [22] to train our models. All models are trained on an NVIDIA RTX 4090 24 GB GPU for 1000 epochs, and the batch size of the models is set to 8. We use the CNN-based models with the upsampling module removed as the backbone. For the model with SwinIR [21] as the

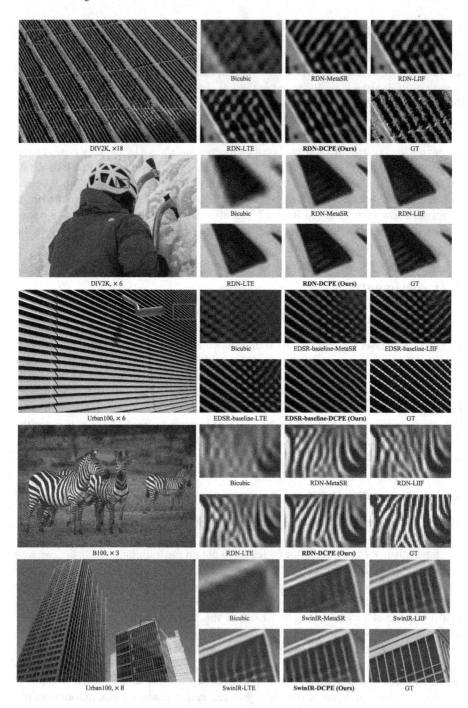

Fig. 3. Qualitative comparison of different arbitrary-scale SR methods. In the large image on the left side, red boxes indicate the selected area for comparison, and the source dataset of the images and the corresponding scale factor used for the comparison are labeled below the large image. The smaller images on the right side display detailed SR images generated by each method, with the respective backbone and method name indicated below each small image. (Color figure online)

backbone, the initial learning rate is set to 2e−4 and decayed by a factor of 0.5 at epochs of [500, 800, 900, 950], respectively. For the models with EDSR-baseline [22] or RDN [43] as the backbone, the initial learning rate is set to 1e−4 and decays to half of the previous learning rate for every 200 epochs of training.

4.3   Evaluation

Quantitative Results. Table 1 compares the performance of several arbitrary-scale SR methods (Meta-SR [13], LIIF [6], LTE [20], and our DCPE) on the DIV2K validation set, using EDSR-baseline [22], RDN [43], and SwinIR [21] as the backbone respectively. The table shows that our model outperforms the other models at all scales with EDSR-baseline [22] and RDN [43] as backbones. With SwinIR [21] as the backbone, our model is slightly lower than LTE [20] by 0.01 dB in the in-scale distribution, but achieves the best performance in the out-of-scale distribution with a maximum difference of 0.09 dB (×30). DCPE also has a more significant improvement in SR performance at large scales regardless of the backbone used, especially at ×30 with EDSR-baseline as the backbone, where DCPE achieves a maximum improvement of 0.13 dB over LTE. Table 2 compares the performance of each method on benchmark datasets. Our method achieves superior performance in most cases compared to other methods.

Qualitative Results. Figure 3 shows the qualitative analysis of the benchmark dataset and the DIV2K dataset. The figure demonstrates that our method generates SR images with more accurate texture and fewer artifacts than other arbitrary-scale SR methods, both in the in-scale and out-of-scale distributions. The figure also compares various methods using EDSR-baseline, RDN or SwinIR as the backbone, and reveals that our method significantly outperforms other methods on various datasets, regardless of the backbone. This excellent performance can be attributed to our proposed DCPE, which effectively mitigates distortion of texture and maximizes the recovery of texture from the ground-truths.

Table 3. Quantitative ablation study on module validity validation of DCPE. We evaluated the results on the DIV2K validation set (PSNR (dB)), and used EDSR-baseline [22] as the backbone for all DCPE models. DCPE(-D) denotes the model without the DFU module, DCPE(-F) denotes the model without the FPE module, and DCPE(-R) denotes the model without the Deep ResMLP module.

Method	In-scale			Out-of-scale		
	×2	×3	×4	×6	×12	×18
DCPE	**34.78**	**31.07**	**29.11**	**26.87**	**23.84**	**22.33**
DCPE(-D)	34.74	31.03	29.06	26.82	23.78	22.25
DCPE(-F)	34.75	31.05	29.09	26.85	23.83	22.32
DCPE(-R)	34.72	31.02	29.06	26.83	23.81	22.30

4.4   Ablation Study

In this section, we conduct a series of experiments to demonstrate the effectiveness of the various modules of DCPE and to select the optimal parameters for the model, using EDSR-baseline [22] as the backbone for all models.

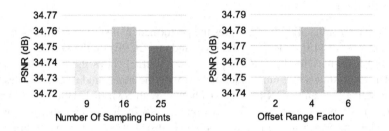

Fig. 4. This figure shows the effect of the number of sampling points (left) and the offset range factor (right) in the DFU module on DIV2K (×2).

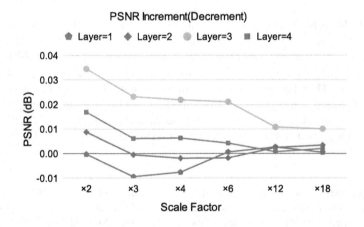

Fig. 5. This figure shows the change in model performance when the number of layers of MLP in the FPE module is 1, 2, 3, and 4, respectively. The increment/decrement refers to the difference between the results from these ablation studies and the DCPE(-F) in Table 3.

Module Validity Validation. We conducted a series of experiments to assess the effectiveness of different modules within DCPE. We removed various modules individually and retrained new models with the remaining components kept unchanged. Table 3 shows the results. Regarding implementation details, for DCPE(-D), we applied nearest-neighbor interpolation to upsample V to $M' \in \mathbb{R}^{sH \times sW \times PC}$, then fused M' with PE' and fed it to f_θ; for DCPE(-F), we stacked the position information (δx) and scale factor together on M and fed it to f_θ; for DCPE(-R), we removed the Deep ResMLP module and used the same decoder settings as LIIF [6], that is, the network in Fig. 2 (left) as

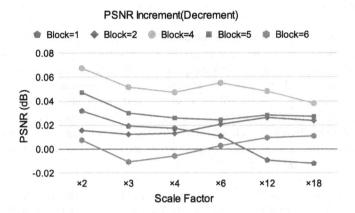

Fig. 6. This figure shows the change in model performance when the number of residual blocks in the Deep ResMLP module is 1, 2, 4, 5, and 6, respectively. The increment/decrement refers to the difference between the results from these ablation studies and the EDSR-baseline-LIIF in Table 1.

f_θ. The experimental findings reveal that each module has a positive impact on SR performance. Notably, the DFU module exhibits the most significant enhancement effect in the out-of-scale distribution, and the Deep ResMLP module notably improves SR performance in the in-scale distribution.

Parameter Selection. We conducted a series of individual ablation studies to determine the optimal parameters for the DFU module, the FPE module, and the Deep ResMLP module. For the DFU module, we investigated the impact of varying the number of sampling points P and the offset range factor o on model performance, as illustrated in Fig. 4. The results indicate that the model performs significantly better when employing sixteen sampling points, and the optimal offset range factor is four. To produce the final sampling offsets that cover the $k \times k$ region around the reference point, we set $k = o + 1$. Hence, we use a convolutional layer with a kernel size of 5×5 to extract the offset estimation feature map, i.e., $k = 5$. For the FPE module, we varied the number of layers in MLP and measured the model performance. Figure 5 shows the results. The figure indicates that the model with three layers of MLP performs better than the others in all scales. For the Deep ResMLP module, we concentrated on assessing the impact of the number of residual blocks on model performance. We only kept the Deep ResMLP module and removed the other two modules for this experiment, so we compared our results with EDSR-baseline-LIIF [6] in Table 1. Figure 6 shows the results. The results revealed that employing four residual blocks consistently yielded superior performance across all scales. We used the optimal parameters from these experiments to get the final results in previous experiments.

5   Conclusion

In this paper, we have proposed a deformable CNN with position encoding for arbitrary-scale super-resolution. Our network correctly concatenates image feature information using the DFU module, and obtains the position encoding with the same dimension as the image features through the FPE module, which promotes the fusion of position information with image features. We also use deep residual connections to improve the expressive power of the local implicit image function. We conducted extensive experiments on the DIV2K and benchmark datasets. The experimental results demonstrate that our method achieves superior SR performance compared to other arbitrary-scale SR methods in both quantitative and qualitative assessments.

Acknowledgments. This work is supported in part by the National Natural Science Foundation of China under Grant 62101480 and 62162067, the Yunnan Foundational Research Project under Grant No. 202201AU070034 and No. 202201AT070173, Research and Application of Object detection based on Artificial Intelligence, in part by the Yunnan Province expert workstations under Grant202305AF150078.

References

1. Agustsson, E., Timofte, R.: NTIRE 2017 challenge on single image super-resolution: dataset and study. In: Proceedings of the IEEE Conference on Computer Vision and Pattern Recognition Workshops, pp. 126–135 (2017)
2. Atzmon, M., Lipman, Y.: SAL: sign agnostic learning of shapes from raw data. In: Proceedings of the IEEE/CVF Conference on Computer Vision and Pattern Recognition, pp. 2565–2574 (2020)
3. Barron, J.T., Mildenhall, B., Tancik, M., Hedman, P., Martin-Brualla, R., Srinivasan, P.P.: Mip-NeRF: a multiscale representation for anti-aliasing neural radiance fields. In: Proceedings of the IEEE/CVF International Conference on Computer Vision, pp. 5855–5864 (2021)
4. Bevilacqua, M., Roumy, A., Guillemot, C., Alberi-Morel, M.L.: Low-complexity single-image super-resolution based on nonnegative neighbor embedding (2012)
5. Chen, H., et al.: Pre-trained image processing transformer. In: Proceedings of the IEEE/CVF Conference on Computer Vision and Pattern Recognition, pp. 12299–12310 (2021)
6. Chen, Y., Liu, S., Wang, X.: Learning continuous image representation with local implicit image function. In: Proceedings of the IEEE/CVF Conference on Computer Vision and Pattern Recognition, pp. 8628–8638 (2021)
7. Chen, Z., Tagliasacchi, A., Zhang, H.: BSP-Net: generating compact meshes via binary space partitioning. In: Proceedings of the IEEE/CVF Conference on Computer Vision and Pattern Recognition, pp. 45–54 (2020)
8. Chen, Z., Zhang, H.: Learning implicit fields for generative shape modeling. In: Proceedings of the IEEE/CVF Conference on Computer Vision and Pattern Recognition, pp. 5939–5948 (2019)
9. Dai, T., Cai, J., Zhang, Y., Xia, S.T., Zhang, L.: Second-order attention network for single image super-resolution. In: Proceedings of the IEEE/CVF Conference on Computer Vision and Pattern Recognition, pp. 11065–11074 (2019)
10. Dong, C., Loy, C.C., He, K., Tang, X.: Image super-resolution using deep convolutional networks. IEEE Trans. Pattern Anal. Mach. Intell. **38**(2), 295–307 (2015)

11. Fu, Y., Chen, J., Zhang, T., Lin, Y.: Residual scale attention network for arbitrary scale image super-resolution. Neurocomputing **427**, 201–211 (2021)

12. Genova, K., Cole, F., Vlasic, D., Sarna, A., Freeman, W.T., Funkhouser, T.: Learning shape templates with structured implicit functions. In: Proceedings of the IEEE/CVF International Conference on Computer Vision, pp. 7154–7164 (2019)

13. Hu, X., Mu, H., Zhang, X., Wang, Z., Tan, T., Sun, J.: Meta-SR: a magnification-arbitrary network for super-resolution. In: Proceedings of the IEEE/CVF Conference on Computer Vision and Pattern Recognition, pp. 1575–1584 (2019)

14. Huang, J.B., Singh, A., Ahuja, N.: Single image super-resolution from transformed self-exemplars. In: Proceedings of the IEEE Conference on Computer Vision and Pattern Recognition, pp. 5197–5206 (2015)

15. Jiang, C., et al.: Local implicit grid representations for 3d scenes. In: Proceedings of the IEEE/CVF Conference on Computer Vision and Pattern Recognition, pp. 6001–6010 (2020)

16. Kim, J., Lee, J.K., Lee, K.M.: Accurate image super-resolution using very deep convolutional networks. In: Proceedings of the IEEE Conference on Computer Vision and Pattern Recognition, pp. 1646–1654 (2016)

17. Kim, J., Lee, J.K., Lee, K.M.: Deeply-recursive convolutional network for image super-resolution. In: Proceedings of the IEEE Conference on Computer Vision and Pattern Recognition, pp. 1637–1645 (2016)

18. Kingma, D.P., Ba, J.: Adam: a method for stochastic optimization. arXiv preprint arXiv:1412.6980 (2014)

19. Ledig, C., et al.: Photo-realistic single image super-resolution using a generative adversarial network. In: Proceedings of the IEEE Conference on Computer Vision and Pattern Recognition, pp. 4681–4690 (2017)

20. Lee, J., Jin, K.H.: Local texture estimator for implicit representation function. In: Proceedings of the IEEE/CVF Conference on Computer Vision and Pattern Recognition, pp. 1929–1938 (2022)

21. Liang, J., Cao, J., Sun, G., Zhang, K., Van Gool, L., Timofte, R.: SwinIR: image restoration using Swin transformer. In: Proceedings of the IEEE/CVF International Conference on Computer Vision, pp. 1833–1844 (2021)

22. Lim, B., Son, S., Kim, H., Nah, S., Mu Lee, K.: Enhanced deep residual networks for single image super-resolution. In: Proceedings of the IEEE Conference on Computer Vision and Pattern Recognition Workshops, pp. 136–144 (2017)

23. Liu, L., Gu, J., Zaw Lin, K., Chua, T.S., Theobalt, C.: Neural sparse voxel fields. Adv. Neural. Inf. Process. Syst. **33**, 15651–15663 (2020)

24. Liu, Y.T., Guo, Y.C., Zhang, S.H.: Enhancing multi-scale implicit learning in image super-resolution with integrated positional encoding. arXiv e-prints, pp. arXiv–2112 (2021)

25. Martin, D., Fowlkes, C., Tal, D., Malik, J.: A database of human segmented natural images and its application to evaluating segmentation algorithms and measuring ecological statistics. In: Proceedings Eighth IEEE International Conference on Computer Vision, ICCV 2001, vol. 2, pp. 416–423. IEEE (2001)

26. Mescheder, L., Oechsle, M., Niemeyer, M., Nowozin, S., Geiger, A.: Occupancy networks: learning 3D reconstruction in function space. In: Proceedings of the IEEE/CVF Conference on Computer Vision and Pattern Recognition, pp. 4460–4470 (2019)

27. Mildenhall, B., Srinivasan, P.P., Tancik, M., Barron, J.T., Ramamoorthi, R., Ng, R.: NeRF: representing scenes as neural radiance fields for view synthesis. Commun. ACM **65**(1), 99–106 (2021)

28. Niemeyer, M., Mescheder, L., Oechsle, M., Geiger, A.: Differentiable volumetric rendering: learning implicit 3D representations without 3D supervision. In: Proceedings of the IEEE/CVF Conference on Computer Vision and Pattern Recognition, pp. 3504–3515 (2020)

29. Paszke, A., et al.: PyTorch: an imperative style, high-performance deep learning library. In: Advances in Neural Information Processing Systems, vol. 32 (2019)
30. Sarmad, M., Ruspini, L., Lindseth, F.: Photo-realistic continuous image super-resolution with implicit neural networks and generative adversarial networks. In: Proceedings of the Northern Lights Deep Learning Workshop, vol. 3 (2022)
31. Shi, W., et al.: Real-time single image and video super-resolution using an efficient sub-pixel convolutional neural network. In: Proceedings of the IEEE Conference on Computer Vision and Pattern Recognition, pp. 1874–1883 (2016)
32. Sitzmann, V., Zollhöfer, M., Wetzstein, G.: Scene representation networks: continuous 3D-structure-aware neural scene representations. In: Advances in Neural Information Processing Systems, vol. 32 (2019)
33. Tai, Y., Yang, J., Liu, X.: Image super-resolution via deep recursive residual network. In: Proceedings of the IEEE Conference on Computer Vision and Pattern Recognition, pp. 3147–3155 (2017)
34. Vaswani, A., et al.: Attention is all you need. In: Advances in Neural Information Processing Systems, vol. 30 (2017)
35. Wang, L., Wang, Y., Lin, Z., Yang, J., An, W., Guo, Y.: Learning a single network for scale-arbitrary super-resolution. In: Proceedings of the IEEE/CVF International Conference on Computer Vision, pp. 4801–4810 (2021)
36. Wang, X., et al.: ESRGAN: enhanced super-resolution generative adversarial networks. In: Leal-Taixé, L., Roth, S. (eds.) ECCV 2018. LNCS, vol. 11133, pp. 63–79. Springer, Cham (2019). https://doi.org/10.1007/978-3-030-11021-5_5
37. Xia, Z., Pan, X., Song, S., Li, L.E., Huang, G.: Vision transformer with deformable attention. In: Proceedings of the IEEE/CVF Conference on Computer Vision and Pattern Recognition, pp. 4794–4803 (2022)
38. Xu, X., Wang, Z., Shi, H.: UltraSR: spatial encoding is a missing key for implicit image function-based arbitrary-scale super-resolution. arXiv preprint arXiv:2103.12716 (2021)
39. Zeyde, R., Elad, M., Protter, M.: On single image scale-up using sparse-representations. In: Boissonnat, J.D., et al. (eds.) Curves and Surfaces: 7th International Conference, Avignon, France, 24–30 June 2010, Revised Selected Papers 7, vol. 6920, pp. 711–730. Springer, Cham (2012). https://doi.org/10.1007/978-3-642-27413-8_47
40. Zhang, D., Huang, F., Liu, S., Wang, X., Jin, Z.: SwinFIR: revisiting the SwinIR with fast fourier convolution and improved training for image super-resolution. arXiv preprint arXiv:2208.11247 (2022)
41. Zhang, K., Zuo, W., Gu, S., Zhang, L.: Learning deep CNN denoiser prior for image restoration. In: Proceedings of the IEEE Conference on Computer Vision and Pattern Recognition, pp. 3929–3938 (2017)
42. Zhang, Y., Li, K., Li, K., Wang, L., Zhong, B., Fu, Y.: Image super-resolution using very deep residual channel attention networks. In: Ferrari, V., Hebert, M., Sminchisescu, C., Weiss, Y. (eds.) ECCV 2018. LNCS, vol. 11211, pp. 294–310. Springer, Cham (2018). https://doi.org/10.1007/978-3-030-01234-2_18
43. Zhang, Y., Tian, Y., Kong, Y., Zhong, B., Fu, Y.: Residual dense network for image super-resolution. In: Proceedings of the IEEE Conference on Computer Vision and Pattern Recognition, pp. 2472–2481 (2018)

Single-Video Temporal Consistency Enhancement with Rolling Guidance

Xiaonan Fang[1]([⊠])[iD] and Song-Hai Zhang[2][iD]

[1] Macau University of Science and Technology, Taipa 999078, Macau, China
xnfang@must.edu.mo
[2] Tsinghua University, Beijing 100084, China
shz@tsinghua.edu.cn

Abstract. Image/video synthesis has been extensively studied in academics, and computer-generated videos are becoming increasingly popular among the general public. However, ensuring the temporal consistency of generated videos is still a challenging problem. Most existing algorithms for temporal consistency enhancement rely on the motion cues from a guidance video to filter the temporally inconsistent video. This paper proposes a novel approach that processes single-video input to achieve temporal consistency. The key observation is that we can obtain a coarse guidance video through temporal smoothing and refine its visual quality using a rolling guidance pipeline. We only use an off-the-shelf optical-flow estimation model as external visual knowledge. The proposed algorithm has been evaluated on a wide range of videos synthesized by various methods, including single-image processing models and text-to-video models. Our method effectively eliminates temporal inconsistency while preserving the input visual content.

Keywords: temporal consistency · video enhancement · video filtering

1 Introduction

Video shot represents a realistic or virtual scene in a period. In most scenarios, the shading and reflectance of the scene remain almost unchanged, leading to temporally consistent content in the image domain. Videos captured by cameras or synthesized by realistic rendering algorithms usually have good temporal consistency. However, the rapid development of image processing algorithms and neural synthesis techniques brings new challenges to temporal consistency. Humans are sensitive to flickering effects in the generated videos and usually prefer temporally consistent presentations. Some videos are created from source videos with an image processing algorithm executed frame by frame. These videos often suffer from poor temporal consistency because the adopted algorithms are unstable under the camera and object motion. Some videos are synthesized with more abstract guidance information, such as label maps, edge maps [33,40,52] and text description [9,14,35], and in these cases, it is more difficult to achieve temporal consistency.

F.-L. Zhang and A. Sharf (Eds.): CVM 2024, LNCS 14593, pp. 109–130, 2024.
https://doi.org/10.1007/978-981-97-2092-7_6

Currently, there are two main-stream strategies to enhance the temporal consistency of synthesized videos. The first one is adding some temporal constraints in a specific synthesis algorithm. For example, when training a neural network, people can add a loss term that requires two pixels corresponding to the same physical location in consecutive frames to have similar color [16]. Another strategy is to apply a post-processing filter to deal with different types of inconsistency brought by various algorithms [4]. The latter category of methods can transfer the inter-frame correspondence from a source video to a target one. Here the target video is generated by some algorithm from the temporally consistent counterpart. However, the source videos are not always available, and some input representations, such as edge maps and textual descriptions cannot provide temporal correspondence. Therefore, it is of great value to develop an algorithm for temporal consistency enhancement with single-video input. We notice that a few recent papers [1, 24] have similar motivations, but our solution is quite different from those and has its advantages. We will give the theoretical and experimental comparison with the method proposed in [24].

The temporally inconsistent video input is denoted as $\mathcal{I} = \{I_1, I_2, \cdots, I_T\}$, where T is the number of frames. The image resolution is $W \times H$. Our goal is to find another sequence $\mathcal{J} = \{J_1, J_2, \cdots, J_T\}$ with the same resolution that maintains the video content and removes as much temporal inconsistency as possible. A straightforward approach to ensure temporal consistency is smoothing the video content temporally. To tackle view changes and object motion, we can adopt an optical-flow estimation method to find pixel correspondence between consecutive frames and apply a 1D filter on each temporal trajectory independently. However, this operation will inevitably smooth every frame in the spatial domain because the flow estimation is imprecise. In addition, the estimated flow becomes less reliable when there exists a flickering effect.

High-quality temporal filtering is possible if there exists an appropriate guidance video. The blind video consistency method (BVC) [4] and Deep Video Prior (DVP) method [25] are two major solutions. BVC uses gradient-domain optimization, while DVP regards the architecture of neural networks as a kind of regularization. Directly using input $\mathcal{I}$ as guidance is unsuitable for these two algorithms. The weights for warping error in [4] are determined by the pixel similarity in the guidance video, so the guidance video must be stable enough. The DVP algorithm requires more properties of guidance video. It must contain the correct structures and textures. Otherwise, the network will produce blurry results. For example, the DVP algorithm does not work when using edge maps as guidance. The three candidate approaches above have their drawbacks, but we will show that the video temporal consistency can be effectively enhanced if they are carefully combined. Besides, it is difficult to resolve the temporal consistency problem in a single-stage neural network such as [22] because of the lack of precise inter-frame correspondences. Thus, we design a multi-stage method to tackle different aspects of challenges progressively.

Our solution brings a few ideas from image filters. Image filters are designed to reduce the spatial variation, while in this task we need to reduce the

Input video   Enhanced video

Fig. 1. Example of single-video temporal consistency enhancement. Our algorithm only takes the temporally inconsistent video (left) as input and creates a consistent version (right) with the rolling guidance framework.

temporal variation. Image filtering algorithms can utilize structural information from a guidance image [21]. Similarly, previous video temporal filters need a guidance video with sufficient temporal consistency. The problem we encounter is how to construct an appropriate guidance video from unstable input. Inspired by the Rolling Guidance Filter [49], we propose a pipeline that generates a coarse guidance video at first and refines the video content gradually. The pipeline consists of three stages. In the first stage, we apply a temporal version of domain transform filter [10]. The filtered video can provide a more precise optical flow map so that we can apply the filter repeatedly with the refined temporal correspondence. After a few steps of temporal filtering, we obtain a coarse but temporally stable video. Then we recover the image structures using gradient-domain optimization, which is modified from the method proposed in [4]. The filtered video from the previous step can serve as guidance and provide inter-frame correspondence. In the final stage, we refine the global consistency and suppress visual artifacts using Deep Video Prior [25], where we still use the result from the previous stage as the guidance video. An example of temporal consistency enhancement result is presented in Fig. 1. The temporal color inconsistency in the input is introduced by an image operator, and our algorithm can remove it and achieve a visually pleasing result.

We conducted experiments on a wide range of synthesized videos. We tested single image operators including colorization, enhancement, spatial white balancing, and dehazing algorithms. We also evaluated videos generated by the text-to-video model, line art colorization model, and neural shading model. We exhibit that our algorithm can effectively improve temporal consistency while maintaining the original image content. Our algorithm does not require guidance videos, and we do not need to train any new network on external datasets. The model only relies on a relatively reliable optical-flow estimation model [37]. The main contributions of this paper are:

- We propose a novel rolling guidance framework of temporal consistency enhancement with single-video input.
- Our algorithm achieves better temporal consistency and visual quality compared with previous methods on a wide range of videos.

2   Related Work

We briefly review the representative papers for temporally consistent video processing and synthesis. Some algorithms are designed for specific tasks, and others are task-agnostic, which could serve as a post-processing filter for various types of processed videos. We also discuss some relevant papers about spatial filters that inspired us to do this work.

2.1   Temporal Consistency for Specific Tasks

Optical flow is widely used in video synthesis algorithms. The accuracy of flow estimation is significantly improved by neural networks such as FlowNet [8,17], PWC-Net [36] and RAFT model [37]. The most popular method to enhance temporal consistency is using a warping loss between consecutive frames as regularization during network training. Usually, an optical-flow estimation model is adopted to determine the warping function. The warping loss could be used for video style transfer [16], colorization [23], scene illumination [43] and low-light enhancement [47]. Besides, test-time training with geometric constraints was proposed to improve the consistency of depth-map estimation [28].

There are some other strategies to ensure temporal consistency in video synthesis. TecoGAN [7] predicts the video sequence with a forward pass and a backward pass, then a ping-pong loss is used to ensure long-range temporal consistency. This network is trained for video super-resolution and video translation. Vid2vid [40] is built upon the Pix2pix model [18,41]. It fuses the image warped from previous predictions and a synthesized image with a predicted occlusion map. This method can be accelerated by spatial compression and frame interpolation technique [52]. Video translation model can also be trained on unpaired dataset [5] using cycle consistency for both reconstructed frames and their flow maps.

2.2   Blind Video Temporal Consistency

A temporally inconsistent video is usually the processing result of a source video. Bonneel et al. [4] provided the first blind video temporal consistency (BVC) algorithm, which is independent of how the target video is generated. They optimize the video content with a gradient term to maintain the contrast of processed video and a weighted warping term between consecutive frames. Yao et al. [46] constructed the warped frame from a few keyframes and used a content compensation method to refine detail structures. They also proposed a new metric for temporal consistency considering the warping error on both the source video and the target video. Lai et al. [22] trained a ConvLSTM network on DAVIS dataset [30] to achieve fast blind video consistency (FBVC). They adopted the perceptual loss [19] and warping loss as supervision. Deep Video Prior (DVP) [25] extended the concept of Deep Image Prior [26]. A neural network (e.g., U-Net [31]) is trained to reconstruct the processed frame from the input frame. Since the model fits only one sequence, it can implicitly transfer the temporal correspondence of input frames to the processed frames, leading to a temporally smooth output. The thought of DVP can also be adapted to specific tasks such as video segmentation [51]. Recently, researchers have been considering how to improve temporal consistency when the source video is unavailable. Lei et al. [24] proposed the blind video deflickering algorithm, which uses a neural filter to improve the flawed neural atlases [20]. Ali et al. [1] proposed another framework for task-agnostic consistency with a novel tri-frame design for stable flow estimation on flickering data.

2.3 Spatial Smoothing Filters and Rolling Guidance

Smoothing filters in the image domain are extensively studied, but we will only introduce some widely-used filters here. Bilateral filter [38] is probably the most famous tool for edge-preserving smoothing. Some methods are formulated as minimizing the data term and some regularization terms such as L_0 gradient norm [44], L_1 gradient norm [3] and Relative Total Variation [45]. Domain transform filter [10] explicitly defines the smoothing operation and is more efficient for computation.

The smoothing process can also be conducted with a guidance image. A classical formulation is the joint bilateral filter [21], and the guided filter [13] is another famous tool. The guidance map can be constructed in a more sophisticated way, deriving other filters such as bilateral texture filter [6]. Rolling Guidance Filter [49] uses a Gaussian filter to generate the initial guidance and refine the guidance with the joint bilateral filter iteratively. The converged guidance image is also the smoothed version of the input image. The idea of rolling guidance is also applied to geometry processing, known as the rolling guidance normal filter [39].

3   Method

3.1   Overview

The pipeline of our temporal consistency enhancement algorithm is illustrated in Fig. 2. The input video is denoted as $\mathcal{I} = \{I_1, I_2, \cdots, I_T\}$. Similar to the

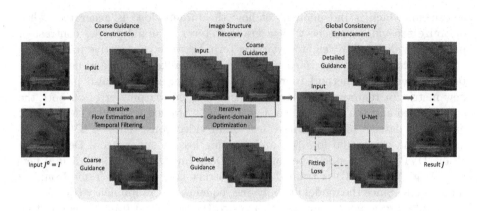

Fig. 2. The pipeline of our algorithm. We adopt the framework of Rolling Guidance Filter [49]. We start with the input video $\mathcal{J}^0 = \mathcal{I}$ and apply a series of operators to filter the input video with guidance iteratively. Specifically, we apply the temporal domain transform filter to get the coarse guidance in the first stage, apply gradient-domain optimization to get detailed guidance in the second stage and enhance the global consistency using the deep-video-prior of a U-Net in the last stage. The final output is denoted by $\mathcal{J}$.

Rolling Guidance Filter [49], we compute a series of videos $\mathcal{J}^1, \mathcal{J}^2, \cdots$ step by step. Each video could serve as guidance for the next step. Let $\mathcal{J}^0 = \mathcal{I}$, we can formulate the process as:

$$\mathcal{J}^i = \text{Filter}_i(\mathcal{J}^{i-1}, I), \tag{1}$$

where the function $\text{Filter}_i(\cdot, \cdot)$ represents a joint filter that uses the guidance information inside $\mathcal{J}^{i-1}$ to refine $\mathcal{I}$. However, unlike the pipeline in [49], we adopt three filters in the entire process for different purposes.

Firstly, the input sequence $\mathcal{I}$ is smoothed by a temporal version of domain transform filter [10], resulting in a coarse but temporally stable guidance video $\mathcal{J}^1$. Then it is possible to use $\mathcal{J}^1$ to compute more precise flow maps and reuse the domain transform filter. We repeat this process for s times to obtain $\mathcal{J}^1, \cdots, \mathcal{J}^s$.

Secondly, we try to recover the image structure. In this stage, we adopt a gradient-domain optimization framework modified from BVC [4]. We use $\mathcal{J}^s$ as guidance to filter the target video $\mathcal{I}$ from frame 1 to frame T, obtaining $\mathcal{J}^{s+1}$. Then we regard $\mathcal{J}^{s+1}$ as a new guidance video and apply the optimization algorithm in the opposite direction, obtaining video $\mathcal{J}^{s+2}$ with improving structures.

The final stage is designed to refine $\mathcal{J}^{s+2}$ for global consistency. We use Deep Video Prior [25] to reconstruct $\mathcal{I}$ from $\mathcal{J}^{s+2}$ by training a convolutional neural network from scratch. The final result is denoted by $\mathcal{J}$.

3.2   Constructing Coarse Guidance Video

In this stage, we adopt the domain transform filter [10] to smooth the video content in the temporal order. The basic idea of domain transform is mapping the data points to a line while maintaining the geodesic distance. Given a pixel $p = (x, y)$ in the t-th frame, we can find its corresponding point q in the $(t-1)$-th frame. We adopt the RAFT model [37] for optical flow estimation. The geodesic distance between these two points is defined as:

$$d = 1 + \frac{\sigma_s}{\sigma_r} \|I_t(p) - I_{t-1}(q)\|_1. \tag{2}$$

Parameters σ_s and σ_r represent the variance on the temporal axis and RGB color space. Increasing σ_r will make the result smoother. Since the point q might not lie on the image grid, we cannot efficiently construct the whole trajectory through the video. Therefore, we apply the recursive form of the domain transform filter to smooth the value at p. Since it is not the contribution of this work, please refer to [10] for the detailed implementation. The color at position q is estimated by bilinear interpolation.

Sometimes the content at p in the t-th frame does not appear in the previous frame. One possible situation is that the corresponding position q is outside the image domain, namely $q \notin [0, W-1] \times [0, H-1]$. Another situation is that the point is occluded in the previous frame. We estimate the occlusion by analyzing the optical flow f from the $(t-1)$-th frame to the t-th frame. The visibility map V is constructed as proposed in [42]:

$$V(x, y) = \sum_{i=1}^{W} \sum_{j=1}^{H} \max(0, 1 - |x - i - f^x(i, j)|) \tag{3}$$
$$\cdot \max(0, 1 - |y - j - f^y(i, j)|).$$

Then the binary occlusion map O is defined as:

$$O(p) = \begin{cases} 1, & V(p) > 0.5 \text{ and } q \in [1, H] \times [1, W] \\ 0, & \text{otherwise.} \end{cases} \tag{4}$$

Let Z_t be the output of the recursive filter in a forward pass, and O_t the occlusion map for the t-th frame, we define

$$Z_t(p) = (1 - O_t(p)a^d)I_t(p) + O_t(p)a^d Z_{t-1}(q). \tag{5}$$

Here the factor a is used to control the amount of local smoothing and is related to σ_s. Similarly, we can filter the video content in the opposite direction. The video is filtered back and forth with parameter a gradually decreasing. We adopt the same updating rule of a as proposed in [10]. The result of the initial temporal domain transform filter is denoted by $\mathcal{J}^1 = \{J_1^1, J_2^1, \cdots, J_T^1\}$. More accurate optical flow can be estimated on $\mathcal{J}^1$, and we replace the initial flow computed from $\mathcal{I}$. Then we can apply the domain transform filter on $\mathcal{I}$ again, but with new temporal correspondence. We repeat the filtering process for s times. Hence sequence $\mathcal{J}^s$ is the result of this stage. In our experiment, we find that $s = 3$ is adequate to remove most artifacts.

Figure 3 exhibits the evolution of video content after three iterations. Though the result of the first step (the second row) has serious artifacts, it provides better inter-frame matching (i.e., the artifacts between two frames are also consistent). Thus, the rolling guidance strategy can recover the content gradually.

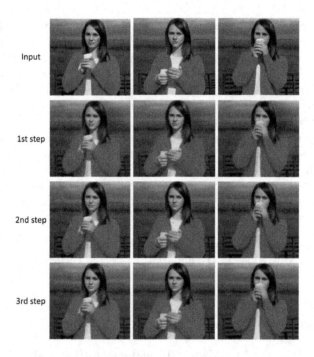

Fig. 3. Example of domain transform filtering in the first stage. The spatial artifact can be significantly reduced using rolling guidance.

3.3   Recovering Image Details

Due to the inherent limitation of optical flow, the result $\mathcal{J}^s$ from the previous stage is usually blurry and might have structural error. The goal of this stage is to recover the clear image structure by optimization. Inspired by the work of blind video consistency [4], we adopt a modified gradient-domain optimization scheme. The key point is to reconstruct the gradient field of the original frame, namely ∇I_t. Meanwhile, the color at pixel p in the t-th frame is supposed to be similar to a reference point in the neighboring frame. We use $\mathcal{J}^{i-1}$ to represent the result from the previous step. It serves as the guidance video to find the pixel correspondence, and the optimized video is denoted by $\mathcal{J}^i$. For the optimization in a forward pass, our target is to minimize

$$\sum_p \|\nabla J_t^i(p) - \nabla I_t(p)\|^2 + w(p)\|J_t^i(p) - r(p)\|^2. \tag{6}$$

Here $r(p)$ is the reference color for current location p, and weight $w(p)$ is the confidence value of such a reference. The reference could be obtained by warping with the optical flow computed on guidance video $\mathcal{J}^{i-1}$. Let $q_1(p)$ be the corresponding location in the previous frame. The optical-flow estimation is not always correct, so we provide another candidate position $q_2(p)$ in the previous frame found by PatchMatch [2]. Now we have two candidates for reference:

$$r_k(p) = J_{t-1}^i(q_k(p)), k \in \{1, 2\}. \tag{7}$$

Then we define the confidence value as color affinity in the guidance video:

$$w_k(p) = e^{-\|J_t^{i-1}(p) - J_{t-1}^{i-1}(q_k(p))\|^2/2\sigma^2}, k \in \{1, 2\}. \tag{8}$$

The term $w_k(p)$ represents the similarity between position p and $q_k(p)$ in the two consecutive frames. If this value is not high enough or the pixel p is occluded (verified by the value of $O_t(p)$), we consider that the correspondence in the guidance video is inaccurate. Therefore, we compare the similarity with a threshold α. If the similarity is less than α, we will use the color value $I_t(p)$ in the original video as a reference. Specifically, we define

$$r(p) = \begin{cases} r_1(p), w_1(p) \geq w_2(p) \wedge w_1(p) > \alpha \wedge O_t(p), \\ r_2(p), w_2(p) > w_1(p) \wedge w_2(p) > \alpha \wedge O_t(p), \\ I_t(p), \text{ otherwise.} \end{cases} \tag{9}$$

Here the occlusion index $O_t(p)$ is given by Eq. 4. We choose the weight $w(p)$ with the same criteria:

$$w(p) = \begin{cases} w_1(p), w_1(p) \geq w_2(p) \wedge w_1(p) > \alpha \wedge O_t(p), \\ w_2(p), w_2(p) > w_1(p) \wedge w_2(p) > \alpha \wedge O_t(p), \\ \alpha, \text{ otherwise.} \end{cases} \tag{10}$$

We set $\alpha = 0.75$ for all test videos used in the experiment. However, people may choose a lower threshold if the flow estimation is good enough. Moreover, it is possible to use $J_t^{i-1}(p)$ instead of $I_t(p)$ as reference color. Using this alternative leads to results with smoother changes but larger differences from the input video.

The objective in Eq. 6 has a quadratic form and could be converted into a linear system. We initialize $J_1^i = J_1^{i-1}$ and adopt the Gauss-Seidel method to solve $J_2^i, ..., J_T^i$ in order. The result $\mathcal{J}^i$ can serve as the new guidance video for solving $\mathcal{J}^{i+1}$ in the opposite direction, i.e., fixing the last frame and computing the t-th frame from the $(t+1)$-th frame. In this way, we will obtain $\mathcal{J}^{s+2}$ as the output of this stage.

Figure 4 shows how the detail structures are recovered by gradient-domain optimization. Note that the color of the wall is flickering in the input sequence (first column). The first filtering stage removed the inconsistency but produced blurry textures (second column). The second stage recovered the details while maintaining the color consistency (last column).

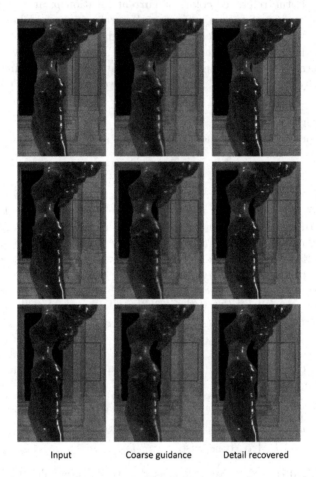

Input   Coarse guidance   Detail recovered

Fig. 4. The effect of image detail recovery via gradient-domain optimization. The coarse guidance video is provided by the previous stage.

3.4   Global Refinement

In the previous stage, the video content is updated sequentially, meaning that the error might accumulate gradually and the later frames will diverge from the original one. Therefore, it is necessary to refine the output video with global optimization. The result of the previous stage will serve as a detailed guidance video to filter the input one. Deep Video Prior [25] has been verified as an effective tool to regularize the visual content and eliminate temporal flickering if a high-quality guidance video is available. A convolutional neural network F is trained from scratch to reconstruct the unstable video $\mathcal{I}$ from some stable input sequence. Each frame is processed independently. In this work, we adopt the U-Net structure [31]. We use the result $\mathcal{J}^{s+2}$ from the second stage as the input of network F. Regarding the video frames as training data, the objective is to minimize the following reconstruction error:

$$\mathcal{L} = \sum_{t=1}^{T} L(F(J_t^{s+2}), I_t). \tag{11}$$

The reconstruction term is defined as the combination of L_1 loss and perceptual loss [19] of VGG-Net features [34]:

$$\begin{aligned} L(F(J_t^{s+2}), I_t) &= \|F(J_t^{s+2}) - I_t\|_1 \\ &+ \sum_{l=1}^{5} \lambda_l \|\phi_l(F(J_t^{s+2})) - \phi_l(I_t)\|_1. \end{aligned} \tag{12}$$

Here $\phi_l(\cdot)$ represents the feature maps in the l-th convolutional block of VGG-Net.

The network is trained through 25 epochs with a learning rate of 10^{-4}. The final enhanced video $\mathcal{J} = \{J_1, J_2, \cdots, J_T\}$ is obtained by applying the trained model F frame by frame.

$$J_t = F(J_t^{s+2}), t \in \{1, 2, \cdots, T\}. \tag{13}$$

3.5   Comparison with the Deflickering Algorithm

The Deflickering algorithm proposed by Lei et al. [24] also aims to improve the temporal consistency using single-video input. Their pipeline also contains three stages, but different techniques are adopted. In both methods, the first stage is designed to obtain a temporally stable intermediate result, but we choose a concise way without tedious training. In the second stage, Lei et al. use a network trained on MS COCO [27] to correct image structures. However, this network is trained on single-image input, so temporal consistency is not explicitly guaranteed. In the last stage, they adopt a network similar to [22]. The advantage is that video can be processed in sequential order by one pass, but the model trained on an external dataset is not as stable as an internal learning method like DVP [25].

4   Experiment

4.1   Dataset

We evaluate our method on two types of data. For the first type, we know the source video from which the target video was generated. We collect the paired test videos from [25], which is generated by colorization [50], dehazing [12], spatial white balancing [15] and enhancement algorithm [11]. We also add a few colorized videos generated by the single image model provided by [23].

For some video generation algorithms, there is no input video, or the input cannot provide sufficient guidance to improve the temporal consistency of the generated video. We collect the text-to-video data from CogVideo [14], Make-A-Video [35] and Gen-2 model [9]. We also consider specific tasks including neural shading [29,43] and line art colorization [33]. The unpaired dataset contains 31 videos in total.

For most data, we kept the same parameters in the pipeline. We set $\sigma_s = 60$ and $\sigma_r = 1.0$ for stage 1 by default. However, we observe that some videos in the paired dataset have large temporal color variation, so we set $\sigma_s = 300$ and $\sigma_r = 6.0$ to handle these challenging cases.

Fig. 5. Comparison on paired data. For the colorization task, the guidance video used in BVC [4], FBVC [22], and DVP [25] is the grayscale version of the input. The Deflickering algorithm [24] and our method do not use the guidance video.

4.2   Quality Assessment

Similar to the DVP paper [25], we assess the quality of refined videos in two aspects: the temporal consistency and the similarity to the input video. We use warping error to measure the temporal consistency. The warping error between two frames J_s, J_t with resolution $W \times H$ is defined as:

$$e(J_s, J_t) = \frac{1}{W \times H} \|M_{s,t}(J_t - \mathrm{warp}(J_s))\|^2. \tag{14}$$

For paired data, the frame J_s is warped by the optical flow computed on the original video. The flow map is predicted by the RAFT model [37], and the occlusion map is estimated using the method proposed in [32]. Then we construct the temporal consistency measure E_w for video $\mathcal{J}$:

$$E_w(\mathcal{J}) = \frac{1}{2(T-1)} \sum_{t=2}^{T} \left(e(J_{t-1}, J_t) + e(J_1, J_t)\right). \tag{15}$$

The error between consecutive frames reflects the short-range consistency, while the error between the first frame and every other frame represents the long-range consistency.

Apart from temporal consistency, it is also important to maintain the input video content with little appearance change. Thus we define the fidelity term E_f as the average PSNR between input and output frames:

$$E_f(\mathcal{J},\mathcal{I}) = \frac{1}{T-1} \sum_{i=2}^{T} \text{PSNR}(J_t, I_t). \tag{16}$$

We neglect the first frame because for some methods the first frame is kept the same as the input, and the PSNR value for it is infinity.

As for unpaired videos, there is no temporally stable guidance video for optical-flow estimation. Therefore, we estimate the flow on the output itself as an approximation, and evaluate the following term:

$$\hat{E}_w(\mathcal{J}) = \frac{1}{T-1} \sum_{t=2}^{T} \frac{1}{W \times H} ||J_t - \text{warp}(J_{t-1})||^2. \tag{17}$$

Note that for videos processed by different algorithms, the involved optical flow is also different, and the occlusion map estimated by [32] is not always reliable. So we do not use the occlusion map and the long-range term for unpaired videos. We also use metric E_f to evaluate the fidelity of unpaired videos. Since there is no well-accepted temporal consistency metric for unpaired data, we conduct a user study.

Table 1. Evaluation on Paired Videos. We report the warping error E_w and the fidelity term E_f of different algorithms.

Method	Input	E_w (lower the better)	E_f (higher the better)
Processed	–	0.1877	Inf
BVC [4]	Paired	0.1513	25.30
FBVC [22]	Paired	0.2692	22.88
DVP [25]	Paired	0.1341	32.25
DeFlickering [24]	Single	0.1160	27.05
Ours	Single	0.1264	30.65

4.3   Comparison to State-of-the-Art Methods

For the paired data, we test previous algorithms including BVC [4], FBVC [22], and DVP [25], which require the original video to provide inter-frame correspondence explicitly or implicitly. For the Deflickering algorithm proposed by Lei et al. [24] and our method, the original input video is neglected. The evaluation result is reported in Table 1. The Deflickering algorithm achieved a lower warping error than ours, but our method can better maintain the video content, with a much higher E_f index. All algorithms using paired videos have higher warping

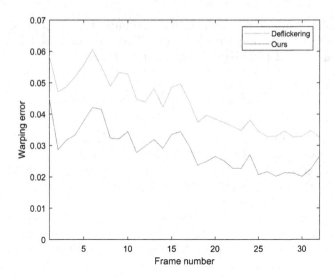

Fig. 6. Frame-by-frame warping error compared to the Deflickering algorithm [24] in one video sequence.

Table 2. Evaluation on Unpaired Videos. We report the warping error with the optical flow computed on the output video, as well as the fidelity term.

Data Type	Processed	Deflickering		Ours	
	$\hat{E}_w$	$\hat{E}_w$	E_f	$\hat{E}_w$	E_f
Make-a-video	0.0624	0.0541	28.90	0.0396	31.45
CogVideo	0.0996	0.0573	31.68	0.0447	30.15
Gen2	0.0487	0.0440	27.75	0.0414	31.31
Shading	0.0304	0.0237	31.71	0.0229	37.36
Colorization	0.0387	0.0297	38.07	0.0249	31.97

errors than ours. We also list the initial errors of the input videos ("Processed" in the table). Figure 5 shows an example. The Deflickering algorithm produced color-blending artifacts as highlighted in the image.

For the unpaired data, we evaluate our method and the Deflickering algorithm [24]. Table 2 lists the two metrics on each type of video respectively. Due to the large domain difference, the performance on these videos varies a lot. In general, our method is superior to the Deflickering algorithm on $\hat{E}_w$ for all types of videos. The PSNR of our method is similar across different video styles while the Deflickering algorithm is not that stable. We randomly choose 15 videos from the unpaired dataset for the user study. The results generated by our method and Deflickering algorithm were played to users in parallel in random order. Then the users were required to assess the temporal consistency and the general visual quality. We invited 28 users to attend the study and obtained 397 judgments in

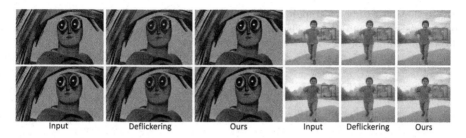

Fig. 7. Comparison between the Deflickering algorithm [24] and our method on unpaired data. Note that the Deflickering algorithm might blend the color among different objects.

Fig. 8. Example of the ablation study. We adopt DVP [25] and an improved version of BVC [4] as components in our pipeline. However, directly applying BVC or DVP using a single video as guidance cannot achieve temporal consistency.

total. The result is summarized in Table 3. Our method is preferred by more participants on both temporal consistency and visual quality. Figure 7 exhibits two examples, in which the Deflickering algorithm tends to blend the color of different objects. Compared with the neural filter in [24], our detail recovery scheme can better preserve the original image appearance while improving the temporal consistency. Figure 6 provides the comparison of warping errors at every frame of one sequence, which is the same one as displayed in Fig. 8. More visual results on long sequences are provided in Fig. 11 and the supplementary material.

4.4 Ablation Study

We analyze the intermediate results of our method to verify the effectiveness of our pipeline. In specific, we evaluated the result $\mathcal{J}^s$ of stage 1 and the result $\mathcal{J}^{s+2}$ of stage 2. Since we adopt the BVC method [4] and DVP method [25] as components in our pipeline, we also evaluate these two methods using the input video $\mathcal{I}$ as guidance. We test all these alternatives on the CogVideo dataset [14] containing 13 sequences. The quantitative result is displayed in Table 4 and Fig. 8 provides an example. The output of stage 1 is the most consistent under our

Table 3. User Study on Unpaired Videos. Users were required to compare the temporal consistency and general visual quality between our method and the Deflickering algorithm [24]. Then they reported their preferences.

Preference on	Ours	Deflickering	Same
Temporal Consistency	33%	20%	47%
General Visual Quality	45%	21%	34%

Table 4. Results of Ablation Study. We report the warping error and fidelity term.

Method	$\hat{E}_w$	E_f
Processed	0.0996	Inf.
Single-input BVC [4]	0.0861	26.66
Single-input DVP [25]	0.0964	37.13
Ours (stage 1)	0.0258	29.60
Ours (stage 2)	0.0512	31.51
Ours (final)	0.0447	30.15

metric. However, the content is also smoothed in the spatial domain, and some visual artifacts are introduced. The detail recovery process in stage 2 can improve the visual quality and remove most artifacts. The warping error will also increase to some extent. The global optimization in stage 3 can reduce the warping error created by the previous step. Note that using the same video as guidance for BVC [4] or DVP [25] is useless because the inconsistent video cannot provide good visual correspondence.

The first stage aims to obtain a guidance video with reliable optical flow. The definition of the occlusion map in Eq. 4 implies that the forward flow and backward flow should be consistent if the content is not occluded. Therefore, the average value of this map, Avg(O), can reflect the quality of the estimated flow. Ideally, it should be equal to the actual non-occlusion rate, which is usually close to 1. Figure 9 shows the change of Avg(O) for sequences $\mathcal{J}^0$ to $\mathcal{J}^3$ displayed in Fig. 3. A higher value implies that the forward flow and backward flow are more consistent, and hence more reliable. We also visualize the flow maps before and after filtering in Fig. 10. The sequences can be found in the supplementary material.

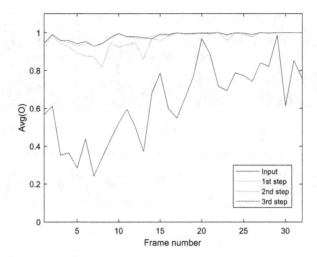

Fig. 9. Average value of the occlusion map O computed from input and intermediate video sequences. A higher value implies a more reliable optical flow estimation.

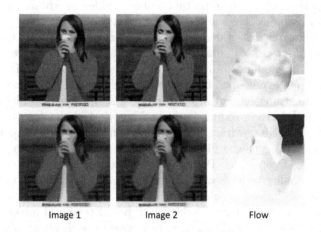

Fig. 10. Visualization of flow maps. The first row shows the input flickering images and the corresponding flow, and the second row shows the result after one-step filtering. It is worth noting that though the initial filtering brings artifacts in the image domain, the updated flow is more accurate and aligned with object boundaries.

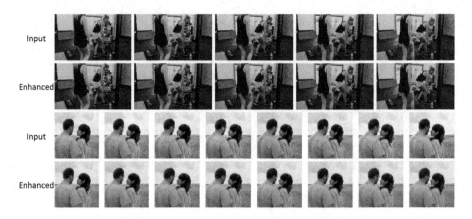

Fig. 11. Additional sequential results of temporal consistency enhancement.

5   Discussion and Conclusion

Temporal consistency is an important issue in video synthesis. Although AI-generated videos have been widely spread on the Internet, there is no unified framework to ensure temporal consistency on synthesized videos. In this paper, we present a framework to enhance the temporal consistency of a single input video without the guidance of a temporally consistent video. This method can serve as a post-processing operator for a wide range of video synthesis algorithms. We analyze the strengths and drawbacks of existing temporal filters requiring paired input and derive a rolling guidance framework that improves the quality of filtered video with a few iterations. Our pipeline consists of temporal smoothing with a domain transform filter, gradient-domain reconstruction, and global refinement using Deep Video Prior. We evaluate the proposed algorithm with warping error, fidelity term as well as user study, and exhibit that our algorithm can create visually pleasant video content.

Our algorithm cannot handle arbitrary types of temporal inconsistency. For example, Large-scale semantic change in the video is difficult to eliminate (e.g., the frame-by-frame processing result of ControlNet [48]), and we would like to study how to reduce the semantic-level inconsistency in the future. We hope the progress in single-video consistency enhancement can contribute to the whole video synthesis community. If temporal consistency could be achieved by post-processing, the designers of video synthesis models can focus on other aspects of visual quality, such as semantic and aesthetic metrics.

Acknowledgement. This work was supported by the Natural Science Foundation of China (No. 62132012, 62361146854), Macau Unversity of Science and Technology (FRG-24-028-FIE). We also thank Xiaoxiong Fan and Guan Luo for their work in data collection and processing.

References

1. Ali, M.K., Kim, D., Kim, T.H.: Learning task agnostic temporal consistency correction (2022)
2. Barnes, C., Shechtman, E., Finkelstein, A., Goldman, D.B.: PatchMatch: a randomized correspondence algorithm for structural image editing. ACM Trans. Graph. (Proc. SIGGRAPH) **28**(3), 24 (2009)
3. Bi, S., Han, X., Yu, Y.: An L1 image transform for edge-preserving smoothing and scene-level intrinsic decomposition. ACM Trans. Graph. **34**(4), 78 (2015)
4. Bonneel, N., Tompkin, J., Sunkavalli, K., Sun, D., Paris, S., Pfister, H.: Blind video temporal consistency. ACM Trans. Graph. (TOG) **34**(6), 1–9 (2015)
5. Chen, Y., Pan, Y., Yao, T., Tian, X., Mei, T.: Mocycle-GAN: unpaired video-to-video translation. In: Proceedings of the 27th ACM International Conference on Multimedia, MM 2019, pp. 647–655. Association for Computing Machinery, New York, NY, USA (2019). https://doi.org/10.1145/3343031.3350937
6. Cho, H., Lee, H., Kang, H., Lee, S.: Bilateral texture filtering. ACM Trans. Graph. (TOG) **33**(4), 1–8 (2014)
7. Chu, M., Xie, Y., Mayer, J., Leal-Taixé, L., Thuerey, N.: Learning temporal coherence via self-supervision for GAN-based video generation. ACM Trans. Graph. **39**(4), 75-1 (2020). https://doi.org/10.1145/3386569.3392457
8. Dosovitskiy, A., et al.: FlowNet: learning optical flow with convolutional networks. In: 2015 IEEE International Conference on Computer Vision (ICCV), pp. 2758–2766 (2015). https://doi.org/10.1109/ICCV.2015.316
9. Esser, P., Chiu, J., Atighehchian, P., Granskog, J., Germanidis, A.: Structure and content-guided video synthesis with diffusion models. arXiv preprint arXiv:2302.03011 (2023)
10. Gastal, E.S., Oliveira, M.M.: Domain transform for edge-aware image and video processing. In: ACM SIGGRAPH 2011 Papers, pp. 1–12 (2011)
11. Gharbi, M., Chen, J., Barron, J.T., Hasinoff, S.W., Durand, F.: Deep bilateral learning for real-time image enhancement. ACM Trans. Graph. **36**(4), 1–12 (2017). https://doi.org/10.1145/3072959.3073592
12. He, K., Sun, J., Tang, X.: Single image haze removal using dark channel prior. IEEE Trans. Pattern Anal. Mach. Intell. **33**(12), 2341–2353 (2011). https://doi.org/10.1109/TPAMI.2010.168
13. He, K., Sun, J., Tang, X.: Guided image filtering. IEEE Trans. Pattern Anal. Mach. Intell. **35**(6), 1397–1409 (2013). https://doi.org/10.1109/TPAMI.2012.213
14. Hong, W., Ding, M., Zheng, W., Liu, X., Tang, J.: CogVideo: large-scale pretraining for text-to-video generation via transformers. arXiv preprint arXiv:2205.15868 (2022)
15. Hsu, E., Mertens, T., Paris, S., Avidan, S., Durand, F.: Light mixture estimation for spatially varying white balance. In: ACM SIGGRAPH 2008 Papers, SIGGRAPH 2008. Association for Computing Machinery, New York, NY, USA (2008). https://doi.org/10.1145/1399504.1360669
16. Huang, H., et al.: Real-time neural style transfer for videos. In: 2017 IEEE Conference on Computer Vision and Pattern Recognition (CVPR), pp. 7044–7052 (2017). https://doi.org/10.1109/CVPR.2017.745
17. Ilg, E., Mayer, N., Saikia, T., Keuper, M., Dosovitskiy, A., Brox, T.: FlowNet 2.0: evolution of optical flow estimation with deep networks. In: IEEE Conference on Computer Vision and Pattern Recognition (CVPR), July 2017. http://lmb.informatik.uni-freiburg.de//Publications/2017/IMKDB17

18. Isola, P., Zhu, J.Y., Zhou, T., Efros, A.A.: Image-to-image translation with conditional adversarial networks. In: 2017 IEEE Conference on Computer Vision and Pattern Recognition (CVPR), pp. 1125–1134 (2017)
19. Johnson, J., Alahi, A., Fei-Fei, L.: Perceptual losses for real-time style transfer and super-resolution. In: Leibe, B., Matas, J., Sebe, N., Welling, M. (eds.) ECCV 2016. LNCS, vol. 9906, pp. 694–711. Springer, Cham (2016). https://doi.org/10.1007/978-3-319-46475-6_43
20. Kasten, Y., Ofri, D., Wang, O., Dekel, T.: Layered neural atlases for consistent video editing. ACM Trans. Graph. **40**(6), 1–12 (2021). https://doi.org/10.1145/3478513.3480546
21. Kopf, J., Cohen, M.F., Lischinski, D., Uyttendaele, M.: Joint bilateral upsampling. ACM Trans. Graph. (ToG) **26**, 96 (2007)
22. Lai, W.-S., Huang, J.-B., Wang, O., Shechtman, E., Yumer, E., Yang, M.-H.: Learning blind video temporal consistency. In: Ferrari, V., Hebert, M., Sminchisescu, C., Weiss, Y. (eds.) ECCV 2018. LNCS, vol. 11219, pp. 179–195. Springer, Cham (2018). https://doi.org/10.1007/978-3-030-01267-0_11
23. Lei, C., Chen, Q.: Fully automatic video colorization with self-regularization and diversity. In: The IEEE Conference on Computer Vision and Pattern Recognition (CVPR), June 2019
24. Lei, C., Ren, X., Zhang, Z., Chen, Q.: Blind video deflickering by neural filtering with a flawed atlas. In: Proceedings of the IEEE/CVF Conference on Computer Vision and Pattern Recognition, pp. 10439–10448 (2023)
25. Lei, C., Xing, Y., Chen, Q.: Blind video temporal consistency via deep video prior. Adv. Neural. Inf. Process. Syst. **33**, 1083–1093 (2020)
26. Lempitsky, V., Vedaldi, A., Ulyanov, D.: Deep image prior. In: 2018 IEEE/CVF Conference on Computer Vision and Pattern Recognition, pp. 9446–9454 (2018). https://doi.org/10.1109/CVPR.2018.00984
27. Lin, T.Y., et al.: Microsoft COCO: common objects in context. In: Fleet, D., Pajdla, T., Schiele, B., Tuytelaars, T. (eds.) Computer Vision–ECCV 2014: 13th European Conference, Zurich, Switzerland, 6–12 September 2014, Proceedings, Part V 13, vol. 8693, pp. 740–755. Springer, Cham (2014). https://doi.org/10.1007/978-3-319-10602-1_48
28. Luo, X., Huang, J.B., Szeliski, R., Matzen, K., Kopf, J.: Consistent video depth estimation. ACM Trans. Graph. (ToG) **39**(4), 71–1 (2020)
29. Nalbach, O., Arabadzhiyska, E., Mehta, D., Seidel, H.P., Ritschel, T.: Deep shading: convolutional neural networks for screen space shading. Comput. Graph. Forum **36**(4), 65–78 (2017). https://doi.org/10.1111/cgf.13225
30. Perazzi, F., Pont-Tuset, J., McWilliams, B., Van Gool, L., Gross, M., Sorkine-Hornung, A.: A benchmark dataset and evaluation methodology for video object segmentation. In: 2016 IEEE Conference on Computer Vision and Pattern Recognition (CVPR), pp. 724–732 (2016). https://doi.org/10.1109/CVPR.2016.85
31. Ronneberger, O., Fischer, P., Brox, T.: U-Net: convolutional networks for biomedical image segmentation. In: Navab, N., Hornegger, J., Wells, W.M., Frangi, A.F. (eds.) Medical Image Computing and Computer-Assisted Intervention - MICCAI 2015, pp. 234–241. Springer, Cham (2015). https://doi.org/10.1007/978-3-319-24574-4_28
32. Ruder, M., Dosovitskiy, A., Brox, T.: Artistic style transfer for videos. In: Rosenhahn, B., Andres, B. (eds.) GCPR 2016. LNCS, vol. 9796, pp. 26–36. Springer, Cham (2016). https://doi.org/10.1007/978-3-319-45886-1_3
33. Shi, M., Zhang, J.Q., Chen, S.Y., Gao, L., Lai, Y., Zhang, F.L.: Reference-based deep line art video colorization. IEEE Trans. Vis. Comput. Graph. **20**(1) (2022)

34. Simonyan, K., Zisserman, A.: Very deep convolutional networks for large-scale image recognition (2015)
35. Singer, U., et al.: Make-a-video: text-to-video generation without text-video data (2022)
36. Sun, D., Yang, X., Liu, M.Y., Kautz, J.: PWC-Net: CNNs for optical flow using pyramid, warping, and cost volume. In: 2018 IEEE/CVF Conference on Computer Vision and Pattern Recognition, pp. 8934–8943 (2018). https://doi.org/10.1109/CVPR.2018.00931
37. Teed, Z., Deng, J.: RAFT: recurrent all-pairs field transforms for optical flow. In: Vedaldi, A., Bischof, H., Brox, T., Frahm, J.-M. (eds.) ECCV 2020. LNCS, vol. 12347, pp. 402–419. Springer, Cham (2020). https://doi.org/10.1007/978-3-030-58536-5_24
38. Tomasi, C., Manduchi, R.: Bilateral filtering for gray and color images. In: Sixth International Conference on Computer Vision, pp. 839–846. IEEE (1998)
39. Wang, P.S., Fu, X.M., Liu, Y., Tong, X., Liu, S.L., Guo, B.: Rolling guidance normal filter for geometric processing. ACM Trans. Graph. (TOG) 34(6), 1–9 (2015)
40. Wang, T.C., et al.: Video-to-video synthesis. In: Advances in Neural Information Processing Systems (NeurIPS) (2018)
41. Wang, T.C., Liu, M.Y., Zhu, J.Y., Tao, A., Kautz, J., Catanzaro, B.: High-resolution image synthesis and semantic manipulation with conditional GANs. In: Proceedings of the IEEE Conference on Computer Vision and Pattern Recognition (2018)
42. Wang, Y., Yang, Y., Yang, Z., Zhao, L., Wang, P., Xu, W.: Occlusion aware unsupervised learning of optical flow. In: Proceedings of the IEEE Conference on Computer Vision and Pattern Recognition, pp. 4884–4893 (2018)
43. Xin, H., Zheng, S., Xu, K., Yan, L.Q.: Lightweight bilateral convolutional neural networks for interactive single-bounce diffuse indirect illumination. IEEE Trans. Visual Comput. Graph. 28(4), 1824–1834 (2022). https://doi.org/10.1109/TVCG.2020.3023129
44. Xu, L., Lu, C., Xu, Y., Jia, J.: Image smoothing via L0 gradient minimization. ACM Trans. Graph. 30(6), 1–12 (2011)
45. Xu, L., Yan, Q., Xia, Y., Jia, J.: Structure extraction from texture via relative total variation. ACM Trans. Graph. 31(6), 1–10 (2012)
46. Yao, C.H., Chang, C.Y., Chien, S.Y.: Occlusion-aware video temporal consistency. In: Proceedings of the 25th ACM International Conference on Multimedia, MM 2017, pp. 777–785. Association for Computing Machinery, New York, NY, USA (2017). https://doi.org/10.1145/3123266.3123363
47. Zhang, F., Li, Y., You, S., Fu, Y.: Learning temporal consistency for low light video enhancement from single images. In: 2021 IEEE/CVF Conference on Computer Vision and Pattern Recognition (CVPR), pp. 4965–4974 (2021). https://doi.org/10.1109/CVPR46437.2021.00493
48. Zhang, L., Agrawala, M.: Adding conditional control to text-to-image diffusion models. arXiv preprint arXiv:2302.05543 (2023)
49. Zhang, Q., Shen, X., Xu, L., Jia, J.: Rolling guidance filter. In: Fleet, D., Pajdla, T., Schiele, B., Tuytelaars, T. (eds.) Computer Vision–ECCV 2014: 13th European Conference, Zurich, Switzerland, 6–12 September 2014, Proceedings, Part III 13, vol. 8691, pp. 815–830. Springer, Cham (2014). https://doi.org/10.1007/978-3-319-10578-9_53

50. Zhang, R., Isola, P., Efros, A.A.: Colorful image colorization. In: Leibe, B., Matas, J., Sebe, N., Welling, M. (eds.) ECCV 2016. LNCS, vol. 9907, pp. 649–666. Springer, Cham (2016). https://doi.org/10.1007/978-3-319-46487-9_40

51. Zhang, Y., Borse, S., Cai, H., Porikli, F.: AuxAdapt: stable and efficient test-time adaptation for temporally consistent video semantic segmentation. In: 2022 IEEE/CVF Winter Conference on Applications of Computer Vision (WACV), pp. 2633–2642 (2022). https://doi.org/10.1109/WACV51458.2022.00269

52. Zhuo, L., Wang, G., Li, S., Wu, W., Liu, Z.: Fast-Vid2Vid: spatial-temporal compression for video-to-video synthesis. In: Avidan, S., Brostow, G., Cissé, M., Farinella, G.M., Hassner, T. (eds.) Computer Vision – ECCV 2022. ECCV 2022. LNCS, vol. 13675, pp. 289–305. Springer, Cham (2022). https://doi.org/10.1007/978-3-031-19784-0_17

GTLayout: Learning General Trees for Structured Grid Layout Generation

Pengfei Xu[1(✉)], Weiran Shi[1], Xin Hu[1], Hongbo Fu[2], and Hui Huang[1]

[1] Shenzhen University, Shenzhen, China
xupengfei.cg@gmail.com, hhzhiyan@gmail.com
[2] City University of Hong Kong, Hong Kong, China

Abstract. Structured grid layouts are preferable in many scenarios of 2D visual content creation since their structures facilitate further layout editing. Multiple geometry-based methods can effectively create structured grid layouts but require user-provided constraints or rules. Existing data-driven approaches have achieved remarkable performance on layout generation, but fail to produce appropriate layout structures. We present *GTLayout*, a novel generative model for structured grid layout generation. We adopt general trees to represent structured grid layouts and exploit a recursive neural network (RvNN) for this generation task. Our model can handle grid layouts with varied structures and regular arrangements. Qualitative and quantitative experiments on public grid layout datasets show that our method outperforms several baselines in the tasks of layout reconstruction and layout generation, especially when the datasets contain a small number of samples. We also demonstrate that the structured layout space constructed by our method enables structure blending between structured layouts. We will release our code upon the acceptance of the paper.

Keywords: Grid layout · Recursive neural network · Layout structure · Layout generation · Layout interpolation

1 Introduction

Creating grid layouts [30,33] is a fundamental step for creating 2D visual content in various forms, including documents, magazines, webpages, GUIs, *etc.*. Grid lines can be used to regularize such layouts' structures, including the spatial relations and organizations of graphical layout elements [5]. These structures can be abstracted as graphs [8,44] or trees [14,20] and can facilitate further editing (see Fig. 1), *e.g.*, adjusting elements in a structure-preserving manner [8], adapting layouts to various display configurations [14], *etc.*Given the great usability of layout structures, multiple geometry-based methods have been proposed to effectively create structured layouts interactively [44,47] or automatically [5,40,43]. However, they are not always preferable since the interactive methods require heavy labor inputs and the automatic ones demand high-level constraints or rules provided by users. It seems more natural to address these problems with data-driven approaches.

Very recently, learning techniques, including GAN [9], VAE [23], Transformer [41], GNN [38], Diffusion model [11], *etc.*, have benefited the generation of layouts [1,4,

© The Author(s), under exclusive license to Springer Nature Singapore Pte Ltd. 2024
F.-L. Zhang and A. Sharf (Eds.): CVM 2024, LNCS 14593, pp. 131–153, 2024.
https://doi.org/10.1007/978-981-97-2092-7_7

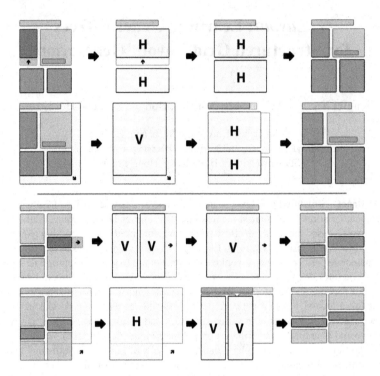

Fig. 1. Structured layouts can facilitate further editing, *e.g.*, adjusting elements in a structure-preserving manner (Row 1 and 3) and adapting layouts to various display configurations (Row 2 and 4).

10, 12, 13, 17, 18, 21, 24, 48]. These layout generation methods have achieved remarkable results in automatic layout creation with different problem formulations. Early methods [48] consider layouts as raster images and represent graphic layout elements as color regions. The succeeding methods often adopt a parametric representation of layouts, *i.e.*, representing graphic layout elements as bounding boxes with semantic labels. This parametric representation enables convenient applications of the generated layouts since the bounding boxes can be replaced with semantic elements to synthesize realistic visual content. However, this procedure requires the semantic elements to possess the same geometries as the corresponding bounding boxes. This requirement cannot be achieved in some scenarios. For example, when synthesizing a magazine page, the image aspect ratio or the text length might not be consistent with the corresponding bounding boxes in the generated layouts. In this case, the layout structures that explicitly indicate the spatial relations and organizations of graphic elements can help automatically adjust the layout geometries. Nevertheless, none of the above layout generation methods can produce such layout structures.

Recursive neural networks (RvNNs) [39] are effective in generating structured data and have succeeded in several generation problems, *e.g.*, 3D shape generation [28, 32, 50] and indoor scene generation [29]. They are also suitable for the problem of structured grid layout generation. READ [35] is the first learning-based method that

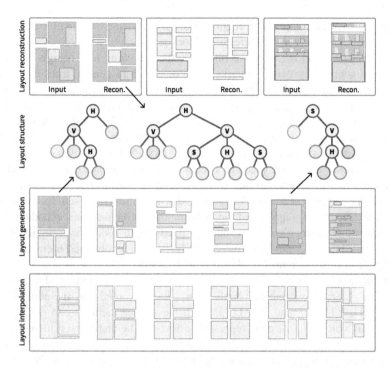

Fig. 2. Our method is effective in producing high-quality structured grid layouts. Row 1: layout reconstruction with our method. Row 2: layout structures produced by our method. Row 3: layouts generated by our method with randomly sampled latent codes. Row 4: structured layout blending achieved by our method. The leftmost and rightmost layouts are the inputs for blending.

recognizes the importance of layout structures. It adopts RvNN for structured document layout generation and can produce realistic document layouts. However, READ focuses more on exploiting the structures as tools for layout generation, instead of generating plausible layout structures. It adopts binary trees as the representation of layout structures. Although this structural representation is effective in the layout generation task, it deviates from people's perceptions of layout structures. A more appropriate representation for grid layout structures would be general trees [7,15,17,20,34,43], in which leaf nodes represent graphic elements and internal nodes represent horizontal or vertical arrangements of their children. However, READ fails to produce layouts with such structures.

This paper presents *GTLayout*, a novel generative model for the structured grid layout generation (Fig. 2). Inspired by the recent structured object generation methods [28,29,32,35,50], we also adopt RvNN for our generation task. Compared with existing RvNN-based generative models, our model needs to address the following new challenges. First, compared with 3D shapes, the grid layout structures are highly varied and involve spatial relations among different numbers of elements. Second, high-quality grid layouts are often composed of regular arrangements from local to global, while this regularity only exists in substructures of indoor scenes.

To address these challenges, we introduce the following new designs. Instead of binary trees adopted by existing works [28,35], we adopt general trees as the structural representation of grid layouts. The hierarchical structures of grid layouts are estimated using a method similar to the one described in [15,17,43]. In addition, different from existing works [29,32], we do not constrain the structures of these trees, and thus they can represent any structured grid layouts. With a dataset of structured grid layouts, we train a variational recursive autoencoder (RvNN-VAE), which embeds layouts into a structure-aware layout space in a recursive bottom-up manner. Specifically, we introduce a set of encoders and decoders, including geometry encoder/decoder, label encoder/decoder, element encoder/decoder, and arrangement encoders/decoders. These encoders are recursively applied to the substructures of layouts and encode the overall structures and geometries of layouts into fixed-length codes that roughly follow a Gaussian distribution. A new structured grid layout can be obtained hierarchically by decoding a randomly generated code with the decoders.

Our method is effective in producing high-quality structured grid layouts (see Fig. 2). We compare our method with several baseline methods, including Layout-GAN++ [21], VTN [1], and READ [35]. All these three methods can construct layout spaces in which a latent code represents a layout. The comparison includes layout generation, layout reconstruction, and layout interpolation. The experiments are conducted on three public layout datasets, including Magazine [48], PubLayNet [49], and RICO [6]. To better examine how these methods are affected by the datasets' scales, we prepare a series of datasets by gradually reducing the samples in these three public layout datasets. The experiments show that our method outperforms these methods qualitatively and quantitatively in the tasks of layout generation and reconstruction. The superiority of our method is more significant for the datasets of small scales, indicating that our method is more suitable for practical usage. For the layout interpolation task, only our method achieves smooth and reasonable structure blending. To the best of our knowledge, this is accomplished for the first time by a learning-based method.

2   Related Work

Interactive Layout Creation.   Grid layouts exist in various forms of 2D visual content and usually possess regular structures. Many techniques have focused on facilitating the interactive creation of such layouts, *e.g.*, snapping tools [2,3], arrangement commands [37,42]. These techniques help create regular grid layouts incrementally but do not extract the layout structures. Xu *et al.* [44] proposed a framework for globally beautifying roughly aligned grid layouts. The spatial relations among the elements in a layout were inferred and could serve as the layout structures. Zeidler *et al.* [47] proposed the Auckland layout editor to help users interactively create structured GUI layouts. Although these techniques have improved the efficiency of structured layout creation, they still require heavy labor input. This problem becomes severer when producing a large number of layouts.

Geometry-Based Layout Generation. Several geometry-based methods have been proposed for the automatic generation of structured grid layouts. For example, O'Donovan *et al.* [34] presented an optimization method for generating structured grid layouts based on the design principles extracted from existing layouts. Kikuchi *et al.* [20] introduced a method for generating webpage layouts by formulating the layout generation as a hierarchical optimization problem. The framework named Grids proposed by Dayama *et al.* [5] adopted a mixed integer linear programming solution to automatically generate structured grid layouts based on only several heuristic rules. Swearngin *et al.* [40] presented Scout, a system that helped designers explore structured grid layouts, which were generated based on user-provided high-level constraints. Xu *et al.* [43] introduced a method for creating novel structured grid layouts by blending existing ones. The core of their method was a correspondence algorithm devised according to high-level rules. Although these methods have achieved the automatic generation of structured grid layouts, the high-level constraints or rules may not be available or preferable for different types of grid layouts. Yang *et al.* [46] presented a method for generating urban layouts by recursively splitting regions. Although their method was not designed for grid layout generation, we were inspired by their idea of the recursive procedure for layout generation.

Learning-Based Layout Generation. Learning techniques have benefited the task of layout generation in recent years. A pioneer work was LayoutGAN [27], which adopted a generative adversarial network [9] for layout generation. LayoutGAN++ [21] adopted a similar network and further improved the quality of generated layouts. Layout-VAE [18] exploited two variational autoencoders [23], *i.e.*, CountVAE and BBoxVAE, to generate layouts. LayoutTransformer [10] and VTN [1] leveraged Transformer [41] to produce layouts and achieved remarkable results. Based on layout generation, CanvasVAE [45] provided a Transformer-based method for vector graphic document generation. Jiang *et al.* [17] also exploited Transformer for layout generation. Their coarse-to-fine strategy was insightful. NDN [26] adopted a graph neural network [38] for generating layouts satisfying user constraints. Recently, several works focused on controllable layout generation. BLT [24] extended BERT [19] to the layout generation task. It learned to predict the masked attributes of layouts based on known attributes. Layoutformer++ [16] could take geometric relations among layout elements as conditions for the layout generation. Two LayoutDMs [4, 13] and LDGM [12] adopted Diffusion model [11] for the layout generation. They also enabled controllable layout generation. These recent works have greatly advanced the research on layout generation, However, none of them can produce layout structures that explicitly indicate the spatial relations and organizations of graphic elements, though some of them [4, 12, 16, 26] exploited layout structures as conditions for layout generation. READ [35] was the first learning-based layout generation method that exploited and produced layout structures. However, its adopted layout structures were represented as binary trees, which deviated from peoples' perceptions. In contrast, our method adopts general trees as a more appropriate representation of layout structures, constructs a structure-aware layout space, and achieves better performance in the tasks of layout reconstruction, layout generation, and layout blending (Sect. 4).

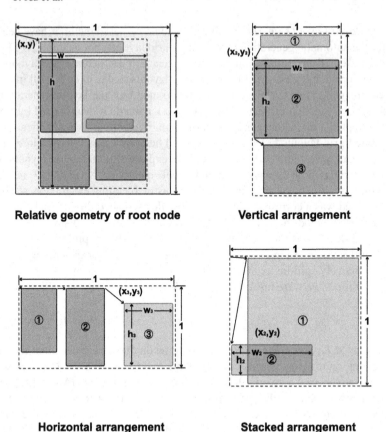

Fig. 3. To better capture arrangement patterns, we store the relative positions and sizes of node bounding boxes. The four sub-figures show how we compute the relative geometries in different arrangements. Top left: the relative geometry of the root node of a layout. Top right: vertical arrangement. Bottom left: horizontal arrangement. Bottom right: stacked arrangement.

RvNN for Structure Generation. We adopt RvNN [39] for our structured layout generation task. This network has been proven effective in various structured data generation tasks. For example, Li *et al.* [28] presented GRASS, the first work for exploiting RvNN for structured 3D shape synthesis. Zhu *et al.* [50] presented SCORES that leveraged RvNN for structured 3D shape composition. The shape structures were represented as binary trees in both works. StructureNet [32] was another RvNN-based method for structured shape generation. It adopted general trees to represent shape structures. However, it was designed to handle shapes in the same categories, i.e., shapes with similar structures. Li *et al.* [29] presented GRAINS, an RvNN-based method for synthesizing indoor scenes. This method aimed to produce 2D layouts in natural. Compared with indoor scene layouts, grid layouts possess more varied and regular structures, thus posing new challenges to layout generation.

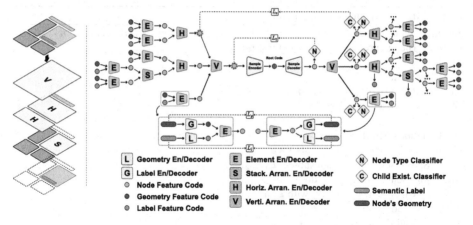

Fig. 4. Left: the procedure for extracting a layout tree from a grid layout. Right: the architecture of our generative model illustrated with an example. The encoders in our generative model map a structured grid layout to a latent feature code. The encoding is achieved in a recursive bottom-up manner. The decoders covert a latent feature code to a structured grid layout reversely.

3   Method

Our method adopts RvNN-VAE to embed structured grid layouts into a structure-aware layout space in a recursive bottom-up manner. In this space, layouts are represented as fixed-length codes that roughly follow a Gaussian distribution. Novel structured layouts can be obtained by decoding randomly generated codes. We first describe the structural representation adopted by our method and how we extract such a representation (Sect. 3.1). Then we introduce our generative model, including the encoders, the decoders, and the encoding/decoding procedures (Sect. 3.2). Finally, we explain the training objective and training details of our generative model (Sect. 3.3).

3.1   Structural Layout Representation

Most existing learning-based layout generation techniques consider a layout as a set of bounding boxes with semantic labels. READ [35] exploits layout structures for layout generation but adopts binary trees as a structural representation. As discussed in [15, 43], structured grid layouts are naturally hierarchical and can be represented by general trees. We thus adopt general trees, which we term layout trees, as the representation of structured layouts.

To extract a layout tree from a grid layout, in which elements are represented as labeled bounding boxes, we use a method similar to the one described in [15,43], but allows elements to stack. Figure 4 (left) shows an example to illustrate this procedure. Specifically, we recursively split a layout horizontally and vertically with grid lines that do not traverse elements. If a sub-layout contains multiple elements but cannot be split, we consider that it contains stacked elements. We then decompose this sub-layout into two parts with the first part being the largest element in this sub-layout and the

---

Algorithm 1. Layout Tree Extraction

Input: A set of layout elements $\mathcal{T} = \{e_i\}$, each e_i having attributes $\{label, x, y, w, h\}$.
Output: Hierarchical structured layout tree root node N.
 1:
 2: **Class** Node:
 3:     Attributes: $children, parent, elements$
 4:     Method: add_child(node)
 5:
 6: **Function** ExtractTree($\mathcal{L}, N$):
 7: **if** $\mathcal{L}$ can be divided horizontally **then**
 8:     Split $\mathcal{L}$ horizontally into subsets $\mathcal{L}_1, \mathcal{L}_2, \ldots, \mathcal{L}_n$.
 9:     **for** each subset $\mathcal{L}_i \subseteq \mathcal{L}$ **do**
10:         Create a new Node N_i with $\mathcal{L}_i$ as $elements$.
11:         N.add_child(N_i).
12:         Call ExtractTree($\mathcal{L}_i, N_i$).
13: **else if** $\mathcal{L}$ can be divided vertically **then**
14:     Split $\mathcal{L}$ vertically into subsets $\mathcal{L}_1, \mathcal{L}_2, \ldots, \mathcal{L}_n$.
15:     **for** each subset $\mathcal{L}_i \subseteq \mathcal{L}$ **do**
16:         Create a new Node N_i with $\mathcal{L}_i$ as $elements$.
17:         N.add_child(N_i).
18:         Call ExtractTree($\mathcal{L}_i, N_i$).
19: **else**
20:     Let e_{max} be the largest element in $\mathcal{L}$.
21:     Let $\mathcal{L}_{remain} = \mathcal{L} \setminus \{e_{max}\}$.
22:     Create a new Node N_{max} with e_{max} as $elements$.
23:     N.add_child(N_{max}).
24:     **if** $\mathcal{L}_{remain}$ is not empty **then**
25:         Create a new Node N_{remain} with $\mathcal{L}_{remain}$ as $elements$.
26:         N.add_child(N_{remain}).
27:         Call ExtractTree($\mathcal{L}_{remain}, N_{remain}$).
28:
29: Initialize root node N_{root} as ExtractTree($\mathcal{T}, N_{root}$).

---

second part being the rest elements. The elements in the second part can be further split recursively. This procedure stops when all elements are separated. Algorithm 1 shows this procedure as pseudocode.

In the extracted layout trees, the internal nodes represent arrangements of elements, including horizontal arrangements, vertical arrangements, and stacked arrangements. The leaf nodes represent graphical layout elements. The node types, *i.e.*, the arrangement or element types, and the bounding box geometries are stored in the nodes. To better capture the arrangement patterns, we store the relative positions and sizes of the bounding boxes in the nodes, instead of absolute ones. Please see Fig. 3 for an illustration. Specifically, for an internal node and its children in a layout, we first normalize the children's geometries with their parent's geometry. Then the first child's position is relative to the parent, and the other children's positions are relative to their left neighbored siblings. The root node stores the relative geometry of the layout regarding a fixed-geometry canvas.

3.2   Generative Model for Structured Grid Layouts

The encoders in our generative model map a structured grid layout to a latent feature code $f \in \mathbb{R}^N$. In our experiments, we set N as 256. The encoding is achieved in a recursive bottom-up manner. The decoders convert a latent feature code to a structured grid layout reversely. Please see Fig. 4 for an illustration. Below we describe the encoders/decoders in detail.

Geometry Encoder/Decoder. The geometry encoder is used to map the relative geometries of a node i in a layout tree to a geometry feature code $f_i^g \in \mathbb{R}^N$:

$$f_i^g = e^g([x_i, y_i, w_i, h_i]), \tag{1}$$

where the input is the node i's geometry vector obtained by concatenating its relative position and size. The geometry decoder converts a geometry feature code f_i^g to a node i's relative geometries:

$$[x_i, y_i, w_i, h_i] = d^g(f_i^g). \tag{2}$$

We employ single-layer perceptrons (SLPs) for the geometry encoder/decoder since they are sufficient for the tasks.

Label Encoder/Decoder. The label encoder is used to map the semantic label of a leaf node i in a layout tree to a label feature code $f_i^l \in \mathbb{R}^N$:

$$f_i^l = e^l(l_i), \tag{3}$$

where the input is the leaf node i's semantic label represented as a one-hot vector. The label decoder converts a label feature code f_i^l to a leaf node i's semantic label:

$$l_i = d^l(f_i^l). \tag{4}$$

The networks for the label encoder/decoder are SLPs.

Element Encoder/Decoder. The element encoder combines the geometry feature code f_i^g and the label feature code f_i^l of a leaf node i into a node feature code $f_i \in \mathbb{R}^N$:

$$f_i = e^e([f_i^g, f_i^l]), \tag{5}$$

where the input is a vector obtained by concatenating f_i^g and f_i^l. The element decoder does the reverse task:

$$[f_i^g, f_i^l] = d^e(f_i). \tag{6}$$

The networks for the element encoder/decoder are SLPs.

Arrangement Encoders/Decoders. We consider three types of arrangement encoders/ decoders, *i.e.*, horizontal arrangement encoder/decoder, vertical arrangement encoder/ decoder, and stacked arrangement encoder/decoder. The networks for these encoders/decoders are all MLPs with one hidden layer. The encoders/decoders are distinguished since the nodes' relative geometries in different arrangements are defined in different ways (see Fig. 3). Given an internal node j and its child nodes $\{i_1, i_2, ..., i_K\}$, the encoders combine the child nodes' feature codes $\{f_{i_1}, f_{i_2}, ..., f_{i_K}\}$ and the internal node j's geometry feature code f_j^g into a new node feature code $f_j \in \mathbb{R}^N$:

$$f_j = e^*([f_{i_1}, f_{i_2}, ..., f_{i_K}, f_j^g]), \tag{7}$$

where $* \in \{h, v, s\}$, corresponding to the horizontal, vertical, or stacked arrangements, respectively. K is the maximum children number that is dataset-dependent. If an internal node has K' children, where $K' < K$, we append zero feature codes to obtain a vector $[f_{i_1}, ..., f_{i_{K'}}, \mathbf{0}, ..., \mathbf{0}, f_j^g]$ whose length is still $(K+1)N$.

The decoders convert a node feature code f_j into its child nodes' feature codes and its geometry feature code. Before applying the decoders, we need to first determine which decoder should be selected. We thus design an auxiliary node type classifier c^n (to be described latter) that predicts the node j's type. According to the output of this classifier, an appropriate decoder is applied to f_j:

$$[f_{i_1}, f_{i_2}, ..., f_{i_K}, f_j^g] = d^*(f_j), \tag{8}$$

where $* \in \{h, v, s\}$. Note that f_j may also be a leaf node's feature code. In this case, this code is fed to the element decoder. After applying an arrangement decoder, the obtained long feature vector is then split into several new node feature codes and a geometry feature code. Since the number of child nodes of an internal node is not fixed, we introduce a child existence classifier c^c to discard the invalid children.

Auxiliary Classifiers. We have two auxiliary classifiers in our model, *i.e.*, the node type classifier and the child existence classifier. The node type classifier c^n is an MLP with one hidden layer. It takes as input a node feature code and outputs a vector indicating the node type. The child existence classifier c^c is an SLP. It takes a child feature code as input and outputs a value to indicate the validity of this child.

3.3   Training

We train our model on structured layout datasets. The goal is to train the encoders and decoders so that they can perform a reversible mapping between a structured layout and a feature code. Given structured layouts, we recursively apply appropriate encoders at the nodes of the corresponding layout trees until reaching the root nodes. The feature codes of the roots are approximated to a Gaussian distribution by the VAE. We then reverse the process by feeding randomly sampled feature codes to the decoders. Finally we can obtain structured layouts in the form of layout trees.

Loss. We adopt several losses in our training procedure. The total training loss is:

$$\mathcal{L} = \lambda_g \mathcal{L}_g + \lambda_t \mathcal{L}_t + \lambda_l \mathcal{L}_l + \lambda_e \mathcal{L}_e + \lambda_{KL} \mathcal{L}_{KL}, \tag{9}$$

where $(\lambda_g, \lambda_t, \lambda_l, \lambda_e, \lambda_{KL})$ is set as $(1, 0.3, 0.3, 0.4, 0.004)$ in our experiments. $\mathcal{L}_g$ is the geometry loss formulated as the sum of squared difference between the nodes' relative geometries in the input and output layout trees. $\mathcal{L}_t$ is the node type loss formulated as a cross-entropy loss between the nodes' types in the input and output layout trees. $\mathcal{L}_l$ is the semantic label loss formulated as a cross-entropy loss between the leaf nodes' semantic labels in the input and output layout trees. $\mathcal{L}_e$ is the child existence loss formulated as a binary cross-entropy with logits loss between the child existence values in the input and output layout trees. $\mathcal{L}_{KL}$ is the KL-divergence loss for approximating the space of all root node feature codes.

Other Details. We implement our *GTLayout* in PyTorch. We use Adam optimizer [22] with an initial learning rate of 10^{-3} reduced by a factor of 0.9. The batch size is 128.

4   Evaluation

Our method constructs a structure-aware layout space in which a latent code represents a structured layout. With this space, our method can generate novel structured layouts by decoding randomly sampled codes. We also demonstrate that this layout space is an appropriate representation of structured layouts by faithfully reconstructing them with their latent codes. In addition, this layout space enables interpolation between given structured layouts. In this section, we evaluate our method in the tasks of layout generation, layout reconstruction, and layout interpolation respectively. We also conducted an ablation study to verify the design of our method.

Baselines. Many existing learning-based works have already achieved novel layout generation with given layout datasets. As discussed in Sect. 2, these works adopt different learning techniques, *e.g.*, GAN, VAE, Transformer, GNN, Diffusion model, *etc.*. Only a few of them, *e.g.*, LayoutGAN++ [21], VTN [1], and READ [35], have explicitly constructed latent spaces to represent layouts. With their constructed layout spaces, they can perform layout generation, layout reconstruction, and layout interpolation similarly to our method. In contrast, other methods that fail to construct such spaces can only accomplish parts of these three tasks using different strategies. We thus compare our method with LayoutGAN++, VTN, and READ in the tasks of layout generation, reconstruction, and interpolation to demonstrate the superiority of our method and its constructed layout space.

Datasets. The evaluation is conducted on several public grid layout datasets, including Magazine [48] which includes 3, 919 layouts with 5 labels, PubLayNet [49] which includes 330K layouts with 5 labels, and RICO [6] which includes 66K layouts with 27 labels. Due to memory limit, we remove the layouts that contain excessive elements

Table 1. The statistics, including the number of layouts, the number of labels, and the maximum number of elements per layout, of the constructed datasets. These datasets are used in the experiments included in the paper.

Datasets		Layouts (#)	Labels (#)	Elements (#)
Magazine	0.5K	500	4	30
	1.0K	1,000	4	30
	1.9K	1,929	4	30
	2.5K	2,705	4	30
PubLayNet	0.5K	500	5	24
	5K	5,000	5	27
	40K	40,000	5	32
	297K	297,066	5	48
RICO	0.5K	500	14	10
	2K	2,000	17	13
	10K	10,000	21	66
	46K	46,086	23	74

and labels as existing works [16,21] did. We also remove the trivial layouts that contain less than 3 elements. After this filtering, we have the following datasets: Magazine (2,705 layouts, 4 labels, up to 30 elements per layout), PubLayNet (297,066 layouts, 5 labels, up to 48 elements per layout), and RICO (46,086 layouts, 23 labels, up to 74 elements per layout). To exhaustively examine how the compared methods are affected by the scales of the datasets, we further construct a series of datasets by gradually removing the layouts in the original datasets. Table 1 shows the statistics of the constructed datasets that are used in the experiments included in the paper. The training/testing ratio for all these datasets is 9 : 1.

4.1 Layout Generation

Since all the compared methods can construct layout spaces in which a latent code represents a layout, the layout generation task is achieved by decoding randomly sampled codes. It is worth noting that, besides a latent code, LayoutGAN++ also needs a list of labels as input to generate a layout. We adopt the same strategy as described in [21] to get such a list, *i.e.*, randomly selecting a layout in the testing set and using this layout's label list as input.

Evaluation Metrics. We evaluate the generated layouts in three aspects. The first is the arrangement quality of the generated layouts. We use the overlap score (*Overlap*) and the alignment score (*Align*) for the evaluation. Since *Overlap* and *Align* have different definitions in existing works, we reiterate our adopted definitions as below.

Overlap is defined on a layout T as:

$$Overlap(T) = \frac{1}{|T|(|T| - 1)} \sum_{i \in T} \sum_{j \in T, j \neq i} \frac{A(b_i \cap b_j)}{A(b_i \cup b_j)}, \tag{10}$$

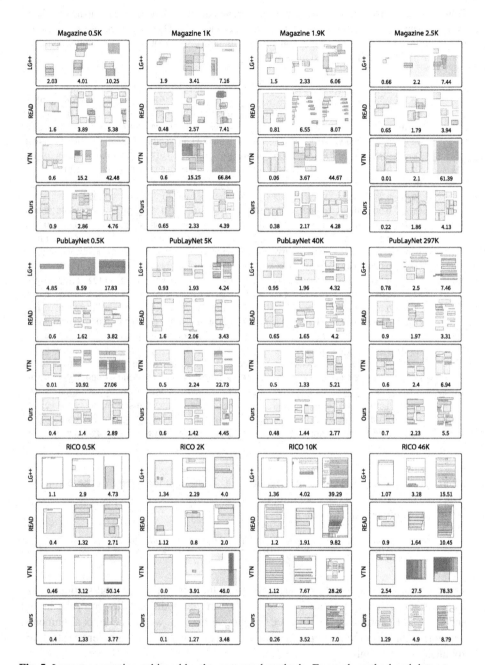

Fig. 5. Layout generation achieved by the compared methods. For each method and dataset, we select three representative layouts according to the layout similarity scores (displayed under each layout). Our method is stable in producing high-quality layouts across all datasets. In contrast, the other methods may produce low-quality layouts.

Table 2. Quantitative comparisons on the layout generation task between the compared methods. In most metrics, our method outperforms the other methods. The advantage of our method is more significant for the datasets that contain a small number of layouts. The first and second best scores are highlighted in bold and underline.

		Magazine				PubLayNet				RICO			
		0.5K	1.0K	1.9K	2.5K	0.5K	5K	40K	297K	0.5K	2K	10K	46K
Align ↓	LG++	0.057	0.066	0.080	0.075	0.011	0.034	0.034	0.034	0.034	0.037	0.031	0.036
	READ	0.068	0.068	0.077	0.056	0.061	0.039	0.032	0.033	0.066	0.057	0.038	0.039
	VTN	**0.009**	**0.006**	0.026	0.024	0.013	**0.004**	**0.004**	**0.003**	0.007	0.033	0.027	**0.006**
	Ours	0.027	0.028	0.029	0.029	**0.010**	0.011	0.011	0.017	0.014	**0.018**	**0.018**	0.016
Overlap ↓	LG++	0.090	0.067	0.022	0.042	0.421	0.008	0.004	0.009	0.019	0.019	0.011	0.013
	READ	0.016	0.018	0.013	0.084	0.004	0.001	0.007	0.007	**0.007**	0.007	0.008	0.007
	VTN	0.267	0.291	0.154	0.103	0.117	0.089	0.044	10^{-4}	0.227	0.127	0.079	0.105
	Ours	**0.002**	**0.002**	**0.002**	**0.003**	10^{-4}	10^{-4}	10^{-4}	10^{-4}	0.010	**0.006**	**0.005**	**0.006**
W label ↓	LG++	0.053	0.071	0.047	0.040	**0.070**	0.034	0.013	0.096	**0.231**	**0.192**	0.451	**0.418**
	READ	0.338	0.179	0.310	0.396	0.241	0.350	0.069	**0.029**	0.864	0.689	1.014	1.081
	VTN	0.058	0.080	0.097	0.057	0.099	0.091	0.093	0.041	1.243	0.408	7.906	12.779
	Ours	**0.044**	**0.021**	**0.019**	**0.030**	0.188	**0.022**	0.097	0.115	0.336	0.275	**0.143**	0.608
W bbox ↓	LG++	0.162	0.153	0.087	0.094	0.469	0.079	0.073	0.075	0.142	0.122	0.107	0.099
	READ	0.083	0.068	0.099	0.132	**0.040**	0.062	0.053	0.051	0.098	0.087	0.053	**0.051**
	VTN	0.171	0.232	0.129	0.083	0.082	0.080	0.075	**0.006**	0.194	0.155	0.343	0.442
	Ours	**0.037**	**0.027**	**0.026**	**0.021**	0.052	**0.014**	**0.024**	0.022	**0.071**	**0.039**	**0.023**	0.117
LaySim ↓	LG++	5.544	3.456	2.974	2.804	9.475	2.175	**2.188**	3.569	1.850	1.862	6.367	**4.877**
	READ	4.200	3.235	6.012	9.280	2.377	3.088	2.557	2.550	2.154	1.970	5.426	5.357
	VTN	34.470	38.625	17.327	9.607	25.760	8.875	2.195	2.381	20.794	9.237	7.696	23.464
	Ours	**2.839**	**2.534**	**2.641**	**2.431**	**1.400**	2.054	2.429	3.526	**1.206**	**1.609**	5.848	6.369
LayDiv ↑	LG++	2.557	1.838	2.460	1.692	1.257	1.172	1.480	1.961	0.166	1.198	4.130	3.659
	READ	0.860	1.411	0.957	1.796	1.176	0.392	1.814	1.928	**0.862**	0.946	2.506	2.327
	VTN	1.910	1.065	1.781	1.650	**1.473**	1.065	1.959	2.466	0.752	0.979	1.597	5.055
	Ours	**2.795**	**2.400**	**2.528**	**2.311**	0.652	**1.923**	**2.115**	**3.213**	0.684	**1.426**	**5.744**	**5.109**

where i and j are elements in the layout $\mathcal{T}$. b_i is the bounding box of the element i. $A(b_i)$ means the area of the bounding box b_i.

Align is defined on a layout $\mathcal{T}$ as:

$$Align(\mathcal{T}) = \frac{1}{|\mathcal{T}|} \sum_{i \in \mathcal{T}} (\min_j \frac{D_h(b_i, b_j)}{h_{\mathcal{T}}} + \min_j \frac{D_v(b_i, b_j)}{w_{\mathcal{T}}}), \quad (11)$$

where $D_h(b_i, b_j)$ and $D_v(b_i, b_j)$ are defined as the minimal horizontal/vertical alignment distances between b_i and b_j. $w_{\mathcal{T}}$ and $h_{\mathcal{T}}$ are the width and height of the layout and are used to normalize the distance. In our comparison, we consider six alignments, *i.e.*, horizontal alignments: top, vertical center, bottom; vertical alignments: left, horizontal center, and right.

The second aspect of the evaluation is the similarity between the generated and existing layouts. We adopt the Wasserstein distance [1] to measure the distribution similarity between these two layout sets. Specifically, we compute the Wasserstein distances between the generated and testing layouts for the label distribution (*W label*) and the bounding box distribution (*W bbox*). Besides the distribution similarity, we want to measure the layout appearance similarity between the generated and existing layouts. Intuitively, the generated layouts should possess similar appearances to the existing layouts. This layout appearance similarity, termed *LaySim*, can be defined as:

$$LaySim(\mathcal{S}, \mathcal{S}') = \frac{1}{|\mathcal{S}|} \sum_{\mathcal{T} \in \mathcal{S}} \min_{\mathcal{T}' \in \mathcal{S}'} M(\mathcal{T}, \mathcal{T}'), \tag{12}$$

where $\mathcal{S}$ and $\mathcal{S}'$ are the generated and testing layout sets. $M(\mathcal{T}, \mathcal{T}')$ is the similarity measure between a pair of layouts $\mathcal{T}$ and $\mathcal{T}'$. Several works [31,35,36,43] have investigated the similarity measures between layouts. Patil *et al.* [35] introduced a combinatorial layout similarity measure called *DocSim*. This measure is effective for finding the nearest neighbors of a given layout, but the computed scores are inconsistent across different layouts. For example, the self-similarity scores of different layouts may vary in a large range; the similarity scores of two distinct pairs of layouts can not be compared directly. Xu *et al.* [43] introduced another combinatorial layout similarity measure that produces consistent similarity scores. However, it requires layouts to possess hierarchical structures. LayoutGMN [36] and GCN-CNN [31] are two learning-based methods that can predict the similarity between two layouts. They require a heavy load of training before using them to measure specific layouts' similarities. For convenient computation, we combine the combinatorial methods introduced in [35,43] to define the layout similarity measure $M(\mathcal{T}, \mathcal{T}')$. Specifically, we treat layouts as sets of elements [35] and use the Hungarian algorithm [25] to compute the optimal matching cost as the layout similarity measure between a pair of layouts. The element matching cost follows the definition in [43] and an element can correspond to a void.

The third aspect of the evaluation is the diversity of the generated layouts. This can be reflected by the similarities among the generated layouts, *i.e.*, the average similarity score among all pairs of layouts in the generated layout set $\mathcal{S}$. We term the layout diversity *LayDiv* and define it as:

$$LayDiv(\mathcal{S}) = \frac{1}{|\mathcal{S}|(|\mathcal{S}| - 1)} \sum_{\mathcal{T} \in \mathcal{S}} \sum_{\mathcal{T}' \in \mathcal{S}, \mathcal{T}' \neq \mathcal{T}} M(\mathcal{T}, \mathcal{T}'). \tag{13}$$

Results. For each method and each dataset, we randomly generate $1,000$ layouts for comparison. As discussed earlier, the generation is achieved by decoding randomly sampled codes. Table 2 shows the quantitative comparisons of the methods on different datasets. Figure 5 shows some representative layouts selected from the generated layouts. For each dataset and method, we select three layouts according to the similarity measures between the generated and existing layouts, *i.e.*, the most, the least, and the medially similar ones:

$$\mathcal{T}_{\text{most}} = \arg\min_{\mathcal{T} \in \mathcal{S}} (\min_{\mathcal{T}' \in \mathcal{S}'} M(\mathcal{T}, \mathcal{T}')),$$

$$\mathcal{T}_{\text{least}} = \arg\max_{\mathcal{T} \in \mathcal{S}} (\min_{\mathcal{T}' \in \mathcal{S}'} M(\mathcal{T}, \mathcal{T}')), \qquad (14)$$

$$\mathcal{T}_{\text{median}} = \arg\operatorname*{median}_{\mathcal{T} \in \mathcal{S}} (\min_{\mathcal{T}' \in \mathcal{S}'} M(\mathcal{T}, \mathcal{T}')),$$

where $\mathcal{S}$ and $\mathcal{S}'$ are the generated and testing layout sets. From these quantitive and qualitative results, we have the following findings. First, in most metrics, our method outperforms the other methods. The advantage of our method is more significant for the datasets that contain a small number of layouts. For the datasets that contain a large number of layouts (*e.g.*, PubLayNet 297K), our method outperforms or is comparable to the other methods in most metrics. For *Overlap*, our method outperforms the other methods on almost all the datasets. This should be attributed to our recursive structure generation procedure and the design of relative geometry. For *Align*, our method is slightly behind VTN. VTN adopts discrete coordinates to represent element geometry, and thus greatly improves its performance on alignment. According to *W label* and *W bbox*, our method also achieves comparable performance in these two metrics. Since these two metrics only consider the distribution of labels and box geometries, we introduce *LaySim* to measure the appearance similarity. For *LaySim*, our method also achieves the best performance in most datasets. According to *LaySim* and *LayDiv*, we can conclude that our method produces more diverse layouts with higher qualities, especially for small datasets. In terms of qualitative comparison, all the methods can produce reasonable layouts, *e.g.*, the layouts that are most similar to the testing layout sets. However, our method is more stable than the other methods in producing high-quality layouts. As illustrated in Fig. 5, all the representative layouts generated by our method, including the ones that are most, medially, and least similar to the testing layout sets, are of high quality. In contrast, some of the representative layouts generated by the other methods, including the ones that are medially or least similar to the testing layout sets, are of low quality, especially for the datasets that contain a small number of layouts (*e.g.*, Magzine 0.5K). READ also adopts RvNN as the network architecture, therefore its performance is better when training with small datasets. For large datasets, its performance degrades since the layouts in these datasets contain excessive elements, leading to over-deep binary layout trees, and resulting in the collapse of the model. VTN archives comparable performance to our method, especially for large datasets, indicating the advantage of the transformer architecture. Due to the memory limit, the training of VTN with RICO 46K dataset fails, resulting in low-quality results. In the supplemental material, we provided more results, including the generated layouts' nearest neighbors selected from the testing sets. These additional results confirm that our method can produce novel layouts that are visually similar to the existing ones.

4.2   Layout Reconstruction

In this task, the reconstruction is achieved by first encoding a layout to obtain a latent code and then decoding this code to reconstruct the layout. The reconstruction quality indicates whether the latent code is an appropriate representation of the layout. Since

Table 3. Quantitative comparisons on the layout reconstruction task between the compared methods, in terms of the Chamfer distance (*CD*) and the Intersecion-over-Union (*IoU*). Our method achieves the best performance for almost all the datasets. The best scores are highlighted in bold.

		Magazine				PubLayNet				RICO			
		0.5K	1.0K	1.9K	2.5K	0.5K	5K	40K	297K	0.5K	2K	10K	46K
CD ↓	READ	0.057	0.076	0.082	0.194	0.047	0.072	0.022	0.023	0.131	0.052	0.093	0.082
	VTN	0.084	0.149	0.156	0.111	0.043	0.039	0.033	**0.013**	0.379	0.230	0.460	1.948
	Ours	**0.023**	**0.031**	**0.019**	**0.022**	**0.030**	**0.017**	**0.014**	0.021	**0.037**	**0.024**	**0.014**	**0.034**
IoU ↑	READ	0.237	0.251	0.195	0.250	0.281	0.222	0.422	0.416	0.207	0.410	0.266	0.267
	VTN	0.172	0.201	0.232	0.318	0.353	0.318	0.374	**0.479**	0.372	0.484	0.165	0.115
	Ours	**0.455**	**0.480**	**0.527**	**0.537**	**0.382**	**0.416**	**0.446**	0.356	**0.422**	**0.548**	**0.366**	**0.338**

LayoutGAN++ does not have an encoder, it can not perform this reconstruction task. Therefore, we compare our method with VTN and READ.

Evaluation Metrics. We adopt the Chamfer distance (*CD*) [17] and Intersection-over-Union score (*IoU*) [31,35] between the ground-truth layouts and the reconstructed layouts as the evaluation metrics.

Results. For each testing dataset, we randomly select and reconstruct 1, 000 layouts (or all layouts for small datasets) using the compared methods. Table 3 shows the quantitative comparisons between the compared methods. According to *CD* and *IoU*, our method achieves the best performance on layout reconstruction for almost all the datasets. Figure 6 shows some representative reconstruction results obtained by the compared methods. For each dataset, we obtain three groups of layouts, each of which contains an input layout and three layouts reconstructed by the compared methods. The three input layouts are selected according to the *CD* score: for each method, we select the input layout with the best *CD* score after reconstruction. This strategy avoids the bias of manual selection. This qualitative comparison also confirmed that the reconstructed layouts obtained by our method are more visually similar to the input layouts compared with the other methods. VTN also achieves satisfactory results when training with large datasets (*e.g.*, PubLayNet 120K), but its performance degrades significantly for small datasets (*e.g.*, Magazine 0.5K). These quantitative and qualitative comparisons confirm that the latent code computed by our method is an appropriate neural representation of layouts.

4.3   Layout Interpolation

Layout interpolation is achieved by interpolating the latent codes of existing layouts and then decoding the interpolated codes. We compare our method with VTN and READ in this task.

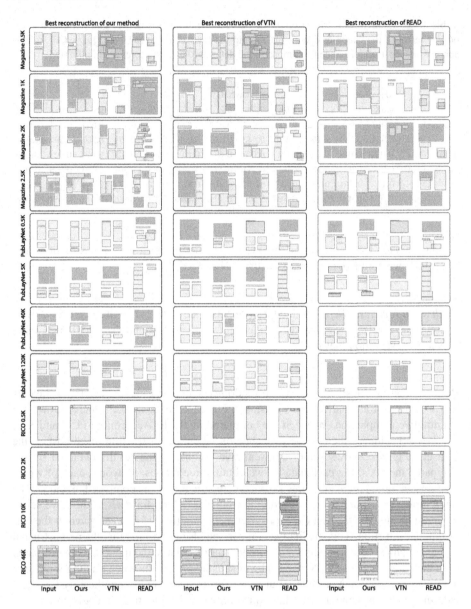

Fig. 6. The layout reconstruction achieved by the compared methods. For each dataset, we obtain three groups of layouts, according to the best reconstruction of each method. Our method outperforms the other methods in this task.

Results. Figure 7 gives a few interpolation examples. These results are obtained by training the compared methods with Magazine 2.5K and PubLayNet 297K respectively. We do not include RICO in this task since the variation of the layouts in this dataset is overly high and all the methods can not achieve satisfactory interpolation.

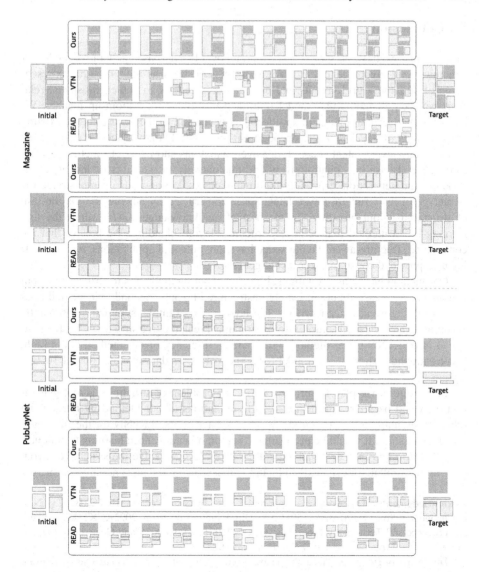

Fig. 7. The layout interpolation achieved by the compared methods. All the methods can produce satisfactory layouts by interpolation. However, only our method achieves smooth and reasonable structure blending. It confirms that the latent space constructed by our method is structure-aware.

This qualitative comparison shows that all the methods can produce satisfactory layouts by interpolation. However, only our method achieves smooth and reasonable structure blending, since it exploits the structural information when embedding layouts into the latent space. These results confirm that the latent space constructed by our method is structure-aware. Please refer to the supplemental material for the animation of the layout interpolation.

5   Conclusion

In this paper, we have presented *GTLayout*, a novel RvNN-based generative model for structured grid layout generation. We adopt general trees as the structural representation of structured grid layouts and use relative geometry to depict the spatial relations between elements. Our model is trained in a recursive bottom-up manner. We have designed several encoders and decoders according to the arrangements existing in structured gird layouts. These encoders can successfully map structured grid layouts to a structure-aware latent space. Extensive evaluations show that our method outperforms several baselines quantitatively and qualitatively in the tasks of layout reconstruction and generation, especially for small datasets. We have also demonstrated the advantage of the structure-aware latent space constructed by our method via the task of structured layout blending. To the best of our knowledge, *GTLayout* is the first learning-based method that achieves structured layout blending. We believe that the constructed structure-aware layout space has more potential applications, *e.g.*, exploiting user-provided constraints for layout generation.

Our method has some limitations. First, since our method aims to structured layout generation, it is less reliable to handle unstructured layouts. Second, our method does not consider more advanced structures in layouts, for example, symmetry or semantic groupings, since these structural information may break the tree structures. Lastly, similar to other RvNN-based methods, the training efficiency of our method is not high. It takes around 20 h to train a model for 200 epochs on a dataset composed of $10,000$ layouts.

In the future, we plan to further explore the problem of structured layout generation. It would be interesting to resolve the limitations of our method by introducing other representations of structured layouts. We have adopted RvNN for the structured layout generation. It would be promising to exploit other advanced learning techniques, *e.g.*, Transformers [41] or Graph Neural Network [38], to solve the structured layout generation problem, or even extend them to other structured data generation problems.

Acknowledgments. This work was supported in parts by NSFC (62072316, U21B2023), NSF of Guangdong Province (2023A1515011297), DEGP Innovation Team (2022KCXTD025), Shenzhen Science and Technology Program (KQTD20210811090044003), and Guangdong Laboratory of Artificial Intelligence and Digital Economy (SZ).

Disclosure of Interests. The authors have no competing interests to declare that are relevant to the content of this article.

References

1. Arroyo, D.M., Postels, J., Tombari, F.: Variational transformer networks for layout generation. In: Proceedings of the IEEE/CVF Conference on Computer Vision and Pattern Recognition, pp. 13642–13652 (2021)
2. Baudisch, P., Cutrell, E., Hinckley, K., Eversole, A.: Snap-and-go: helping users align objects without the modality of traditional snapping. In: Proceedings of the SIGCHI Conference on Human Factors in Computing Systems, pp. 301–310 (2005)
3. Bier, E.A., Stone, M.C.: Snap-dragging. ACM SIGGRAPH. Comput. Graph. **20**(4), 233–240 (1986)

4. Chai, S., Zhuang, L., Yan, F.: Layoutdm: transformer-based diffusion model for layout gener-
     ation. In: Proceedings of the IEEE/CVF Conference on Computer Vision and Pattern Recog-
     nition, pp. 18349–18358 (2023)
5. Dayama, N.R., Todi, K., Saarelainen, T., Oulasvirta, A.: Grids: interactive layout design
     with integer programming. In: Proceedings of the 2020 CHI Conference on Human Factors
     in Computing Systems, pp. 1–13 (2020)
6. Deka, B., et al.: Rico: a mobile app dataset for building data-driven design applications. In:
     Proceedings of the 30th Annual ACM Symposium on User Interface Software and Technol-
     ogy, pp. 845–854 (2017)
7. Dixon, M., Leventhal, D., Fogarty, J.: Content and hierarchy in pixel-based methods for
     reverse engineering interface structure. In: Proceedings of the SIGCHI Conference on
     Human Factors in Computing Systems, pp. 969–978 (2011)
8. Frisch, M., Kleinau, S., Langner, R., Dachselt, R.: Grids & guides: multi-touch layout and
     alignment tools. In: Proceedings of the SIGCHI Conference on Human Factors in Computing
     Systems, pp. 1615–1618 (2011)
9. Goodfellow, I., et al.: Generative adversarial nets. In: Ghahramani, Z., Welling, M., Cortes,
     C., Lawrence, N., Weinberger, K. (eds.) Advances in Neural Information Processing Sys-
     tems, vol. 27. Curran Associates, Inc. (2014). https://proceedings.neurips.cc/paper/2014/file/
     5ca3e9b122f61f8f06494c97b1afccf3-Paper.pdf
10. Gupta, K., Lazarow, J., Achille, A., Davis, L.S., Mahadevan, V., Shrivastava, A.: Layout-
     transformer: layout generation and completion with self-attention. In: Proceedings of the
     IEEE/CVF International Conference on Computer Vision, pp. 1004–1014 (2021)
11. Ho, J., Jain, A., Abbeel, P.: Denoising diffusion probabilistic models. Adv. Neural. Inf. Pro-
     cess. Syst. **33**, 6840–6851 (2020)
12. Hui, M., Zhang, Z., Zhang, X., Xie, W., Wang, Y., Lu, Y.: Unifying layout generation with
     a decoupled diffusion model. In: Proceedings of the IEEE/CVF Conference on Computer
     Vision and Pattern Recognition, pp. 1942–1951 (2023)
13. Inoue, N., Kikuchi, K., Simo-Serra, E., Otani, M., Yamaguchi, K.: LayoutDM: discrete diffu-
     sion model for controllable layout generation. In: Proceedings of the IEEE/CVF Conference
     on Computer Vision and Pattern Recognition, pp. 10167–10176 (2023)
14. Jiang, Y., Du, R., Lutteroth, C., Stuerzlinger, W.: Orc layout: adaptive GUI layout with or-
     constraints. In: Proceedings of the 2019 CHI Conference on Human Factors in Computing
     Systems, pp. 1–12 (2019)
15. Jiang, Y., Stuerzlinger, W., Lutteroth, C.: Reverseorc: reverse engineering of resizable user
     interface layouts with or-constraints. In: Proceedings of the 2021 CHI Conference on Human
     Factors in Computing Systems, pp. 1–18 (2021)
16. Jiang, Z., et al.: Layoutformer++: conditional graphic layout generation via constraint seri-
     alization and decoding space restriction. In: Proceedings of the IEEE/CVF Conference on
     Computer Vision and Pattern Recognition, pp. 18403–18412 (2023)
17. Jiang, Z., Sun, S., Zhu, J., Lou, J.G., Zhang, D.: Coarse-to-fine generative modeling for
     graphic layouts. In: AAAI 2022 (2022)
18. Jyothi, A.A., Durand, T., He, J., Sigal, L., Mori, G.: Layoutvae: stochastic scene layout gen-
     eration from a label set. In: Proceedings of the IEEE/CVF International Conference on Com-
     puter Vision, pp. 9895–9904 (2019)
19. Kenton, J.D.M.W.C., Toutanova, L.K.: Bert: pre-training of deep bidirectional transformers
     for language understanding. In: Proceedings of NAACL-HLT, pp. 4171–4186 (2019)
20. Kikuchi, K., Otani, M., Yamaguchi, K., Simo-Serra, E.: Modeling visual containment for
     web page layout optimization. In: Computer Graphics Forum, vol. 40, pp. 33–44. Wiley
     Online Library (2021)

21. Kikuchi, K., Simo-Serra, E., Otani, M., Yamaguchi, K.: Constrained graphic layout generation via latent optimization. In: Proceedings of the 29th ACM International Conference on Multimedia, pp. 88–96 (2021)
22. Kingma, D.P., Ba, J.: Adam: a method for stochastic optimization. In: Bengio, Y., LeCun, Y. (eds.) 3rd International Conference on Learning Representations, ICLR 2015, San Diego, 7–9 May 2015, Conference Track Proceedings (2015). http://arxiv.org/abs/1412.6980
23. Kingma, D.P., Welling, M.: Auto-encoding variational bayes. In: International Conference on Learning Representations (2013)
24. Kong, X., et al.: BLT: bidirectional layout transformer for controllable layout generation. In: Avidan, S., Brostow, G., Cissé, M., Farinella, G.M., Hassner, T. (eds.) Computer Vision – ECCV 2022: 17th European Conference, Tel Aviv, 23–27 October 2022, Proceedings, Part XVII, pp. 474–490. Springer, Cham (2022). https://doi.org/10.1007/978-3-031-19790-1_29
25. Kuhn, H.W.: The Hungarian method for the assignment problem. Naval Res. Logist. Quart. 2(1–2), 83–97 (1955)
26. Lee, H.-Y., et al.: Neural design network: graphic layout generation with constraints. In: Vedaldi, A., Bischof, H., Brox, T., Frahm, J.-M. (eds.) Computer Vision – ECCV 2020: 16th European Conference, Glasgow, 23–28 August 2020, Proceedings, Part III, pp. 491–506. Springer, Cham (2020). https://doi.org/10.1007/978-3-030-58580-8_29
27. Li, J., Yang, J., Hertzmann, A., Zhang, J., Xu, T.: Layoutgan: generating graphic layouts with wireframe discriminators. arXiv preprint arXiv:1901.06767 (2019)
28. Li, J., Xu, K., Chaudhuri, S., Yumer, E., Zhang, H., Guibas, L.: Grass: generative recursive autoencoders for shape structures. ACM Trans. Graph. 36(4), 1–14 (2017)
29. Li, M., et al.: Grains: generative recursive autoencoders for indoor scenes. ACM Trans. Graph. 38(2), 1–16 (2019)
30. Lupton, E.: Thinking with Type: A Critical Guide for Designers, Writers, Editors, & Students. Chronicle Books (2014)
31. Manandhar, D., Ruta, D., Collomosse, J.: Learning structural similarity of user interface layouts using graph networks. In: Vedaldi, A., Bischof, H., Brox, T., Frahm, J.-M. (eds.) Computer Vision – ECCV 2020: 16th European Conference, Glasgow, 23–28 August 2020, Proceedings, Part XXII, pp. 730–746. Springer, Cham (2020). https://doi.org/10.1007/978-3-030-58542-6_44
32. Mo, K., et al.: Structurenet: hierarchical graph networks for 3d shape generation. arXiv preprint arXiv:1908.00575 (2019)
33. Müller-Brockmann, J.: Grid systems in graphic design: a visual communication manual for graphic designers, typographers and three dimensional designers. Arthur Niggli (1996)
34. O'Donovan, P., Agarwala, A., Hertzmann, A.: Learning layouts for single-page graphic designs. IEEE Trans. Visual Comput. Graph. 20(8), 1200–1213 (2014)
35. Patil, A.G., Ben-Eliezer, O., Perel, O., Averbuch-Elor, H.: Read: recursive autoencoders for document layout generation. In: Proceedings of the IEEE/CVF Conference on Computer Vision and Pattern Recognition Workshops, pp. 544–545 (2020)
36. Patil, A.G., Li, M., Fisher, M., Savva, M., Zhang, H.: Layoutgmn: neural graph matching for structural layout similarity. In: Proceedings of the IEEE/CVF Conference on Computer Vision and Pattern Recognition, pp. 11048–11057 (2021)
37. Raisamo, R., Räihä, K.J.: A new direct manipulation technique for aligning objects in drawing programs. In: Proceedings of the 9th Annual ACM Symposium on User Interface Software and Technology, pp. 157–164 (1996)
38. Scarselli, F., Gori, M., Tsoi, A.C., Hagenbuchner, M., Monfardini, G.: The graph neural network model. IEEE Trans. Neural Networks 20(1), 61–80 (2008)
39. Socher, R., Lin, C.C., Manning, C., Ng, A.Y.: Parsing natural scenes and natural language with recursive neural networks. In: Proceedings of the 28th International Conference on Machine Learning (ICML-11), pp. 129–136 (2011)

40. Swearngin, A., Wang, C., Oleson, A., Fogarty, J., Ko, A.J.: Scout: rapid exploration of interface layout alternatives through high-level design constraints. In: Proceedings of the 2020 CHI Conference on Human Factors in Computing Systems, pp. 1–13 (2020)
41. Vaswani, A., et al.: Attention is all you need. In: Guyon, I., et al. (eds.) Advances in Neural Information Processing Systems, vol. 30. Curran Associates, Inc. (2017). https://proceedings.neurips.cc/paper/2017/file/3f5ee243547dee91fbd053c1c4a845aa-Paper.pdf
42. Xu, P., Fu, H., Tai, C.L., Igarashi, T.: GACA: group-aware command-based arrangement of graphic elements. In: Proceedings of the 33rd Annual ACM Conference on Human Factors in Computing Systems, pp. 2787–2795 (2015)
43. Xu, P., Li, Y., Yang, Z., Shi, W., Fu, H., Huang, H.: Hierarchical layout blending with recursive optimal correspondence. ACM Trans. Graph. (Proc. SIGGRAPH ASIA) **41**(6), 249:1–249:15 (2022)
44. Xu, P., Yan, G., Fu, H., Igarashi, T., Tai, C.L., Huang, H.: Global beautification of 2d and 3d layouts with interactive ambiguity resolution. IEEE Trans. Visual Comput. Graph. **27**(4), 2355–2368 (2019)
45. Yamaguchi, K.: Canvasvae: learning to generate vector graphic documents. In: Proceedings of the IEEE/CVF International Conference on Computer Vision, pp. 5481–5489 (2021)
46. Yang, Y.L., Wang, J., Vouga, E., Wonka, P.: Urban pattern: layout design by hierarchical domain splitting. ACM Trans. Graph. **32**(6), 1–12 (2013)
47. Zeidler, C., Lutteroth, C., Sturzlinger, W., Weber, G.: The Auckland layout editor: an improved GUI layout specification process. In: Proceedings of the 26th Annual ACM Symposium on User Interface Software and Technology, pp. 343–352 (2013)
48. Zheng, X., Qiao, X., Cao, Y., Lau, R.W.: Content-aware generative modeling of graphic design layouts. ACM Trans. Graph. **38**(4), 1–15 (2019)
49. Zhong, X., Tang, J., Yepes, A.J.: Publaynet: largest dataset ever for document layout analysis. In: 2019 International Conference on Document Analysis and Recognition (ICDAR), pp. 1015–1022. IEEE (2019)
50. Zhu, C., Xu, K., Chaudhuri, S., Yi, R., Zhang, H.: Scores: shape composition with recursive substructure priors. ACM Trans. Graph. **37**(6), 1–14 (2018)

Image Understanding

Silhouette-Based 6D Object Pose Estimation

Xiao Cui[ID], Nan Li, Chi Zhang, Qian Zhang, Wei Feng, and Liang Wan[✉]

Tianjin University, Tianjin, China
{cuixiao1998,linan94,zhangchi1736,qianz,lwan}@tju.edu.cn, wfeng@ieee.org

Abstract. For a long time, deep learning-based 6D object pose estimation networks have lacked the ability to address the problem of pose estimation of the unknown objects beyond the training datasets, due to the closed-set assumption and the expensive cost of high-quality annotation. Conversely, traditional methods struggle to achieve accurate pose estimation for texture-less objects. In this work, we propose a silhouette-based 6D object pose estimation method. being a conventional method As a traditional method, our approach achieves high accuracy without any need of annotation data, demonstrating excellent generalization. Additionally, we employ silhouette to mitigate texture dependency issues, ensuring effectiveness even in the case of textureless objects. In the method, we introduce a dimensionality reduction strategy for $SE(3)$ pose space, accompanied by theoretical proofs, which make it possible to perform pose estimation through search, rendering, and comparison in a reduced-dimensional space efficiently and accurately. Experimental results demonstrate the high precision and generalization of the proposed method. Our code is available at *https://github.com/worldTester/STI-Pose*.

Keywords: Object pose estimation · generalization · silhouette · texture-independent

1 Introduction

6D object pose estimation from a single image is a classical problem in computer vision. Its objective is to accurately estimate the precise 6D pose of a target object relative to the current camera. This problem plays a crucial role in various tasks, including robotic technology(e.g. automatic manufacturing [22], cooperative assistance [4,9]), where precise object poses are required to guide grasping, and augmented reality (AR) technology, which relies on determining the real-world object poses for seamless integration with the virtual world [19,23].

In traditional approaches to object pose estimation, the most common methods are based on correspondence [17]. These methods establish the 2D-3D correspondences between the object in the image and its 3D model and then estimate the object pose through the PnP [15]/RANSAC framework. They typically

F.-L. Zhang and A. Sharf (Eds.): CVM 2024, LNCS 14593, pp. 157–179, 2024.
https://doi.org/10.1007/978-981-97-2092-7_8

employ texture-dependent feature point extracting and matching algorithms like SIFT [17] and ORB [24] to establish the 2D-3D correspondences. Consequently, they struggle to handle pose estimation for those objects with weak or no texture. To address this issue, one approach is to adopt template matching-based methods [10,20]. These methods require generating a collection of images with ground truth object poses from different views prior to usage. Thus, transforming the 6D object pose estimation problem into an image retrieval problem. However, the accuracy of the result obtained through these methods heavily relies on the density of the constructed templates. Another approach to tackle the challenge of pose estimation for weakly-textured or textureless objects involves leveraging depth information [7,25]. It begins by extracting local shape descriptors of the partial-view point cloud of objects in the image from the current perspective and the complete point cloud on the 3D model. Subsequently, registration is performed to obtain the pose estimation result, thereby circumventing the reliance on object surface texture. However, the limited precision of depth sensors and the constraints of applicable scenarios hinder the widespread usage of these methods.

In recent years, significant progress has been made in the field of object pose estimation, thanks to the advancements in computer vision and deep learning. Numerous deep learning-based approaches have been proposed for pose estimation [6,13,21,26,29–31], alleviating many of the challenges encountered by traditional methods. One category of methods involves directly training a single object pose estimation network. These methods employ deep convolutional neural networks to directly regress the position and rotation of the object [6,13,29,31]. Alternatively, an approach is proposed aiming to make the PnP/RANSAC module differentiable [12], enabling end-to-end training of pose estimation networks. Another category of methods achieves higher accuracy in object pose estimation by leveraging neural network outputs that establish sparse or dense 2D-3D correspondence relationships. These methods subsequently estimate the object pose using traditional PnP/RANSAC algorithms [21,26,30].

However, deep learning-based approaches inevitably suffer from the closed-set assumption issues, which limit the widespread application of object pose estimation methods. Firstly, such methods require datasets [3,5,11] with highly accurate annotations of object poses. The task of annotating 6D poses for individual objects is expensive and the precision is limited. Secondly, training a single object pose estimation network requires a significant amount of time. The state-of-the-art methods that achieve high accuracy often sacrifice the generalization between object instances. They train a network that exclusively serves a single object instance, aiming to maximize the pose estimation capability for that specific object. However, when faced with pose estimation tasks involving multiple objects, it becomes necessary to train multiple network models. Lastly, many downstream tasks of object pose estimation do not prioritize texture but instead focus on the shape information of object, such as robotic arm grasping. These methods heavily rely on texture, requiring the construction of new dataset and retraining networks even for objects with the same shape but different textures.

In response to these issues, we propose a silhouette-based texture-independent object pose estimation method (STI-Pose), which employs an iterative rendering and comparing methodology. By utilizing the 3D model of the object, STI-Pose renders the silhouette in the 6D pose space and compares it with the silhouette of the target object in the reference image, seeking the pose corresponding with the strongest consistency as the estimation result. The method solely relies on silhouettes, which not only avoids the need for object appearance texture but also eliminates the requirement for annotated object poses, exhibiting impressive generalization capabilities.

To address the search problem in the 6D pose space, we introduce a Homography-based Spherical Intersection over Union method (HSIoU), which determines the similarity of camera poses corresponding to two silhouette images while equivalently reducing the search task of the six degrees of freedom in $SE(3)$ space to three, significantly enhancing the computational efficiency. We provide theoretical derivations to demonstrate the equivalence of this dimensionality reduction strategy. Furthermore, we propose an Optimized Particle Swarm Optimization algorithm, denoted as O-PSO, designed for efficient and robust search within the reduced-dimensional object pose space.

We approach silhouette extraction as an image segmentation task, which is a relatively simpler task compared to object pose estimation. The silhouettes required by our method can be obtained through various means: for cases with a straightforward background, green screen extraction or foreground segmentation methods suffice; for more complex backgrounds, universal segmentation methods such as SAM [14] or SEEM [33] can be employed. None of these segmentation methods impose a closed-set assumption, allowing for segmentation of arbitrary objects.

We validated our method on commonly used datasets [3,5] for object pose estimation and datasets specifically created for pose estimation of objects with various textures. The results demonstrate that our method is independent of object surface texture, while simultaneously exhibiting high precision and generalizability. Our contributions can be summarized as follows:

1. We propose a silhouette-based object pose estimation method that achieves high accuracy without the requirement of annotated object poses. This breakthrough surpasses the limitation of current networks that can only handle objects in the datasets.
2. Through extensive experiments, we demonstrate the robustness of our method to variations in object appearance, making it highly suitable for real-world applications involving numerous objects with similar geometric structures but different appearances.

2 Related Work

In this section, we will discuss the pose estimation methods most relevant to our work with the input of RGB image, dividing them into two parts: traditional methods and deep learning methods.

2.1 Traditional Methods

Traditional methods often rely on establishing 2D-3D correspondences and utilize the PnP/RANSAC framework to solve object pose estimation, such as [18], achieving high-precision results. However, these methods require the use of feature descriptors such as SIFT [17], SURF [1], or ORB [24], hence struggle to handle textureless objects. To address this issue, a template matching method called LineMod [10] has been proposed. LineMod constructs a large number of templates and utilizes image gradients for template matching, transforming the pose estimation problem into an image retrieval problem. This approach effectively handles textureless objects. However, the accuracy ceiling of template matching methods depends on the density of the templates.

[32] proposed a contour-based pose estimation method for textureless space objects. This method involves extracting the contour of the target object and performing an initial coarse matching with a pre-built library of contour templates. Subsequently, the ORB [24] algorithm is used to establish 2D-2D correspondences between the contours, and the 3D information within the contour templates is used to establish 2D-3D correspondences. The object pose is then computed using the PnP/RANSAC algorithm, thereby improving the accuracy ceiling of template matching methods. However, this method places higher demands on the object's shape, as the contours should not be excessively smooth, as it may cause the 2D-2D correspondences between the contours to fail.

2.2 Methods with Deep Learning

Deep learning methods surpass traditional approaches in terms of both accuracy and computational speed, and they exhibit excellent capability in handling textureless objects.

End-to-end approaches, such as PoseCNN [31], DenseFusion [29], directly regress the pose of the object. [12] attempt to transform PnP/RANSAC into a differentiable module. The end-to-end architecture of these methods enhances their flexibility, enabling them to serve as differentiable pose estimation modules that can be applied to a wider range of tasks.

Non-direct methods, which leverage the powerful regression capability of neural networks, achieve higher prediction accuracy. These methods predict sparse or dense 2D-3D correspondence relationships and subsequently utilize PnP/RANSAC methods to compute the object's pose. Each of these methods employs different approaches to predict the 2D-3D correspondence relationships. PVNet [21] predicts the pixel coordinates of 3D feature points, generating sparse correspondence relationships. GDR-Net [30] divides the object surface into multiple fragments, initially classifying 2D pixel points into a specific fragment and then regressing the offset within that fragment. ZebraPose [26] employs binary encoding for the object's vertices, and the network predicts the corresponding encoding for 2D pixel points, thereby establishing the 2D-3D correspondence relationships. GDR-Net and ZebraPose generate dense correspondence relationships, exhibiting superior performance.

Despite the significant advancements of deep learning methods compared to traditional approaches, they do have certain drawbacks due to their reliance on data. Firstly, these methods necessitate lengthy training on meticulously annotated pose estimation datasets, which can be time-consuming for both dataset creation and training. Secondly, they lack generalizability and can hardly estimate poses for unknown objects not present in the training dataset.

3   The Method

In this section, we propose a silhouette-based object pose estimation method that is texture-independent (STI-Pose). As shown in Fig. 1, STI-Pose takes as input the silhouette image of an object in a reference image, along with the corresponding 3D model of the object.

We introduce a homography-based spherical intersection over union (HSIoU) method to determine the proximity of the camera poses corresponding to the two silhouette images. By reducing the dimensionality of the object pose space from six dimensions to three, with the help of HSIoU, we use an optimized particle swarm optimization algorithm (O-PSO) in the reduced space to obtain the optimal pose. In the following, we will describe the method in detail.

3.1   Problem Formulation and Notation

In this paper, we use a 3D rotation $\mathbf{R} \in \mathrm{SO}\,(3)$ and a 3D translation $\mathbf{t} \in \mathbb{R}^3$ to indicate the pose $\mathbf{P} \in \mathrm{SE}\,(3)$, i.e., $\mathbf{P} = \begin{bmatrix} \mathbf{R} & \mathbf{t} \\ \mathbf{0}^{\mathrm{T}} & 1 \end{bmatrix} \simeq \langle \mathbf{R}, \mathbf{t} \rangle$. We use the uppercase and lowercase subscripts to indicate the relative relationship, specifically, $\mathbf{P}_{\mathrm{A}}^{\mathrm{B}}$ denotes the pose of coordinate system B relative to coordinate system A. We use the capital letter C to indicate the camera while the capital letter O to indicate the object. In addition, we utilize Euler angles to represent the rotation matrix, denoted as r_x, r_y, and r_z, respectively. For the camera model, we denote the intrinsic parameter matrix as $\mathbf{K} = \begin{bmatrix} f_x & 0 & c_x \\ 0 & f_y & c_y \\ 0 & 0 & 1 \end{bmatrix}$. In addition, the homogeneous coordinates of a 3D point $\mathbf{X} \in \mathbb{R}^3$ are represented as $\tilde{\mathbf{X}} = [x, y, z, 1]^{\mathrm{T}}$, while the homogeneous coordinates of a 2D pixel point $\mathbf{p} \in \mathbb{R}^2$ are represented as $\tilde{\mathbf{p}} = [u, v, 1]^{\mathrm{T}}$.

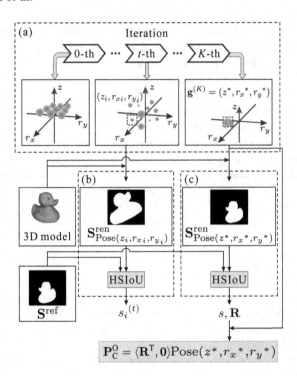

Fig. 1. Working flow of the silhouette-based object pose estimation (STI-Pose). The input is silhouette $\mathbf{S}^{\text{ref}}$ and 3D model. (a) is the optimized particle swarm optimization (O-PSO) algorithm to obtain the optimal pose in the reduced space. (b) and (c) are homography-based spherical intersection over union (HSIoU) method to determine the proximity of the camera poses corresponding to the two silhouette images.

We transform the pose estimation problem into an optimization problem in SE(3) space, specifically as follows:

$$\mathbf{P}_{\text{C}}^{\text{O}*} = \underset{\mathbf{P}_{\text{C}}^{\text{O}} \in \text{SE}(3)}{\arg\min} \left\| \mathbf{S}_{\mathbf{P}_{\text{C}}^{\text{O}}}^{\text{ren}} - \mathbf{S}^{\text{ref}} \right\|_2, \tag{1}$$

where $\mathbf{S}^{\text{ref}}$ is the reference silhouette image and $\mathbf{S}_{\mathbf{P}_{\text{C}}^{\text{O}}}^{\text{ren}}$ is the rendered silhouette image using object pose $\mathbf{P}_{\text{C}}^{\text{O}}$. Obtaining the global maximum in the six-dimensional SE(3) space is indeed a hard task. However, STI-Pose allows for efficient and stable identification of the optimal pose. It is worth mentioning that the 3D models used in this paper consist of triangular mesh representations, containing solely geometric shape information and devoid of any texture information.

3.2   Dimensionality Reduction

The key factor to the accurate object pose estimation through iterative search, rendering, and comparison is to determine the similarity of the camera pose corresponding to the reference silhouette image and the rendered silhouette image, thereby deciding the search termination, and obtaining the final estimated object pose. In this section, we propose a homography-based spherical intersection over union (HSIoU) method to determine the proximity of the camera poses corresponding to the two silhouette images. At the same time, we provide detailed instructions on how to effectively reduce the search task of six degrees of freedom in SE (3) space to three degrees.

Homography-Based Spherical Intersection over Union. The process of the HSIoU is illustrated in Fig. 2. Given two camera images of an object silhouette, $\mathbf{S}_1$ and $\mathbf{S}_2$, captured by cameras with the same intrinsic parameters $\mathbf{K}$ but different poses, HSIoU computes the proximity of the translation vectors $\mathbf{t}_1$ and $\mathbf{t}_2$ between the unknown camera poses $\mathbf{P}_O^{C_1} \simeq \langle \mathbf{R}_1, \mathbf{t}_1 \rangle$ and $\mathbf{P}_O^{C_2} \simeq \langle \mathbf{R}_2, \mathbf{t}_2 \rangle$. Additionally, the algorithm also outputs the relative rotation $\mathbf{R} = \mathbf{R}_1^T * \mathbf{R}_2$ when the proximity s is high enough.

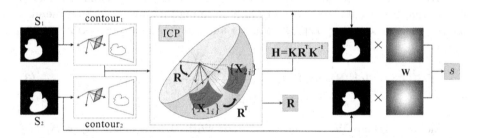

Fig. 2. Illustration of the homography-based spherical intersection over union (HSIoU) method.

Theorem 1. *When $\mathbf{t}_1$ is equal to $\mathbf{t}_2$ and the only difference between $\mathbf{P}_O^{C_1}$ and $\mathbf{P}_O^{C_2}$ lies in rotation $\mathbf{R}$, there exists a transformation relationship between $\mathbf{S}_1$ and $\mathbf{S}_2$ through a homography matrix $\mathbf{H}$. Applying $\mathbf{H}$ to $\mathbf{S}_1$ yields $\mathbf{S}_1'$, which perfectly aligns with $\mathbf{S}_2$.*

The proof is as follows.

Proof. For the 2D pixel points $\tilde{\mathbf{p}}_1, \tilde{\mathbf{p}}_2$ which are projections of a spatial point $\mathbf{X}$ onto the two image planes of the cameras, we have

$$
\begin{aligned}
\tilde{\mathbf{p}}_1 &= \mathbf{K}\mathbf{X}, \\
\tilde{\mathbf{p}}_2 &= \mathbf{K}\mathbf{R}^T\mathbf{X} = \mathbf{K}\mathbf{R}^T\mathbf{K}^{-1}\tilde{\mathbf{p}}_1.
\end{aligned}
\tag{2}
$$

Thus, $\tilde{p}_2 = H\tilde{p}_1$ when defining $H = KR^T K^{-1}$. Hence, there exists a homography transformation between the pixel points of S_1 and S_2. Applying this transformation to S_1 yields S_1', the Intersection over Union (IoU) between S_1' and S_2 is always 1.

The H matrix is easily computable. Firstly, we utilize the contour extraction algorithm [27] to extract the contour points from S_1 and S_2. We then back-project these points onto the unit sphere using the camera intrinsic parameters K, resulting in point clouds $\{X_{1i}\}$ and $\{X_{2i}\}$. Next, we employ a specialized ICP [2] algorithm to align the two point clouds and obtain R, from which we derive H. The specialized ICP algorithm only applies rotation operations to the point clouds, disregarding translation. It is important to note that the projection onto the unit sphere is necessary to ensure that all points in $\{X_{1i}\}$ and $\{X_{2i}\}$ have equal distances from the camera optical center. This requirement satisfies the prerequisites of the specialized ICP algorithm for aligning the point clouds. When t_1 is not equal to t_2, we can still calculate the IoU using the aforementioned process. Note that, in this case, the IoU value will always be less than 1, and we can use it to quantify the proximity between t_1 and t_2.

However, performing IoU calculations on a pixel plane can be susceptible to the influence of the perspective effect, leading to unstable IoU values. Consequently, we have introduced a weight map W during the IoU computation to ensure that the results are equivalent to performing IoU calculations on the unit sphere, as represented by Eq. (3), where i and j represent pixel coordinates.

$$\text{IoU}(S_1, S_2, W) = \frac{\sum\limits_{(i,j) \in S_1 \cap S_2} W(i,j)}{\sum\limits_{(i,j) \in S_1 \cup S_2} W(i,j)} \in (0, 1]. \tag{3}$$

The weight map W has the same size (width W and height H) as S_1 and S_2, where the value of each pixel represents the ratio of the area occupied by that pixel on the unit sphere to its area on the normalized plane. The creation of W is solely dependent on the camera intrinsic parameters K. Figure 3 and Eqs. (4-6) give the derivation process.

According to the back-projection relationship of camera internal parameters, we have the coordinate (x, y) of the point T in the normalized plane,

$$x = \frac{i - c_x}{f_x}, \qquad y = \frac{j - c_y}{f_y}, \tag{4}$$

where $1 \leq i \leq W, 1 \leq j \leq H$. Thus, The distance between T and the vertical point M of the optical center O on the normalized plane is

$$\|MT\| = l = \tan(\theta) = \sqrt{x^2 + y^2}. \tag{5}$$

Hence, the weight map W (the ratio of the infinitesimal area element dS_1 on the unit sphere to the corresponding infinitesimal area element dS_2 on the normalized

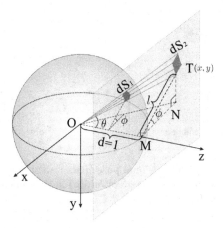

Fig. 3. Derivation illustration of the weight map $\mathbf{W}$

plane) can be calculated by

$$\mathbf{W}(i,j) = \frac{\mathrm{dS}_1}{\mathrm{dS}_2} = \frac{\sin(\theta) \cdot \mathrm{d}\phi \cdot \mathrm{d}\theta}{l \cdot \mathrm{d}\phi \cdot \mathrm{d}l} = \frac{\sin(\theta)}{\tan(\theta) \cdot \frac{\mathrm{d}l}{\mathrm{d}\theta}}$$

$$= \cos^3(\theta) \qquad (6)$$

$$= ((\frac{i - c_x}{f_x})^2 + (\frac{j - c_y}{f_y})^2 + 1)^{-\frac{3}{2}} \in (0, 1].$$

By introducing the weight map $\mathbf{W}$ and modifying the IoU calculation, we refer to the algorithmic process described above as HSIoU, which can be represented by Eq. (7).

$$s, \mathbf{R} = \mathrm{HSIoU}(\mathbf{S}_1, \mathbf{S}_2, \mathbf{K}), \qquad (7)$$

where the proximity s is the result of Eq. (3), it solely reflects the proximity between $\mathbf{t}_1$ and $\mathbf{t}_2$, with no relation to $\mathbf{R}_1$ and $\mathbf{R}_2$. On the other hand, $\mathbf{R} = \mathbf{R}_1^{\mathrm{T}}\mathbf{R}_2$ represents the disparity between the unknown $\mathbf{R}_1$ and $\mathbf{R}_2$, and its value is meaningful only when s approaches 1.

The Dimensionality Reduction by HSIoU. HSIoU gives a naive method for object pose estimation, it can effectively reduce the search task of six degrees of freedom in SE (3) space to three. It allows us to first determine the translation $\mathbf{t}$ of the camera pose, and then obtain the rotation R to accomplish pose estimation. To obtain the accurate translation vector $\mathbf{t}$ of the camera pose $\mathbf{P}_O^C \simeq \langle \mathbf{R}, \mathbf{t} \rangle$, we traverse the $\mathbb{R}^3$ space. When $\mathbf{t}$ takes the value $\mathbf{t}_i$, since the rotation $\mathbf{R}$ does not affect the computation of HSIoU, we can set it as an arbitrary rotation matrix $\mathbf{R}_i$. We set the z-axis of camera points towards the origin of the object coordinate system for convenience. This configuration is illustrated in Fig. 4 (a).

We denote these poses as $\{\mathbf{R}_i, \mathbf{t}_i\}$ and use them to render silhouettes $\{\mathbf{S}_{\langle \mathbf{R}_i, \mathbf{t}_i \rangle}^{\mathrm{ren}}\}$. We then compute HSIoU with respect to the reference silhouette

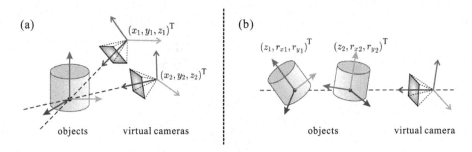

Fig. 4. Two types of reduced-dimensional pose spaces. (a) is the dimensionality reduction of the **camera pose space** after reduction. (b) is the dimensionality reduction of the **object pose space** after reduction.

$\mathbf{S}^{\text{ref}}$. Then, we can obtain the pose $\langle \mathbf{R}^*, \mathbf{t}^* \rangle$ that yields the maximum $s \approx 1$, along with the corresponding $\mathbf{R}$. This can be expressed using Eq. (8).

$$s, \mathbf{R} = \text{HSIoU}(\mathbf{S}^{\text{ren}}_{\langle \mathbf{R}^*, \mathbf{t}^* \rangle}, \mathbf{S}^{\text{ref}}, \mathbf{K}). \qquad (8)$$

In this way, the camera pose can be represented as $\mathbf{P}^C_O \simeq \langle \mathbf{R}^* \mathbf{R}, \mathbf{t}^* \rangle$, and the object's pose can be obtained as $\mathbf{P}^O_C = \mathbf{P}^{C^{-1}}_O$. During this computation process, we traverse only the translation vector $\mathbf{t} = [x, y, z]^T \in \mathbb{R}^3$, thus, reducing the dimensions that need to be searched in the pose space.

However, this approach has several limitations. Firstly, traversing only the translation vector $\mathbf{t}$ is not the optimal choice. Considering that the individual influence of the three dimensions of $\mathbf{t}$ on the silhouette does not vary significantly, expressing $\mathbf{t}$ in spherical coordinates (r, θ, ϕ) would magnify this difference. Specifically, r primarily influences the size of the area of $\mathbf{S}^{\text{ren}}$, while θ and ϕ have a greater impact on the shape of $\mathbf{S}^{\text{ren}}$. This representation can achieve a certain level of decoupling, providing better properties for exploration within the pose space. Secondly, the approach calculates the camera pose $\mathbf{P}^C_O$ and then converts it into the object pose $\mathbf{P}^C_O$, which may seem less straightforward.

Based on the aforementioned approach and its shortcomings, we reduce the dimensionality of the pose space and provide a more precise definition. This dimensionality reduction method is more concise and rational. As shown in Fig. 4 (b), the coordinate of the reduced-dimensional space is denoted as (z, r_x, r_y), where z represents the z-coordinate of the object in the camera coordinate system, while r_x and r_y denote the object's Euler angles around the x and y axes, respectively, in the camera coordinate system. The dimensions that have been reduced are x, y, and r_z, which are set to 0. $x = y = 0$ signifies that the origin of the object lies on the z-axis of the camera coordinate system, aligning with the earlier approach. Considering that r_z corresponds to the in-plane rotation of the camera, we can indeed set $r_z = 0$.

Thus, to express the mapping relationship from the reduced-dimensional space to the 6D pose space, we employ the notation $\mathbf{P}^C_O = \text{Pose}(z, r_x, r_y)$. Given $\mathbf{S}^{\text{ref}}$, we traverse the (z, r_x, r_y) coordinate space, rendering $\{\mathbf{S}^{\text{ren}}_{\text{Pose}(z_i, r_{xi}, r_{yi})}\}$

with $\{\text{Pose}(z_i, r_{xi}, r_{y_i})\}$ and calculating the HSIoU with respect to $\mathbf{S}^{\text{ref}}$. This process yields the coordinates $(z^*, r_x{}^*, r_y{}^*)$ that maximize the proximity measure s produced by HSIoU.

$$s, \mathbf{R} = \text{HSIoU}(\mathbf{S}^{\text{ren}}_{\text{Pose}(z^*, r_x{}^*, r_y{}^*)}, \mathbf{S}^{\text{ref}}, \mathbf{K}). \tag{9}$$

Based on the aforementioned calculations, the 6D pose of the object can be expressed as:

$$\mathbf{P}^O_C = \langle \mathbf{R}^T, \mathbf{0} \rangle \text{Pose}(z^*, r_x{}^*, r_y{}^*). \tag{10}$$

3.3   Optimized Particle Swarm Optimization

In the previous section, we discussed how to reduce the dimensionality of the object pose space but did not provide a detailed explanation of how to search for the global maximum of the variable s in the HSIoU algorithm. In this section, we utilize an optimized particle swarm optimization (O-PSO) algorithm to accurately and reliably accomplish this task, thereby achieving a good object pose estimation.

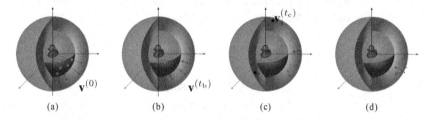

(a)   (b)   (c)   (d)

Fig. 5. Execution process of the optimized particle swarm optimization (O-PSO) algorithm. The color of the particle reflects its corresponding s of HSIoU, with red indicating a larger value and blue indicating a smaller value. (a) depicts the initialization of the particle swarm, which is on the spherical surface with a radius of z_{near} (*Color figure online*) and moving radially. (b) represents the motion during the first stage (prior to P iterations). The particles gradually accelerate in the radial direction until they reach the radius of z_{far}. (c) showcases the motion during the second stage (after P iterations), where particles start acquiring tangential velocity. (d) illustrates the convergence of O-PSO and the particles gather around the peak of s.

Due to the non-differentiability of HSIoU, it is not possible to compute the gradients with respect to (z, r_x, r_y). Therefore, we choose the Particle Swarm Optimization (PSO) algorithm [8], which is suitable for finding maximum points in spaces with unknown gradients. However, PSO is prone to get trapped in local maxima, and to mitigate this issue, we need a larger number of particles to cover a wider range, which can affect the convergence speed of the algorithm. As shown in Fig. 5, taking into account the characteristics of the object pose space after dimensionality reduction, we propose an initialization and movement strategy for the particle swarm. This strategy effectively addresses the local optima problem without introducing an excessive number of particles.

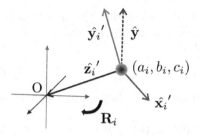

Fig. 6. Initialization for the coordinate of the particle swarm.

Particle Swarm Initialization. Since r_x and r_y in the (z, r_x, r_y) space represent angles, it follows that r_x and r_y are in the interval $(-\pi, \pi]$. For the variable z, we set a search range of $[z_{\text{near}}, z_{\text{far}}]$. Therefore, the search range for the O-PSO algorithm is $[z_{\text{near}}, z_{\text{far}}] \times (-\pi, \pi] \times (-\pi, \pi]$. To initialize the particles, we first assign initial coordinates to each particle. Assuming we have N particles, we utilize the Fibonacci sphere algorithm to uniformly sample N points on a sphere centered at the object with a radius of 1. As shown in Fig. 6, we use (a_i, b_i, c_i) to represent the coordinates of the i-th particle,

$$
\begin{cases}
b_i & = 1 - \frac{2i}{N-1}, \\
a_i & = \sqrt{1 - b_i^2} \cdot \cos(i\phi), \\
c_i & = \sqrt{1 - b_i^2} \cdot \sin(i\phi), \\
\phi & = (\sqrt{5} - 1)\pi,
\end{cases}
\tag{11}
$$

where ϕ represents the golden angle in radians. Then, we convert $\{(a_i, b_i, c_i)\}$ to the reduced object pose space, represented as $\{(z_i, r_{xi}, r_{yi})\}$,

$$
\begin{cases}
\hat{\mathbf{y}} & = [0, 1, 0]^{\mathrm{T}}, \\
\hat{\mathbf{z}}_i{}' & = -[a_i, b_i, c_i]^{\mathrm{T}}, \\
\hat{\mathbf{x}}_i{}' & = \hat{\mathbf{y}} \times \hat{\mathbf{z}}_i{}', \\
\hat{\mathbf{y}}_i{}' & = \hat{\mathbf{z}}_i{}' \times \hat{\mathbf{x}}_i{}'.
\end{cases}
\tag{12}
$$

Hence, we have the rotation matrix $\mathbf{R}_i$ of an object relative to the coordinate system of the i-th particle,

$$
\mathbf{R}_i = [\frac{\hat{\mathbf{x}}_i{}'}{\|\hat{\mathbf{x}}_i{}'\|}, \frac{\hat{\mathbf{y}}_i{}'}{\|\hat{\mathbf{y}}_i{}'\|}, \hat{\mathbf{z}}_i{}']^{\mathrm{T}}.
\tag{13}
$$

In particular, we use the Euler angle to represent the $\mathbf{R}_i$, that is $R_i \simeq \langle r_{xi}, r_{yi}, r_{zi} \rangle$. Subsequently, we replace the z_i values in $\{(z_i, r_{xi}, r_{yi})\}$ with z_{near}, resulting in $\{(z_{\text{near}}, r_{xi}, r_{yi})\}$. This signifies that all N particles are located on a spherical surface with a radius of z_{near} from the center of the object, which is shown in Fig. 5(a). Thus, we consider $\{(z_{\text{near}}, r_{xi}, r_{yi})\}$ as the initial coordinates for the particles.

Particle Swarm Movement Strategy. Firstly, we define a random vector $\mathbf{X}$,

$$\mathbf{X} = (X_1, X_2, X_3) \quad \text{s.t.} \quad X_i \sim U(0,1).$$ (14)

Then the the velocity $\mathbf{v}_i^{(t)} = [v_{zi}, v_{r_x i}, v_{r_y i}]^\mathrm{T}$ of the i-th particle at the t-th iteration can be represented as

$$\mathbf{v}_i^{(t)} = \begin{cases} [(z_{\text{far}} - z_{\text{near}}) \frac{e^{\frac{k}{P-1}} - 1}{e^k - 1} e^{\frac{k}{P-1}(t-1)}, 0, 0]^\mathrm{T}, & t \leq P - 1 \\ \omega \mathbf{v}_i^{(t-1)} + c_1(\mathbf{p}_i^{(t-1)} - \mathbf{x}_i^{(t-1)}) + \\ c_2\mathbf{X}(\mathbf{g}^{(t-1)} - \mathbf{x}_i^{(t-1)}), & P \leq t \leq K \end{cases}$$ (15)

where $\mathbf{p}_i$ represents the position corresponding to the maximum value of s encountered during the traversal by the i-th particle, while $\mathbf{g}$ denotes the one by all particles, k is a hyperparameter. And the coordinate $\mathbf{x}_i^{(t)} = [z_i, r_{xi}, r_{yi}]^\mathrm{T}$ of the i-th particle at the t-th iteration in Eq.(15) is

$$\mathbf{x}_i^{(t)} = \begin{cases} \mathbf{p}_i^{(t-1)}, & t = P \\ \mathbf{x}_i^{(t-1)} + \mathbf{v}_i^{(t-1)}, & t \neq P \end{cases}$$ (16)

In the first P iterations, the algorithm is at the first stage, which is shown in 5 (b). The velocities v_{r_x} and v_{r_y} are set to 0, while v_z increases incrementally. This setting indicates that the particles only accelerate radially in relation to the center of the object. This choice is made because, at larger distances from the center of the object, the impact on silhouette size from the same distance becomes less significant. Hence, we allow v_z to increase with each iteration, resulting in a longer distance. Upon completion of the P iterations, we set the coordinate $\mathbf{x}_i$ of the particle to the maximum point, $\mathbf{p}_i$, it has traversed. After P iterations is the second stage, where we proceed with the standard PSO algorithm. Upon convergence of the particle swarm (as shown in Fig. 5 (d)), we obtain $\mathbf{g} = (z^*, r_x^*, r_y^*)$, which enables us to compute the object pose $\mathbf{P}_\mathrm{C}^\mathrm{O}$ using Eqs. (9-10).

4 Experiments

In this section, we will substantiate the high precision, texture independence, excellent generalization, and numerical stability of STI-Pose through a series of experiments. In this context, the distinctive characteristic of STI-Pose will be emphasized.

4.1 Experiments Setup

Implementation Details. Our approach involves rendering silhouette images based on object poses and comparing them with reference silhouette images. We utilize OpenGL for image rendering and use a fragment shader to output white color, enabling direct rendering of silhouettes. For contour extraction, we employ the "findContours" function from OpenCV. Additionally, if multiple contours are detected, we select the one with the maximum length to eliminate noise interference. The pure rotational ICP algorithm is implemented by adapting the source code of the point cloud registration algorithm from Open3D. We perform dense interpolation on the back-projected point cloud of the reference silhouette image contours, while no processing is applied to the back-projected point cloud of the rendered silhouette image contours. This minimizes point cloud registration errors as much as possible. The scale map can be computed offline and stored since it only depends on the image size and the camera intrinsic $\mathbf{K}$.

We have implemented the particle swarm optimization algorithm ourselves, with the following settings in Eqs. (15,16): $k = 2$, inertia weight $\omega = 0.8$, acceleration coefficients $c_1 = c_2 = 0.5$, and a maximum iteration limit of $K = 200$. For all datasets, the search space for the particle swarm optimization algorithm is constrained with $z_{\text{near}} = 400$ mm, $z_{\text{far}} = 1400$ mm. P is set to 20, and the number of particles N is set to 50.

Datasets. Currently, the commonly used object pose estimation datasets includes LM-O [3] and YCB-V [5]. LM-O consists of 8 objects, with a higher proportion of textureless objects. On the other hand, YCB-V comprises 21 objects, most of which are symmetrical and have textured surfaces. Since our proposed method requires complete silhouettes, we filtered the test sets of these two datasets based on occlusion conditions and conducted experiments only on datasets with occlusion rates below 10%. In our experiments, we employ the combination of bounding box detector FCOS [28] and SAM [14] to obtain the object silhouettes. The FCOS detector is provided by CDPNv2 [16].

To demonstrate the STI-Pose is texture-independent, we created two dataset of objects with various surface textures. The first dataset based on the YCB-V dataset called YCB-V-NT(YCB-V with new texture), which is a virtual rendering dataset. Specifically, we replaced the texture maps of the original objects in YCB-V with three different texture images. We then rendered the objects using the ground truth object poses and synthesized the rendered images with the original ones. The synthesized data is illustrated in Fig. 7. Additionally, we has curated an dataset comprising 155 images collected from the real world, called texture replacement dataset from real world(TR-RW). The dataset includes three variations of identical-shaped cans and two types of industrially molded components with distinct textures. Pose annotations were manually obtained for accurate positioning. The data is illustrated in Fig. 8.

Error Metrics. We employ the commonly utilized ADD(-S) metric for the task of object pose estimation. The ADD metric assesses whether the average deviation of the transformed model points falls below 10% of the object's diameter. In the case of symmetric objects, the ADD-S metric is utilized to measure the error as the average distance to the nearest model point. Additionally, we utilize

Fig. 7. Samples from the dataset YCB-V-NT rendered using three different textures. The first, second, and third rows correspond to the textures of grid, stone, and metal, respectively.

Fig. 8. Samples from the TR-RW dataset.

the Area Under the Curve (AUC) of the ADD(-S) with a maximum threshold of 10 cm.

It is worth noting that, as our method is texture-independent, for objects with shape symmetry, we will consistently use the ADD-S metric for comparison with other methods, without considering symmetry in texture.

4.2   Comparison to State of the Art

We compared our STI-Pose with the state-of-the-art methods on the unoccluded data from YCB-V and LM-O datasets to demonstrate the high accuracy (Fig. 9).

Results on YCB-V. We present the results of ADD(-S) and its corresponding AUC in Table 1. Both ZebraPose [26] and GDR-Net [30] are deep learning approaches based on 2D-3D correspondences, exhibiting exceptional accuracy. Since our method relies solely on silhouettes and does not consider the internal textures of objects, we solely consider the object shape symmetry. In the

Fig. 9. Visualization of pose estimation results using STI-Pose on the YCB-V and LM-O datasets. The estimated poses are represented by blue contours overlaid on the reference images. (a) displays visualizations from the YCB-V dataset, and (b) shows visualizations from the LM-O dataset. (Color figure online)

experimental process, for shape-symmetric objects, Zebrapose, GDR-Net, and the proposed STI-Pose, all employ ADD-S for evaluation. To ensure fair comparisons, Zebrapose and GDR-Net utilize pre-trained models provided by their authors. Additionally, since both methods require RoI as input, we employ the same detector, FCOS [28], to obtain the RoI images.

Experimental results demonstrate that STI-Pose performs the best. Moreover, STI-Pose extremely accurately estimates the poses of textureless objects such as the bowl and banana. Our method outperforms others in both metrics for the bowl object, owing to its symmetry and lack of texture. Thus, deep learning methods struggle to learn pose-related features based on texture or shape, whereas our approach solely utilizes silhouette, eliminating such limitations.

Results on LM-O. We compared the STI-Pose with the methods presented in Table 2. The experiment shows that although STI-Pose does not achieve the highest accuracy, it exhibits performance comparable to state-of-the-art methods. It is noteworthy that in LM-O, a significant portion of the object lacks surfaces texture or have no texture, yet STI-Pose, a conventional approach, achieves sufficiently high precision.

It is noteworthy that our methods were directly tested on the evaluation dataset, confirming the generalization capability of STI-Pose for object pose estimation on various objects.

Table 1. Comparison results between STI-Pose and other state-of-the-art methods on the YCB-V dataset. The table showcases the ADD(-S) and AUC-ADD(-S) metrics for each object in %.

Method	ZebraPose		GDR-Net		STI-Pose	
	ADD(-S)	AUC-ADD(-S)	ADD(-S)	AUC-ADD(-S)	ADD(-S)	AUC-ADD(-S)
master_chef_can	100	94.4	98.3	93.4	100	96.5
cracker_box	100	85.5	100	97.2	100	97
sugar_box	100	94.5	100	95.9	97.3	93.1
tomato_soup_can	100	96.2	100	94.2	100	95
mustard_bottle	100	96.4	100	95.3	100	96
tuna_fish_can	97.3	95.3	94.6	95.4	85	94.1
gelatin_box	86.8	94.7	88.9	94.1	100	94.4
potted_meat_can	100	95.2	100	90.3	100	94.8
banana	100	90.0	100	92.8	100	89.2
pitcher_base	100	92.9	100	90.3	89.7	85.5
bleach_cleanser	100	91.1	97.8	89.7	100	92.4
bowl	62.5	78.5	74.9	81.8	100	95.4
mug	76.0	89.7	72.1	90.5	60	80.8
power_drill	98.8	90.5	100	92.3	100	93.9
large_clamp	98.1	91.0	92.4	83.3	95.2	93.2
extra_large_clamp	100	94.6	100	90.3	93.8	97.6
foam_brick	100	95.2	100	94.6	100	95.8
mean	95.3	92.7	95.2	91.8	**95.4**	**93.2**

4.3   Performance on YCB-V-NT and TR-RW

Although it is evident that utilizing silhouettes allows our method to be texture-agnostic, we still conducted experiments on two self-constructed datasets YCB-V-NT and TR-RW, which fully illustrate that existing methods lack texture generalization.

We conducted comparative experiments on the YCB-V-NT dataset, comparing it with the state-of-the-art ZebraPose, which has shown excellent performance in deep learning approaches. The experimental results are presented in Table 3, where it can be observed that STI-Pose maintains high accuracy even on the texture-replaced dataset, while the deep learning methods struggle to achieve correct pose estimation. This indicates that deep learning approaches fundamentally rely heavily on extracting features from the surface texture of objects, and their training on data with a specific texture does not generalize well to objects with different textures. In contrast, our method only requires the input of silhouettes and is completely independent of object surface textures. As a result, it naturally possesses texture generalization capabilities.

Furthermore, we also tested STI-Pose on our self-constructed TR-RW dataset, as shown in Table 4 The experimental results on cans and injection-molded samples demonstrate that variations in object surface textures, when

Table 2. Comparison with state-of-the-art methods on LM-O. We compare our STI-Pose with these methods using metrics of ADD-S, AUC of ADD-S in %.

Method	ADD-S	AUC of ADD-S
ZebraPose	**91.2**	88.1
GDR-Net	78.1	89.6
RePose	80.4	86.5
SO-Pose	74.3	88.9
Ours	90.4	**90.0**

Table 3. Comparison with ZebraPose on YCB-V and YCB-V-NT. We compared our STI-Pose with the state-of-the-art deep learning pose estimation method, ZebraPose, using the metrics of ADD(-S) and AUC-ADD(-S) in %.

Method	ZebraPose		STI-Pose	
	ADD(-S)	AUC-ADD(-S)	ADD(-S)	AUC-ADD(-S)
YCB-V	95.3	92.7	**95.4**	**93.2**
YCB-V-NT	4.6	13.3	**91.3**	**92.9**

the shapes are the same, have negligible impact on the accuracy of our approach. This further validates the texture-agnostic nature of STI-Pose.

Table 4. The experimental results of STI-Pose on the TR-RW dataset.

Objects/Metrics	ADD(-S)	AUC-ADD(-S)
Coca-Cola can	96.8	97.6
Sprite can	100	98.1
Fanta can	100	97.8
Blue injection-molded part	96.8	90.3
Gray injection-molded part	93.5	88.5

4.4   Silhouette Stability Experiments

Due to the utilization of silhouettes as input in STI-Pose, it is essential to investigate the stability of the algorithm with respect to silhouette extraction accuracy. In this paper, based on the YCB-V and LM-O datasets, we introduce various degrees of perturbations to the silhouette images segmented by SAM and evaluate the accuracy of STI-Pose on perturbed data. We employ the function $\delta = A\cos(x)$ as a random perturbation method. For each silhouette edge point, a random value x is chosen to calculate the perturbation value δ, and the point is displaced along the normal direction by δ to obtain the new silhouette image. In this perturbation data generation method, the amplitude A determines the perturbation magnitude. During actual generation, different values ranging from 0 to 2.5 are used to simulate various silhouette extraction accuracies. The visual effects of silhouettes under different perturbation amplitudes are illustrated in Fig. 10.

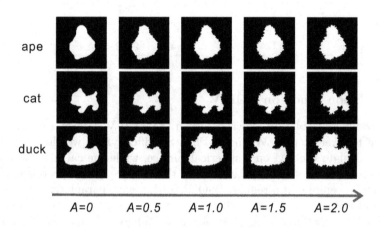

Fig. 10. Silhouette images under different perturbation amplitudes.

Table 5. The relative change in estimation error of STI-Pose as the silhouette perturbation amplitude varies.

Datasets/A	0	0.25	0.5	1	1.5	2	2.5
YCB-V	1	1.06	1.14	1.23	1.33	1.57	1.85
LM-O	1	1.04	1.11	1.18	1.35	1.52	1.77

Table 5 presents the relative changes in the ADD(-S) values of STI-Pose under both unperturbed and perturbed data at different amplitude levels. The data in the table represent the relative change rates of the ADD(-S) distance values. It can be observed that as the perturbation level increases, STI-Pose initially maintains stability until a significant decrease in accuracy occurs when the perturbation becomes excessive. This may be attributed to the calculation of Intersection over Union (IoU). The results indicate that the proposed method exhibits a certain tolerance to silhouette extraction accuracy, effectively addressing potential issues of inaccurate object silhouette extraction in practical applications.

Table 6. Ablation Study on YCB-V. We conducted ablation experiments on the weight map and O-PSO in STI-Pose, and the results are represented in % using ADD(-S) and AUC-ADD(-S).

Exp.	Module Selection		Evaluation Metrics	
	W	O-PSO	ADD(-S)	AUC-ADD(-S)
1			63.7	73.2
2	✓		65.6	75.3
3		✓	85.6	90.4
4	✓	✓	**95.4**	**93.2**

4.5 Ablation Study on YCB-V

We conducted ablation experiments on the YCB-V dataset to examine the effects of the weight map **W** and O-PSO. Specifically, the weight map **W** was used to calculate the IoU on a spherical surface, while the calculation was performed on a planar surface otherwise. In the absence of the proposed O-PSO algorithm, we employed a regular PSO algorithm with parameters aligned with those of O-PSO.

The experimental results, as depicted in Table 6, clearly demonstrate the significant performance improvement achieved with O-PSO. This improvement indicates its ability to assist STI-Pose in reliably locating the global maximum. Furthermore, the inclusion of the weight map **W** leads to further precision enhancement when using O-PSO. However, without O-PSO, the impact of the weight map is less pronounced. This is because, in scenarios near non-global maximum points, the improvement in HSIoU precision brought about by the weight map does not directly translate into improved pose estimation accuracy.

5   Conclusion and Outlook

In summary, we propose a silhouette-based 6D object pose estimation method, achieving high accuracy in the experiments. This method eliminates the need for annotated data, overcoming the limitations of deep learning-based pose estimation methods that can only handle several objects in the datasets. Furthermore, this method does not rely on object surface characteristics, exhibiting excellent generalization on objects with similar structures but different appearances, and demonstrated that achieving reasonably accurate object pose estimation is possible solely through silhouette information.

The use of silhouettes is the key factor in achieving generalization in our approach. However, relying solely on silhouettes comes with several limitations. STI-Pose requires precise and complete silhouette as input, and when an object is occluded, silhouettes may not be effectively extracted, making the method ineffective. In cases where silhouette ambiguity arises due to symmetry, STI-Pose can align silhouettes but may not provide correct pose values. Therefore, we plan to improve the method for assessing silhouette overlap in future work, enhancing the occlusion tolerance of HSIoU. Furthermore, while we have demonstrated that using only silhouette information can achieve satisfactory object pose estimation, completely disregarding texture information is not an optimal choice. We plan to consider object texture as an optional attribute and incorporate it into the HSIoU calculation. This integration aims to address potential silhouette ambiguity issues by leveraging texture information when needed.

References

1. Bay, H., Tuytelaars, T., Van Gool, L.: Surf: speeded up robust features. In: Proceedings of the 9th European Conference on Computer Vision. vol. Part I, pp. 404–417 (2006)
2. Besl, P.J., McKay, N.D.: Method for registration of 3-D shapes. In: Proceedings of the International Society for Optical Engineering. vol. 14, pp. 239–256 (1992)
3. Brachmann, E., Krull, A., Michel, F., Gumhold, S., Shotton, J., Rother, C.: Learning 6D object pose estimation using 3D object coordinates. In: Proceedings of the European Conference on Computer Vision. vol. Part II, pp. 536–551 (2014)
4. Busam, B., Esposito, M., Che'Rose, S., Navab, N., Frisch, B.: A stereo vision approach for cooperative robotic movement therapy. In: Proceedings of the IEEE International Conference on Computer Vision workshops, pp. 127–135 (2015)
5. Calli, B., Singh, A., Walsman, A., Srinivasa, S., Abbeel, P., Dollar, A.M.: The ycb object and model set: towards common benchmarks for manipulation research. In: Proceedings of thr IEEE International Conference on Advanced Robotics, pp. 510–517 (2015)
6. Di, Y., Manhardt, F., Wang, G., Ji, X., Navab, N., Tombari, F.: SO-Pose: exploiting self-occlusion for direct 6D pose estimation. In: Proceedings of the IEEE/CVF International Conference on Computer Vision, pp. 12396–12405 (2021)
7. Drost, B., Ulrich, M., Navab, N., Ilic, S.: Model globally, match locally: efficient and robust 3D object recognition. In: Proceedings of the IEEE Computer Society Conference on Computer Vision and Pattern Recognition, pp. 998–1005 (2010)
8. Eberhart, R., Kennedy, J.: A new optimizer using particle swarm theory. In: Proceedings of the IEEE International Symposium on Micro Machine and Human Science, pp. 39–43 (1995)
9. Ghazaei, G., Laina, I., Rupprecht, C., Tombari, F., Navab, N., Nazarpour, K.: Dealing with ambiguity in robotic grasping via multiple predictions. In: Proceedings of the Asian Conference on Computer Vision, pp. 38–55 (2019)
10. Hinterstoisser, S., et al.: Multimodal templates for real-time detection of texture-less objects in heavily cluttered scenes. In: Proceedings of the IEEE International Conference on Computer Vision, pp. 858–865 (2011)
11. Hodan, T., et al.: T-LESS: An RGB-D dataset for 6D pose estimation of texture-less objects. In: Proceedings of the IEEE Winter Conference on Applications of Computer Vision, pp. 880–888. IEEE (2017)
12. Hu, Y., Fua, P., Wang, W., Salzmann, M.: Single-stage 6D object pose estimation. In: Proceedings of the IEEE/CVF Conference on Computer Vision and Pattern Recognition, pp. 2930–2939 (2020)

13. Kendall, A., Grimes, M., Cipolla, R.: Posenet: a convolutional network for real-time 6-dof camera relocalization. In: Proceedings of the IEEE International Conference on Computer Vision, pp. 2938–2946 (2015)
14. Kirillov, A., et al.: Segment Anything. arXiv:2304.02643 (2023)
15. Lepetit, V., Moreno-Noguer, F., Fua, P.: Epnp: an accurate o (n) solution to the pnp problem. Int. J. Comput. Vision **81**, 155–166 (2009)
16. Li, Z., Wang, G., Ji, X.: CDPN: coordinates-based disentangled pose network for real-time RGB-based 6-DoF object pose estimation. In: Proceedings of the IEEE/CVF international conference on computer vision, pp. 7678–7687 (2019)
17. Lowe, D.G.: Object recognition from local scale-invariant features. In: Proceedings of the Seventh IEEE International Conference On Computer Vision, vol. 2, pp. 1150–1157. IEEE (1999)
18. Lowe, D.G.: Distinctive image features from scale-invariant keypoints. Int. J. Comput. Vision **60**, 91–110 (2004)
19. Marchand, E., Uchiyama, H., Spindler, F.: Pose estimation for augmented reality: a hands-on survey. IEEE Trans. Visual Comput. Graphics **22**(12), 2633–2651 (2015)
20. Olson, C.F., Huttenlocher, D.P.: Automatic target recognition by matching oriented edge pixels. IEEE Trans. Image Process. **6**(1), 103–113 (1997)
21. Peng, S., Liu, Y., Huang, Q., Zhou, X., Bao, H.: PVNet: pixel-wise voting network for 6DoF pose estimation. In: Proceedings of the IEEE/CVF Conference on Computer Vision and Pattern Recognition, pp. 4561–4570 (2019)
22. Pérez, L., Rodríguez, Í., Rodríguez, N., Usamentiaga, R., García, D.F.: Robot guidance using machine vision techniques in industrial environments: a comparative review. Sensors **16**(3), 335 (2016)
23. Rambach, J., Pagani, A., Schneider, M., Artemenko, O., Stricker, D.: 6DoF object tracking based on 3D scans for augmented reality remote live support. Computers **7**(1), 6 (2018)
24. Rublee, E., Rabaud, V., Konolige, K., Bradski, G.: ORB: An efficient alternative to SIFT or SURF. In: Proceedings of the IEEE International Conference on Computer Vision, pp. 2564–2571 (2011)
25. Rusu, R.B., Blodow, N., Marton, Z.C., Beetz, M.: Aligning point cloud views using persistent feature histograms. In: Proceedings of the IEEE/RSJ International Conference on Intelligent Robots and Systems, pp. 3384–3391 (2008)
26. Su, Y., et al.: ZebraPose: coarse to fine surface encoding for 6DoF object pose estimation. In: Proceedings of the IEEE/CVF Conference on Computer Vision and Pattern Recognition, pp. 6738–6748 (2022)
27. Suzuki, S., et al.: Topological structural analysis of digitized binary images by border following. Comput. Vision, Graph. Image Process. **30**(1), 32–46 (1985)
28. Tian, Z., Shen, C., Chen, H., He, T.: FCOS: fully convolutional one-stage object detection. In: Proceedings of the IEEE/CVF International Conference on Computer Vision, pp. 9627–9636 (2019)
29. Wang, C., et al.: DenseFusion: 6D object pose estimation by iterative dense fusion. In: Proceedings of the IEEE/CVF Conference on Computer Vision and Pattern Recognition, pp. 3343–3352 (2019)
30. Wang, G., Manhardt, F., Tombari, F., Ji, X.: GDR-Net: geometry-guided direct regression network for monocular 6D object pose estimation. In: Proceedings of the IEEE/CVF Conference on Computer Vision and Pattern Recognition, pp. 16611–16621 (2021)
31. Xiang, Y., Schmidt, T., Narayanan, V., Fox, D.: PoseCNN: a convolutional neural network for 6D object pose estimation in cluttered scenes. In: Robotics: Science and Systems XIV (2018)

32. Zhang, X., Jiang, Z., Zhang, H., Wei, Q.: Vision-based pose estimation for textureless space objects by contour points matching. IEEE Trans. Aerosp. Electron. Syst. **54**(5), 2342–2355 (2018)
33. Zou, X., et al.: Segment everything everywhere all at once. arXiv preprint arXiv:2304.06718 (2023)

Robust Light Field Depth Estimation over Occluded and Specular Regions

Xuechun Wang, Wentao Chao, and Fuqing Duan[✉]

School of Artificial Intelligence, Beijing Normal University, Beijing 100875, China
fqduan@bnu.edu.cn

Abstract. Traditional methods for light field depth estimation establish the cost data to measure the photo consistency of pixels refocused into a specific depth range, with the highest level of consistency indicating the correct depth. These methods are based on the photo consistency of Lambertian surface. However, the photo consistency is broken when occlusion and specular reflection occur. In this paper, a new depth estimation algorithm is proposed to solve the problem that the photo consistency is broken. Firstly, the central view image is segmented into multiple superpixel regions. The cost ranges of the un-occluded points and occluded points in the refocusing process are analyzed, and a penalty term is added to the pixel whose color deviation exceeds an adaptive threshold to detect the occluded points. Because the un-occluded pixels in the angular sampling image still keeps the photo consistency, we propose a voting method to select the un-occluded pixels to obtain the initial depth of the occluded point. We use a method to determine the specular region based on similar features of color and texture in the superpixel region and then present an optimization energy function to obtain the depth of the specular region. Finally, a more accurate depth map is obtained by using a globally optimization. Experimental results show that the proposed method is superior to other comparison algorithms, especially in the cases of the specular regions and multi-occlusion.

Keywords: Light field · depth estimation · occlusion detection · specluar reflection · 3D reconstruction

1 Introduction

Different from traditional cameras, light field [12] can record spatial and angular information simultaneously by a single shot, and it has been used in microscopic scene [28] for life sciences, the temperature distribution reconstruction [32] and 3D reconstruction [7]. Since a single light field image has multi-view information, it can be applied to surveillance security [33] and fake face recognition [8]. Depth information is essential to accomplish these tasks. At present, many depth estimation methods have been proposed using different light field image formats, such as stereo matching in sub-aperture images [4,6], slope estimation in epipolar plane image (EPI) [29,30] and focusness estimation in focal stacks [2,31]. These methods are based on the property of Lambertian surface that the image of a point obtained from different views should satisfy the photo

ⓒ The Author(s), under exclusive license to Springer Nature Singapore Pte Ltd. 2024
F.-L. Zhang and A. Sharf (Eds.): CVM 2024, LNCS 14593, pp. 180–199, 2024.
https://doi.org/10.1007/978-981-97-2092-7_9

consistency. However, occlusions and specular reflections are always present in real scenes. The photo consistency assumption will be broken on the occlusions or specular reflection regions, which results in inaccurate depth estimation on these regions. Therefore, it is very important to accurately handle occlusion and specular reflection problems for depth estimation. Both the occluded and specular regions violate the photo consistency, so we denote the occluded and specular regions as non-photo consistency regions (NPCR).

The previous works [21,22,34] always used the Canny detector to detect edge points in the central view image and identified these edge points as occlusion points. However, some occlusion points in non-center view images will be missed. These methods are hard to detect occlusion correctly, which limits obtaining an accurate depth map. For the specular regions, the previous works [19,27] estimated an initial depth map based on the assumption of the photo consistency, and each point was refocused to the estimated initial depth. The angular sampling image was clustered into two clusters to remove the specular reflection component for obtaining the final depth. However, the clustering result will be affected by the error of the initial depth, and it is not suitable for the saturated specular points. In addition, it is time-consuming to process each point in the central view image. At present, it is still challenging to well solve the NPCR problem.

In this paper, we propose a novel depth estimation method which can well deal with the NPCR problem. Our main contributions have four aspects, including

- The central view image is segmented into multiple superpixel regions. The NPCR can be determined based on the characteristic of superpixel which can save more time.
- An adaptive threshold is determined by combining the spatial domain and angular domain. We introduce a penalty term for the pixel whose color deviation exceeds the adaptive threshold to detect the occluded points.
- We propose a voting method to choose the un-occluded pixels from the angular sampling image of the occluded point to estimated the initial depth.
- We use the chrominance similarity among pixels in the same superpixel region to detect specular regions. Then, we develop an energy function to compute the depth of the specular region.

2   Related Work

The main reasons that cause the photo consistency of Lambertian surface to be broken are occlusion and specular reflection. A lot of algorithms have been proposed to solve the two problems separately.

Occlusion Problem. Williem et al. [25,26] defined the constrained angular entropy cost and the constrained adaptive defocus cost to estimate the initial depth map. Zhang et al. [14] proved that if the depth of occlusion is constant in the angular sampling image, the occlusion boundary in the angular sampling image is similar to that of the reference image. Therefore, they estimated the depth map by developing an integral guided filter to estimate the occlusion probabilities in angular sampling images. Han et al. [2] estimated the depth map by counting the number of pixels whose deviation from the refocused pixel to the central view pixel was less than an adaptive threshold. Although they used the adaptive threshold to reduce the influence of the occlusion, the threshold will be affected in the real scene with severe noise. Chen et al. [1] detected partially occluded boundary regions based on superpixel segmentation and applied shrinkage operation on the label confidence map and reinforcement operation on the occluded boundary to estimate the depth map. But the whole algorithm process takes a long time. Wang et al. [21,22] demonstrated the occlusion edges in both spatial and angular domains are consistent when refocused to the proper depth. They divided the angular domains into two regions with the guidance of the spatial domain, and the depth is estimated using the region with less variance. Their method is limited to a single occluder and is highly dependent on edge detection. Zhu et al. [34] improved the occlusion model of Wang et al. [21,22], and proposed a model suitable for both single-occluder and multi-occluder occlusions. They selected the un-occluded pixels using the K-means strategy to estimate the depth map. However, it is time-consuming and is not always effective when multiple occluders are distributed at different depths.

All of these methods use Canny detector to detect the occlusion points in the central view image, but the occlusion points in the other views may be neglected. Different from these methods, we analyze the range of data cost and add a penalty term to a pixel whose color difference exceeds the adaptive threshold to detect the occluded points. We choose the un-occluded pixels in the angular sampling image of the occluded point according to the voting method using an adaptive threshold.

Specular Reflection. Wang et al. [19] used the depth estimation method by Tao et al. [17] to obtain initial depth. Each point is refocused to the initial depth to classify its angular sampling image into two clusters using k-means clustering. Light source was estimated using the difference between two clusters through several iterations to remove the specular reflection component. Wang et al. [27] used a threshold strategy to classify the points in the central view image into saturated specular points and unsaturated specular points, after estimating initial depth using the method by Tao et al. [17]. For unsaturated specular points, they used k-means clustering to divide the angular sampling image into the part without specular and the part with specular. The specular components will be removed using the difference between the two clusters. These methods all use initial depth obtained based on photo consistency to remove specularity. Moreover, all these methods can not handle the saturated specular points. Wang et al. [18] proposed point-consistency to estimate the initial depth and line-consistency to estimate light source color through analyzing the dichromatic reflection model. They estimated the specular intensity using light source color and removed the specular components. Unlike these methods, we utilize the characteristic of superpixel and energy function to estimate the depth of the specular reflection region.

Deep Learning Methods. There are also some learning based methods for light field depth estimation. Shin et al. [15] used a multi-stream convolutional neural network to estimate accurate depth maps with subpixel accuracy. However, their network fails to infer accurate disparities in reflection and textureless regions. Tsai et al. [20] fused multi-view information using an attention-based views selection module and used a spatial pyramid pooling to extract more context information of the image for depth estimation. Huang et al. [5] designed a lightweight disparity estimation model with physical-based multi-disparity-scale cost volume aggregation to estimate depth map.

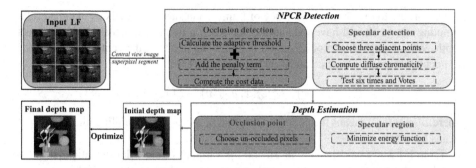

Fig. 1. The proposed algorithm overview. The proposed method mainly consists of four parts: Segment the central view image using SLIC algorithm; Detect the NPCR including occlusion and specular regions; For the occlusion, the un-occluded pixels in the angular sampling image are used to compute the initial depth; For the specular regions, the depth is estimated according to the depth of the adjacent non-specular regions; Depth optimization.

It significantly improved the geometric details near edges by introducing a sub-network of edge guidance. Wang et al. [23] constructed an occlusion-aware cost by modulating pixels from different views and integrated pixels by using the convolutions with specifically designed dilation rates. They aggregated these costs constructed via convolutions to estimate the depth map.

The above methods only consider the occlusion or specular regions, so they cannot handle the two cases well at the same time. In this paper, we unify the two cases into a NPCR problem, and propose a new depth estimation algorithm to solve this problem better.

3   The Depth Estimation

In this section, we first segment the central view image using the SLIC superpixel algorithm. The initial depth map is estimated based on the characteristic of the superpixel region. The final depth map is obtained after optimization. The complete algorithm flow chart is shown in Fig. 1.

3.1   Consistency Data and Confidence

A 4D light field image can be represented as $L(x, y, u, v)$, where (x, y) means the spatial coordinate in the sub-aperture image, and (u, v) means the angular coordinate. According to the imaging characteristic of the light field, the light field image can be refocused to a new imaging plane [12]. Therefore, the refocused light field image $L_\alpha(x, y, u, v)$ is represented as

$$L_\alpha(x, y, u, v) = L(x + u(1 - \frac{1}{\alpha}), y + v(1 - \frac{1}{\alpha}), u, v) \tag{1}$$

where α is the candidate depth label.

According to the photo consistency of Lambertian surface, the pixels in the angular sampling image should have the same color when a point is refocused to the correct depth. We calculate the color deviation between the pixels in the central view and the non-central view in different candidate depths using Eq. 2.

$$d_\alpha(x, y, u, v) = \|L_\alpha(x, y, u, v) - L(x, y, 0, 0)\| \tag{2}$$

where $L(x, y, 0, 0)$ means the central view pixel of the angular sampling image, and $\|\cdot\|$ means L2-norm.

From Eq. 2, we calculate the mean and the variance of the color deviations to measure the consistency of the angular sampling image in different candidate depths,

$$D_\alpha(x, y) = \frac{1}{N} \sum_{u,v} \rho(d_\alpha(x, y, u, v)) \tag{3}$$

and

$$C_\alpha(x, y) = \frac{1}{N-1} \sum_{u,v} \{\rho(d_\alpha(x, y, u, v)) - D_\alpha(x, y)\}^2 \tag{4}$$

where N is the number of pixels in the angular sampling image. $\rho(x) = 1 - e^{-\frac{x^2}{2\sigma^2}}$ is the distance function, and σ controls the sensitivity of the function to large color difference.

The initial depth α^* of point (x, y) can be obtained using Eq. 5.

$$\alpha^*(x, y) = \arg\min_\alpha W_\alpha(x, y) \tag{5}$$

where $W_\alpha(x, y) = D_\alpha(x, y) + C_\alpha(x, y)$. The depth confidence is defined using the mean and minimum of data costs $W_\alpha(x, y)$ among all the candidates as Eq. 6.

$$w(x, y) = 1 - \exp(-\frac{mean\{W_\alpha(x, y)\}/\min\{W_\alpha(x, y)\}}{2\delta_w^2}) \tag{6}$$

where δ_w controls the sensitivity of ratio.

3.2 NPCR Depth Estimation

The occluded region is a small part of the image, and the un-occluded pixels in the angular sampling image still satisfy the photo consistency. Moreover, the specular region is a small part of most images, except when most of the objects in the image are metal or transparent. Therefore, we need to detect the occluded points and specular regions to reduce computational time.

A superpixel is a small region consisting of a series of adjacent points with similar features such as color, brightness, and texture. We use the SLIC superpixel segmentation algorithm [13] to segment the central view image. In the experiments, the size of superpixel segmentation is set as 15. We take the light field image *Mona* as an example shown in Fig. 2(a). From Fig. 2(a), we can find that the light field image is divided to many tiny regions, and each region is a superpixel.

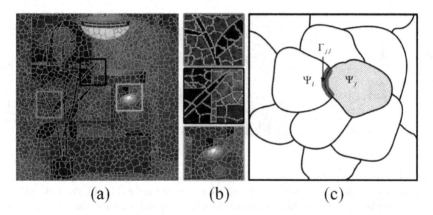

Fig. 2. (a) The superpixel segmentation result of the light field image *Mona*. (b) Zoom in on some small regions that contains occlusion and specular for a clearer observation. (c) The illustration of boundary points set $\Gamma_{j,l}$ between two adjacent superpixels Ψ_j and Ψ_l.

To more clearly show the relationship of adjacent superpixels and their boundary points, a concise illustration is shown in Fig. 2(c). These superpixels are noted as $\Psi_j, j = 1, 2, ..., n$. It is not difficult to find that the occluded points only exist at the boundary of two adjacent superpixel regions, as shown in the green region $\Gamma_{j,l}$ in Fig. 2(c). We define these pixels as the boundary region by dilating the edge of two adjacent superpixels. From Fig. 2, the occluded points are located at the boundary of the superpixel and in the region near the boundary of the superpixel, and the specular points are clustered in a superpixel. In conclusion, we identify occluded points and specular points from the superpixel boundary to the interior. It can reduce the time of detecting occluded points and specular regions.

Occluded Points. If there exist occluded pixels in the angular sampling image, the photo consistency will be broken. It is key that the occluded points should be detected accurately. There is an important prior condition that the occluder and the occluded point have a large color difference.

We take the light field image *Mona* as an example, and the illustration is shown in Fig. 3. From Fig. 3(a), the photo consistency of the angular sampling image is the highest when the un-occluded point is focused at the correct depth, and the corresponding data cost is also the minimum of all data costs. From Fig. 3(c), the un-occluded pixels in the angular sampling image of the green point have the highest photo consistency when the occluded point is focused at the correct depth. However, the corresponding data cost is not the minimum among all data costs. In addition, from Fig. 3(a) and (c), we can observe that the ranges of data cost between the occluded point and the un-occluded point are different.

For a more intuitive comparison, we plot the cost curves of the occluded points and the un-occluded points in the same graph. The illustration is shown in Fig. 4. There are four points in Fig. 4(a), which are un-occluded points **A, B** and the occluded points **C, D**. From Fig. 4(b), we can find that the maximum cost $W_{\max}$ and the minimum cost

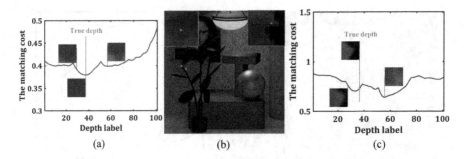

Fig. 3. The cost curves of the occluded point and the un-occluded point in the light field image *Mona* focused on different depth. (a) The cost curve of the red point. (b) The red and green rectangles are the spatial sampling images of the two points in the central view image. (c) The cost curve of the green point. (Color figure online)

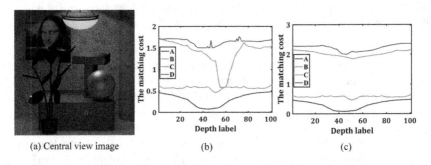

Fig. 4. The trend of the data cost of the four points in the light field image *Mona*. (b) The cost curves of four points A, B, C and D. (c) The cost curves of four points A, B, C and D after adding the penalty term.

$W_{\min}$ of the points **C, D** are greater than those of the points **A, B**. We can identify the occluded point according to the minimum cost. However, the difference between the minimum cost of point **C** and the minimum cost of points **A, B** is small. The reason is that there are fewer occluded pixels in the angular sampling image of point **C**.

To avoid the impact of this case on determining occlusion, we add a penalty weight to pixels that the color deviation $d_\alpha(u, v)$ is too large. We propose an adaptive threshold $\Delta\varepsilon$ to control the color deviation $d_\alpha(u, v)$, which can increase the impact of the occluded pixel on the data cost. The new color deviation $\tilde{d}_\alpha$ can be obtained using Eq. 7, if the color deviation $d_\alpha(u, v)$ is greater than the adaptive threshold $\Delta\varepsilon$.

$$\tilde{d}_\alpha(u, v) = d_\alpha(u, v) + \varsigma(u, v) \tag{7}$$

where $\varsigma(u, v) = |d_\alpha(u, v) - \Delta\varepsilon|$ is the penalty term.

Because different occlusion situations have different color differences, we use an adaptive threshold to judge whether the pixel in the angular sampling image is from the occluder. In Wang's method [22], they proved that the occlusion edge of the spatial domain is consistent with that of the angular sampling image when refocused to the correct depth. We build the local square window W_{UV} centered at $p = (x, y)$ in the central view image, and $U * V$ is same as the angular resolution of the light field image. We compute the color difference $E(p)$ between point p and each point $q = (s, t)$ in the local square window W_{UV},

$$E(p) = \|L(s, t, 0, 0) - L(x, y, 0, 0)\|, q \in W_{UV} \tag{8}$$

To avoid the effect of large color differences caused by occlusion or overly small color differences between point p and its adjacent points, we sort these color difference values and define them as a set A_{UV}. We take these values in the middle third of set A_{UV}. According to Eq. 9, the average of these color differences is calculated as the adaptive threshold.

$$\Delta\varepsilon = \frac{1}{k} \sum_{i=k+1}^{2k} A_i \tag{9}$$

where $k = \left\lceil UV/3 \right\rceil$.

We can obtain the new cost curves of the points **A, B, C, D** from Eq. 7 as shown in Fig. 4(c). From this figure, we can find that the difference between the minimum cost of point **C** and the minimum cost of points **A, B** is greater than before. We can use Eq. 10 and the threshold δ_1 (set as 0.5 in the experiments) to determine whether the point $p = (x, y)$ is the occluded point,

$$t(p) = f\{[W_{\min}(p) < \delta_1]\} \tag{10}$$

If $t(p) = 1$, the point p is an occluded point.

When a point is determined as the occluded point. It is obvious that the pixels from the occluder no longer satisfy the photo consistency with the central pixel in the angular sampling image. To obtain the accurate depth of the occluded point, we need to choose the un-occluded pixels from the angular sampling image. The color deviation $d_\alpha(u, v)$ of each pixel (u, v) in different label α is calculated using Eq. 2. If the color deviation $d_\alpha(u, v)$ is greater than the adaptive threshold $\Delta\varepsilon$, we set 0 as the label of this pixel (u, v). Otherwise, we set 1 as the label of this pixel (u, v).

$$label^\alpha_{(u,v)} = \begin{cases} 1, & d_\alpha(u, v) \le \Delta\varepsilon \\ 0, & d_\alpha(u, v) > \Delta\varepsilon \end{cases} \tag{11}$$

Using Eq. 11, we can obtain all the labels of pixel (u, v) in the angular sampling image. The sum of these labels of pixel (u, v) is noted as $s(x, y, u, v)$. If $s(x, y, u, v)$ is more than half of the total number of candidate depth labels, the pixel (u, v) is un-occluded. Therefore, the un-occluded pixels can be accurately chosen using a threshold ξ (set as 60 in the experiments). That is

$$occ(u, v) = \begin{cases} 0, & s(x, y, u, v) \le \xi \\ 1, & s(x, y, u, v) > \xi \end{cases} \tag{12}$$

From Eq. 12, the pixel can be determined as an un-occluded pixel when $occ(u, v) = 1$. Therefore, the initial depth of the occluded point can be determined using these un-occluded pixels in the angular sampling image by Eq. 5.

Specular Region. As shown in the purple rectangle of Fig. 2(b), the specular region is a small part of the image. The point p in the specular region can be described using the dichromatic reflection model [13],

$$I_c(p) = m_d(p)\Lambda_c(p) + m_s(p)T_c(p) \tag{13}$$

where $c \in \{R, G, B\}$ denotes the color channels. $\Lambda_c(p)$ and $T_c(p)$ represent diffuse and specular reflection components, respectively. $m_d(p)$ and $m_s(p)$ are the corresponding weight factors, respectively.

The diffuse components of adjacent diffuse points in the same superpixel region are very close. In addition, because of the small proportion of the specular component in the diffuse point, the weight factor $m_s(p)$ is very small. As shown in Fig. 2(c), if there are three adjacent diffuse points p, p_1 and p_2 in the superpixel Ψ_j, $\Lambda_c(p)$, $\Lambda_c(p_1)$ and $\Lambda_c(p_2)$ should be approximately equal. For the two points p and p_1, we have

$$I_c(p_1) - I_c(p) \cong [m_d(p_1) - m_d(p)]\Lambda_c(p_1, p) \tag{14}$$

where $\Lambda_c(p_1, p)$ means either of $\Lambda_c(p)$ and $\Lambda_c(p_1)$, because $\Lambda_c(p)$ and $\Lambda_c(p_1)$ are approximately equal.

Combining the three color channels, we have

$$\sum_c [I_c(p_1) - I_c(p)] = [m_d(p_1) - m_d(p)]\sum_c \Lambda_c \tag{15}$$

Let $\Lambda_R + \Lambda_G + \Lambda_B = 1$, Eq. 15 can be rewritten as

$$\sum_c [I_c(p_1) - I_c(p)] = m_d(p_1) - m_d(p) \tag{16}$$

Combining Eq. 14 and Eq. 16, we can compute the diffuse chromaticity of p and p_1 in the superpixel Ψ_j,

$$\Lambda_c(p_1, p) = \frac{I_c(p_1) - I_c(p)}{\sum_c [I_c(p_1) - I_c(p)]} \tag{17}$$

Similarly, $\Lambda_c(p_2, p)$ can be also obtained. If the superpixel Ψ_j is not a specular region, the difference in chromaticity values should be very small. Therefore, we have $\Delta\kappa = |\Lambda_c(p_1, p) - \Lambda_c(p_2, p)|$. If $\Delta\kappa$ is larger than a predefined threshold (set as 0.1 in the experiments), the three points p, p_1, and p_2 are voted as the specular points. Because the point p has four adjacent points, each point in the superpixel Ψ_j is tested six times. If the number of votes for the point is greater than 4, then the point is a specular point. If the number of points with votes greater than 4 is more than half of the total points in the boundary region of Ψ_j, the superpixel Ψ_j is a specular region.

Let M_j be the set of all adjacent superpixels of the specular reflection region Ψ_j, and $\Gamma_{j,l}$ be the set of boundary points between Ψ_j and $\Psi_l(\Psi_l \in M_j)$. Therefore, the depth of the specular reflection region Ψ_j is computed by minimizing the following energy function,

$$\sum_{p \in \Psi_j} w(p) \|\psi(j) - \alpha^*(p)\|^2 + \lambda \sum_{\Psi_l \in M_j} \sum_{q \in \Gamma_{j,l}} \frac{\|\psi(j) - \psi(\Psi_l)\|^2}{|\nabla I(q)|} \tag{18}$$

where $\nabla I(q)$ is the gradient of the boundary point $\Gamma_{j,l}$, $\alpha^*(p)$ is the initial depth of point p, and λ (set as 0.05 in the experiments) is a weight of the depth of the adjacent superpixel. $\psi(\Psi_l)$ is the weighted mean depth of the superpixel Ψ_l. It is calculated using the following equation,

$$\psi(\Psi_l) = \frac{\sum_{t \in \Psi_l} \alpha^*(t) / \min\{W_\alpha(t)\}}{\sum_{t \in \Psi_l} 1 / \min\{W_\alpha(t)\}} \tag{19}$$

In order to avoid the depth difference of adjacent superpixel regions in the specular region being too large, which will affect the depth accuracy of the specular region, a depth difference threshold is added when optimizing the energy function to discard the unreliable adjacent region. The depth of $\psi(j)$ can be solved efficiently using Eq. 18 within a weighted least squares framework [16].

3.3   Depth Refinement

We optimize the initial depth map using the global optimization. The energy function is

$$E = E_1(p, \alpha^*(p)) + \lambda_s E_2(p, q, \alpha^*(p), \alpha^*(q)) \tag{20}$$

where q is the adjacent point of point p, λ_s is a weight factor (set as 5 in the experiments). The unary term E_1 is defined as Eq. 21

$$E_1 = \sum_p w(p) \|\alpha(p) - \alpha^*(p)\|^2 \tag{21}$$

The smooth regularization term E_2 is defined as Eq. 22

$$E_2 = \sum_{p,q} \frac{\exp(-\frac{(\alpha(p) - \alpha(q))^2}{2\delta^2})}{|\nabla I(p) - \nabla I(q)| + \mu |t(p) - t(q)|} \tag{22}$$

where μ is a weighting factor, $t(p)$ and $t(q)$ mean whether the two points are occlusion points or not, which can be obtained from Eq. 10. $\nabla I(q)$ is the gradient of the point q. The final depth can be derived by solving Eq. 20 using the standard graph cut algorithm [9].

4   Experiment

In this section, the proposed algorithm is evaluated on the synthetic and real light field images. The synthetic light field images are from Wang et al. [22], Wanner et al. [24]

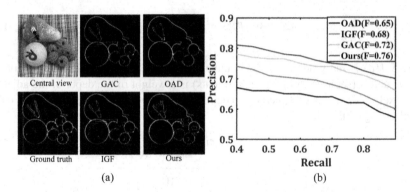

Fig. 5. (a) The visual comparisons of occlusion detection results. (b) The PR-curves of occlusion detection results using OAD [22], GAC [34], IGF [14], and Ours on the dataset from Wanner et al. [24].

and Honauer et al. [3], and the real light field images are collected using Lytro Illum camera [11] and Lytro camera [10]. We compare the proposed algorithm with traditional estimation methods including Wang et al. [22] (OAD), Zhu et al. [34] (GAC), Shen et al. [14] (IGF), Han et al. [2] (OAVC) and Wang et al. [18] (PLC), and the learning based methods including Shin et al. [15] (Epinet), Wang et al. [23] (OACC), Tsai et al. [20] (LFnet) and Huang et al. [5] (Fastnet). Because there are ground truth in synthetic light field datasets, we use the mean squared error (MSE) and badpixel(0.07) error [3] to evaluate the estimated depth results. F-measure [15] is computed to evaluate the performance of the occlusion detection methods. The values of the hyperparameters have been stated in Sect. 3. The values of the hyperparameters in the experiments are the ones that have been tested many times or generally recognized, and we will not describe them in detail due to the lack of space.

4.1 Occlusion Processing Comparisons

We detect the occluded points using different occlusion-aware methods including OAD [22], IGF [14], and GAC [34]. The comparison results are shown in Fig. 5(a), which takes the light field image *StillLife* from Wanner et al. [24] as an example. From Fig. 6(a), we can see our method can get more completed occluded points than the other three comparison methods. In addition, we quantitatively evaluate the occluded point detection method compared with OAD [22], IGF [14], and GAC [34] by computing the recall and precision to obtain the PR-curve, and the result is shown in Fig. 5(b). The PR-curve also demonstrates the proposed method performs best. Experimental results shown in Fig. 5 demonstrate that the performance of the proposed method is better than these comparison algorithms. The reason is that the proposed method detects the occluded points according to the minimum cost of each point, while OAD [22] and GAC [34] use the Canny detector to determine the occluded points in the central view image, and the occlusions in other views may be ignored. For IGF [14], the accuracy of occluded point detection is highly dependent on the central view image. If there are too

Table 1. The badpix error of the occlusion points on the synthetic datasets [22, 24].

	Buddha	Medieval	Papillon	Buddha2	Horses	Mona	StillLife	Bedroom	Livingroom	Outdoor	Plant
Epinet [15]	18.22	27.67	43.97	58.71	23.91	22.51	25.81	16.51	13.24	32.56	21.74
OACC [23]	12.71	25.53	31.55	43.67	20.14	18.53	22.17	12.31	10.56	26.73	17.60
Fastnet [5]	16.13	28.93	35.45	55.12	22.88	21.74	24.37	15.55	13.33	30.28	20.91
LFnet [20]	14.39	26.44	37.98	50.52	21.16	23.13	25.66	15.33	14.47	28.77	19.16
OAD [22]	15.01	13.29	24.44	20.70	23.75	20.75	28.82	8.38	10.78	9.87	7.33
IGF [14]	8.34	9.96	20.83	15.79	9.62	12.67	19.63	7.42	10.75	10.85	9.57
GAC [34]	13.64	12.57	15.16	13.85	15.80	18.81	21.71	7.41	11.79	13.88	10.18
PLC [18]	21.13	19.15	25.65	27.64	23.59	22.78	28.93	49.13	22.14	32.65	27.17
OAVC [2]	7.67	12.43	8.91	**12.25**	9.96	10.71	13.32	7.35	9.95	8.87	8.89
Ours	**7.59**	**9.72**	**7.50**	13.89	**8.85**	**8.77**	**12.83**	**6.51**	**7.85**	**6.89**	**5.87**

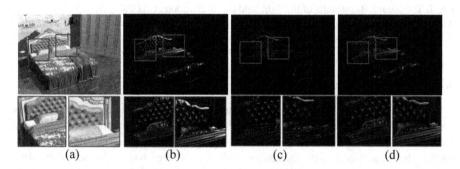

(a)   (b)   (c)   (d)

Fig. 6. The comparison results of the detection of the specular regions in the light field image *Bedroom*. (a) The central view image, (b) The ground truth, (c) Wang et al. [27], (d) Ours.

many noisy and complex occlusions in the central view image, the detection method may fail.

After the occluded points are determined, the accuracy of the depth estimation of the occluded points has a great influence on the final depth map. To quantitatively evaluate the performance of our occlusion detection and processing method, we calculate the badpix error of all comparison algorithms at the occluded points on the synthetic datasets [22, 24] according to the ground truth, and the results are shown in Table 1. From Table 1, we can find the error of the proposed algorithm is much lower than that of other comparison algorithms. OAD [22] can not handle the case of multiple occlusions, and GAC [34] is affected by the distribution of multiple occlusions. However, PLC [18] does not deal with occlusion in the depth estimation algorithm. The proposed method selects the un-occluded pixels in the angular sampling image using an adaptive threshold. It is not affected by different images and occlusion conditions.

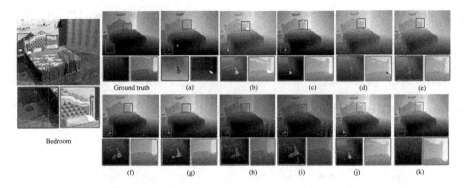

Fig. 7. The comparison results of the light field image *Bedroom*. (a) GAC [34], (b) OAD [22], (c) IGF [14], (d) OAVC [2], (e) PLC [18], (f) Epinet [15], (g) Fastnet [5], (h) LFnet [20], (i) OACC [23], (j) Ours without processing specular, (k) Ours.

4.2 Specular Regions Processing

In this subsection, we evaluate the performance of our specular region detection method compared with that of Wang et al. [27]. The detection results of image *Bedroom* are shown in Fig. 6. From Fig. 6, we can find the proposed method can detect more accurately. The reason is that the detection method of Wang et al. [27] used a threshold value strategy based on the initial depth, and the initial depth is obtained based on the assumption of the photo consistency, while the initial depth in the specular region had a large error. The proposed method uses superpixel segmentation to segment the central view image into several tiny regions. According to the similarity of points in the same superpixel region, each point in the superpixel region is judged without the initial depth, thus improving the detection accuracy.

We also use the compared algorithms, the proposed method without processing the specular points and the proposed method to estimate the depth map of image *Bedroom*. The results are shown in Fig. 7. From Fig. 7, it can be found that there are some holes in the depth maps of all the algorithms except the proposed method. Learning based meth-

Table 2. The badpixel error of the points in the specular regions on synthetic datasets [22, 24].

	Buddha	Medieval	Papillon	Buddha2	Horses	Mona	StillLife	Bedroom	Livingroom	Outdoor	Plant
Epinet [15]	25.81	19.95	21.71	43.37	27.18	33.37	28.19	62.78	58.19	23.67	56.81
OACC [23]	22.11	18.98	20.13	40.17	25.57	29.19	26.76	58.18	53.27	18.87	52.98
Fastnet [5]	26.25	18.82	20.91	42.18	24.57	28.88	26.65	60.19	55.77	22.18	58.91
LFnet [20]	24.13	20.13	21.72	41.18	26.64	31.88	27.71	61.18	59.89	21.36	54.46
OAD [22]	22.13	15.57	13.37	28.97	15.75	18.16	16.56	42.88	32.18	19.97	43.17
IGF [14]	21.87	16.61	14.87	25.61	16.88	17.73	15.58	39.97	28.75	18.53	40.11
GAC [34]	23.33	14.76	15.57	26.73	15.79	18.81	14.34	38.87	26.65	17.73	38.87
PLC [18]	13.36	8.89	9.26	13.86	9.13	10.30	8.87	22.27	13.34	11.23	28.91
OAVC [2]	23.17	12.25	16.36	22.27	16.88	16.73	15.51	36.55	23.73	16.59	32.28
Ours	**9.73**	**7.92**	**7.68**	**10.40**	**7.98**	**9.57**	**10.33**	**16.85**	**9.78**	**8.81**	**18.45**

Table 3. The MSE errors of the estimated depth for the light field images from the synthetic datasets [3,24]. The first set of images is from Wanner et al. [24], and the seconde set of images is from Honauer et al. [3] (Red means the best result in learning based methods, and blue means the best result in traditional methods.)

Image	Epinet [15]	OACC [23]	Fastnet [5]	LFnet [20]	OAD [22]	IGF [14]	GAC [34]	PLC [18]	OAVC [2]	Ours
Papillon	6.12	3.38	7.42	4.98	0.23	0.81	0.41	2.31	0.84	0.32
Medieval	2.28	1.61	3.37	0.50	0.18	1.03	0.67	1.27	0.88	0.09
StillLife	2.43	2.07	23.2	14.1	0.21	1.46	0.23	1.63	1.07	0.17
Mona	1.33	2.33	1.56	0.79	0.25	0.44	0.46	0.79	0.44	0.36
Buddha	0.36	0.78	0.42	0.33	0.38	0.59	0.29	0.64	0.36	0.19
Buddha2	6.64	4.31	5.06	6.06	1.18	0.64	1.02	2.42	1.29	0.53
Hourse	7.35	2.21	5.67	6.32	1.36	1.21	1.37	2.08	0.53	0.77
Average	3.79	2.24	6.67	4.72	0.68	0.88	0.64	1.59	0.77	0.35
Cotton	0.27	0.18	0.32	0.21	0.32	4.31	1.56	2.07	0.60	0.25
Boxes	6.09	3.32	4.39	3.99	9.85	12.32	9.42	10.31	6.99	8.18
Pyramids	0.010	0.004	0.018	0.004	0.021	0.039	0.098	0.21	0.04	0.013
Bakgmamon	2.62	2.69	1.52	3.65	3.71	5.83	6.08	4.67	3.84	2.94
Dots	2.52	1.01	3.17	1.63	3.01	3.89	5.82	3.87	16.6	2.61
Dino	0.17	0.08	0.19	0.09	1.14	0.12	0.31	0.41	0.27	0.54
Sideboard	0.83	0.54	0.75	0.53	2.30	0.13	1.02	0.99	1.05	0.32
Stripes	0.95	0.84	0.98	0.89	8.13	22.81	6.96	4.62	1.32	5.58
Average	1.68	1.08	1.42	1.37	3.56	6.18	3.91	3.39	3.84	2.55

ods also do not work well with specular regions. The main reason is that the learning based methods do not consider the effect of specular regions and the dataset used for training contains fewer specular regions. That means the performance of deep learning methods will be affected by the image characteristics of the training dataset, which has the generalization problems. The experimental results again prove the effectiveness of the proposed method in the specular reflection region.

In order to further test the proposed energy function for estimating the depth of the specular region, we calculate the badpix error of the estimated depth in the specular region using all depth estimation algorithms. The specular regions are detected using the proposed detection algorithm. The results are shown in Table 2. From Table 2, it can be found that compared with other estimation algorithms, PLC [18] and our method have smaller badpix errors. However, the average error of PLC [18] is higher than our method. This mainly because PLC [18] is based on the differences between the specular components in multiple views, but the baseline between the sub-aperture images of the light field camera is too short, which results in a small difference. In addition, PLC [18] can not deal with saturated specular points. Our method uses the proposed energy function to obtain the depth of the specular region based on the depth of adjacent non-specular regions. It also can estimate the depth of saturated specular point.

Table 4. The badpix error of the estimated depth for the light field images from the synthetic datasets [3,24]. The first set of images is from Wanner et al. [24], and the seconde set of images is from Honauer et al. [3] (Red means the best result in learning based methods, and blue means the best result in traditional methods.)

Image	Epinet [15]	OACC [23]	Fastnet [5]	LFnet [20]	OAD [22]	IGF [14]	GAC [34]	PLC [18]	OAVC [2]	Ours
Papillon	35.6	23.6	31.8	34.8	6.35	15.2	7.17	22.7	14.4	5.58
Medieval	18.8	15.4	16.6	11.7	2.22	8.04	2.13	2.49	10.9	0.78
StillLife	11.4	12.7	11.5	11.7	1.72	8.14	2.37	8.67	5.97	2.11
Mona	10.8	9.56	8.89	10.8	4.92	9.79	5.13	9.79	6.01	4.75
Buddha	1.55	3.33	2.23	2.02	7.21	6.85	2.34	3.09	1.78	1.68
Buddha2	34.8	28.6	31.4	34.2	14.4	9.35	10.2	19.1	11.7	8.68
Hourse	16.4	13.7	15.8	16.2	17.7	9.03	6.38	29.2	5.45	7.54
Average	18.5	15.3	16.9	17.4	8.92	9.48	5.12	13.7	8.03	4.44
Cotton	0.51	0.49	0.71	0.27	7.61	7.76	4.37	7.19	2.55	3.38
Boxes	6.09	13.31	18.70	11.04	9.85	12.32	9.42	24.06	16.1	12.36
Pyramids	0.29	0.11	0.61	0.19	0.34	0.41	0.57	0.44	0.83	0.22
Bakgmamon	2.29	4.81	3.75	3.13	3.49	5.15	5.21	5.48	3.12	3.15
Dots	5.36	1.65	21.06	1.43	7.49	7.98	12.41	8.84	69.1	5.85
Dino	1.29	0.97	2.41	0.85	14.91	1.94	2.18	4.08	3.94	2.65
Sideboard	4.81	3.35	7.03	2.87	18.49	2.13	9.29	8.65	12.4	7.96
Stripes	2.46	2.92	9.44	2.93	18.41	29.31	14.99	5.12	29.31	6.88
Average	2.89	3.45	7.96	2.89	10.07	8.38	7.31	7.98	17.17	5.31

4.3 Depth Map

To further evaluate the performance of the proposed algorithm, we use the different comparison algorithms to estimate the depth map on the synthetic datasets [3,24]. We compute the MSE and badpix error to quantitatively analyze the estimated depth map. The results are shown in Table 3 and Table 4. From Table 3 and Table 4, the proposed method achieves the best result compared with those traditional algorithms. Moreover, although the deep learning methods obtain less error in Honauer et al. [3], which is the trianing dataset of these methods, they obtain large errors on Wannar's dataset [24]. To make a qualitative comparison, Fig. 8 shows the estimated depth maps of three light field images. As shown in Fig. 8, the results of the proposed method have clearer boundaries. The depth map results obtained by other compared traditional methods have more noise and fuzzy boundaries. The learning based methods get poor results in the three light field images because their methods are not trained on this dataset [24]. That means the deep learning methods have generalization problems in some other datasets.

Table 5. The running time of all the estimation algorithms. (unit:s)

	Epinet [15]	OACC [23]	Fastnet [5]	LFnet [20]	OAD [22]	IGF [14]	GAC [34]	PLC [18]	OAVC [2]	Ours (w/o specular)	Ours
Time	3.51	0.049	1.71	2.77	362.38	425.93	635.17	398.42	105.58	315.33	371.88
Language	Python/CUDA	Python/CUDA	Python/CUDA	Python/CUDA	Matlab/C++	Matlab/C++	Matlab/C++	Matlab/C++	Python/CUDA	Matlab/C++	Matlab/C++

We also accomplish a lot of experiments to evaluate the performance of our method in real scenes. The estimated depth maps of four images with occlusion and specular

Fig. 8. Depth estimation for synthetic light field images. The first two images are from the dataset [24], and the third image is from the dataset [3]. (a) GAC [34], (b) OAD [22], (c) IGF [14], (d) OAVC [2], (e) PLC [18], (f) Epinet [15], (g) LFnet [20], (h) Fastnet [5], (i) OACC [23], (j) Ours.

regions from the real datasets [10,11] as shown in Fig. 9. The results of the first two images demonstrate our method is effective in occlusion modeling, whether for single occluders or multiple occluders. The results of the last two images show that our method is effective for depth estimation of the specular regions. Although PLC [18] performs better in the specular regions, the method gets too smooth occlusion boundary. The other traditional methods and deep learning methods all produce some holes in the specular regions. The experiment results verify the proposed method can handle occlusions and specular regions effectively.

4.4 Computational Time

The proposed method is implemented on a notebook computer with an Intel i5 2.50 GHz CPU and 16 GB RAM. The running platform is Matlab R2016b. The running time and

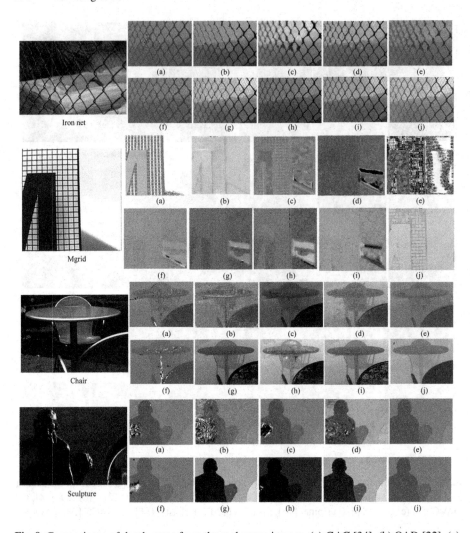

Fig. 9. Comparisons of depth maps from the real-scene images. (a) GAC [34], (b) OAD [22], (c) IGF [14], (d) OAVC [2], (e) PLC [18], (f) Epinet [15], (g) LFnet [20], (h) Fastnet [5], (i) OACC [23], (j) Ours.

running platforms of all comparison algorithms are shown in Table 5. Depth estimation of the specular region is performed by minimizing the energy function using the weighted least square method, which is a time-consuming step in the complete algorithm. We also show the running time with or without specular processing in Table 5. LFnet [20] needs a long time to load the model. OAVC [2] takes less time using Python with CUDA. From Table 5, we can see that compared with traditional algorithms, the proposed method takes less time. The time taken to estimate the depth of the specular region does not affect the running speed of the whole algorithm. In general, the proposed method is faster than most of these compared algorithms.

5   Conclusion and Limitation

In this paper, we present a novel depth estimation method for light field cameras to handle occlusion and specular reflection problems. Firstly, the central view image is segmented using superpixel segmentation algorithm. The occluded point is determined according to the minimum cost value of this point after adding a penalty term to the pixel in the angular sampling image whose color difference exceeds an adaptive threshold. We propose a voting method using label accumulation to select the un-occluded pixels for depth estimation of occlusion points. The specular regions are detected using the properties that the pixels in the same superpixel region have similar diffuse chromaticity. Finally, the depth of the specular region is estimated by minimizing the energy function. The proposed method can detect the occlusion and specular regions accurately and estimate the depth of these regions accurately. Compared with the previous works, experimental results demonstrate that the proposed method has better performance on both synthetic and real light-field datasets, especially in multi-occluder occlusions and specular regions.

The proposed method can accurately estimate the depth of NPCR. However, the depth of the specular region is estimated based on the adjacent superpixel regions. If the specular region is too large or distributed extensively around the scene, the proposed method can not handle such cases. Although we can consider adjusting the parameters of the superpixel segmentation, this would make the depth map too smooth. In addition, this will increase the running time of the proposed algorithm.

Acknowledgments. This work is supported by National Key Research and Development Project Grant, Grant/Award Number: 2018AAA0100802, Opening Foundation of National Engineering Laboratory for Intelligent Video Analysis and Application.

Disclosure of Interests. The authors have no competing interests to declare that are relevant to the content of this article.

References

1. Chen, J., Hou, J., Ni, Y., Chau, L.P.: Accurate light field depth estimation with superpixel regularization over partially occluded regions. IEEE Trans. Image Process. **27**(10), 4889–4900 (2018). https://doi.org/10.1109/TIP.2018.2839524
2. Han, K., Xiang, W., Wang, E., Huang, T.: A novel occlusion-aware vote cost for light field depth estimation. IEEE Trans. Pattern Anal. Mach. Intell. **44**(11), 8022–8035 (2022). https://doi.org/10.1109/TPAMI.2021.3105523
3. Honauer, K., Johannsen, O., Kondermann, D., Goldluecke, B.: A dataset and evaluation methodology for depth estimation on 4d light fields. In: Asian Conference on Computer Vision (2016)
4. Huang, C.T.: Empirical bayesian light-field stereo matching by robust pseudo random field modeling. IEEE Trans. Pattern Anal. Mach. Intell. **41**(3), 552–565 (2019)
5. Huang, Z., Hu, X., Xue, Z., Xu, W., Yue, T.: Fast light-field disparity estimation with multi-disparity-scale cost aggregation. In: 2021 IEEE/CVF International Conference on Computer Vision, ICCV, pp. 6300–6309. IEEE (2021)

6. Jeon, H.G., et al.: Accurate depth map estimation from a lenslet light field camera. In: 2015 IEEE Conference on Computer Vision and Pattern Recognition (CVPR), pp. 1547–1555 (2015). https://doi.org/10.1109/CVPR.2015.7298762

7. Kim, C., Zimmer, H., Pritch, Y., Sorkine-Hornung, A., Gross, M.: Scene reconstruction from high spatio-angular resolution light fields. ACM Trans. Graph. **32**(4), 1 (2013)

8. Kim, S., Ban, Y., Lee, S.: Face liveness detection using a light field camera. Sensors **14**(12), 22471–22499 (2014)

9. Kolmogorov, V., Zabih, R.: What energy functions can be minimizedvia graph cuts? IEEE Trans. Pattern Anal. Mach. Intell. **26**(2), 147–159 (2004)

10. Mousnier, A., Vural, E., Guillemot, C.: Partial light field tomographic reconstruction from a fixed-camera focal stack. Computer Science (2015)

11. Raj, A.S., Lowney, M., Shah, R., Wetzstein, G.: Stanford light field archives (2016). http://lightfields.stanford.edu/

12. Ren, N., Levoy, M., Bredif, M., Duval, G., Hanrahan, P.: Light Field Photography with a Hand-Held Plenoptic Camera. Stanford University CSTR (2005)

13. Shafer, S.A.: Using color to separate reflection components. Color Res. Appl. **10**(4), 210–218 (1985)

14. Sheng, H., Zhang, S., Cao, X., Fang, Y., Xiong, Z.: Geometric occlusion analysis in depth estimation using integral guided filter for light-field image. IEEE Trans. Image Process. **26**(12), 5758–5771 (2017). https://doi.org/10.1109/TIP.2017.2745100

15. Shin, C., Jeon, H.G., Yoon, Y., Kweon, I.S., Kim, S.J.: Epinet: a fully-convolutional neural network using epipolar geometry for depth from light field images. In: 2018 IEEE/CVF Conference on Computer Vision and Pattern Recognition, pp. 4748–4757 (2018). https://doi.org/10.1109/CVPR.2018.00499

16. Strutz, T.: Data Fitting and Uncertainty: A Practical Introduction to Weighted Least Squares and Beyond. Springer (2011)

17. Tao, M.W., Hadap, S., Malik, J., Ramamoorthi, R.: Depth from combining defocus and correspondence using light-field cameras. In: 2013 IEEE International Conference on Computer Vision, pp. 673–680 (2013).https://doi.org/10.1109/ICCV.2013.89

18. Tao, M.W., Su, J.C., Wang, T.C., Malik, J., Ramamoorthi, R.: Depth estimation and specular removal for glossy surfaces using point and line consistency with light-field cameras. IEEE Trans. Pattern Anal. Mach. Intell. **38**(6), 1155–1169 (2015)

19. Tao, M.W., Wang, T.-C., Malik, J., Ramamoorthi, R.: Depth estimation for glossy surfaces with light-field cameras. In: Agapito, L., Bronstein, M.M., Rother, C. (eds.) Computer Vision - ECCV 2014. LNCS, vol. 8926, pp. 533–547. Springer, Cham (2015). https://doi.org/10.1007/978-3-319-16181-5_41

20. Tsai, Y.J., Liu, Y.L., Ouhyoung, M., Chuang, Y.Y.: Attention-based view selection networks for light-field disparity estimation. In: Proceedings of the AAAI Conference on Artificial Intelligence, vol. 34, pp. 12095–12103 (2020)

21. Wang, T.C., Efros, A.A., Ramamoorthi, R.: Occlusion-aware depth estimation using light-field cameras. In: IEEE International Conference on Computer Vision (2016)

22. Wang, T.C., Efros, A.A., Ramamoorthi, R.: Depth estimation with occlusion modeling using light-field cameras. IEEE Trans. Pattern Anal. Mach. Intell. **38**(11), 2170–2181 (2016). https://doi.org/10.1109/TPAMI.2016.2515615

23. Wang, Y., Wang, L., Liang, Z., Yang, J., An, W., Guo, Y.: Occlusion-aware cost constructor for light field depth estimation. In: Proceedings of the IEEE/CVF Conference on Computer Vision and Pattern Recognition (CVPR), pp. 19809–19818 (2022)

24. Wanner, S., Meister, S., Goldluecke, B.: Datasets and benchmarks for densely sampled 4d light fields. In: Vision, Modeling and Visualization, pp. 225–226 (2013)

25. Williem, W., Park, I.K., Lee, K.M.: Robust light field depth estimation using occlusion-noise aware data costs. IEEE Trans. Pattern Anal. Mach. Intell. **40**(10), 2484–2497 (2018).https://doi.org/10.1109/TPAMI.2017.2746858

26. Williem, W., Park, I.K.: Robust light field depth estimation for noisy scene with occlusion. In: Computer Vision and Pattern Recognition, pp. 4396–4404 (2016)

27. Xu, C., Wang, X., Wang, H., Zhang, Y.: Accurate image specular highlight removal based on light field imaging. In: 2015 Visual Communications and Image Processing (VCIP), pp. 1–4. IEEE (2015)

28. Wang, Y., Ji, X., Dai, Q.: Key technologies of light field capture for 3D reconstruction in microscopic scene. Sci. China Inf. Sci. **53**(10), 1917–1930 (2010). https://doi.org/10.1007/s11432-010-4045-2

29. Zhang, S., Sheng, H., Li, C., Zhang, J., Xiong, Z.: Robust depth estimation for light field via spinning parallelogram operator. Comput. Vis. Image Underst. **145**, 148–159 (2016). https://doi.org/10.1016/j.cviu.2015.12.007

30. Zhang, Y., et al.: Light-field depth estimation via epipolar plane image analysis and locally linear embedding. IEEE Trans. Circuits Syst. Video Technol. **27**(4), 739–747 (2017)

31. Zhang, Y., Dai, W., Xu, M., Zou, J., Zhang, X., Xiong, H.: Depth estimation from light field using graph-based structure-aware analysis. IEEE Trans. Circuits Syst. Video Technol. **30**(11), 4269–4283 (2020)

32. Zhao, W., Zhang, B., Xu, C., Duan, L., Wang, S.: Optical sectioning tomographic reconstruction of three-dimensional flame temperature distribution using single light field camera. IEEE (2) (2018)

33. Zhu, H., Wang, Q., Yu, J.: Light field imaging: models, calibrations, reconstructions, and applications. Front. Inf. Technol. Electron. Eng. **18**(9), 1236–1249 (2017)

34. Zhu, H., Wang, Q., Yu, J.: Occlusion-model guided antiocclusion depth estimation in light field. IEEE J. Select. Topics Signal Process. **11**(7), 965–978 (2017). https://doi.org/10.1109/JSTSP.2017.2730818

Foreground and Background Separate Adaptive Equilibrium Gradients Loss for Long-Tail Object Detection

Tianran Hao⬤, Ying Tao⬤, Meng Li⬤, Xiao Ma⬤, Peng Dong⬤,
Lisha Cui⬤, Pei Lv$^{(\boxtimes)}$⬤, and Mingliang Xu⬤

Zhengzhou University, Zhengzhou 450001, Henan, China
`ielvpei@zzu.edu.cn`

Abstract. The current mainstream object detection methods usually tend to implement on datasets where the categories remain balanced, and have made great progress. However, in the presence of long-tail distribution, the performance is still unsatisfactory. Long-tail data distribution means that a few head classes occupy most of the data, while most of the tail classes are not representative, and tail classes are excessive negatively suppressed during training. Existing methods mainly consider suppression from negative samples of the tail classes to improve the detection performance of the tail classes, while ignoring suppression from correct background prediction. In this paper, we propose a new Foreground and Background Separate Adaptive Equilibrium Gradients Loss for Long-Tail Object Detection (FBS-AEGL) to deal with the problem mentioned above. Firstly, we introduce the numerical factor among categories to weight different classes, then adaptively leverage the suppression of head classes according to the logit value of the network output. Meanwhile, dynamically adjusting the suppression gradient of the background classes to protect the head and common classes while improving the detection performance of the tail classes. We conduct comprehensive experiments on the challenging LVIS benchmark. FBS-AEGL Loss achieved the competitive results, with 29.8% segmentation AP and 29.4% box AP on LVIS v0.5 and 28.8% segmentation AP and 29.4% box AP on LVIS v1.0 based on ResNet-101.

Keywords: Long-tail distribution · Object detection · Re-weighting · Equilibrium gradients

1 Introduction

Object detection is one of the most representative and challenging tasks in computer vision and plays a central role in other related tasks. Most datasets for

This work was supported in part by the Zhengzhou Major Science and Technology Project under Grant 2021KJZX0060-6, in part by China Postdoctoral Science Foundation under Grant 2021TQ0301, and in part by the National Natural Science Foundation of China under Grant 62372415, 62036010, 62106232.

F.-L. Zhang and A. Sharf (Eds.): CVM 2024, LNCS 14593, pp. 200–218, 2024.
https://doi.org/10.1007/978-981-97-2092-7_10

general-purpose object detection, such as PASCAL VOC [6] and MS COCO [17], are large-scale and manually balanced by collecting common classes, each with a large number of annotations. In realistic scenarios and practical applications, the data usually shows a long-tail distribution [23], and the detection performance of the tail class decreases rapidly.

The reason for this phenomenon is that the performance of deep learning based methods is built on a large amount of data. The data amount of head classes occupies a large proportion of the whole dataset, while that of tail classes can not enable the model to be trained adequately. Moreover, during the training process, other classes often become the negative samples of the tail class, so the gradient of positive and negative samples received by the tail classes are usually in an imbalanced condition and judged as the incorrect classes. In this situation, the performance of using the traditional object detector will be greatly affected, and the prediction results will be more biased towards the head classes.

To overcome the impact generated by this imbalance data distribution, some researchers have proposed re-sampling and re-weighting strategies to address the long-tail distribution. Existing methods use re-sampling [7, 10, 24, 32, 33] to rebalance the dataset and manually change the distribution of the long tail classes of the datasets. Re-weighting methods [12, 27, 28, 31] rebalance the classes by tuning the weights of different classes during the training process. While all these methods improve results to varying degrees, re-sampling may risk over-fitting and under-fitting. Re-weighting methods primarily focus on suppressing negative gradients from incorrect foreground classification, overlooking the importance of negative gradients from correct background classification. In the background case, the loss received by the classification branch suppresses all

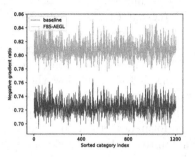

Fig. 1. Percentage of accumulative negative gradients for baseline (blue) and FBS-AEGL (red). The x-axis is the sorted category index of 1203 categories of the LVIS v1.0 dataset. The y-axis is the ratio of accumulative negative gradient for foreground classification and background anchors. We found that the percentage of negative gradients from background is much higher compared to the incorrect foreground prediction.

foreground class prediction scores. Depicted in Fig. 1, we study the effect of such discouraging gradients on the different categories of a long-tail dataset. The curve indicates the ratio of negative gradients generated by the incorrect foreground classes to ground-truth background. A smaller ration represents that background produces more negative gradients. We find that discouraging gradients from background classification contribute a much higher percentage of total discouraging gradients compared to that of incorrect foreground prediction. While re-weighting methods cannot balance multiple factors simultaneously.

In this paper, we propose a foreground and background separate adaptive equilibrium gradients loss (FBS-AEGL) to address above observed problems. FBS-AEGL mainly relies on the weight factor to regulate the learning process of the object detection network. To clearly demonstrate how the FBS-AEGL works in long-tail object detection, we incorporate FBS-AEGL into a two-stage detector, Mask R-CNN, as our baseline in Fig. 2. For the proposals of foreground regions, we first evaluate the quality of samples in each class of the dataset to calculate the number of effective samples in each class. The loss in the prior data volume is rebalanced and reweighted according to the maximum marginal benefit that can be extracted by the network. Then, during the learning process of the model, the logit value of the network output is compared, and a reasonable threshold is set to choose a better sampling level by targeted suppression of the head classes rather than suppressing all negative samples in the tail classes.

Foreground weight factors can effectively mitigate the suppression of classes from foreground region proposals. Considering the balance of gradients for the background region proposals is also essential, we propose background weighting factor for the foreground region proposals. In detail, the Bernoulli distribution is introduced to combine the background weighting factor and foreground weighting factor, and allow the network to fine-tune the overall weights in a stochastic manner. This combination of weighting factors by FBS-AEGL can effectively improve the attention of the network to the tail classes and protect the performance of the head and common classes from excessive suppression while improving the performance of the tail classes.

The proposed FBS-AEGL is trained on two versions of LVIS dataset and evaluated accordingly. Comprehensive experiments demonstrate the effectiveness of FBS-AEGL, with a more competitive performance relative to previous methods. Our main contributions are as follows:

- We propose a new loss function that firstly adopts the weighting factors based on the learning state output of the network and the quality of the dataset, which can efficiently deal with the long-tail object detection problem.
- The loss function is further extended by equalizing the negative gradients generated in the background class, which improves the prediction results of those negative samples in the tail classes.
- We conduct the experiments on the LVIS dataset with a long-tail distribution, and achieve significant improvements, which validate the effectiveness of our method.

2   Related Works

2.1   General Object Detection

With the emergence of convolutional neural networks, many deep learning-based object detection algorithms have achieved quite good detection results. In

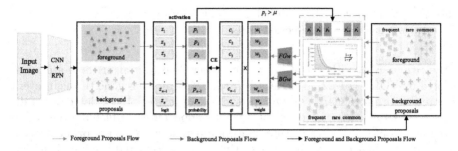

Fig. 2. An illustration of our proposed adaptive foreground and background class suppression loss with two-stage detector. For the proposals, different shapes represent different categories, and different colors of the same category represent different stages. The logit represents the output of the network. Different re-weighting strategies for the foreground and background proposals are adopted, which are FGw and BGw, respectively. Activation means the activation function, such as sigmoid and softmax. CE denotes the cross-entropy function.

general, deep learning-based object detection algorithms can be divided into tow-stage [2,8,11,25] and one-stage methods [16,18,22]. The key difference between the two methods is that the two-stage algorithm needs to generate a proposal (a pre-selected box that could potentially contain the object to be detected) and then perform fine-grained object detection, while the one-stage algorithm extracts feature directly in the network to predict object classification and location.

Two-Stage Methods. The regional-based convolutional neural network (R-CNN) series of work is the most representative work of two-stage object detection methods. The R-CNN [9] first generates 2,000 candidate detections that are most likely to be objects using a selective search method [29], then extracts the depth features of these candidate detection using a deep convolutional neural network, and finally performs classification and regression using a support vector machine. Since R-CNN extracts the depth features of each candidate detection separately, it suffers from the problem of slow inference speed. Fast R-CNN [8] is an improved work of R-CNN. Fast R-CNN first extracts the depth features of the whole image, then scales the features of the candidate detection to a fixed size using region of interest (RoI) pooling operation, and finally performs classification and regression using the fully connected layer. Unlike the previous Fast R-CNN [8], which relies on selective search algorithm, Faster R-CNN [25] introduces the Region Proposal Network (RPN), and unifies the generation of candidate windows with the classification and regression of candidate windows into a single network for learning together. Via adding a mask prediction branch in the Faster R-CNN architecture, Mask R-CNN [11] bridges the gap between object detection and instance segmentation. Different with the two-stage methods, the one-stage methods does not need to get the proposal box stage and directly generates the class probability and position coordinate values of the object, so it has a faster detection speed.

One-Stage Methods. The one-stage object detection algorithms are represented by YOLO [20–22,30] series and SSD [18], which has gone through several iterations. In particular, YOLOv5 provides a variety of object detectors of different sizes to satisfy the needs of different applications, and has been widely used in real-life. SSD uses feature maps of different scales to perform detection, with large scale feature maps for detecting small objects and small scale feature maps for detecting large objects. In general, two-stage methods are more precise in detection, while one-stage methods are faster in inference.

2.2   Long-Tail Object Detection

Re-sampling. Re-sampling [10,26,32,33] is a most intuitive solution by randomly duplicating more target data from the tail classes for training or removing a certain amount of target data from head classes to tackle the long-tail distribution problem. While those methods achieve significant improvement, they may still have significant over-fitting problems among them. Other works [7,24,34] balance data distribute through meta-learning or memory augmentation. For example, they introduce a new quality ranking of candidate regions to enhance the datasets.

Re-weighting. Another typical strategy re-weighting [5,27,28] is to give different weights to different classes by the loss function, giving a relatively high weight to the loss of the tail class to expand the impact on the training samples of the tail class, or more fine-grained adjustment at the sample level by multiplying different weights on different training samples to reweight the network loss at the category level. Seesaw loss [31] dynamically rebalances the positive and negative gradients of each sample using a mitigation factor and a compensation factor. EFL [14] focuses on the degree of imbalance between positive and negative samples of each category by introducing a category-dependent moderator. However, the above methods do not take into account the different prediction results of the background and foreground classes, and ignore the treatment of the background classes.

Other-Methods. GOL [1] points out that the use of Sigmoid or Softmax functions is responsible for the poor performance of long-tail object detection, and the use of Gumbel activation functions that are more suitable for long-tail data distribution. AHRL [13] visualizes the feature representation of each category in the learned feature space to address the long-tail problem in a coarse-to-fine manner. LDAM [3] is minimized based on the marginal generalization bound. Balanced Group Softmax (BAGS) [15] divides classes with similar number of samples into groups and applies a softmax function to each group, but with inconsistent training between neighboring classes of similar size. NORCAL [19] investigates a post-processing calibration of confidence scores. ROG [35] design a generalized average precision (GAP) lossto explicitly optimize the global-level score ranking across different objects.

Unlike the above methods, our method focuses on both foreground and background categories. We start from the impact of the data volume of the dataset itself on the model, and adaptively adjust the suppression gradient of each class according to the logit value of the model output, so that the model focuses more on the tail class and improves the discriminative ability between semantically similar categories of the head classes and tail ones.

3   Methodology

As mentioned in Sect. 1, for long-tail object detection, equilibrium gradients from foreground and background region proposals for categories are two intertwined and equally vital parts, while the quantity and difficulty of data is root cause. In this work, we propose Foreground and Background Separate Adaptive Equilibrium Gradients Loss to balance gradient for each category, which consists of two components: 1) adaptive dynamically adjusts gradient for each class from foreground region proposals, 2) adaptive further balances gradient for each class from background region proposals. The proposed FBS-AEGL is flexible enough to be applied to existing detectors.

3.1   Revisiting Sigmoid Cross-Entropy Loss

The sigmoid cross-entropy loss is widely adopted in object detection, so we first revisit it:

$$p_i = \frac{1}{1 + e^{-z_i}}, \tag{1}$$

$$L_{BCE} = -\sum_{i=1}^{C} \log\left(\hat{p}_i\right), \quad \hat{p}_i = \begin{cases} p_i, & \text{if } i = c, \\ 1 - p_i, & \text{otherwise,} \end{cases} \tag{2}$$

where C is the number of categories. z_i denotes the logit of the network output of class i. p_i denotes the probability that the current sample belongs to class i as calculated by Eq. 1. The gradient of the loss function with respect to z_i is derived as:

$$\frac{\partial L_{BCE}}{\partial z_i} = \begin{cases} p_i - 1, \text{if } i = c, \\ p_i, \quad \text{otherwise.} \end{cases} \tag{3}$$

The sigmoid cross-entropy application with long-tail object detection, giving a sample which foreground prediction of category c, for rare categories $i(i \neq c)$, they will receive negative suppression gradients and result in a low probability of network output. Such negative gradients will occur in large numbers from the frequent classes and impede the positive activation of tail classes. On the other hand, the background samples are negative samples for all categories. Our core idea is to mitigate the negative gradients of each category, both in terms of foreground and background predictions.

3.2 Foreground and Background Separate Adaptive Equilibrium Gradients Loss

In this section, we introduce FBS-AEGL to balance gradients for each category from foreground and background proposals, which considers class sizes and the network learning status.

Formally, we introduce a weight term w to the original sigmoid cross-entropy loss function, and the Foreground and Background Separate Adaptive Equilibrium Gradients Loss as:

$$L_{FBS-AEGL} = -\sum_{i=1}^{C} w_i \log\left(\hat{p}_i\right), \tag{4}$$

$$\hat{p}_i = \begin{cases} p_i, & \text{if } i = c, \\ 1 - p_i, & \text{otherwise.} \end{cases} \tag{5}$$

For a region proposal r, we set w_i with the following as:

$$w_i = \begin{cases} FGw_i, & \text{if } E(r) = 1, \\ BGw_i, & \text{otherwise,} \end{cases} \tag{6}$$

where FGw_i denotes the weight generated by FGw for class i of foreground proposal, BGw_i denotes the weight generated by BGw for class i of background proposal. $E(r)$ indicates whether the proposal is foreground or background. $E(r)$ equals to 1 means r is a foreground region and vice versa is background. FGw and BGw denote the re-weighting strategies for the foreground and background proposals, respectively. The gradient of FBS-AEGL with respect to z_i can be derived as:

$$\frac{\partial L_{FBS-AEGL}}{\partial z_i} = \begin{cases} w_i p_i - 1, & \text{if } i = c, \\ w_i p_i, & \text{otherwise.} \end{cases} \tag{7}$$

We will discuss the FGw and BGw in detail, respectively.

Foreground Weight (FGw). FGw focuses on foreground region proposals to adjust gradients for each class. First, we adopt the weighting factor $(1-\gamma)/(1-\gamma^n)$ that uses the effective number of actual training instances per category to re-balance the loss from class sizes following CB loss function [5]. Where n denotes the number of instances and $\gamma \in [0, 1)$ is a hyper-parameter. Then, we allow the model to more accurately adjust the loss based on the learning status. Finally, we multiply FGw_i by the loss term $-log(\hat{p}_i)$ for category i. The formulation of FGw_i is designed as:

$$FGw_i = \begin{cases} (1-\gamma)/(1-\gamma^{n_i}), & \text{if } i = c, \\ (1-\gamma)/(1-\gamma^{n_i}), & \text{if } i \neq c \quad and \quad p_i \geq \mu, \\ 0, & \text{if } i \neq c \quad and \quad p_i < \mu, \end{cases} \tag{8}$$

where n_i denotes the number of instances belonging to category i in dataset. As category c, FGw_i is set to $(1-\gamma)/(1-\gamma^{n_i})$, if the current proposal belongs to

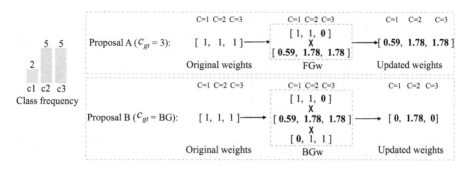

Fig. 3. Illustration of an example which leverages the suppression gradients from our proposed FBS-AEGL. The upper part describes the FGw and the lower part describes the BGw. Here we assume there are three possible foreground classed, and show the ground-truth classes (i.e., c_{gt}) and original weights for foreground proposal and background proposal. Green numbers, blue numbers, and grey numbers are handled by category probabilities, the weighting factor, and Bernoulli, respectively. Red numbers indicate final weights (Color figure online).

category c. For other categories i ($i \neq c$), we apply the sigmoid probability p_i as a signal to decide whether to suppress category i. The sigmoid probability works well because it does not assume mutual exclusivity between classes and can be a good representation of fine-grained features. If p_i is bigger than μ, that means the network considers category i as similar to c, then we set FGw_i to $(1-\gamma)/(1-\gamma^{n_i})$ for discriminative learning. Otherwise, FGw_i equals to 0, FGw_i will be set as 0 to alleviate needless negative suppression. Our proposed FGw integrates the data quantity and the network output probability to adjust the gradient with each class more precisely. Let us consider a three-class example (see Fig. 3), in which c=1 is a tail class, and c=2 and c=3 are head classes. Assuming that foreground proposal A is found from an image: proposal A has original weights [1 ,1 ,1]. Let us suppose c1 = 2, c2 = c3 = 5, and by applying Eq. 8, we get the new weights for proposal A as [0.59, 1.78, 1.78], which reduced tail category suppression for c = 1.

Background Weight (BGw). FGw effectively alleviates negative suppression gradients for each class from foreground region proposals. However, the gradients balanced from the background region proposals is more important, as they occupy a large proportion of the train learning.

Therefore, we design BGw to mitigate negative suppression gradients from the background proposals. Similar to the design of the FGw, we seek to further optimize to determine the category of suppression. The role of BGw is to mitigate the accumulation of small but non-negligible discouraging gradients from the background. We introduce a Bernoulli distribution to better combine with FGw, allowing the network to fine-tune the weights in a stochastic manner [12], thus dynamically balancing the effect of background suppression gradients for rare/common/frequent categories. We formulate BGw_i as follows:

$$BGw_i = \begin{cases} w_{Ber}^i \cdot \frac{(1-\gamma)}{(1-\gamma^{n_i})}, & \text{if } p_i \geq \mu, \\ 0, & \text{if } p_i < \mu, \end{cases} \tag{9}$$

$$w_{Ber}^i = \begin{cases} 1, \text{ if } z_i = 1 \quad and \quad Ber(\sigma_{z_i}) < \sigma_{z_i}, \\ 1, \text{ if } z_i \neq 1, \\ 0, \text{ otherwise,} \end{cases} \tag{10}$$

where $w_{Ber}^i \in \{0, 1\}$ which as a signal to decide whether to suppress category i. If the region proposal r belongs to the background, w_{Ber}^i is drawn from Bernoulli distribution $Ber(\sigma_{z_i})$ which denotes the random value of the class i. The parameter σ_{z_i} determined by the number of low-frequency categories in the current batch of region proposals. If z_i equals to 1 means the network output logit of category i belong to low frequency category, $\sigma_{z_i} = (n_r + n_c)/n_{all}$, else, z_i not equals to 1 means the network output logit of category i belongs to frequent category, $\sigma_{z_i} = (n_f)/n_{all}$, where n_r, n_c, and n_f indicate the number of rare, common, and frequent foreground region proposals in the current training batch, respectively. n_{all} indicates the total number of foreground region proposals, which is equal to the sum of n_r, n_c, and n_f. As shown in the lower part of Fig. 3, assuming that background proposal B is found from an image: proposal B has initial weights [1, 1, 1], by applying Eq. 9, we get the new weights for proposal B as [0, 1.78, 0] that eliminate the suppression of the tail category.

In summary, we design FGw and BGw strategies for the foreground and background, respectively, which takes into class sizes and the network learning status to balance gradients for each category.

4   Experiments on LVIS

4.1   Datasets and Evaluation Metric

We perform experiments on the long-tail and large-scale dataset LVIS [10], which has accurate bounding box and mask annotations each categories. We mainly conduct experiments on the challenging LVIS v1.0 dataset that contains 1203 categories. We train our model on the training set (100K images) and evaluate it on the validation set (19.8K images). LVIS counts the number of images in each category and then divides all categories into three groups: frequent category with more than 100 images, common category with 11–100 images, and rare category with less than 10 images. In addition to the widely used IoU threshold (0.5 - 0.95) for the metric AP, LVIS also reports AP_r (rare category), AP_c (common category), and AP_f (frequent category) to portray the performance of long-tail classes. Like most existing works, we have experimented predominantly with the LVIS v1.0 dataset and present extra key results on LVIS v0.5 dataset. As shown in Fig. 4, we visualize the number of training instances for categories in LVIS v0.5 and v1.0 training set.

4.2   Implementation Details

For our experiments, we choose Mask R-CNN detector with FPN structure. To compare with the state-of-the-art methods, we also employ Mask R-CNN on LVIS v0.5 and v1.0 datasets, using different backbones, in combination with our proposed FBS-AEGL. The ResNet backbone is initialized by the ImageNet pre-training model. During the training phase, scale jitter and random horizontal flipping are adopted as the default data augmentation. We use 4 GPUs (NVIDIA Tesla V100) with a batch size of 16 (4 images on each GPU). The optimizer is set to stochastic gradient descent (SGD) with 0.9 momentum and 0.0001 weight decay. The initial learning rate is set to 0.02 and is warmed up with 500 iterations. The learning rate decays to 0.002 at epoch 16 and to 0.0002 at epoch 22. The total number of training epochs is 24. During the inference phase, we first resize the images used to shortside of 800 pixels

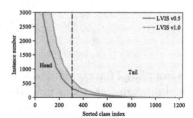

Fig. 4. Statistics of instance number for each category on LVIS v0.5 and v1.0 training set.

and longside of no more than 1333 pixels. We begin by applying Non-Maximal Suppression, with an IoU threshold of 0.5, to eliminate duplicate items. After that the first 300 detections will be chosen to be final result. The other hyper-parameter settings, such as anchor scale and anchor ratio, are consistent with the same default settings in MMDetection [4]. We concentrate on the classification sub-network of the Mask R-CNN in our experiments using FBS-AEGL Loss and replace the original softmax cross-entropy loss using our proposed loss function for long-tail datasets with repeat factor sampling (RFS) [10].

4.3   Ablation Studies

In order to better analyze FBS-AEGL, we set up the following groups of ablation experiments:

Effectiveness of FGw and BGw. In addition to this, we perform ablation experiments to verify the performance of the core strategy in our method with Mask R-CNN ResNet-50-FPN backbone. FGw, BGw denote foreground and background suppression factor, respectively. FGw focuses on foreground region proposals to adjust gradients for each class. BGw effectively alleviates negative suppression gradients each class from background region proposals. As shown in Table 1, the 6.4% box AP and 9.3% box AR improvement is achieved on the network with FGw, BGw which demonstrate the effectiveness of its two factors.

Sampling Factor γ and Suppressing Factor μ. FBS-AEGL introduces two hyper-parameters, which are the sampling factor and the suppressing factor.

Table 1. Ablation study of FGw, BGw in FBS-AEGL with Mask R-CNN and ResNet-50-FPN as the backbone for LVIS v1.0 val set. FGw, BGw indicate foreground and background suppression factor respectively.

FGw	BGw	AP^b	AP	AP_r	AP_c	AP_f	AR^b
		21.4	20.5	1.1	18.6	31.0	28.4
√		26.6	26.9	16.2	27.3	29.7	37.0
	√	26.8	27.0	18.0	26.6	31.0	37.1
√	√	**27.8**	**27.6**	**19.1**	**27.0**	**32.5**	**37.7**

The sampling factor γ defines the effective number of actual training instances. The suppressing factor μ indicates the degree of suppression for each category which is a trade-off between reliving over-suppression on tail classes and chasing discriminative learning. A small μ means that most of the categories will be suppressed, which will suppress too much on tail categories. However, for an extremely large μ, the network will only suppress categories with extremely high confidences while ignore most of the other categories, thus will weaken the classifier's discriminative power. For all experiments we mainly use ResNet-50 Mask R-CNN and LVIS v1.0 dataset. To explore how γ and μ influence the predicted results, we experiment with several different values and the results are reported in Table 2. As shown in Table 2, both the sampling factor and the suppressing factor have played an essential role in FBS-AEGL. Through the two components working in synergy, FBS-AEGL dramatically improves the performance of improved baseline from 21.4% box AP to 27.8% box AP. We empirically find $\gamma = 0.7$ and $\mu = 0.7$ works best under current setting.

Table 2. Ablation study of the hyper-parameter γ and μ.

μ	γ	AP^b	AP	AP_r	AP_c	AP_f
0.01	0.7	25.1	25.6	16.0	24.3	31.3
0.1	0.7	25.6	25.2	17.7	24.4	30.4
0.3	0.7	26.7	26.7	18.9	25.8	31.2
0.5	0.7	27.3	27.1	19.4	26.6	31.0
0.7	0.7	**27.8**	**27.6**	19.1	27.0	**32.5**
0.9	0.7	27.1	27.0	17.7	26.3	32.2
0.7	0.5	27.4	27.1	18.1	27.0	31.2
0.7	0.6	27.6	27.4	19.6	**27.1**	31.2
0.7	0.8	27.7	27.5	**20.4**	27.0	31.2
0.7	0.9	27.6	27.1	18.8	26.8	31.1

Table 3. Comparative results for LVIS v1.0 val set using random sampler and RFS sampler in FBS-AEGL with Mask R-CNN and ResNet-50-FPN as the backbone.

Sampler	AP^b	AP	AP_r	AP_c	AP_f
Random	27.4	27.1	18.1	27.0	31.2
RFS	27.8	27.6	19.1	27.0	32.5

Table 4. Ablation study of the weighting factor in FBS-AEGL with Mask R-CNN and ResNet-50-FPN as the backbone.

Method	AP^b	AP	AP_r	AP_c	AP_f
w/o WF	27.0	27.0	18.1	26.0	31.9
w/ WF	27.8	27.6	19.1	27.0	32.5

Table 5. Comparisons our proposed method plugged into various loss functions for LVIS v1.0 val set. # indicated used RFS sampler.

Method	backbone	AP^b	AP	AP_r	AP_c	AP_f
Mask R-CNN# w/CE	ResNet-50-FPN	24.7	23.7	13.3	23.0	29.0
FBS-AEGL# w/CE	ResNet-50-FPN	27.8	27.6	19.1	27.0	32.5
FBS-AEGL# w/GOL	ResNet-50-FPN	28.0	27.8	21.9	27.9	32.5
Mask R-CNN# w/CE	ResNet-101-FPN	27.0	25.7	17.5	24.6	30.6
FBS-AEGL# w/CE	ResNet-101-FPN	29.4	28.8	21.6	28.4	33.8
FBS-AEGL# w/GOL	ResNet-101-FPN	30.4	30.0	23.2	30.4	34.1

Random Sampler and RFS Sampler. We conduct ablation experiments for different sampling strategies, as shown in Table 3, using random sampler and RFS sampler respectively, and achieved 0.3% box AP improvement using RFS sampler with the same backbone network.

Effectiveness of Weighting Factor. We perform ablation experiments for the effectiveness of the weighting factor (WF) formula $(1-\gamma)/(1-\gamma^n)$, as shown in Table 4, we first ignore the WF in calculating the FBS-AEGL loss, the statistics of a single batch are not representative of the entire training set. In the face of a long-tailed distribution, it cannot optimize the AP for all categories, which leads to suboptimal results. When WF is introduced based on the predefined category distribution of the dataset, the AP gains brings improvements (0.8 points on AP^b and 1.0 points on AP_r). The experimental results verify the effectiveness of the weighting factor, which achieve AP^b of 27.8% and AP_r of 19.1%.

Effectiveness of FBS-AEGL. Our proposed FBS-AEGL is can be used alongside with other loss functions, we perform experiments plugged into GOL methods to confirm the effectiveness of our approach. As shown in Table 5 , the experimental results validate that our method can achieve better results inserted into GOL method. For the baseline model trained with sigmoid CE loss and RFS sampler using ResNet-50 as the backbone, FBS-AEGL loss could improve the AP of object detection. It is noted that the AP for rare categories rises 5.8%. Furthermore, we apply our FBS-AEGL loss with the GOL. We find that FBS-AEGL loss still brings solid improvements (e.g., $+8.6\ AP_r$). We replace ResNet-50 with ResNet-101. Insertion of FBS-AEGL into GOL method which achieves 30.4% box AP, outperforming other competitive methods including GOL (29.2%), ROG (29.3) by 1.2%, 1.1%, respectively. The experimental results have verified the effectiveness of our method.

4.4   Generalization on Stronger Models

We perform further experiments by replacing larger backbones in order to confirm the generalization of our approach. We replace ResNet-50 with ResNet-101 and Swin-Transformer. The experimental results are as the concluded in Table 6. The experimental results validate that our method can achieve good results in better backbone as well. In the case of using ResNet-101 and Swin-Transformer as the backbone, the box AP improves by 8.0% and 10.1%, respectively, compared to the baseline model. In addition, by observing the experimental results, it can also be seen that FBS-AEGL has a huge improvement in handling rare categories under different backbones (e.g., the improved AP_r for ResNet-50 is 19.1%, for ResNet-101 is 21.6% and for Swin-Transformer is 23.0%.), which indicates that FBS-AEGL has an excellent performance in handling long-tail data.

Table 6. Comparisons between our proposed method and the baseline Mask R-CNN based on various backbones for LVIS v1.0 val set.

Method	backbone	AP^b	AP	AP_r	AP_c	AP_f
Mask R-CNN	ResNet-50-FPN	21.4	20.5	1.1	18.6	31.0
FBS-AEGL(ours)	ResNet-50-FPN	**27.8**	**27.6**	**19.1**	**27.0**	**32.5**
Mask R-CNN	ResNet-101-FPN	22.8	21.8	1.4	20.3	32.5
FBS-AEGL(ours)	ResNet-101-FPN	**29.4**	**28.8**	**21.6**	**28.4**	**33.8**
Mask R-CNN	Swin-Transformer	24.6	24.2	2.6	22.5	35.4
FBS-AEGL(ours)	Swin-Transformer	**31.5**	**31.0**	**23.0**	**30.5**	**36.2**

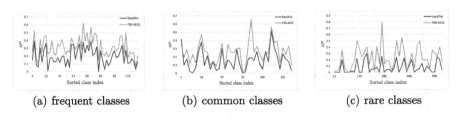

| (a) frequent classes | (b) common classes | (c) rare classes |

Fig. 5. The box AP for the baseline and FBS-AEGL on frequent, common, and rare classes, respectively. For both models, the ResNet-50-FPN backbone is used for training. The x-axis represents the sorted class index. The y-axis represents the accuracy.

4.5   Performance Analysis

As shown in Fig. 5, we exhibit the result of baseline and FBS-AEGL on rare, common, and frequent categories on the LVIS v1.0 dataset. Figure 5(a) displays the AP for the frequent category. The two curves are nearly overlapping each other, indicating that our approach does not compromise the performance of the head category. For the common categories (Fig. 5(b)), our method starts to demonstrate advantages and can even detect many categories that the baseline model cannot detect. As shown in Fig. 5(c), our performance is significantly

Table 7. Comparison with state-of-the-art methods on LVIS v0.5 and v1.0. All models use Mask R-CNN. * denotes that the experimental results in the table are directly from the reference. # indicates that the experimental results are trained with the RFS sampler.

Method	Backbone	Dataset	AP^b	AP	AP_r	AP_c	AP_f
RFS* # [10]	R-50-FPN	LVIS v0.5	25.4	25.4	16.3	25.7	28.7
EQL* [28]	R-50-FPN	LVIS v0.5	23.3	22.8	11.3	24.7	25.1
SimCal* [32]	R-50-FPN	LVIS v0.5	22.6	23.4	16.4	22.5	27.2
Forest R-CNN* [33]	R-50-FPN	LVIS v0.5	25.9	25.6	18.3	26.4	27.6
BAGS* [15]	R-50-FPN	LVIS v0.5	25.8	26.3	18.0	26.9	28.7
LOCE* [7]	R-50-FPN	LVIS v0.5	28.2	28.4	**22.0**	29.0	30.2
DropLoss* [12]	R-50-FPN	LVIS v0.5	25.1	25.5	13.2	27.9	27.3
EQL v2* [27]	R-50-FPN	LVIS v0.5	27.0	27.1	18.6	27.6	29.9
AHRL* # [13]	R-50-FPN	LVIS v0.5	27.4	27.3	17.5	29.0	29.1
FBS-AEGL(ours) #	R-50-FPN	LVIS v0.5	**28.5**	**28.9**	20.9	**30.0**	**30.6**
DropLoss* [12]	R-101-FPN	LVIS v0.5	26.8	26.9	14.8	29.7	28.3
EQL v2* [27]	R-101-FPN	LVIS v0.5	28.1	28.1	20.7	28.3	30.9
AHRL* [13]	R-101-FPN	LVIS v0.5	29.3	29.1	**21.3**	30.7	30.3
FBS-AEGL(ours) #	R-101-FPN	LVIS v0.5	**29.4**	**29.8**	20.7	**31.0**	**31.9**
RFS* # [10]	R-50-FPN	LVIS v1.0	24.7	23.7	13.5	22.8	29.3
LOCE* [7]	R-50-FPN	LVIS v1.0	27.4	26.6	18.5	26.2	30.7
DropLoss* # [12]	R-50-FPN	LVIS v1.0	22.9	22.3	12.4	22.3	26.5
EQL v2* # [27]	R-50-FPN	LVIS v1.0	26.1	25.5	17.7	24.3	30.2
Seesaw* [31]	R-50-FPN	LVIS v1.0	27.4	26.4	19.6	26.1	29.8
FREESEG* [34]	R-50-FPN	LVIS v1.0	26.0	25.2	20.2	23.8	28.9
AHRL* # [13]	R-50-FPN	LVIS v1.0	26.4	25.7	–	–	–
GOL* # [1]	R-50-FPN	LVIS v1.0	27.5	**27.7**	**21.4**	**27.7**	30.4
ROG* # [35]	R-50-FPN	LVIS v1.0	27.2	26.9	20.1	26.8	30.0
FBS-AEGL(ours) #	R-50-FPN	LVIS v1.0	**27.8**	27.6	19.1	27.0	**32.5**
RFS* # [10]	R-101-FPN	LVIS v1.0	26.6	25.5	16.6	24.5	30.6
LOCE* [7]	R-101-FPN	LVIS v1.0	29.0	28.0	19.5	27.8	32.0
EQL v2* [27]	R-101-FPN	LVIS v1.0	27.9	27.2	20.6	25.9	31.4
Seesaw* # [31]	R-101-FPN	LVIS v1.0	28.9	28.1	20.0	28.0	31.8
FREESEG* [34]	R-101-FPN	LVIS v1.0	28.6	27.5	**23.0**	26.5	30.7
AHRL* # [13]	R-101-FPN	LVIS v1.0	28.7	27.6	–	–	–
GOL* # [1]	R-101-FPN	LVIS v1.0	29.2	**29.0**	22.8	29.0	31.7
ROG* # [35]	R-101-FPN	LVIS v1.0	29.3	28.8	21.1	**29.1**	31.8
FBS-AEGL(ours) #	R-101-FPN	LVIS v1.0	**29.4**	28.8	21.6	28.4	**33.8**

better than the baseline. The orange curve (ours) has a considerably larger area of integration than the blue curve (baseline). This indicates that our method protects and even improves the head and common classes, while enhancing the tail classes' performance.

4.6   Comparison with State-of-the-Art Methods

We compare the proposed FBS-AEGL with Mask R-CNN in our experiments and perform with other competitive methods on LVIS v0.5 and LVIS v1.0, and presents the results in Table 7. For LVIS v0.5, we present the results of Mask R-CNN with ResNet50-FPN backbone. Our method achieves 28.5% box AP and segmentation performance of 28.9%AP, outperforming other competitive methods including EQL v2 [27] (27.0%), LOCE* [7] (28.2%) and AHRL [13] (27.4%) by 1.5%, 0.3%, and 1.1%, respectively. These results demonstrate that our method effectively protects the performance of the common class (30.0%) and head class (30.6%) while also improving the performance of the tail classes. Notably, other methods were unable to achieve this level of performance protection for both the head and common classes, further validating the effectiveness of our approach. For LVIS v1.0, we present the results of using the ResNet50-FPN and ResNet101-FPN backbones with Mask R-CNN. For ResNet50-FPN, FBS-AEGL achieved the best performance with 27.8% box AP, outperforming other methods such as ROG [35], AHRL [13], and GOL [1]. With the larger ResNet101-FPN backbone, our method achieved the best results with 29.4% box AP and 28.8% segmentation AP. Although FBS-AEGL Loss doesn't achieve the best result of AP_r, it obtains the competitive result on AP_c or AP_f, leading to the highest overall performance. We speculate the reason is that other methods focus on optimizing the performance of the tail categories at the expense of the performance of common and head categories. While our method focuses all categories, thus can achieve the best overall performance.

Table 8. Results on COCO-LT minival set. AP^m and AP^b indicate the Mask mAP and Bbox mAP, respectively. AP_1^b, AP_2^b, AP_3^b, AP_4^b refer to bin of [1,20), [20,400), [400,8000), [8000,-) training instances.

Method	AP_1^m	AP_2^m	AP_3^m	AP_4^m	AP^m	AP_1^b	AP_2^b	AP_3^b	AP_4^b	AP^b
Mask R-CNN	0.0	8.2	24.4	26.0	18.1	0.0	9.5	27.5	30.3	21.4
SimCal	15.0	16.2	24.3	26.0	21.8	14.5	18.0	27.3	30.3	24.6
FASA	13.5	19.0	25.2	27.5	23.4	–	–	–	–	26.0
FREESEG	15.8	20.6	27.6	28.8	25.1	–	–	–	–	–
FBS-AEGL(ours)	**18.6**	**21.9**	**28.0**	**29.0**	**26.0**	**16.6**	**21.3**	**30.5**	**32.4**	**27.5**

4.7   Evaluation on COCO-LT

To confirm the generalization ability to other datasets, we evaluated FBS-AEGL on COCO-LT dataset [32]. The COCO-LT contains 80 classes and about 100K images. COCO-LT dataset defines four class groups [1, 20), [20, 400), [400, 8000), [8000, -) and reports performance as AP_1, AP_2, AP_3, AP_4. For a fair comparison, we used the same experimental setup as SimCal [32]. As shown in Table 8, FBS-AEGL (with Mask R-CNN as baseline) achieves AP^b of 27.5 with the ResNet-50 backbone, which outperforms SimCal and FASA by 2.9% AP^b and 1.5% AP^b, respectively. And, the rare categories (AP_1^b and AP_2^b) has also been significantly gains. All experimental results demonstrate the advantages and generalizability of our method.

Fig. 6. Prediction results of Mask R-CNN framework without and with FBS-AEGL on the LVIS v1.0 validation set. Compared to the baseline method, our method shows significant improvement on tail, common and frequent classes, and detects many classes that are not detected by the baseline method.(e.g., horse_buggy, gargoyle, silo, steak_(food), walking_cane, telephone). We use red arrows to indicate where we did correct while Mask R-CNN did wrong, and blue arrows to show where we detect while the ground truth is not labeled. (e.g., sunhat, wagon_wheel, dog, sheep). Blue/Green/Red boxes indicate frequent/common/rare category labels. (Color figure online)

4.8   Result Visualization

FBS-AEGL not only improves the performance of the tail classes, but also does not compromise the performance of the head classes and additionally detects some classes that were not detected in the baseline. To better interpret the result, we provide qualizative results on LVIS v1.0 in Fig. 6. We show the (predicted) bounding boxes from the ground truth annotations, the baseline Mask R-CNN, and FBS-AEGL. We observe that our method can accurately identify more objects in rare and common categories that may be ignored by the baseline detector. For example, FBS-AEGL can correctly detect horse_buggy, gargoyle, silo and steak_(food). They are rare or common categories and the baseline detector fails to make any correct detection on them.

5   Conclusion

In this paper, we propose an foreground and background separate adaptive equilibrium gradients Loss (FBS-AEGL) that is introduced with weight factors based on the learning state output of the network and the quality of the dataset itself. FBS-AEGL mitigates the issue of oversuppression of tail classes by head and common classes in long-tail object detection. This improvement aims to enhance the performance of tail classes without compromising the performance of head and common classes. The proposed method further equalizes against the negative suppression gradients generated by the background class. The experimental results on the long-tail dataset LVIS validate the effectiveness of our method and provide a simple and effective solution for long-tail object detection. A future study will explore the use of the proposed FBS-AEGL for other long-tail distributed vision tasks, such as one/few shot learning, and active learning.

Limitations. In FBS-AEGL, we introduced two hyper-parameters γ and μ that need to be tuned for different datasets. In the future, we plan to extend our method by incorporating reasonable assumptions on the data distribution or designing learning-based, adaptive methods. Currently, we focus on the two-stage detector to address long-tail detection, after which we plan to explore simple and fast one-stage detectors that are widely used in the industry.

References

1. Alexandridis, K.P., Deng, J., Nguyen, A., Luo, S.: Long-tailed instance segmentation using Gumbel optimized loss. In: Avidan, S., Brostow, G., Cissé, M., Farinella, G.M., Hassner, T. (eds.) Computer Vision – ECCV 2022. LNCS, vol. 13670, pp. 353–369. Springer, Cham (2022). https://doi.org/10.1007/978-3-031-20080-9_21
2. Cai, Z., Vasconcelos, N.: Cascade r-cnn: High quality object detection and instance segmentation. IEEE Trans. Pattern Anal. Mach. Intell. **43**(5), 1483–1498 (2019)
3. Cao, K., Wei, C., Gaidon, A., Arechiga, N., Ma, T.: Learning imbalanced datasets with label-distribution-aware margin loss. Adv. Neural Inf. Process. Syst. **32** (2019)

4. Chen, K., et al.: MMdetection: open MMLAB detection toolbox and benchmark. arXiv preprint arXiv:1906.07155 (2019)
5. Cui, Y., Jia, M., Lin, T.Y., Song, Y., Belongie, S.: Class-balanced loss based on effective number of samples. In: Proceedings of the IEEE/CVF Conference on Computer Vision and Pattern Recognition, pp. 9268–9277 (2019)
6. Everingham, M., Eslami, S.A., Van Gool, L., Williams, C.K., Winn, J., Zisserman, A.: The pascal visual object classes challenge: a retrospective. Int. J. Comput. Vision 111, 98–136 (2015)
7. Feng, C., Zhong, Y., Huang, W.: Exploring classification equilibrium in long-tailed object detection. In: Proceedings of the IEEE/CVF International Conference on Computer Vision, pp. 3417–3426 (2021)
8. Girshick, R.: Fast r-cnn. In: Proceedings of the IEEE International Conference on Computer Vision (ICCV) (2015)
9. Girshick, R., Donahue, J., Darrell, T., Malik, J.: Rich feature hierarchies for accurate object detection and semantic segmentation. In: Proceedings of the IEEE Conference on Computer Vision and Pattern Recognition, pp. 580–587 (2014)
10. Gupta, A., Dollar, P., Girshick, R.: Lvis: a dataset for large vocabulary instance segmentation. In: Proceedings of the IEEE/CVF Conference on Computer Vision and Pattern Recognition, pp. 5356–5364 (2019)
11. He, K., Gkioxari, G., Dollár, P., Girshick, R.: Mask r-cnn. In: Proceedings of the IEEE International Conference on Computer Vision, pp. 2961–2969 (2017)
12. Hsieh, T.I., Robb, E., Chen, H.T., Huang, J.B.: Droploss for long-tail instance segmentation. In: Proceedings of the AAAI Conference on Artificial Intelligence, vol. 35, pp. 1549–1557 (2021)
13. Li, B.: Adaptive hierarchical representation learning for long-tailed object detection. In: Proceedings of the IEEE/CVF Conference on Computer Vision and Pattern Recognition, pp. 2313–2322 (2022)
14. Li, B., et al.: Equalized focal loss for dense long-tailed object detection. In: Proceedings of the IEEE/CVF Conference on Computer Vision and Pattern Recognition, pp. 6990–6999 (2022)
15. Li, Y., et al.: Overcoming classifier imbalance for long-tail object detection with balanced group softmax. In: Proceedings of the IEEE/CVF Conference on Computer Vision and Pattern Recognition, pp. 10991–11000 (2020)
16. Lin, T.Y., Goyal, P., Girshick, R., He, K., Dollár, P.: Focal loss for dense object detection. In: Proceedings of the IEEE International Conference on Computer Vision, pp. 2980–2988 (2017)
17. Lin, T.-Y., et al.: Microsoft COCO: common objects in context. In: Fleet, D., Pajdla, T., Schiele, B., Tuytelaars, T. (eds.) Computer Vision – ECCV 2014. LNCS, vol. 8693, pp. 740–755. Springer, Cham (2014). https://doi.org/10.1007/978-3-319-10602-1_48
18. Liu, W., et al.: SSD: single shot multibox detector. In: Leibe, B., Matas, J., Sebe, N., Welling, M. (eds.) Computer Vision – ECCV 2016. LNCS, vol. 9905, pp. 21–37. Springer, Cham (2016). https://doi.org/10.1007/978-3-319-46448-0_2
19. Pan, T.Y., et al.: On model calibration for long-tailed object detection and instance segmentation. Adv. Neural. Inf. Process. Syst. 34, 2529–2542 (2021)
20. Redmon, J., Divvala, S., Girshick, R., Farhadi, A.: You only look once: unified, real-time object detection. In: Proceedings of the IEEE Conference on Computer Vision and Pattern Recognition, pp. 779–788 (2016)
21. Redmon, J., Farhadi, A.: Yolo9000: better, faster, stronger. In: Proceedings of the IEEE Conference on Computer Vision and Pattern Recognition, pp. 7263–7271 (2017)

22. Redmon, J., Farhadi, A.: Yolov3: an incremental improvement. arXiv preprint arXiv:1804.02767 (2018)
23. Reed, W.J.: The pareto, zipf and other power laws. Econ. Lett. **74**(1), 15–19 (2001)
24. Ren, J., Yu, C., Ma, X., Zhao, H., Yi, S., et al.: Balanced meta-softmax for long-tailed visual recognition. Adv. Neural. Inf. Process. Syst. **33**, 4175–4186 (2020)
25. Ren, S., He, K., Girshick, R., Sun, J.: Faster r-cnn: towards real-time object detection with region proposal networks. Adv. Neural Inf. Process. Syst. **28** (2015)
26. Shen, L., Lin, Z., Huang, Q.: Relay backpropagation for effective learning of deep convolutional neural networks. In: Leibe, B., Matas, J., Sebe, N., Welling, M. (eds.) Computer Vision. ECCV 2016. LNCS, vol. 9911, pp. 467–482. Springer, Cham (2016). https://doi.org/10.1007/978-3-319-46478-7_29
27. Tan, J., Lu, X., Zhang, G., Yin, C., Li, Q.: Equalization loss v2: a new gradient balance approach for long-tailed object detection. In: Proceedings of the IEEE/CVF Conference on Computer Vision and Pattern Recognition, pp. 1685–1694 (2021)
28. Tan, J., et al.: Equalization loss for long-tailed object recognition. In: Proceedings of the IEEE/CVF Conference on Computer Vision and Pattern Recognition, pp. 11662–11671 (2020)
29. Uijlings, J.R., Van De Sande, K.E., Gevers, T., Smeulders, A.W.: Selective search for object recognition. Int. J. Comput. Vision **104**, 154–171 (2013)
30. Wang, C.Y., Bochkovskiy, A., Liao, H.Y.M.: Yolov7: trainable bag-of-freebies sets new state-of-the-art for real-time object detectors. In: Proceedings of the IEEE/CVF Conference on Computer Vision and Pattern Recognition, pp. 7464–7475 (2023)
31. Wang, J., et al.: Seesaw loss for long-tailed instance segmentation. In: Proceedings of the IEEE/CVF Conference on Computer Vision and Pattern Recognition, pp. 9695–9704 (2021)
32. Wang, T., et al.: The devil is in cassification: a simple framework for long-tail instance segmentation. In: Vedaldi, A., Bischof, H., Brox, T., Frahm, J.-M. (eds.) Computer Vision. ECCV 2020. LNCS, vol. 12359, pp. 728–744. Springer, Cham (2020). https://doi.org/10.1007/978-3-030-58568-6_43
33. Wu, J., Song, L., Wang, T., Zhang, Q., Yuan, J.: Forest r-cnn: large-vocabulary long-tailed object detection and instance segmentation. In: Proceedings of the 28th ACM International Conference on Multimedia, pp. 1570–1578 (2020)
34. Zhang, C., Pan, T.-Y., Chen, T., Zhong, J., Fu, W., Chao, W.-L.: Learning with free object segments for long-tailed instance segmentation. In: Avidan, S., Brostow, G., Cissé, M., Farinella, G.M., Hassner, T. (eds.) Computer Vision. ECCV 2022. LNCS, vol. 13670, pp. 655–672. Springer, Cham (2022). https://doi.org/10.1007/978-3-031-20080-9_38
35. Zhang, S., Chen, C., Peng, S.: Reconciling object-level and global-level objectives for long-tail detection. In: Proceedings of the IEEE/CVF International Conference on Computer Vision (ICCV), pp. 18982–18992 (2023)

Stylization

Multi-level Patch Transformer for Style Transfer with Single Reference Image

Yue He[1,2], Lan Chen[2,3], Yu-Jie Yuan[1,2], Shu-Yu Chen[1,2], and Lin Gao[1,2(✉)]

[1] Institute of Computing Technology, CAS, Beijing, China
gaolin@ict.ac.cn
[2] University of Chinese Academy of Sciences, Beijing, China
[3] Institute of Automation, CAS, Beijing, China

Abstract. Despite the recent success of image style transfer with Generative Adversarial Networks (GANs), this task remains challenging due to the requirements of large volumes of style image data. In this work, we present a deep model called *CycleTransformer* to optimize the mapping between a content image and a single style image by leveraging the strengths of transformer encoders and generative adversarial networks, where we advocate for patch-level operations. Our proposed network contains a Multi-level Patch Transformer encoder (MPT), which enables effective utilization of the style features of different scales. We combine the patch-based features with global feature maps to avoid overfitting to local style patterns, and feed them to a dynamic filtering decoder to adapt to different styles when generating the final result. Furthermore, we use a cycle-consistent training scheme to ensure the balance between content preservation and stylizing effects. Experiments and a user study confirm that our method substantially outperforms the state-of-the-art style transfer methods when both the style and content domain only contain one image each.

1 Introduction

Image Style transfer is a long-standing problem that seeks to convert an image to the style of a reference image. Despite the success of Generative Adversarial Networks (GANs) [12] in generating high-quality results, the requirement of an image database with the same style makes most of them cost prohibitive in real-world applications. To cope with a wide variety of unseen styles provided by common users that do not possess large datasets, some recent works [32,37,42] focus on modeling the internal statistics of patches contained in a content image and an arbitrary style image. They demonstrate the feasibility of exploiting only the information from the single content and style images by deep neural networks for the style transfer task.

Y. He and L. Chen—Authors contributed equally.

Supplementary Information The online version contains supplementary material available at https://doi.org/10.1007/978-981-97-2092-7_11.

F.-L. Zhang and A. Sharf (Eds.): CVM 2024, LNCS 14593, pp. 221–239, 2024.
https://doi.org/10.1007/978-981-97-2092-7_11

Limited by the descriptive capability of the deep features learned by convolutional kernels with restricted local perceptual field and fixed structure, existing methods always generate undesirable stylized results when the reference style uses different patterns to depict the entire scene. Inspired by the powerful abilities of Transformer-based models [7,11,16,31] on encoding rich relationships existing in the input signals for various tasks, we consider that the self-attention mechanism is suitable to explore the internal relationships within the multi-scale image patches by capturing the long-distance dependencies among input elements. Another challenge for the style transfer task is the lack of paired training data. CycleGAN [47] has demonstrated to be effective in learning the style mappings between unpaired data by learning from large stylized image datasets. However, both our source and target domain only have one image each. To optimize the style mappings between two single unpaired images, we introduce a patch-level cycle-consistent learning scheme, which ensures high-quality stylization results that preserve the original semantic content.

In this work, we present *CycleTransformer*, a transformer-based neural method to deal with the style transfer from a single style image to a content image. CycleTransformer leverages patch-level self-attention and cross-level attention information for style mapping function optimization. More concretely, after extracting features using convolutional layers from randomly sampled nested patches of the input image, we not only learn the self-attention information within patches but also learn the attention across the patches of different scales in our novel Multi-level Patch Transformer encoder (MPT). MPT can exploit the possible relationships within and across the sampled patches to describe the style information carried by the input image. Since there is no prior restriction on the learning style, our network needs to cope with the large diversity in image styles, such as different sizes of color pieces and lengths of strokes, we integrate a dynamic filtering module [13] in our decoder to adaptively learn the filters for different styles when synthesizing the final results. Furthermore, To avoid getting stuck to certain local style modes, the learned embeddings by MPTs are combined with global features before being interpreted by decoding layers. When training our model, the cycle-consistent learning scheme is employed to optimize two mappings: mapping from the original image to the reference style and vice versa. Our network has the minimal requirement for common users in image stylization applications, and outperforms state-of-the-art methods on image-translation task when only one target domain image is available. Our main technical contributions are as follows:

- We propose a novel style transfer method with only one reference image.
- We propose a Multi-level Patch Transformer encoder to model the pixel-wise relationships within and across patches of multiple scales for effective patch-level style feature learning.
- A dynamic filtering module is applied for adapting to a broad range of image styles, that cooperates with our cycle-consistent learning framework to balance the content preservation and stylizing effects.

2   Related Work

Neural Style Transfer. Style transfer originated from non-photorealistic rendering [20] and has many applications such as natural image stylization [37,38], augmented reality [1] and human face make-up [23], etc.Gatys et al.are the pioneers who discovered that the features from a VGG-19 model lead to natural stylized results in the seminal works [8,10], booming the development of optimization-based style transfer methods [21,24,35]. Instead of iterative optimization, feed-forward neural networks are proposed to accelerate the transfer process. Early works [17,22,40] train an independent network for each style, while the single network is further extended to multiple or arbitrary style transfer [2,6,25,27,37,44] later on. Other approaches [18,28,30] are based on analogy or deformation, but require similar semantic structures between style and content images. According to the levels of stylization patterns, arbitrary style transfer can be further classified into two lines, *artistic stylization* and *photorealistic stylization*. The first line includes parameterized feature statistics by adaptive instance normalization (AdaIN) [15] and whitening and coloring transformation (WCT) [26]. To generate more sophisticated patterns, Sheng et al.[37] introduce a patch-based style decorator to reserve the detailed styles. The second line both gains stylization results and preserves photorealistic structural information via variants of WCT, e.g. coarse-to-fine recursive filtering [27] and wavelet corrected transfer network [44]. Alternatively, CycleGAN [47] uses a cycle consistency loss to constrain the GAN-based mappings from a source domain to a target domain and vice versa. However, CycleGAN needs large datasets to learn the bi-directional mappings. Park et al.[33] use patch-wise contrastive learning to do one-side image translation and can operate in a single image manner. Their method concentrates on the containing of structure information. Recently, the diffusion model [36] has achieved remarkable results in cross-modal image generation, and it has also been applied to image style transfer. For example, InST [45] uses textual inversion to obtain style-related embeddings from style images and then applies them to the conditional generation of stylized images. While our CycleTransformer aims to discover detailed style patterns with patchwise attention in a cycle approach. Our CycleTransformer can generate both artistic stylization and realistic images in a single-image manner, and allow input images to have different style types and semantic structures.

Deep Vision Transformer. In computer vision, researchers propose attention-based networks to capture long-range dependencies of pixels in images/videos which are beneficial to both classification [5] and regression [7,16,34], especially when coping with comparatively complex images. For image style transfer, some recent works utilize the self-attention mechanism to alleviate inductive bias caused by CNN kernel's priority for local interaction. For example, SANET [32] and AdaAttN [29] propose to learn correlations between the content and style feature maps by a learnable attention module. However, those feature transformation methods always fail to maintain content structures since they simply transfer features across all spatial locations for each channel. Yao et al.[43] add a transformer encoder into an autoencoder network to capture long-range region

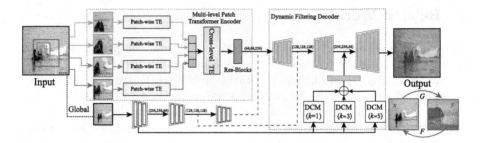

Fig. 1. The architecture of the generator of CycleTransformer. We use a multi-level Patch Transformer Encoder (MPT) to extract features from nested patches. Note that the sub-regions of the patch are randomly selected in the training stage. Thus it can robustly exploit different scales of contextual information at inference with randomly cropped patches. A dynamic filtering decoder interprets the patch-level and global features for result generation. We train two generators sharing the same structure with two discriminators in a cycle-consistent adversarial manner.

relations of the input image. But the patch-by-patch style swap and fusion in their method cause blurring. Deng *et al.*[4] introduce the transformer module into style transfer, taking image patches as words just like in NLP tasks, along with a progressive upsampling decoder to obtain clearer transfer results. Our work uses a transformer-based approach to learn patch-wise style-related attention information for the image translation task.

3   Methodology

Given a content image x and a style image y, our goal is to transfer the style of y to x while maintaining the original semantic content. To achieve that for the two unpaired images, our network is designed to learn the bidirectional mappings between x and y to ensure that the generated image has both appropriate style features and preserves semantic content. Our network contains two mappings G and F sharing the same architecture, where G aims to transfer the style of y to x and F for vice versa. Fig. 1 shows the architecture of the generator of CycleTransformer. Instead of using one global image with a single cropped patch, we utilize the sub-regions of that patch to exploit different scales of contextual information as input. With extracted coarse- and fine-grained style features from *multi-level patch transformer encoders*, a *dynamic filter-based decoder* interprets the local and global features and produces the final translated image. During the inference stage, just randomly sampling one group of local nested patches with global features adequately generates good transfer results because the training stage exploits comprehensive contextual information.

3.1   Multi-level Patch Transformer Encoder

The distinguishable visual characteristics of different styles may exist within different spatial scales. For example, images with some painting styles may have

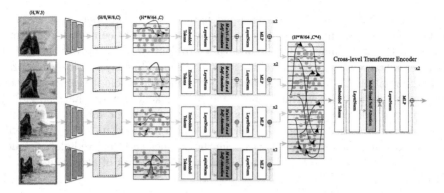

Fig. 2. The structure of Multi-level Patch Transformer (MPT) encoder. We use four patch-wise transformer encoders to learn the relationships within individual patches, and one cross-level transformer encoder to learn the relationships across different scales. The black arrows indicate the feature interactions based on the attention mechanism.

small pen strokes to express their content, while other styles could use much larger color blocks. To enhance the ability to capture visual patterns of different scales, we design a Multi-level Patch Transformer Encoder (MPT). The structure of MPT is shown in Fig. 2. The inputs of MPT are K nested patches of designated sizes, where we set K as 4 in all our experiments. The k-th patch p_k is firstly fed into convolutional layers to obtain its feature maps z^{p_k}, then the element-wise relationships within the patch feature maps are learned by a transformer encoder T, denoted by $t^{p_k} = T(z^{p_k})$. After learning the relationships inside each patch, we concatenate the transformed features and learn the attention information across all the patches through another transformer encoder. More specifically, the K cropped patches are resized to $256 \times 256 \times 3$ and fed to the downsampling sub-modules, each of which consists of one 3×3 convolution (padding=1), a normalization layer and a rectified linear unit (ReLU). We first convolve and downsample the feature maps twice and double the number of feature channels at each downsampling step. The size of the final feature map is $32 \times 32 \times 64$ (H/8, W/8, C). Directly feeding such a feature map to a transformer encoder would result in a huge memory cost. Instead, we unfold the feature map into a length-C sequence of $H \times W$-dimensional tokens to explore the channel-wise relationships in each patch encoder. The learned patch-level features t^{p_k} (k=1,2,3,4) are then concatenated in the channel dimension to generate a feature map of size $(H \times W/64, KC)$. Then we form the tokens representing features from different scales for the final transformer encoder to learn cross-level element relationships.

The structure of the transformer encoder [41] used in our network is shown in Fig. 2, which consists of $M = 2$ blocks containing a multi-head self-attention module and a feed-forward MLP layer. The positional encoding mechanism of Transformer strengthens its ability to exploit the relationships between the elements by considering their relative positions. But the side effect of positional encoding is that if we only feed cropped patches to transformer encoders, the learned patch mapping would be too strong and directly convert the content image to the style image. To alleviate that problem, we incorporate the global features extracted from the entire image in all the decoding layers, since they provide the relationship between a cropped patch and the whole image so that the irrelevant relationships within patches can be weakened. Note that the global features are not utilized in MPT, as MPT is designed for investigating only patch-level features. If the global features are also included in MPT, MPT will tend to focus on the relationships between the patches and the fixed global structural features, leading to to a blurred result due to the lack of attention to style details.

3.2 Dynamic Filter-Based Decoder

We introduce a dynamic filtering-based decoder to dynamically decide how the global features should be decoded when generating the final image. Previous works relying on convolutional layers with fixed kernels to decode features failed to infer different image styles adaptively [9,10], as their filters cannot handle the large diversity of style-related features. Adapting to different kinds of styles is an essential requirement for the arbitrary style transfer task since we cannot assume any style prior before learning from the input images. Dynamic filtering module (DCM) [13,46] simultaneously learns how to dynamically generate filtering kernels of different sizes for different input features. Then the deconvolution kernels applied on the feature maps can be customized based on the style of the input data. As shown in Fig. 1, we normally use 1, 3, and 5 as the sizes of the dynamically generated kernels to capture features of different scales. The three sub-modules to learn the dynamic filters are arranged in parallel. We feed the shallow global feature map to DCMs and concatenate the output with their input for the further decoding process.

3.3 Loss Functions

Our method has two mapping functions to learn, $G : x \to y$ and $F : y \to x$. The discriminators and generators for G and F are trained under adversarial losses. The learning objective for G is:

$$\mathcal{L}_{GAN}(G, D_y, x, y) = E_y[log D_y(y)]$$
$$+ E_{x,\{x(p_k)\}}[log(1 - D_y(G(x, \{x(p_k)\})))], \tag{1}$$

where $x(p_k) \sim P_{data}[x(p)]$, representing the sampled patches from the data distribution $P_{data}[x(p)]$ of the patches with the same style of x. Similarly, for the mapping $F : y \to x$, we define the adversarial loss as $\mathcal{L}_{GAN}(F, D_x, x, y)$.

The adversarial losses are sufficient for generating plausible images in the target domain, but they cannot ensure the preservation of the original semantic content. Therefore, the two GANs need to be further updated using cycle consistency losses to encourage the synthesis of translations of the input image

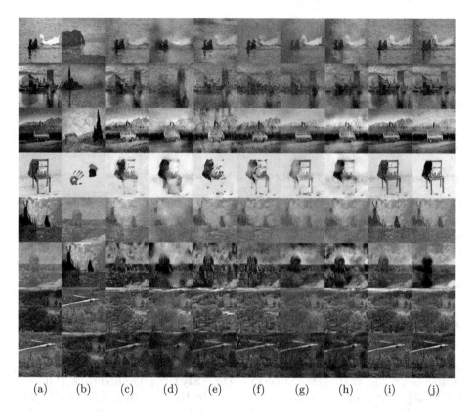

(a)   (b)   (c)   (d)   (e)   (f)   (g)   (h)   (i)   (j)

Fig. 3. Results of the state-of-the-art algorithms and CycleTransformer on photo stylization. The first and second columns are content and style images. The remaining columns are stylized results by (c) AdaIN [15], (d) AAMS [43], (e) SANET [32], (f) StyleFormer [42], (g) photoWCT [27], (h) Avatar-Net [37], (i) DST [18] and (j) Ours.

x. In the forward cycle, cycle consistency loss aims at translating the image $\widetilde{x}$ generated by G back to itself through F, which means using L_1 norm to measure the differences between $F(G(x, \{x(p_k)\}))$ and x. In the backward cycle, it calculates the differences between $G(F(y, \{y(q_k)\})$ and y, where $\{y(q_k)\}$ denotes the sampled patches from the data distribution $P_{data}[y(q)]$ with the style of y. The loss can be expressed as below:

$$\mathcal{L}_{cyc}(G, F, x, y) = E_{x, \{x(p_k)\}}[\|F(G(x, \{x(p_k)\})) - x\|_1] \\ + E_{y, \{y(q_k)\}}[\|G(F(y, \{y(q_k)\})) - y\|_1] \tag{2}$$

To maintain the content of the content image, we add a reconstruction loss [47] to restrict the backward generation effect by L_1 loss. Since G is aimed at enabling converting any content to the reference style of y, it should transform y back to itself, and so does the mapping F. The losses are defined as follows:

$$\mathcal{L}_{idt}(G, F, x, y) = E_{x, \{x(p_k)\}}[\|F(x) - x\|_1] \\ + E_{y, \{y(p_k)\}}[\|G(y) - y\|_1] \tag{3}$$

In summary, the full objective function is:

$$\mathcal{L} = \mathcal{L}_{GAN}(G, D_y, x, y) + \mathcal{L}_{GAN}(F, D_x, y, x)$$
$$+\lambda_{idt}\mathcal{L}_{idt}(G, F, x, y) + \lambda_{cyc}\mathcal{L}_{cyc}(G, F, x, y), \tag{4}$$

where the weights λ_{idt} and λ_{cyc} are set to 100.

4   Experiments and Evaluations

4.1   Implementation Details

Our method only needs one content image and one style image to learn the bi-directional mappings, which facilitates our data collection. Most results presented in this paper are generated using images randomly selected from the CycleGAN dataset and downloaded from the internet. In our experiments, the four patch sizes are normally set as 4, 8, 16, and 32 respectively. All the cropped patches are first resized to 256*256 before being fed into the convolutional layers.

4.2   Qualitative Evaluation

We compare our method with state-of-the-art image stylization methods, including AdaIN [15], AAMS [43], SANET [32], StyleFormer [42], photoWCT [27], Avatar-net [37], DST [18], SpliceViT [39], StyTr^2 [4], QuantArt [14] and InST [45]. Our models are trained using only the two given images. We ran author-released implementations with their default settings for all the other methods. The first four rows in Fig. 3 are photo stylization results, where the content images are real photos and the style images do not contain similar semantic objects. The results of AdaIN [15] and Avatar-Net [37] cannot generate consistent patterns for similar regions, such as the sky regions in the fourth row and the building regions in the second row. PhotoWCT [27] fails to introduce the strokes or the color blocks to express the given styles in all the shown examples. AAMS [43] can integrate multiple stroke patterns and properly adopt the patterns in different regions of the output image. However, their image quality is not satisfactory due to the blurriness all over the picture. Since there is no obvious semantic correspondence between the two images, DST [18] transfers style like a color filter with a high retention of original appearances. In contrast, our method preserves the original content while producing appropriate style details. Cycle style transfer results are shown in the last four rows in Fig. 3 with artistic and photorealistic stylization. Since our network is powerful in learning positional relationships, and thus the style information extracted from style images can be properly distributed according to the content. The other methods either fail to learn the visual characteristics of the styles (AdaIN, photoWCT, and DST), or change the structure of the content (AAMS and Avatar-Net), leading to worse results than ours.

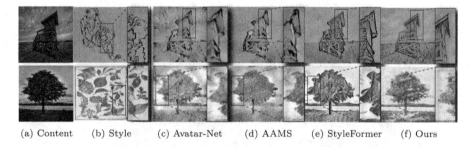

(a) Content   (b) Style   (c) Avatar-Net   (d) AAMS   (e) StyleFormer   (f) Ours

Fig. 4. More comparisons on sketch styles. (a) and (b) are content and style images. We show the results of (c) Avatar-Net [37], (d) AAMS [43], (e) StyleFormer [42] and (f) Ours. It can be seen in the zoom-in windows that our method reveals the original stroke style in the best way.

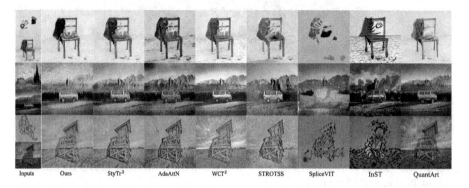

Inputs   Ours   StyTr^2 AdaAttN   WCT^2 STROTSS   SpliceVIT   InST   QuantArt

Fig. 5. More comparison results. Compared to StyTr^2 [4], AdaAttN [29], WCT^2 [44], STROTSS [19], SpliceViT [39], QuantArt [14] and InST [45], our method performs better in style transfer and content preservation.

On the photo stylization for the challenging sketch styles (see Fig. 4), other methods are struggling to produce clean sketches and preserve the content structure properly at the same time. They leave original colors in the background except for photoWCT, which however produces blurred sketch lines. Our method is in a very advantageous position for this kind of style. In our results, only the grey-scale strokes from the style images are utilized to express the content, and the structural features are all well maintained. We also show more comparison results with StyTr^2 [4], AdaAttN [29], WCT^2 [44], STROTSS [19], SpliceViT [39], QuantArt [14] and InST [45] in Fig. 5, and our method performs better in style transfer and content preservation.

Fig. 6. Our photo-to-photo transfer results. We applied different styles to the same content image, and vice versa.

We demonstrate the ability of our methods in image translation between real-life photos. As shown in Fig. 6, our method can generate high-quality translated photos when the two images do not share semantically similar contents. By combining the global features with the features from dynamic filters as mentioned in Sec. 4.1, the details of the content images are well preserved. Figure 6 shows the translated results when we use the images of four seasons as style image. By inspecting the four results of each example, we can see the content is consistent across the four seasons with properly altered appearances.

4.3   Ablation Study

We study the impact of different ingredients in our method and evaluate the structure of MPT. More experiments on the choice of hyper-parameters are shown in the supplementary materials.

CycleTransformer Architecture. Figure 7 illustrates the generated results without MPT and/or Dynamic Filter Decoder. We take the CycleGAN trained by two single images (c) as our baseline. As CycleGAN is originally designed for

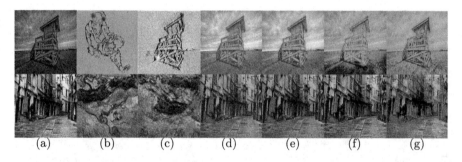

Fig. 7. Ablation study of the architecture of CycleTransformer. Given the content image (a) and the style image (b), we demonstrate the results where (c) the original CycleGAN is trained in a one-shot manner, (d) a random patch is added to extract convolutional features, (e) multiple patches are used to extract convolutional features, (f) multiple patches with dynamic filtering and our full model (g) with both MPT and dynamic filtering.

transferring a style learned from a large number of unpaired images, their one-shot results suffer from noises and blurriness. On the contrary, CycleTransformer achieves a much higher visual quality. To validate the benefits gained from the attention-based patch features extracted by MPT, we remove the MPT module and just feed one patch or nested patches to CNN layers to extract features and then combine them with global features to decode. We show the corresponding results in (d) and (e), where the generated blurred images both look like processed by a local color filter, which demonstrates the importance of the patch-wise self-attention and cross-level attention information learned by MPT when describing the intrinsic style-related features. We also validate the effectiveness of the Dynamic Filter Decoder, which adaptively interprets the shallow features to generate the final results. As shown in (f), the results generated by the model without dynamic filters have much weaker stylization effects. Compared with the results produced by the full model, they are less desirable due to the lack of artistic characteristics. The above study shows the irreplaceable roles of MPT and Dynamic Filter Decoder in CycleTransformer.

Multi-level Patch Transformer Encoder. We evaluate other alternative ways of using Transformer encoders and show the corresponding results in Fig. 8. If we simply use a Transformer encoder to process the global features, the network fails to learn delicate details and just generates weakly stylized results instead, as in Fig. 8(a). The reason is that it only learns the attention information globally and ignores the local pixel-wise relationships. We also evaluate the performance of only processing individual patches and directly feeding the concatenated multi-level patches to the cross-level Transformer encoder. As shown in the results of Fig. 8(b), if we learn only the self-attention information within patches, the network tends to apply a certain pattern universally, failing to adapt to the content. In the cross-level Transformer, the relationships between patches of different levels can be automatically revealed, which improves the stylization

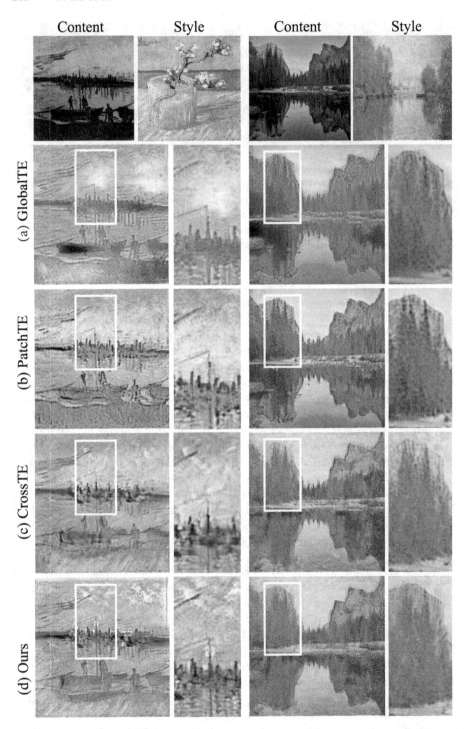

Fig. 8. Ablation study of MPT's structure. We compare the results of our method (d) with (a) "GlobalTE": only global features are fed to a transformer encoder (TE); (b)"PatchTE": patches are only processed by TEs individually; and (c) "CrossTE": patch features are directly processed by the cross-level TE.

effect as in Fig. 8(c). However, results from the full MPT are still superior to its results, because the relationships within the patches themselves are also essential for producing reasonable style details. Furthermore, MPT avoids the problem of duplicated patterns in some regions. As shown in the last column, using our MPT module, we can obtain rich style details with a reasonable distribution. Therefore, we can conclude that our MPT encoder module is able to effectively extract the relationships among pixels and patches of different scales for the arbitrary style transfer task.

Nested Multilevel Patches. Figure 1 in the *supplementary* shows that nested multi-level patches produce better results than a single patch and the image quality improves with the number of nested patches. Compared with the ViT-based patch splitting schemes such as StyTr^2 (Fig. 5), our results show better brush textures. To further investigate the effects of "nested patches", we add an experiment where we replace the nested patches with the Gaussian pyramid of a randomly selected patch. Figure 10 shows the results using patch pyramids, where the details are blurred with obvious artifacts which demonstrate the advantages of nested multi-level patches.

4.4   User Study

To evaluate the visual quality and the faithfulness of stylized images, we conducted a user study. We prepared 18 pairs of images, including 4 pairs in a cycle manner. We generated 22 groups of style transfer results using our method and seven state-of-the-art methods [15,18,27,32,37,42,43]. In total, 46 participants (including 29 males, 17 females, aged from 18 to 33) were recruited in this study and we got 46 (participants) × 22 (questions) = 1012 subjective evaluation results for each method.

The statistics of the user study results were plotted in Fig. 9. We performed one-way ANOVA tests on six methods with respect of "Style Consistency", "Content Consistency" and "Least Artifacts" corresponding to the three criteria above. We found significant effects of our method for all three criteria: style consistency ($F_{(5,126)} = 6.8, p < 0.0001$), content consistency ($F_{(5,126)} = 3.44, p < 0.05$) and least artifacts ($F_{(5,126)} = 2.36, p < 0.05$). Our method has obvious advantages in"Style Consistency", has a more consistent style with the reference image, and produces the least artifacts based on subjective evaluations. We also show a radar plot summarizing the user selections of the images with the best overall visual quality, where our method also got the most votes.

4.5   Quantitative Evaluations

We also sought image-translation tasks where we could get the ground truth translation results to evaluate our method quantitatively.

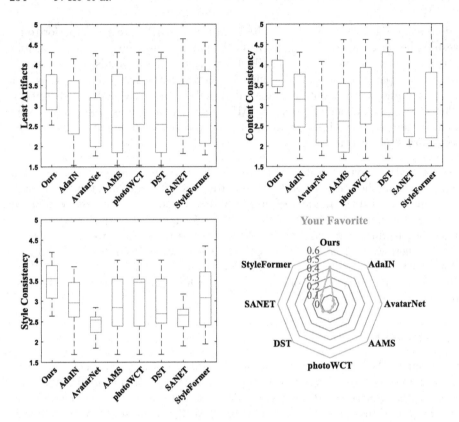

Fig. 9. Subjective scores on the similarity between the generated images of different methods and the corresponding content and style images, as well as the visual realism of the generated images. The additional radar plot summarizes the user selections of the images with the best overall visual quality.

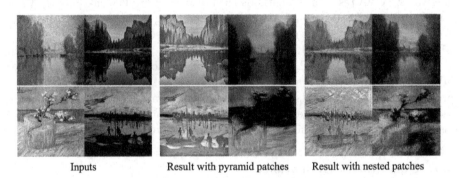

Inputs   Result with pyramid patches   Result with nested patches

Fig. 10. Comparisons of patch pyramids and nested patches.

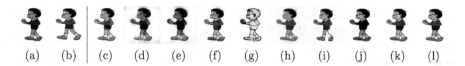

(a)   (b)   (c)   (d)   (e)   (f)   (g)   (h)   (i)   (j)   (k)   (l)

Fig. 11. Comparison of one-shot image colorization. (a) is the input grey image and (b) is the reference color image. The results of (c) AdaIN [15] (Color figure online), (h) photoWCT [27], (g) StyleFormer [42] and (j) DST [18] generate results similar to global color filtering. The results of (d) Avatar-Net [37], (e) AAMS [43], (f) SANET [32] and (i) CycleGAN [47] suffer from blurry artifacts surrounding edges. Our method (k) is able to generate clean results and respect the boundaries in grey images well. (l) is the ground truth

Visual Effect on Both Style and Content. We show quantitative comparisons with previous methods in Table 2 using the content/style perceptual losses (L_c and L_s) used in StyTr^2 [4] and FID on results generated using 300 style and content image pairs. WCT^2, STROTSS, and AdaIN gets the best L_c, L_s and FID, respectively. Note that our method outperforms SpliceViT which has the same single image setting. In addition, we propose patchFID as a quantitative metric for style consistency (Table 2) since the artistic style features usually exist at the patch level. We randomly sampled 100 64×64 patches from the reference style image and regularly picked 16 64×64 patches from the stylized result, and took the mean of the FIDs between these patches as patchFID. We achieve the best patchFID. Note that there have not been any widely accepted metric for quantitative evaluation of style transfer, especially for artistic styles. We believe a user study that relies on human perceptual evaluation as in our paper is a meaningful and important measure (Table 1).

Table 1. Quantitative evaluation.

Methods	Ours	StyTr^2	AdaAttN	WCT^2	STROTSS	SpliceViT	AdaIN	AAMS	SANET	StyleFormer	DST	photoWCT	Avatar-Net
L_c	2.31	1.00	2.55	**0.33**	2.19	3.01	1.76	2.50	2.46	2.41	0.69	1.16	2.12
L_s ↓	0.93	0.80	0.90	1.83	**0.34**	2.28	0.89	2.02	0.90	0.56	1.32	2.19	2.02
FID	2.77	1.73	5.81	1.26	5.42	8.58	**0.74**	4.12	2.33	1.74	4.88	7.64	7.83
patchFID ↓	**2.61**	3.21	2.78	4.05	3.33	7.62	3.74	3.72	4.57	3.31	3.49	5.20	6.17

Rationality of Color Distribution. We chose the colorization task since the paired grey-scale images and the colorized images are all available. We use the three datasets of different cartoon characters provided by [3] as our evaluation data. We randomly select 10 sets of unpaired color and grey-scale images as style and content images respectively from each of the three datasets. We train the models of CycleTransformer and the previous methods (*i.e.* AdaIN, Avatar-Net, AAMS, SANET, StyleFormer, photoWCT, DST, CycleGAN) in the same manner as mentioned in Sec. 4.2. Table 2 reports the performance of all the tested methods measured by the peak signal-to-noise ratio (PSNR) and the structural similarity index measure (SSIM). Our CycleTransformer significantly outperforms existing methods both in PSNR and SSIM. Figure 11 shows some of the colorization results. It seems difficult for previous style transfer methods without cycle consistency (*i.e.* AdaIN, Avatar-Net, AAMS, photoWCT, DST) to learn complex patch-wise correspondences, leading to badly saturated colors. Compared to our method, CycleGAN is unable to achieve compelling results without being trained on large datasets.

4.6   Discussion CycleTransformer vs CycleGAN

CycleGAN is a successful approach for unpaired cycle image translation. But it still needs plenty of images for each domain in training. As shown in Fig. 7, their one-shot bi-directional mapping is unable to converge, thus the results suffer from noises and blurriness. The same artifacts can be seen in Fig. 11, a colorization task. Based on this work and the observed challenges, our work aims at using multi-level patch features for single reference image style transfer. For both photo stylization and colorization, CycleTransformer achieves a much higher visual quality on the contrary.

Table 2. Quantitative validation on the colorization task.

Method	character1		character2		character3	
	PSNR↑	SSIM↑	PSNR↑	SSIM↑	PSNR↑	SSIM↑
Ours	22.327	**0.889**	**26.134**	**0.932**	**26.917**	0.920
AdaIN	16.724	0.809	17.315	0.863	17.865	0.850
AAMS	**22.626**	0.888	15.161	0.705	16.944	0.712
SANET	22.606	0.720	17.435	0.768	19.252	0.872
StyleFormer	13.243	0.433	12.338	0.705	15.324	0.657
DST	20.993	0.863	20.636	0.852	20.118	0.832
photoWCT	18.98	0.878	22.011	0.931	23.303	**0.928**
Avatar-Net	14.971	0.693	16.868	0.720	15.697	0.729
CycleGAN	12.484	0.472	14.762	0.472	12.754	0.556

5   Conclusion and Future Work

We focus on the challenge of learning to transfer style with only a single reference image. We introduce CycleTransformer, a deep model based on Transformers and the cycle-consistent learning scheme to model complex relationships within multi-level patches and across these patches. We integrate them with global features in a dynamic filter-based decoder to achieve a rich stylization effect and better content preservation. Our method uses randomly sampled patches to successfully model the distribution of the visual content with a certain style when only one style image is available. Experiments show the superiority of our method over the state-of-the-art methods on the single-image-based style transfer task. In the future, we will extend CycleTransformer to learn semantic-related patch-level features and utilize our feature learning scheme for other related tasks, such as sketch-based image synthesis.

Acknowledgments. This work was supported by the Beijing Municipal Natural Science Foundation for Distinguished Young Scholars (No. JQ21013), the National Natural Science Foundation of China (No. 62061136007) and the Youth Innovation Promotion Association CAS.

References

1. Castillo, C., De, S., Han, X., Singh, B., Yadav, A.K., Goldstein, T.: Son of zorn's lemma: targeted style transfer using instance-aware semantic segmentation. In: 2017 IEEE International Conference on Acoustics, Speech and Signal Processing (ICASSP), pp. 1348–1352. IEEE (2017)
2. Chen, D., Yuan, L., Liao, J., Yu, N., Hua, G.: Stylebank: an explicit representation for neural image style transfer. In: 2017 IEEE Conference on Computer Vision and Pattern Recognition (CVPR), pp. 2770–2779 (2017)
3. Chen, S.Y., et al.: Active colorization for cartoon line drawings. IEEE Trans. Visual. Comput. Graph. **28**(2), 1198–1208 (2020)
4. Deng, Y., Tang, F., Pan, X., Dong, W., Xu, C., et al.: Stytr: unbiased image style transfer with transformers. arXiv preprint arXiv:2105.14576 (2021)
5. Dosovitskiy, A., et al.: An image is worth 16x16 words: Transformers for image recognition at scale. ArXiv abs/2010.11929 (2020)
6. Dumoulin, V., Shlens, J., Kudlur, M.: A learned representation for artistic style. ArXiv abs/1610.07629 (2017)
7. Esser, P., Rombach, R., Ommer, B.: Taming transformers for high-resolution image synthesis. arXiv preprint arXiv:2012.09841 (2020)
8. Gatys, L.A., Ecker, A.S., Bethge, M.: Texture synthesis using convolutional neural networks. In: NIPS (2015)
9. Gatys, L.A., Ecker, A.S., Bethge, M.: A neural algorithm of artistic style. arXiv preprint arXiv:1508.06576 (2015)
10. Gatys, L.A., Ecker, A.S., Bethge, M.: Image style transfer using convolutional neural networks. In: Conference on Computer Vision and Pattern Recognition (CVPR), pp. 2414–2423 (2016)
11. Girdhar, R., Carreira, J., Doersch, C., Zisserman, A.: Video action transformer network. In: Proceedings of the IEEE/CVF Conference on Computer Vision and Pattern Recognition, pp. 244–253 (2019)
12. Goodfellow, I.J., et al.: Generative adversarial nets. In: NIPS (2014)
13. He, J., Deng, Z., Qiao, Y.: Dynamic multi-scale filters for semantic segmentation. In: Proceedings of the IEEE/CVF International Conference on Computer Vision, pp. 3562–3572 (2019)
14. Huang, S., An, J., Wei, D., Luo, J., Pfister, H.: Quantart: Quantizing image style transfer towards high visual fidelity. In: Proceedings of the IEEE Conference on Computer Vision and Pattern Recognition (June 2023)
15. Huang, X., Belongie, S.: Arbitrary style transfer in real-time with adaptive instance normalization. In: Proceedings of the IEEE International Conference on Computer Vision, pp. 1501–1510 (2017)

16. Jiang, Y., Chang, S., Wang, Z.: Transgan: Two transformers can make one strong gan. arXiv preprint arXiv:2102.07074 (2021)

17. Johnson, J., Alahi, A., Li, F.: Perceptual losses for real-time style transfer and super-resolution. In: European Conference on Computer Vision (ECCV), pp. 694–711 (2016)

18. Kim, S.S.Y., Kolkin, N., Salavon, J., Shakhnarovich, G.: Deformable Style Transfer. In: Vedaldi, A., Bischof, H., Brox, T., Frahm, J.-M. (eds.) Computer Vision – ECCV 2020: 16th European Conference, Glasgow, UK, August 23–28, 2020, Proceedings, Part XXVI, pp. 246–261. Springer International Publishing, Cham (2020). https://doi.org/10.1007/978-3-030-58574-7_15

19. Kolkin, N., Salavon, J., Shakhnarovich, G.: Style transfer by relaxed optimal transport and self-similarity. In: Conference on Computer Vision and Pattern Recognition (CVPR), pp. 10051–10060 (2019)

20. Kyprianidis, J.E., Collomosse, J., Wang, T., Isenberg, T.: State of the 'art': A taxonomy of artistic stylization techniques for images and video? (2012)

21. Li, C., Wand, M.: Combining markov random fields and convolutional neural networks for image synthesis. In: Conference on Computer Vision and Pattern Recognition (CVPR), pp. 2479–2486 (2016)

22. Li, C., Wand, M.: Precomputed real-time texture synthesis with Markovian generative adversarial networks. ArXiv abs/1604.04382 (2016)

23. Li, T., et al.: Beautygan: Instance-level facial makeup transfer with deep generative adversarial network. In: Proceedings of the 26th ACM International Conference on Multimedia, pp. 645–653 (2018)

24. Li, Y., Wang, N., Liu, J., Hou, X.: Demystifying neural style transfer. arXiv preprint arXiv:1701.01036 (2017)

25. Li, Y., Fang, C., Yang, J., Wang, Z., Lu, X., Yang, M.H.: Diversified texture synthesis with feed-forward networks. 2017 IEEE Conference on Computer Vision and Pattern Recognition (CVPR), pp. 266–274 (2017)

26. Li, Y., Fang, C., Yang, J., Wang, Z., Lu, X., Yang, M.: Universal style transfer via feature transforms. In: Advances in Neural Information Processing Systems (NIPS), pp. 386–396 (2017)

27. Li, Y., Liu, M.Y., Li, X., Yang, M.H., Kautz, J.: A closed-form solution to photorealistic image stylization. In: Proceedings of the European Conference on Computer Vision (ECCV), pp. 453–468 (2018)

28. Liao, J., Yao, Y., Yuan, L., Hua, G., Kang, S.B.: Visual attribute transfer through deep image analogy. ACM Trans. Graph. **36**(4), 120:1–120:15 (2017)

29. Liu, S., et al.: Adaattn: revisit attention mechanism in arbitrary neural style transfer. In: Proceedings of the IEEE/CVF International Conference on Computer Vision, pp. 6649–6658 (2021)

30. Liu, X.C., Yang, Y.L., Hall, P.: Learning to warp for style transfer. In: Proceedings of the IEEE/CVF Conference on Computer Vision and Pattern Recognition. pp. 3702–3711 (2021)

31. Okamoto, T., Toda, T., Shiga, Y., Kawai, H.: Transformer-based text-to-speech with weighted forced attention. In: ICASSP 2020–2020 IEEE International Conference on Acoustics, Speech and Signal Processing (ICASSP), pp. 6729–6733. IEEE (2020)

32. Park, D.Y., Lee, K.H.: Arbitrary style transfer with style-attentional networks. In: Proceedings of the IEEE/CVF Conference on Computer Vision and Pattern Recognition, pp. 5880–5888 (2019)

33. Park, T., Efros, A.A., Zhang, R., Zhu, J.-Y.: Contrastive learning for unpaired image-to-image translation. In: Vedaldi, A., Bischof, H., Brox, T., Frahm, J.-M. (eds.) ECCV 2020. LNCS, vol. 12354, pp. 319–345. Springer, Cham (2020). https://doi.org/10.1007/978-3-030-58545-7_19
34. Parmar, N., Vaswani, A., Uszkoreit, J., Kaiser, L., Shazeer, N.M., Ku, A., Tran, D.: Image transformer. ArXiv abs/1802.05751 (2018)
35. Risser, E., Wilmot, P., Barnes, C.: Stable and controllable neural texture synthesis and style transfer using histogram losses. arXiv preprint arXiv:1701.08893 (2017)
36. Rombach, R., Blattmann, A., Lorenz, D., Esser, P., Ommer, B.: High-resolution image synthesis with latent diffusion models. In: Proceedings of the IEEE/CVF Conference on Computer Vision and Pattern Recognition, pp. 10684–10695 (2022)
37. Sheng, L., Lin, Z., Shao, J., Wang, X.: Avatar-net: Multi-scale zero-shot style transfer by feature decoration. In: Proceedings of the IEEE Conference on Computer Vision and Pattern Recognition, pp. 8242–8250 (2018)
38. Texler, O., et al.: Interactive video stylization using few-shot patch-based training. ACM Trans. Graph. (TOG) 39(4), 1–73 (2020)
39. Tumanyan, N., Bar-Tal, O., Bagon, S., Dekel, T.: Splicing vit features for semantic appearance transfer. In: Proceedings of the IEEE/CVF Conference on Computer Vision and Pattern Recognition, pp. 10748–10757 (2022)
40. Ulyanov, D., Lebedev, V., Vedaldi, A., Lempitsky, V.: Texture networks: Feed-forward synthesis of textures and stylized images. In: ICML (2016)
41. Vaswani, A., et al.: Attention is all you need. In: Advances in Neural Information Processing Systems, pp. 5998–6008 (2017)
42. Wu, X., Hu, Z., Sheng, L., Xu, D.: Styleformer: real-time arbitrary style transfer via parametric style composition. In: Proceedings of the IEEE/CVF International Conference on Computer Vision, pp. 14618–14627 (2021)
43. Yao, Y., Ren, J., Xie, X., Liu, W., Liu, Y., Wang, J.: Attention-aware multi-stroke style transfer. 2019 IEEE/CVF Conference on Computer Vision and Pattern Recognition (CVPR), pp. 1467–1475 (2019)
44. Yoo, J., Uh, Y., Chun, S., Kang, B., Ha, J.W.: Photorealistic style transfer via wavelet transforms. In: International Conference on Computer Vision (ICCV), pp. 9035–9044 (2019)
45. Zhang, Y., et al.: Inversion-based style transfer with diffusion models. In: Proceedings of the IEEE/CVF Conference on Computer Vision and Pattern Recognition (CVPR), pp. 10146–10156 (June 2023)
46. Zhao, J., Chalmers, A., Rhee, T.: Adaptive light estimation using dynamic filtering for diverse lighting conditions. IEEE Trans. Visual Comput. Graph. 27(11), 4097–4106 (2021)
47. Zhu, J.Y., Park, T., Isola, P., Efros, A.A.: Unpaired image-to-image translation using cycle-consistent adversarial networks. In: Proceedings of the IEEE International Conference on Computer Vision, pp. 2223–2232 (2017)

Palette-Based Content-Aware Image Recoloring

Zheng-Jun Du[1,2]🆔, Jia-Wei Zhou[1]🆔, Zi-Xun Xia[1]🆔, Bing-Feng Seng[1]🆔, and Kun Xu[3]([✉])🆔

[1] Department of Computer Technology and Application, Qinghai University, Xining 810016, China
{dzj,zjw,xia.zixun,sbf}@qhu.edu.cn
[2] Qinghai Provincial Key Laboratory of Media Integration Technology and Communication, Xining 810016, China
[3] BNRist, Department of CS&T, Tsinghua University, Beijing 100084, China
xukun@tsinghua.edu.cn

Abstract. Palette-based image recoloring is a popular image editing technique in recent years. It allows users to perform global color edits to an image by manipulating a small set of representative colors. Many approaches have been proposed for palette extraction and palette-based image recoloring. However, existing methods primarily leverage low-level visual information to extract color palettes, so that different objects with similar colors will share the same palette colors. It is impossible to individually recolor one of multiple objects with similar colors, as altering a specific palette color may cause unwanted color changes to many non-interesting objects. To address this issue, in this paper, we present a novel, palette-based content-aware image recoloring approach. Different from previous methods, we extract the color palette of an image in a high-dimensional space that combines low-level visual features and high-level semantic features, allowing generating separate palette colors for different objects with similar colors. This enables users to perform targeted local editing, i.e., distinguish and recolor objects with similar colors separately, without producing unexpected global color changes. Extensive experiments demonstrate the flexibility, local control, and effectiveness of our method.

Keywords: palette · recoloring · content-aware · semantic · local editing

1 Introduction

Palette-based image recoloring has attracted increasing attention in recent years. Many approaches have been proposed for palette extraction and recoloring, and have demonstrated promising results in color editing. In these approaches, a color palette consisting of a small set of colors is first extracted from the input image, to characterize its color distribution. Subsequently, a predetermined mapping

F.-L. Zhang and A. Sharf (Eds.): CVM 2024, LNCS 14593, pp. 240–258, 2024.
https://doi.org/10.1007/978-981-97-2092-7_12

function is employed to transfer the modifications made to the color palette to the entire image. So that users could easily adjust the image by modifying the palette colors. These methods are generally efficient, easy to use and learn, and can generate natural, artifact-free results.

Despite these advantages, a long-standing problem is that these methods are limited to handle only global color editing while do not support content-aware local color editing. For example, when an image comprises multiple objects with identical or similar colors, users struggle to alter the color of one object without impacting the others. The primary reason is that existing methods typically extract color palettes in a low-dimensional color space (e.g., RGB or Lab color space), objects with similar colors will share the same palette colors. Therefore, modifying a palette color may cause all objects with similar colors to change at the same time. Existing methods cannot distinguish different objects with similar colors, nor can they recolor each of these objects separately.

To address this problem, in this paper, we present a novel, palette-based content-aware image recoloring method. Our method contains two steps: color palette extraction and content-aware recoloring. In the first step, unlike existing algorithms that usually extract color palettes in 3D RGB or Lab color space, we project the input image into a high-dimensional feature space that contains both low-level visual information and high-level semantic information, and then employ a variant K-means clustering to obtain the palette. So that different objects with similar colors will be associated with different palette colors. In the second step, we design a color transfer function to map the change of the color palette to the whole image. In the color transfer function, the color change of each pixel is defined as a weighted sum of palette color changes, while the weight of a pixel with respect to a specific palette color is determined by their similarity. Our approach is efficient and could generate desirable results that match user edit intention. More importantly, it enables local and content-aware recoloring.

We have demonstrated the effectiveness of our method on extensive experiments. Compared with existing methods, the contributions of our paper lie in:

- We propose to extract the color palette of an image in a high-dimensional space that combines both low-level visual features and high-level semantic features.
- With the extracted color palette, we design a color transfer function to map the changes of palette colors to the whole image. Our approach enables palette-based content-aware recoloring for the first time, allowing users to perform targeted localized editing in complex scenes.

2   Related Works

Image recoloring is a frequent operation executed by graphical designers. Its purpose is to adjust the colors of an image to improve the quality, enhance the artistic effects, or meet some specific design needs. Three types of methods have been proposed for image recoloring, i.e., palette-based methods, stroke-based methods (edit propagation), and example-based methods (style transfer). Next, we will briefly review these three types of methods.

2.1 Palette-Based Image Recoloring

Palette-based image recoloring is a popular topic in image editing. It offers an intuitive yet efficient solution for color adjustment. It enables users to interactively change the color of an image by modifying a color palette.

The pioneering work of palette-based image recoloring was introduced by Chang et al. [4]. They employed a modified K-means clustering to extract the color palette of an image and mapped the changes of the color palette to the entire image with a radial basis function weighted transformation. Similarly, Zhang et al. [29] also used a similar clustering method to obtain the color palette, but they represented image pixels as the weighted sum of palette colors through optimization. During recoloring, the weights are fixed, and users modify the palette colors to change the color of the image. A series of methods based on convex hull in RGB space have been proposed for image recoloring. Tan et al. [25] calculated the simplified convex hull of image colors in RGB space and used its vertices as the color palette. They then decomposed the input image into ordered layers corresponding to the palette colors. Users adjust the image by modifying the layers or the color palette. Later, Tan et al. [23,24] proposed a more efficient method for palette extraction and image recoloring using RGBXY space geometry. Wang et al. [27] further proposed an optimization method to iteratively move the vertices (colors) of the simplified convex hull (palette), to improve the compactness and representativeness of the color palette. Du et al. [9] Extended the palette-based image recoloring to video scenario, and achieved natural yet time-varying color editing. More recently, Chao et al. [5] proposed the "ColorfulCurves" to achieve both color and lightness adjustment. So that users can directly modify palette colors' hue and saturation and per-palette tone curves, or image pixels, to recolor the input image. However, when different objects or regions have similar colors, their method can not recolor them separately. Chao et al. [6] introduced an adaptive solution for recoloring under arbitrary image-space constraints and automatically splits the image into soft sub-regions with more representative local palettes when the constraints cannot be satisfied.

All these methods extract color palettes of input images in RGB or Lab color space. That is to say, they only leverage the low-level color information to obtain the palettes. Different regions or objects that have similar colors necessarily share the same palette color. Thus, modifying some palette color will inevitably result in color changes of multiple regions or objects with similar colors. However, in this paper, we extract the color palette considering both the low-level visual color information and the semantic information. It enables the color palette to incorporate specific semantic information, thereby effectively differentiating between objects with similar colors.

2.2   Edit Propagation (Stroke-Based Image Recoloring)

Edit propagation is a well-studied technique for image recoloring. It allows users to put sparse edits directly onto the image, which are then automatically propagated to the rest of the image. This technique has been widely used in colorization, color editing, material editing, etc.

The first edit propagation method was presented by Levin et al. [16] for stroke-based grayscale image colorization. They started by converting the grayscale image into the YUV color space, and assumed that pixels that have similar luminance (Y) values should receive similar chrominance (UV) values. Based on this assumption, the colorization task is formulated as a quadratic energy optimization problem and further reduced to solving a linear system. Later, Lischinski et al. [18] introduced the idea of edit propagation into tonal adjustment and achieved impressive results. Pellacini et al. [20] further extended this method to edit measured materials. An et al. [3] proposed the first edit propagation-based approach for color editing. They calculated the similarities in all pairs of pixels to achieve distant propagation. All of the above methods require solving large-scale linear systems, which are computationally and storage expensive. To speed up these algorithms and reduce the memory burden, Xu et al. [28] proposed an efficient affinity-based edit propagation using a kd tree, which significantly accelerates this algorithm and saves memory overhead. Li et al. [17] formulated the edit propagation task as an interpolation problem with radial basis functions (RBFs), which first achieved real-time color editing. Recently some deep learning-based approaches have proposed to edit propagation. The first deep learning-based edit propagation method was proposed by Endo et al. [10], termed "DeepProp", which utilizes a convolutional neural network (CNN) to extract high-dimensional features for edit propagation. Gui et al. [12] formulated edit propagation as a multi-class classification problem and utilized a fully convolutional network capable of end-to-end training to extract visual and spatial features and predict the resulting image. These methods are sensitive to user edits and cannot generate results in real-time.

Edit propagation-based approaches typically require users to make density fine-tuned edits, and cannot enable content-aware color editing. Our method only requires users to manipulate a small set of colors to adjust the appearance of an image. Moreover, it can achieve content-aware recoloring.

2.3   Style Transfer (Example-Based Image Recoloring)

Style transfer is another widely researched method for image recoloring, which involves transferring the colors from a reference image to a target image.

A bunch of methods have been proposed for style transfer. For instance, Reinhard et al. [22] mapped the style from the reference image to the target one by aligning their color distributions. Neumann et al. [19] employed a 3D histogram matching technique for color transfer, enabling natural results even when the correspondence between the reference and target images is faint. Pitie et al. [21] developed a continuous transformation that maps one n-dimensional distribution to another, effectively transferring color between two images with varying content. However, these methods primarily focus on low-level visual features, which may lead to significant artifacts when the reference and target images are considerably different. In recent years, deep learning-based algorithms have made substantial advancements in the field of image style transfer. Notable examples include CNN-based style transfer algorithms such as [11,26] and GAN-based style transfer algorithms like [8,30]. These techniques take into account semantic feature correspondence between the reference and target images.

Despite the style transfer is powerful, these approaches offer limited editing controls to users beyond the selection of the reference image. Furthermore, these methods focus on global color editing rather than object-level color adjustment. Whereas palette-based approaches make a better balance between user control and convenience, and support color editing for local objects.

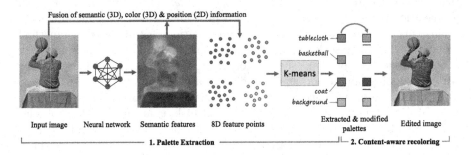

Fig. 1. The pipeline of our approach. Given the input image, we first feed it into a neural network to obtain per-pixel semantic features. Next, we combine it with color and position information, and project them into an 8D feature space, followed by a K-means clustering to extract the palette. Finally, the user modifies the palette colors to locally adjust object colors. In the input image, the man's coat and tablecloth have a similar red color. It is challenging to recolor them separately with existing palette-based methods. Our palette successfully extracts two similar red colors that correspond to the coat and the tablecloth, respectively, so the user can easily recolor the coat and the tablecloth into different colors. (Color figure online)

3   Method

3.1   Overview

The goal of our method is two folded. First, we would like to extract a color palette that can effectively capture the dominant colors of different objects or regions in the input image, so that each palette color can be associated with a specific object or region. Second, we would like to achieve content-aware color editing based on the extracted palette.

Hence, our method could be naturally divided into two stages. The first stage is palette extraction (Sect. 3.2). We first extract per-pixel semantic features from the input image using a neural network. Then, we project the input image into a high-dimensional feature space that incorporates semantic, color, and location information, so that each pixel is regarded as a vertex in this feature space. Finally, we acquire the color palette with a modified K-means clustering method. The second stage is content-ware recoloring (Sect. 3.3). This is achieved by performing a color transfer function to map the changes of the palette colors to corresponding objects or regions of the input image. The pipeline of our method is illustrated in Fig. 1.

3.2 Palette Extraction

Our palette extraction algorithm takes an image along with the palette size as input and outputs a palette. Generally, it consists of two steps, i.e., high-dimensional feature space construction and palette extraction with K-means.

High-Dimensional Feature Space Construction. In this paper, we first utilize the method proposed by Aksoy et al. [2] to generate per-pixel semantic features of the input image. In their work, they designed a feature extractor based on DeepLab-ResNet-101 [7], and cascaded with metric learning [14], to generate features that are as similar as possible if they belong to the same class, and distant from each other otherwise. This feature extraction network takes an image as input and generates a 128-dimensional feature vector for each pixel, and has shown impressive results in semantic segmentation of images.

To remove redundant data and reduce computational overhead, we adopt principal component analysis (PCA) [15] to reduce the dimension of feature vectors from 128 to 3. We visualize the reduced semantic feature map as a three-channel color image and find that it contains some unwanted noise. To reduce noises, we further smooth the extracted semantic features by guided filtering [13] which takes the grayscale image of the input as the guiding image, to better preserve the edges of objects or regions during smoothing. We provide such an example in Fig. 2. From the results, we could find that the features extracted by the neural network are intuitive and can roughly reflect the semantics of different objects in the image. The initial semantic feature image contains a lot of noise, while the filtered feature image is smoother and the boundaries of different objects can be well preserved.

To facilitate the color palette to effectively capture different objects or regions in the image and their representative colors, we project the input image into a high-dimensional feature space for palette extraction. Specifically, we build an 8D feature space that combines semantic, color, and location information together. So any pixel I_i in the input image can be viewed as an 8D point:

$$p_i = \left(r_i, g_i, b_i, x_i, y_i, f_i^1, f_i^2, f_i^3\right) \tag{1}$$

where (r_i, g_i, b_i), (x_i, y_i) and $\left(f_i^1, f_i^2, f_i^3\right)$ are the color, location and semantic features of pixel I_i, respectively. Therefore, the input image can be naturally regarded as a point set in this 8D feature space.

$$\text{(a)}\qquad\qquad\text{(b)}\qquad\qquad\text{(c)}\qquad\qquad\text{(d)}$$

Fig. 2. Visualization of initial and filtered semantic feature maps. (a) Input, (b) Initial semantic feature, (3) The guiding image, (d) Filtered semantic features.

Palette Extraction with K-Means. Next, we employ K-means clustering to extract the palette of the input image. However, directly performing clustering on all pixels is computationally expensive. To speed up, we adopt a classical superpixel segmentation method, i.e., Simple Linear Iterative Clustering (SLIC) [1], to segment the input image into superpixels and use their centroids as the sampling points. Subsequently, we perform K-means clustering on these sampling points.

It is well known that the K-means algorithm is sensitive to the initial cluster centers. To get better initial values, we utilize a similar algorithm to farthest point sampling to choose the initial k cluster centers. The input of the algorithm includes: the sampling point set that contains the centriods of all superpixels $P = \{p_i\}$, and the desired number of palette colors (i.e., desired number of clusters) k. The output is the initial cluster center set C later used for K-means. Initially, $C = \varnothing$. The algorithm performs as follows:

1) For each sampled point $p_i \in P$, assign it a saliency value $\varphi_i = n_i$, where n_i denotes the pixel count of the superpixel where p_i is located.
2) Select the point $p_i \in \{P - C\}$ with the largest saliency value and add it into the clustering center set C.
3) Update the saliency value of all candidate points by:

$$\varphi_j = \left(1 - \exp\left(-\|p_i - p_j\|^2\right)\right) \cdot \varphi_j, \tag{2}$$

where p_i is the newly selected point and p_j iteratives over all sampled points.
4) Return to 2) until k points are selected.

Once the initial cluster center set $C = \{C_i\}$ is determined, we perform K-means clustering on the sampling point set P for further refinement of C.

In the clustering process, the distance $d\left(p_i, C_j\right)$ from a point p_i to a clustering center C_j is defined as the weighted sum of a color term, a location term and a semantic term:

$$d\left(p_i, C_j\right) = \theta_c d\left(p_i^{RGB}, C_j^{RGB}\right) + \theta_p d\left(p_i^{XY}, C_j^{XY}\right) + \theta_s d\left(p_i^{F}, C_j^{F}\right) \tag{3}$$

where $d\left(p_i^{RGB}, C_j^{RGB}\right)$, $d\left(p_i^{XY}, C_j^{XY}\right)$ and $d\left(p_i^F, C_j^F\right)$ denote the L2 distance of color, location and semantic feature between p_i and C_j, respectively. θ_c, θ_p and θ_s denote the relative contributions of these three terms, respectively. We empirically set $\theta_c = 1.0$, $\theta_p = 0.2$ and $\theta_s = 5.0$ in our experiments. Finally, the converged cluster centers $C = \{C_i\}$ is the palette we need for the input image.

The algorithm mentioned above is presented in Algorithm 1. Note that we have actually extended the original definition of a color palette. In our method, each entry of a palette contains a 8D feature (i.e., 3D color + 2D location + 3D semantics), which no longer solely represents a color, but also includes location and semantic information. For the sake of clarity, we will continue to refer to it as the color palette in this paper. Such an extended palette enables performing content-aware recoloring.

Algorithm 1. Palette Extraction

Input:
  an image I and the palette size k
Output:
  an 8D palette $C = \{C_1, C_2, \cdots C_k\}$
 1: build an 8D vector (3D color + 2D location + 3D semantics) for each pixel (Eq. 1)
 2: segment the input image into superpixels S and sample a set of points P
 3: let $C = \varnothing$
 4: assign each sampled point p_i a saliency value $\phi_i = n_i$
 5: **while** not all k seeds are determined **do**
 6:    Select the point $p_i \in \{P - C\}$ with the largest saliency value and add it into the clustering center set C.
 7:    update the saliency value of all candidate points (Eq. 2)
 8: **end while**
 9: perform K-means clustering on all pixels with the seeds C
10: return the converged centers as the palette of the input image

---

3.3   Content-Aware Recoloring

In this section, we design a color transfer function to map the changes of the palette colors to the input image. Our color transfer function mainly follows the principle of similarity, i.e., when a palette entry is changed during recoloring, the colors of objects or regions that are semantically, chromatically, and spatially similar to it will change accordingly, while other irrelevant objects or regions will be kept as unchanged as possible. Specifically, for any pixel I_i (its corresponding 8D feature point is p_i), its edited color I_i' is defined as:

$$I_i' = I_i + \sum_{j=1}^{k} w_j^{p_i} \left(C_j' - C_j\right)_{0:3} \quad \text{and} \quad \sum_{j=1}^{k} w_j^{p_i} = 1 \qquad (4)$$

where k is the palette size, C_j and C_j' are the j-th palette entry before and after modifying, $(\cdot)_{0:3}$ denotes the color component of an 8D vector, $w_j^{p_i} \in [0, 1]$ denotes the similarity weight of p_i with respect to the palette entry C_j.

Before defining $w_j^{p_i}$, we first define a similarity function $S_j(x)$ for any palette entry C_j, to measure the similarity between any pixel x and it. It is defined as a linear combination of a set of radial basis functions:

$$S_j(x) = \sum_{i=1}^{k} \lambda_{j,i} \phi(x, C_i) \tag{5}$$

where $\lambda_{j,i}$ is the coefficient to be solved, and $\phi(x, C_i)$ is a radial basis function which is defined as the product of three Gaussian kernels:

$$\phi(x, C_i) = \exp\left(\frac{-\left(x^{RGB} - C_i^{RGB}\right)^2}{2\sigma_c^2}\right) \cdot \exp\left(\frac{-\left(x^{XY} - C_i^{XY}\right)^2}{2\sigma_p^2}\right) \cdot$$
$$\exp\left(\frac{-\left(x^F - C_i^F\right)^2}{2\sigma_s^2}\right) \tag{6}$$

These three kernels are used to measure the color, location and semantic similarity between x and C_i, respectively. σ_c, σ_p and σ_s denote the corresponding standard deviation of color, location and semantic feature, respectively. This is derived by calculating the average of the colors, coordinates and semantic features of all palette entries.

We design this radial basis function (Eq. 6) based on the idea that the similarity between a pixel and a palette entry should be determined by a combination of their colors, positions and semantic features. From the definition, we could know that x and C_i are similar if and only if all their features are close.

We would like to constrain that $S_j(x) = 1$ if $x = C_j$, and $S_j(x) = 0$ if $x = C_{i \neq j}$. That is to say, each entry in the palette is most similar to itself (with a similarity of 1) and least similar to other entries in the palette (with a similarity of 0). Given the constraints, we can build a linear system with k^2 equations, and the coefficients $\lambda_{j,i}(j, i \in 1, 2, \cdots k)$ in Eq. 5 can be efficiently obtained by solving this linear system.

Once the similarity function of each palette entry is determined, the similarity weight $w_j^{p_i}$ could be obtained through:

$$w_j^{p_i} = \frac{S_j(p_i)}{\sum_{j=1}^{k} S_j(p_i)} \tag{7}$$

During recoloring, the semantic and location components of each palette entry are fixed, and users are allowed to modify the color components of the palette entries to adjust the appearance of the input image. When users modify a palette color, only objects or regions that are semantically close to it (belonging to the same class of objects), similar in color, and close in position will have color changes, thus achieving good local control in color editing. The process of image recoloring is presented in Algorithm 2.

4   Experiments

We perform all experiments on a desktop computer with an Intel i7-11700 2.5 GHz CPU and 16 GB RAM. Our algorithm is implemented in C++ language. We employ the source code provided by Aksoyet al. [2] to extract per-pixel semantic features from an input image. Besides, we developed a GUI for interactive recoloring using Qt as shown in Fig. 3.

Algorithm 2. Image Recoloring

Input:
    an image I, the palette C, the modified palette C'
Output:
    the recolored image I'
1: solve for the coefficient $\lambda_{j,i}$ of the similarity function (Eq. 5)
2: determine the similarity weights of each pixel to the palette entries (Eq. 7)
3: generate the recolored image (Eq. 4)
4: return the recolored image I'

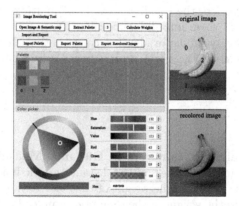

Fig. 3. Our recoloring GUI. Which presents the original and modified color palettes on the left, and the original and recolored images on the right. The numbers below the palette colors correspond to objects or regions in the original image. The color picker (lower left) is used to change the palette colors.

4.1   Results

We generated four recoloring results with our method in Fig. 4. For each example, we provide the input image, the extracted and modified palettes (modified colors are marked with red underlines), and the recolored result. All these examples contain objects or regions with similar colors, and our method is able to modify them to different colors. For example, in Fig. 4 (a), our palette captures two similar blue colors of the sky and balloon, and we can separately alter the sky's

Fig. 4. Recoloring results generated by our method.

color to cyan and change the blue regions in the balloon into purple. In Fig. 4 (c), our method extracts the dominant colors of multiple yellow objects, and successfully recolored them into different colors. Note that while there may be several entries with very similar or identical colors in the palette (e.g., the palette below the input image in Fig. 4 (c)). This is because each entry in the palette is in fact an 8D vector, and the semantic and location components of these entries may be quite different.

4.2   Evaluation

Evaluation of Weight Parameters in Distance Measurement. Here, we evaluate the weighting parameters of the distance metric function (Eq. 3) in the K-means clustering, including the weight of the color term θ_c, the weight of the location term θ_p and the weight of the semantic term θ_s. We give an example in Fig. 5, and provide the extracted palettes and corresponding weight maps with different parameter settings. The results generated with the default parameters ($\theta_c = 1.0, \theta_p = 0.2, \theta_s = 5.0$) are presented in the first row. Followed by the results generated by adjusting θ_c, θ_p and θ_s, respectively. When evaluating one parameter, others are fixed to default values.

Here, a weight map w_i can be viewed as a single-channel grayscale image of the same size as the input image I and is associated with a palette entry C_i. Where any pixel's color $w_i^p \in [0, 1]$ equals the weight of I_p to C_i (Eq. 7).

From the definition of the color transfer function (Eq. 4), the weight map actually denotes the regions affected by the corresponding palette entry during recoloring. In theory, we expect each weight map to contain only a single object

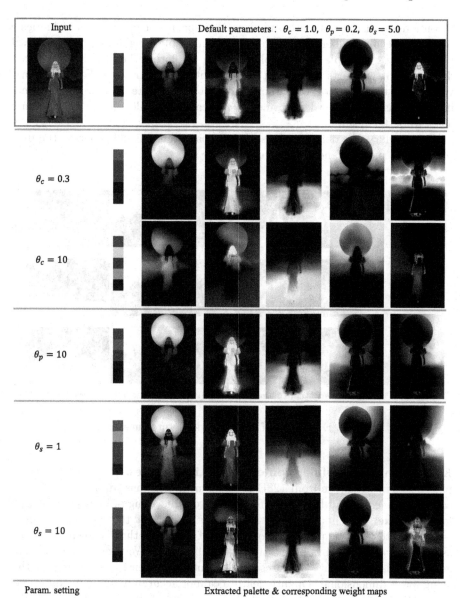

Fig. 5. Parameter evaluation.

with similar semantics and colors, so that this region can be accurately edited by modifying the corresponding palette color.

For θ_c, a small value usually causes the palette entry to affect a larger region containing pixels with quite different colors (i.e., the 2nd weight map in row 2 contains both yellow hair and red skirt), while a larger value leads to the region contains multiple semantically different objects (i.e., the 3rd weight map in row

3 contains both the red skirt and the red carpet). For θ_p, a larger value leads to the same object being scattered across multiple weight maps, thus it will be affected by multiple palette colors during recoloring (i.e., the background is divided into two parts in the last two weight maps in row 4). For θ_s, a small value leads to the region containing different objects (i.e., the 3rd weight map in 5 contains both the red skirt and the red carpet), while a larger value usually leads to better results.

In summary, the default values of these parameters could generate the most satisfactory palettes and weight maps.

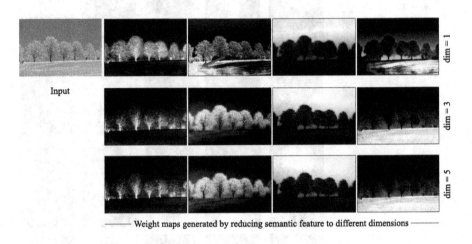

Weight maps generated by reducing semantic feature to different dimensions

Fig. 6. Evaluation of the semantic feature dimension.

Evaluation of the Dimension of Semantic Features. Here we reduce per-pixel's semantic feature from 128D to different dimensions (dim = 1, 3, 5), and combine the color and location information to build a high-dimensional feature for each pixel, and finally perform K-means to extract the palette. In Fig. 6, we expect to extract a palette consisting of 4 entries that correspond to the sky, trunks and branches of the trees, and the earth. We provide weight maps generated using semantic features of different dimensions. It can be seen that using lower dimensional semantic feature cannot accurately distinguish between different objects (e.g., the 2nd weight maps in rows 1). In contrast, using higher dimensional semantic feature yield more accurate distinctions. In this example, it yields improved results when the dimension of the semantic feature is 3 or higher. To reduce storage overhead and effectively differentiate the semantics of various objects, we use the 3D semantic feature along with the 3D color and 2D location as the feature of each pixel.

4.3 Comparisons

Comparison of Palettes and Weight Maps. We first compare the palettes and corresponding weight maps generated by Chang et al. [4] (1st row), Tan

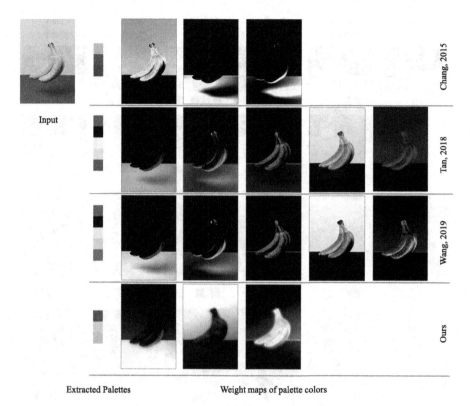

Extracted Palettes   Weight maps of palette colors

Fig. 7. Comparison of color palettes generated by different algorithms.

et al. [23] (2nd row), Wang et al. [27] (3rd row) and our method (4th row) in
Fig. 7. In this example, the banana and background share a similar yellow color.
Existing methods fail to separate them in weight maps. For example, in the 1st
weight map in Chang et al. [4], in the 4th weight map in Tan et al. [23], and in the
4th weight map in Wang et al. [27]), both the banana and upper background are
included in the same weight map. This means users can't edit them individually.
In contrast, our palette captures three primary objects much better: the banana's
yellow, the upper background's yellow, and the lower background's blue, are
presented in three separate weight maps. This allows users to edit the colors of
these objects separately during recoloring without affecting each other.

Comparison of Recoloring Results In Fig. 8 and Fig. 9, we show more recoloring examples to compare our method against approaches proposed by Chang
et al. [4], Tan et al. [23], Wang et al. [27] and Chao et al. [5]. For each example,
we give the input, two editing intends (red and blue texts below the input),
the extracted palettes (1st row), the recoloring results generated by different
methods, and the modified palettes (below the recolored images). The changed
palette colors are marked with red underlines.

Fig. 8. Comparison of recoloring results of different methods.

All provided examples contain at least two objects with similar colors. It is challenging for existing palette-based methods to recolor these objects individually. While our method could effectively capture the dominant features (semantics + color + location) of different objects with similar colors, which thus generates better recoloring results. For example, in Fig. 8 (a), the teddy bear, the chair, and the upper light share similar yellow colors. The two edit intentions

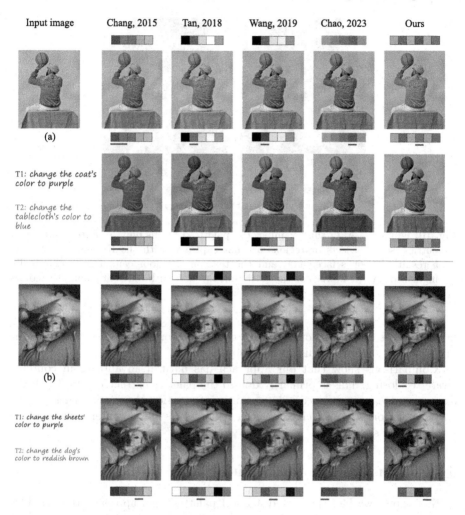

Fig. 9. Comparison of recoloring results of different methods.

given are 1) to change the bear's color to light blue and 2) to change the bench's color to light yellow. Existing methods struggle to recolor them separately without affecting each other, our method accurately recolors them to different colors, aligning well with the user's intent. In Fig. 8 (b), the man's shirts, the TV, and the table have similar colors. When changing the color of a table to beige, existing methods make all these objects' colors unexpectedly beige. Our method successfully adjusts the color of the table without affecting other non-interested objects. In Fig. 8 (c), the input image depicts a beautiful view of the sea melted into the sky. Users want to 1) make the sky's color clear blue and 2) muddy the sea. Existing methods cannot distinguish the sky and the sea effectively, when

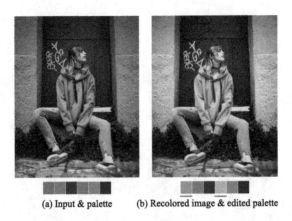

(a) Input & palette   (b) Recolored image & edited palette

Fig. 10. Failure case. In this example, the palette contains only a limited number of six entries, some objects or regions are not captured with the K-means clustering. As a result, the girl's face, hair, and the text on the door cannot be semantically distinguished. When we recolor the cloth and the wall with different colors, the colors of other objects are changed accordingly.

modifying the sky, the color of the sea changes accordingly and vice versa. Our method better fulfills the user's intention.

Comparisons show that our approach has natural advantages in content-aware recoloring. This is primarily due to the palettes extracted from the high-dimensional feature space contain semantic information. As a result, each palette entry corresponds to a specific object or region. This makes content-aware image recoloring possible.

5   Conclusion, Limitation and Future Work

In this paper, we have presented a novel palette-based approach that enables content-aware image recoloring for the first time. To achieve this goal, we first extract the palette of an image in a high-dimensional feature space which fuses the semantic, color and spatial information. This makes our color palette contain semantic information and enables each palette entry to correspond to a particular object or region. We then transfer the changes of palette colors to the input image through a color transfer function. Our method is simple and easy to implement, making it useful for users to perform content-aware local editing. Extensive experiments have demonstrated the effectiveness of our method.

Our method still has two primary limitations to be further improved. First, currently, the palette size k needs to be specified by the user. A color palette with numerous hues might make it challenging to semantically distinguish between different objects, while a limited palette size may result in the inability to accurately represent the colors of certain objects. Therefore, determining the appropriate size of the color palette may require users to invest some time in experimentation. We provide such a failure case in Fig. 10. In the future, it is desirable to explore ways to automatically determine the palette size, by considering both color diversity and semantic complexity of the input image. Second, the accuracy of our palette extraction algorithm builds on top of a semantic feature detection neural network while it is not always accurate, especially for complex scenes. In the future, we would like to explore adaptive palette extraction, and detect semantic features with a more advanced neural network to make the palette extraction and recoloring more robust.

Acknowledgement. We are grateful to the anonymous reviewers for their insightful comments and constructive suggestions, which have significantly contributed to the improvement of our manuscript. This work is supported by the Youth Program of Natural Science Foundation of Qinghai Province (Project Number: 2023-ZJ-951Q).

References

1. Achanta, R., Shaji, A., Smith, K., Lucchi, A., Fua, P., Süsstrunk, S.: Slic superpixels compared to state-of-the-art superpixel methods. IEEE Trans. Pattern Anal. Mach. Intell. **34**(11), 2274–2282 (2012)
2. Aksoy, Y., Oh, T.H., Paris, S., Pollefeys, M., Matusik, W.: Semantic soft segmentation. ACM Trans. Graph. (TOG) **37**(4), 1–13 (2018)
3. An, X., Pellacini, F.: AppProp: all-pairs appearance-space edit propagation. In: ACM SIGGRAPH 2008 papers, pp. 1–9 (2008)
4. Chang, H., Fried, O., Liu, Y., DiVerdi, S., Finkelstein, A.: Palette-based photo recoloring. ACM Trans. Graph. **34**(4), 1–139 (2015)
5. Chao, C.-K.T., Klein, J., Tan, J., Echevarria, J., Gingold, Y.: Colorfulcurves: palette-aware lightness control and color editing via sparse optimization. ACM Trans. Graphics **42**(4), 1–12 (2023). https://doi.org/10.1145/3592405
6. Chao, C.K.T., Klein, J., Tan, J., Echevarria, J., Gingold, Y.: LoCoPalettes: local control for palette-based image editing. Computer Graphics Forum (CGF) **42**(4) (Jun 2023). https://doi.org/10.1111/cgf.14892 special issue for Eurographics Symposium on Rendering (EGSR)
7. Chen, L.C., Papandreou, G., Kokkinos, I., Murphy, K., Yuille, A.L.: Deeplab: semantic image segmentation with deep convolutional nets, atrous convolution, and fully connected crfs. IEEE Trans. Pattern Anal. Mach. Intell. **40**(4), 834–848 (2017)
8. Choi, Y., Choi, M., Kim, M., Ha, J.W., Kim, S., Choo, J.: StarGAN: unified generative adversarial networks for multi-domain image-to-image translation. In: Proceedings of the IEEE Conference on Computer Vision and Pattern Recognition, pp. 8789–8797 (2018)
9. Du, Z.J., Lei, K.X., Xu, K., Tan, J., Gingold, Y.: Video recoloring via spatial-temporal geometric palettes. ACM Trans. Graph. (TOG) **40**(4), 1–16 (2021)
10. Endo, Y., Iizuka, S., Kanamori, Y., Mitani, J.: DeepProp: extracting deep features from a single image for edit propagation. In: Computer Graphics Forum. vol. 35, pp. 189–201. Wiley Online Library (2016)
11. Gatys, L.A., Ecker, A.S., Bethge, M.: Image style transfer using convolutional neural networks. In: Proceedings of the IEEE Conference on Computer Vision and Pattern Recognition, pp. 2414–2423 (2016)
12. Gui, Y., Zeng, G.: Joint learning of visual and spatial features for edit propagation from a single image. Vis. Comput. **36**(3), 469–482 (2020)

13. He, K., Sun, J., Tang, X.: Guided image filtering. IEEE Trans. Pattern Anal. Mach. Intell. **35**(6), 1397–1409 (2012)
14. Hoffer, E., Ailon, N.: Deep metric learning using triplet network. In: Feragen, A., Pelillo, M., Loog, M. (eds.) SIMBAD 2015. LNCS, vol. 9370, pp. 84–92. Springer, Cham (2015). https://doi.org/10.1007/978-3-319-24261-3_7
15. Holland, S.M.: Principal components analysis (PCA). Department of Geology, University of Georgia, Athens, GA 30602, 2501 (2008)
16. Levin, A., Lischinski, D., Weiss, Y.: Colorization using optimization. In: ACM SIGGRAPH 2004 Papers, pp. 689–694 (2004)
17. Li, Y., Ju, T., Hu, S.M.: Instant propagation of sparse edits on images and videos. In: Computer Graphics Forum. vol. 29, pp. 2049–2054. Wiley Online Library (2010)
18. Lischinski, D., Farbman, Z., Uyttendaele, M., Szeliski, R.: Interactive local adjustment of tonal values. ACM Trans. Graph. (TOG) **25**(3), 646–653 (2006)
19. Neumann, L., Neumann, A.: Color style transfer techniques using hue, lightness and saturation histogram matching. In: CAe, pp. 111–122 (2005)
20. Pellacini, F., Lawrence, J.: AppWand: editing measured materials using appearance-driven optimization. In: ACM SIGGRAPH 2007, p. 54 (2007)
21. Pitie, F., Kokaram, A.C., Dahyot, R.: N-dimensional probability density function transfer and its application to color transfer. In: Tenth IEEE International Conference on Computer Vision (ICCV'05) Volume 1. vol. 2, pp. 1434–1439. IEEE (2005)
22. Reinhard, E., Adhikhmin, M., Gooch, B., Shirley, P.: Color transfer between images. IEEE Comput. Graph. Appl. **21**(5), 34–41 (2001). https://doi.org/10.1109/38.946629
23. Tan, J., Echevarria, J., Gingold, Y.: Efficient palette-based decomposition and recoloring of images via RGBXY-space geometry. ACM Trans. Graph. (TOG) **37**(6), 1–10 (2018)
24. Tan, J., Echevarria, J., Gingold, Y.: Palette-based image decomposition, harmonization, and color transfer. arXiv preprint arXiv:1804.01225 (2018)
25. Tan, J., Lien, J.M., Gingold, Y.: Decomposing images into layers via RGB-space geometry. ACM Trans. Graph. (TOG) **36**(1), 1–14 (2016)
26. Ulyanov, D., Lebedev, V., Vedaldi, A., Lempitsky, V.: Texture networks: Feedforward synthesis of textures and stylized images. arXiv preprint arXiv:1603.03417 (2016)
27. Wang, Y., Liu, Y., Xu, K.: An improved geometric approach for palette-based image decomposition and recoloring. In: Computer Graphics Forum. vol. 38, pp. 11–22. Wiley Online Library (2019)
28. Xu, K., Li, Y., Ju, T., Hu, S.M., Liu, T.Q.: Efficient affinity-based edit propagation using kd tree. ACM Trans. Graph. (ToG) **28**(5), 1–6 (2009)
29. Zhang, Q., Xiao, C., Sun, H., Tang, F.: Palette-based image recoloring using color decomposition optimization. IEEE Trans. Image Process. **26**(4), 1952–1964 (2017)
30. Zhu, J.Y., Park, T., Isola, P., Efros, A.A.: Unpaired image-to-image translation using cycle-consistent adversarial networks. In: Proceedings of the IEEE International Conference on Computer Vision, pp. 2223–2232 (2017)

FreeStyler: A Free-Form Stylization Method via Multimodal Vector Quantization

WuQin Liu[1,2] , MinXuan Lin[3] , HaiBin Huang[3] , ChongYang Ma[3] ,
and WeiMing Dong[2(✉)]

[1] School of Artificial Intelligence, University of Chinese Academy of Sciences,
Beijing 101408, China
[2] National Laboratory of Pattern Recognition, Institute of Automation,
Chinese Academy of Sciences, Beijing 100190, China
weiming.dong@ia.ac.cn
[3] Kuaishou Technology, Beijing 100085, China

Abstract. Image stylization refers to the process of transforming an input image into a new one, while retaining its original content but in different styles. However, most existing works only support single-modal guidance, which is not ideal for real-world applications. To tackle this limitation, we propose FreeStyler, a flexible framework for image stylization that is capable of handling various input scenarios. Our approach goes beyond the traditional approach of relying on content and style images to generate a stylized image and supports situations where these references are absent. Specifically, in such cases, FreeStyler allows performing the stylization through text or audio information. The core of FreeStyler is a vector quantized style transfer framework that encodes content and style information into a shared discrete latent feature space, followed by a stylization transformer for style fusion and an image decoder for stylized image reconstruction. To enable free-form stylization, we introduce a novel pseudo-paired token predictor that can estimate tokens from varying input forms without the need for additional text or audio data. Specifically, we leverage Contrastive Language-Image Pre-training (CLIP) as prior knowledge to align discrete representations across different modalities and train the framework using an image and pseudo caption pair provided by Bootstrapping Language-Image Pre-training (BLIP). Through qualitative and quantitative experiments, our method has demonstrated superior performance compared to state-of-the-art stylization methods.

Keywords: Vector quantization · multi-modal stylization · image stylization · contrastive learning

1 Introduction

In this paper, we study the problem of image stylization, which provides a convenient way for amateurs to create vivid artwork without requiring professional skills. One aspect of image stylization work is style transfer, which aims to transform the semantic

F.-L. Zhang and A. Sharf (Eds.): CVM 2024, LNCS 14593, pp. 259–278, 2024.
https://doi.org/10.1007/978-981-97-2092-7_13

Fig. 1. Multimodal guided stylization results generated by our method. In the first row, we show-case images, text, or audio that serve as style information. The first column, on the other hand, presents content information. This approach enables users to guide the stylization process flexibly by selecting input modalities according to their specific content and style preferences.

texture of a style image into a given content image. Initially, Gatys et al. [11] employed a pre-trained VGG network to accomplish style texture transfer by matching the Gram matrices of the content and style images. Subsequent works [15,21,37,42] have built upon and improved this approach. Although these approaches can generate visually appealing artworks by transferring styles of arbitrary artworks into real-world photos, they necessitate the availability of both a reference style image and a content image. However, we argue that this requirement may be impractical in many real-life scenarios where content or style images are unavailable. Consider, for instance, situations where users aim to transfer a specific texture style that only exists in their imagination, without a corresponding content figure. Alternatively, they may lack artistic pictures to stylize a particular photo. Furthermore, users may wish to provide content information in the form of textual descriptions or sounds produced by objects, or convey style information through texture descriptions or sound-to-color synesthesia, or even utilize both modalities simultaneously. These scenarios pose significant challenges to style transfer methods and present noteworthy complexities in image stylization tasks.

To address these challenges, we propose FreeStyler, a general and unified framework for image stylization that explicitly decouples content and style information and supports free-form modality guidance. The key component of FreeStyler is a vector quantization module that bridges the application of style transfer across multi-modalities. Our approach adopts a two-stage learning strategy. In the first stage, we develop a vector quantized style transfer network that employs a shared weight encoder and codebook to project information into a discrete and joint latent space. This is followed by a stylization transformer and decoder module to generate stylization results. In the second stage, we train a pseudo-paired token predictor to reconstruct tokens from various input forms. We leverage the strong prior knowledge of CLIP to align the space using an image and pseudo caption pair generated by BLIP. Figure 1 shows nine combinations of image, text, and audio information used as content and style inputs. Additionally, our model facilitates a range of applications, including mask-guided stylized inpainting and text-driven stylized image editing. In this article, we highlight the results of text-to-image and image-to-image stylization. For more examples, please refer to the supplementary materials.

To summarize, our main contributions are as follows:

- We propose FreeStyler, the first unified image stylization framework that supports free-form multi-modal input as content or style guidance. FreeStyler is designed to cater to a wide range of stylization application scenarios, offering users with enhanced convenience and efficiency.
- To enable free-form multimodal control in image stylization, we present a vector quantization-based approach proposed that establishes a discrete and joint latent space for content and style. This is achieved through a combination of contrastive and adversarial learning techniques. Additionally, we proposed pseudo-paired token predictor that uses a CLIP-based condition transformer to align features across multiple modalities and train the model using an image and pseudo caption pair generated by BLIP.
- Qualitative and quantitative experiments demonstrate that our method can achieve better results in both reference-guided image-to-image style transfer and text-guided image stylization. Moreover, we show the editability of our approach through several novel applications.

2 Related Work

Style Transfer. Inspired by Gatys et al. [11], who defined the distance between two images in the feature space of the VGG network as a measure of style using Gram matrices, several works [15, 21, 37] proposed training end-to-end models by incorporating reasonable content and style constraints without optimization. After that, the arbitrary style transfer (AST) problem has received increasing attention . Li et al. [22, 23] employed the whitening and coloring transform (WCT) method to migrate the distribution of style features, further Yoo et al. [42] proposed a wavelet transform-based WCT to improve the performance in realistic style transfer task. Huang et al. [14] introduced Adaptive Instance Normalization (AdaIN), which replaces the mean and standard deviation of content features with those of style features. With the development of attention mechanism, Park et al. [29] adopted a style-attentional network (SANet) that effectively and flexibly decorates local style patterns based on the semantic spatial distribution of content images. Chen et al. [2] proposed an internal-external and contrastive learning style transfer (IEST) algorithm incorporating two contrastive losses and Zhang et al. [45] proposed CAST approach to address the problem of local distortion and incomplete styles guided by second-order statistics. Furthermore, The QuantArt method by Huang et al. [13] utilizes vector quantization to discretize the latent representation of generated artworks, allowing for flexible control over content preservation, style similarity, and visual fidelity. Later, Liu et al. [28] proposed adaptive attention normalization (AdaAttN) module to enhance visual quality and extend it for video style transfer. Deng et al. [5] employed a transformer-based style transfer framework instead of convolution to focus on the relation of global features. Chen et al. [2] proposed an internal-external and contrastive learning style transfer (IEST) algorithm incorporating two contrastive losses and Zhang et al. [45] proposed CAST approach to address the problem of local distortion and incomplete styles guided by second-order statistics. Furthermore, The QuantArt method by Huang et al. [13] utilizes vector quantization to discretize the latent representation of generated artworks, allowing for flexible control over content preservation, style similarity, and visual fidelity.

In practice, users do not have access to reference style images but still want to mimic a particular painter's texture. Some work [25,27] treated the works of the same painters as a domain and control the results by attribute labels. Kwon et al. [17] proposed CLIPstyler which allows users to enter text to change the style of the content image. Meanwhile, Lee et al. [19] introduced LISA, which uses audio to locate and edit images. However, existing frameworks do not support trimodal input of text, images, and audio, respectively, in the content and style aspects. Therefore, we propose a generic framework to overcome this limitation.

Multimodal-to-Image Generation. The field of multimodal image generation encompasses two main areas: text-to-image generation and audio-to-image generation. The former has been advancing rapidly with the introduction of large-scale pre-trained text-image embedding models like CLIP [31] and the development of diffusion models. However, the latter has received relatively less attention in comparison.

Early approaches to text-guided image generation involved training a convolutional generator that directly predicts pixels from a given text embedding. Later, transformer-based generators [7,9,33] that map text embeddings to discrete representations of images (VQGAN [9] or VQ-VAE [34,38]) achieve significantly improvement on visual quality. And then, diffusion models have been shown to be superior in image generation [6] and gradually take over the main position in digital art generation [8,12,32,35,36]. However, diffusion models have difficulty in generating an image of the specified content, which is consistent with the style of the painting based on a particular painting. Although Kwon et al. [18] attempted to decouple the content and style of an image, it is still a far cry from the performance of traditional style transfer. In terms of audio-guided image generation, attempts have been made to combine wav2clip [40] and VQGAN to generate audio-guided images. However, this area still requires further research and development. Therefore, our approach combines transformer and CLIP to enable users to input arbitrary, images, text and audio as content or style information. Inspired by [39], we train a standard GPT transformer module using pseudo captions to align space without the need for paired text-image data.

Vector-Quantized Image Representation. The vector-quantized generative models, including VQVAE [34,38] and VQGAN [9], were originally designed to achieve compact and efficient image modeling. VQVAE utilizes a vector-quantized autoencoder architecture to represent images using a discrete set of tokens. Building upon VQVAE, VQGAN further enhances the model with an adversarial learning scheme. By discretizing continuous image features, these models offer several advantages, such as enabling smoother post-processing operations. This discretization also empowers the utilization of alternative modalities or expressions to guide the process of image generation, ultimately resulting in more precise and personalized outcomes. In line with these advantages, our approach leverages the power of discretization to expand the applications of style transfer. By providing a more convenient and user-friendly framework, our method aims to facilitate style transfer tasks and empower users with greater control and flexibility over the generated results.

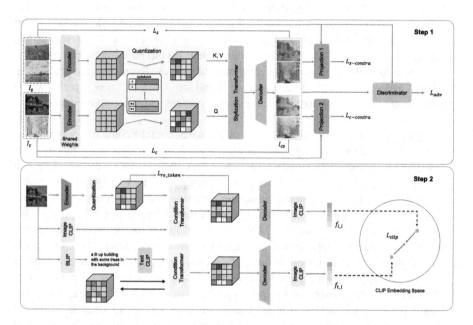

Fig. 2. An overview of our method. It includes a VQGAN model to discretize features, a stylization transformer for style fusion, as well as a condition transformer as the multimodal input guidance module. There are two steps in the training stage: (1) The first step is to train a vector quantization framework, which consists of a pretrained VQGAN encoder and a codebook to quantize the image features. The stylized image is then decoded and sent to two projection modules, which calculate the contrastive loss for content and style respectively. (2) In the second step, we utilize BLIP to provide the pseudo caption for each image and freeze all the modules except the condition transformer to learn the reconstruction of tokens under the CLIP constraint, allowing the user to freely choose the input modality in the inference step.

3   Method

Our goal is to achieve image, text, or audio guided stylization in arbitrary domains for both content and style. To achieve this, our proposed method follows two main steps: (1) training a vector quantized style transfer framework by contrastive and adversarial learning. (2) training a multi-modal guided token predictor in a pseudo-paired approach. Figure 2 illustrates the overall framework of our method.

3.1   Vector Quantization Framework

In our approach, we employ a vector quantization strategy to encode the features of the input image. This strategy ensures a consistent representation between the image and text modalities and makes it easier to construct and manipulate the content and style space in their respective branches. Since all information is discretely represented, we utilize a stylization transformer as an intermediate module to fuse the content and style features. In the context of image style transfer, contrastive learning has been proved to be effective [2]. In this technique, stylized images with the same style should exhibit closer relationships in the style feature space compared to those with different styles. Similarly, stylized images based on the same content should have higher content similarity compared to those based on different content images. To enhance the decoupling of content and style in the feature space, we introduce contrastive loss, which encourages the desired separation and distinctiveness of content and style representations.

Vector Quantization Representation. First of all, we denote the content input image as $I_c \in \mathbb{R}^{H \times W \times 3}$ and the style input image as $I_s \in \mathbb{R}^{H \times W \times 3}$. A shared-weights encoder E is applied to encode both content and style. Then, we construct a perceptually rich codebook $\mathcal{Z} = \{z_k\}_{k=1}^{K} \subset \mathbb{R}^{n_z}$ by adopting a strategy similar to VQGAN [9], where n_z is the dimension of code. In the subsequent training, we freeze the encoder E and the codebook $\mathcal{Z}$ and only optimize the stylization transformer and the decoder G. We use the weights of a pre-trained VQGAN as an initialization for the encoder E and the codebook $\mathcal{Z}$ to reduce computational cost and to provide a good prior. Therefore, given an input content image I_c and a style image I_s, they are mapped into spatial embeddings by the encoder and are then discretized to get z_{qc} and z_{qs} according to the codebook.

It is worth emphasizing that the primary objective of VQ-GAN during the training stage is to reconstruct the original image while preserving its details. To ensure the best reconstruction effect for both real and artistic domains, we carefully selected the pre-trained model from the gallery[1] based on its lowest reconstruction loss as our initial loading checkpoint. This decision guarantees that image details are maintained during the discretization process. In the initial training phase, we keep the encoder and codebook fixed and focus on fine-tuning the remaining modules. We employ a domain discriminator during this phase, which is different from the VQ-GAN discriminator. This domain discriminator specifically enhances the artistic quality of the generated images. It is noteworthy that existing methods similar to VQGAN-CLIP [3] utilize checkpoints trained on ImageNet. Nevertheless, the artistic images generated using our approach still produce satisfactory results. Consequently, using the same codebook does not degrade our generation performance.

Stylization transformer. Discretized image features can be tokenized due to their language-like properties, making transformers a natural choice for feature fusion modules. Recent methods [5,43] have demonstrated that transformer-based style transfer frameworks are better at extracting and preserving global information than CNN-based frameworks. In this work, we utilize a vanilla cross-attention transformer as the feature

---

[1] https://github.com/CompVis/taming-transformers.

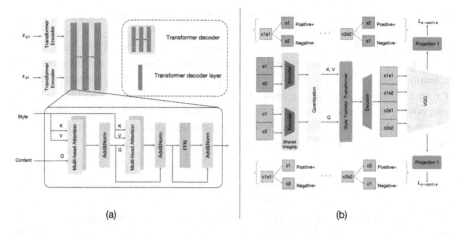

Fig. 3. Two important modules in the framework. (a) The Stylization transformer module proposed for feature style transfer. (b) The contrastive loss used to learn the stylization-to-stylization relations.

fusion module backbone, injecting user-specified style information to modulate content signals.

As illustrated in Fig. 3(a), we utilize two distinct transformer encoders to generate domain-specific sequences for both content and style. Subsequently, a multi-layer transformer decoder is employed to stylize the content sequence by incorporating the style sequence. This process involves taking the discretized features of the content image z_{qc} as the query (Q), while the discretized features of the style image z_{qs} are considered as the key (K) and value (V). Both of them are sent to the stylization transformer in different branches and appended the corresponded position embedding. Finally, we obtain the stylized image I_{cs} using the decoder G.

Contrastive Learning. In recent years, contrastive learning has proved its superiority in style transfer. For example, Chen et al. [2] adopt contrastive learning to enhance the relations of multi-style-single-content and single-style-multi-content results neglected by traditional style transfer methods and In order to improve the generation quality of stylized images, we also leverage contrastive learning to improve the generation quality of stylized images.

As shown in Fig. 3(b), in each training batch, two different content images I_{c_1}, I_{c_2}, and two different style images I_{s_1}, I_{s_2} are processed. We generate all possible combinations of content-style pairs and denote the corresponding results as $I_{c_1 s_1}$, $I_{c_1 s_2}$, $I_{c_2 s_1}$ and $I_{c_2 s_2}$. We utilize a pre-trained VGG19 network as a base projection prior and compute content and style similarity by feeding the features extracted from that into either a content projection network h_c or a style projection network h_s, comprising a two-layer MLP. The content projection is denoted as $l_c = h_c(\phi_{relu4\_1}(*))$ and the style projection as $l_s = h_s(\phi_{relu3\_1}(*))$, where ϕ_i denotes the i-th layer of features extracted from the pre-trained VGG19 model. To simplify the notation, we set the features of projection space as $C_{c_i s_j} = l_c(I_{c_i s_j})$, and $S_{c_i s_j} = l_s(I_{c_i s_j})$. Our approach involves first pushing the stylized image closer to the original content image and further away from other content images in the content projection space, constructing a meaningful and comparable distance space under relationship constraints from opposing directions. The content contrastive loss can be defined as:

$$\mathcal{L}_{c\_contra} = -\log\left(\frac{\exp\left(\frac{C_{c1s1}{}^T C_{c1}}{\tau}\right)}{\exp\left(\frac{C_{c1s1}{}^T C_{c1}}{\tau}\right) + \exp\left(\frac{C_{c1s1}{}^T C_{c2}}{\tau}\right)}\right). \tag{1}$$

where τ is a temperature parameter. At the same time, in the style projection space, we employ the same strategy for style features. The style contrastive loss can be denoted as:

$$\mathcal{L}_{s\_contra} = -\log\left(\frac{\exp\left(\frac{S_{c1s1}{}^T S_{s1}}{\tau}\right)}{\exp\left(\frac{S_{c1s1}{}^T S_{s1}}{\tau}\right) + \exp\left(\frac{S_{c1s1}{}^T S_{s2}}{\tau}\right)}\right). \tag{2}$$

Finally, we obtain the full contrastive loss $\mathcal{L}_{contra}$ as below:

$$\mathcal{L}_{contra} = \mathcal{L}_{c\_contra} + \mathcal{L}_{s\_contra}. \tag{3}$$

Network Training. To ensure the generated results preserve the structure of content branch and texture features of style branch, we construct two perceptual losses. Similar to [1,11,15], we use the pre-trained VGG19 model to extract the features of the image and calculate the content loss and style loss. The content loss and style loss is defined as:

$$\mathcal{L}_c = \frac{1}{N_l} \sum_{i=0}^{N_l} \|\phi_i(I_{cs}) - \phi_i(I_c)\|_2. \tag{4}$$

where N_l denotes the total number of layers. In our experiments, we use features from the layers of relu4_1 and relu5_1 with equal weights.

Meanwhile, the style loss is defined as:

$$\mathcal{L}_s = \frac{1}{N_l} \sum_{i=0}^{N_l} \|\mu(\phi_i(I_{cs})) - \mu(\phi_i(I_s))\|_2$$
$$+ \frac{1}{N_l} \sum_{i=0}^{N_l} \|\sigma(\phi_i(I_{cs})) - \sigma(\phi_i(I_s))\|_2. \tag{5}$$

where μ and σ represent the mean and variance of the extracted features, respectively. In our experiments, we use features from the layers of relu1_1, relu2_1, relu3_1, relu4_1, and relu5_1 with equal weights.

Similar to [24,29,46], we use identity loss terms to make network learning more accurate and rich in content and style information, so that the generated results can maintain more content structure and style features. Therefore, we ensure the similarity in the aspects of pixel space and feature space. The identity loss in the pixel space can be defined as:

$$\mathcal{L}_{identity1} = \|I_{cc} - I_c\|_2 + \|I_{ss} - I_s\|_2 . \tag{6}$$

And the identity loss in the feature space is written as:

$$\mathcal{L}_{identity2} = \frac{1}{N_l} \sum_{i=0}^{N_l} \|\phi_i(I_{cc}) - \phi_i(I_c)\|_2$$

$$+ \frac{1}{N_l} \sum_{i=0}^{N_l} \|\phi_i(I_{ss}) - \phi_i(I_s)\|_2 . \tag{7}$$

where I_{cc} is the output image generated when both the content image and the style image are I_c, and I_{ss} is generated similarly using I_s.

In addition, we use Generative Adversarial Network (GAN) [11,44] to align generated images with the distribution of input art images to learn the human perception of style information, which consists of a generator G and a competing discriminator D. We express the adversarial loss as:

$$\mathcal{L}_{adv} = \mathbb{E}[\log(D(I_s))] + \mathbb{E}[\log(1 - D(I_{cs}))]. \tag{8}$$

So, the overall optimization objective of the model is demonstrated as:

$$\mathcal{L}_{step\_1} = \lambda_1 \mathcal{L}_c + \lambda_2 \mathcal{L}_s + \lambda_3 \mathcal{L}_{identity1} + \lambda_4 \mathcal{L}_{identity2}$$

$$+ \lambda_5 \mathcal{L}_{adv} + \lambda_6 \mathcal{L}_{contra} . \tag{9}$$

In our experiments, we set $\lambda_1 = 8$, $\lambda_2 = 8$, $\lambda_3 = 70$, $\lambda_4 = 1$, $\lambda_5 = 1$ and $\lambda_6 = 2$ to balance different loss terms.

3.2 Pseudo-Paired Token Predictor

To support multimodal control in content and style branches, we adopt the CLIP encoder as a prior to align different modalities during pseudo-paired training. Specifically, we use a condition transformer to predict the token of the image based on the high-level semantic information extracted by CLIP in an autoregressive manner, as inspired by [39]. Given an input image I, we obtain its embedding e_c using the CLIP image encoder and obtain the token $s = \mathcal{Z}(E(I))$ of its discretization feature through the encoder in the step 1. By using the condition transformer, we restore the original image token, which we denote as s'. Using high-level semantic information from CLIP as a guide, we obtain low-level spatial semantic information built from the codebook. Therefore, to achieve our goal in this step, we aim to introduce a token reconstruction loss to enhance the consistency between the original and reconstructed image tokens. The token reconstruction loss $\mathcal{L}_{re\_token}$ is expressed based on the cross-entropy loss $\mathcal{L}_{CE}$ as below:

$$\mathcal{L}_{re\_token} = \mathcal{L}_{CE}(s, s^{'}). \qquad (10)$$

To enhance the performance of image generation, we utilize BLIP to generate a pseudo-caption for the input image I. We then generate the corresponding image $I_t^{'}$ using the network and calculate its similarity with the reconstructed image $I^{'} = G(s^{'})$ in the CLIP space. Thus, we defined the similarity loss as follows:

$$\mathcal{L}_{clip} = \left\| E(I_t^{'}) - E(I^{'}) \right\|_2. \qquad (11)$$

Thus, our overall loss in step 2 is demonstrated as:

$$\mathcal{L}_{step\_2} = \lambda_7 \mathcal{L}_{re\_token} + \lambda_8 \mathcal{L}_{clip}. \qquad (12)$$

where $\lambda_7 = 1$ and $\lambda_8 = 1000$.

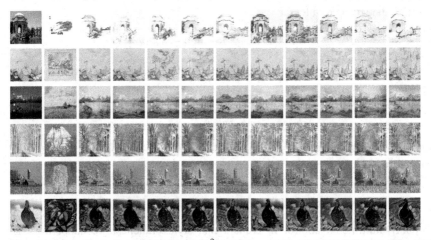

Content Style   Ours   QuartArt CAST StyTr^2 StyleFormer IEST AdaAttN MCCNet ArtFlow AdaIN

Fig. 4. Qualitative comparisons of image style transfer results with several state-of-the-art methods.

4   Experiments

4.1   Implementation Details

In the first stage of our training process, we use MS-COCO [26] as the content dataset and WikiArt [30] as the style dataset. During the training process, all images are first enlarged to 512×512 resolution and then randomly cropped to 256×256 size. We adopt the Adam [16] optimizer and the warm-up adjustment strategy. Meanwhile, the learning rate is set as 5e-4. Then, we train our model on 8 V100 machines with a batch size of 2 and set the number of full training rounds as 40 epochs. In the second stage, we use the MS-COCO dataset as input and train the condition transformer about 200 epochs, the learning rate is also set as 5e-4. We start $\mathcal{L}_{clip}$ after 50 epochs. In this article, we set a standard GPT-2 model of 24 layers as the backbone of the condition transformer.

Baselines. For image style transfer, we compare our approach to AdaIN [14], Art-Flow [1], MCCNet [4], AdaAttN [28], IEST [2], StyleFormer [41], StyTr^2 [5], CAST [45] and QuantArt [13]. All baselines are trained using publicly available implementations with default configurations. For text-guided style transfer, we compare with three state-of-the-art text-guided stylization methods, including CLIPstyler [17], VQGAN-CLIP [3] and LDAST [10].

Fig. 5. Qualitative comparisons of text-guided image stylization results with several state-of-the-art methods.

4.2 Qualitative Results

Image Style Transfer. We first show the visual results of qualitative comparison of our method with state-of-the-art methods in Fig. 4. The comparison shows the superiority of

Freestyler in terms of visual quality and all methods generate stylization images under the same reference image guidance. The results of AdaIN [14] do not preserve the style well and appear crack artifacts, resulting in poor quality of the generated results (e.g., the 3rd, 5th and 6th rows) and ArtFlow [1] may result in insufficient style or inaccuracy (e.g., the 1st and 6th rows). MCCNet [4] can well preserve the content, but there is often a problem of overflow around objects, namely halo artifacts (e.g., the 3rd, 6th and 7th rows). AdaAttN [28] cannot transfer some colors to the generated image, so there will be a style gap between results and reference images (e.g., the 1st, 3rd and 5th rows). IEST [2] can generate high-quality stylization, but it has obvious color distortion problems (e.g., the 1st, 3rd and 7th rows). StyleFormer [41] loses a lot of detail information and generates a number of redundant colors (e.g., the 3rd, 5th and 6th rows). StyTr^2 [5] can generate results with high fidelity, but the learning of style is still difficult, and many colors and textures cannot be transferred (e.g., the 5th, 6th and 7th rows). CAST [45] has a great improvement on both style consistency and content fidelity, however, for some special styles, it is hard to balance the relationship between the style and content, and some detailed textures are distorted(e.g., the 2nd, 5th and 7th rows). QuantArt [13] focuses more on preserving the details of the content, thus retaining the style of many elements such as colors and textures (e.g., the 1st, 4th and 5th rows).

In contrast, our method achieves high quality in both content fidelity and style learning, even with styles containing blank space or large color blocks. By using vector quantization, our decoder only needs to learn a limited number of mapping relationships, improving the quality of stylization images.

Text-Guided Image Stylization. Figure 5 compares our text-guided stylization results with existing baselines that use the same content input. Our method outperforms the baselines in terms of overall quality. CLIPstyler [17] requires model finetuning for each style, which is inconvenient and time-consuming. Additionally, it is challenging for it to learn styles with color blocks (e.g., 1st and 2nd column). VQGAN-CLIP [3] is also an optimization-based method, but its biggest drawback is that the content fidelity gradually decreases as the number of optimization steps increases. In this study, we set the number of optimization steps as 10 to strike a balance, but the content information still cannot be retained as well as our method (e.g., 7th and 8th column). LDAST [10] aims to learn the visual attributes or emotional effects of styles, but it lacks the ability to understand a specific painting style. We observe poor performance in various cases with descriptions from open domains.

In contrast, our method excels in transferring both artistic styles and intentions (e.g., underwater and autumn) effectively to the content image, resulting in visually appealing outcomes. Therefore, our method proficiently disentangles the content and style in separate branches, allowing free-form inputs to guide the structure and texture accordingly. This enables the alignment of text and image features in the discrete space, thereby generating stylized images closely aligned with the provided descriptions.

4.3   Quantitative Results

Image Style Transfer. We present quantitative evaluation results in Table 1, including style and content differences between the generated results and input images, and a

Table 1. Statistical and quantitative comparison of inference time, content and style loss value with state-of-the-art methods. The user study results show the average percentage where other methods perform better than ours in terms of overall quality, content preservation, and style criteria. The best and second-best results are indicated in bold and underlined, respectively.

Method		Ours	QuantArt [13]	CAST [45]	StyTr² [5]	StyleFormer [41]	IEST [2]	AdaAttN [28]	MCCNet [4]	ArtFlow [1]	AdaIN [14]
Inference time(ms/image)		24	32	_11_	530	14	370	71	13	65	**7**
Content loss($\mathcal{L}_c$)		**2.238**	2.332	2.440	2.297	2.808	2.402	2.645	2.334	_2.283_	2.524
style loss($\mathcal{L}_s$)		2.098	2.520	2.488	**1.425**	2.303	2.662	1.958	1.687	2.169	_1.560_
SSIM		_0.598_	0.547	**0.603**	0.538	0.558	0.529	0.465	0.348	0.308	0.319
User Study	Content	-	40.12%	31.88%	27.50%	44.38%	33.75%	34.38%	27.50%	51.25%	10.00%
	Style	-	21.86%	45.00%	43.75%	31.88%	17.50%	19.38%	40.00%	25.63%	18.13%
	Overall	-	33.78%	33.75%	30.00%	41.88%	23.75%	21.25%	30.00%	26.88%	12.50%

user survey assessing the quality of our approach. The first row shows the average inference time of several style transfer methods, and the second and third rows display content and style loss of different methods, respectively. The fourth row shows the SSIM loss of different methods. We calculate content differences according to Eq. 4 and style differences according to Eq. 5 for each method. We generate 900 stylized images by randomly selecting 30 style images and 30 content images. The discrete feature representation derived from vector quantization enables us to achieve optimal performance in measuring content loss, albeit at the expense of a slight loss in style information. However, this does not have any significant impact on visual quality or style similarity, as perceived by humans. In quantitative evaluation, we obtain relatively low scores, striking a suitable balance between content fidelity and style similarity, considering the trade-off between the two.

User Study. We compare our method with nine state-of-the-art style transfer methods to evaluate which method is more favored by humans. We invite 36 users to take part in our survey, and for each participant, 50 questionnaires covering a pair of content and style images are randomly presented, which includes the results of our method and one of the other methods. Each user is asked to answer: (1) which result has better visual quality overall (2) which stylization result preserves the content structure better, and (3) which stylization result transfers style patterns more consistently. We show statistical results in Table 1 and our method outperforms other methods in overall quality and style consistency, achieving the second best result in content preservation.

Text-Guided Image Stylization

User study. We compare our method with the three state-of-the-art stylization methods which support text-guided stylization. The questionnaire contains 29 questions in total, and each question includes a result randomly from the four methods. The participants need to rate from the following three aspects: (1) the content fidelity degree of the stylized result and the content image, (2) the similarity between the stylized result and the style provided by text, and (3) the quality of the generation overall. Each problem will be rated from 1 to 5. We collect 24 valid questionnaires, and we present the results of the user survey in Table 2. The scores demonstrate that our method achieves better

Table 2. The user study of text-guided image stylization in terms of overall quality, content preservation, and style consistency, rating from 1–5. The best and second-best results are highlighted in bold and underlined, respectively.

Method	Ours	CLIPstyler [17]	VQGAN-CLIP [3]	LDAST [10]
Content	4.301	**4.354**	2.656	3.801
Style	**3.966**	3.573	3.531	2.800
Overall	**3.989**	3.801	2.908	3.033

results in style and overall quality than other methods. Compared to the CLIPstyler [17], a slight drop occurs in content due to the lack of sufficient style strength. Generally, our method beats other methods in most comparisons.

4.4 Ablation Study

| Content | Style | w/o $\mathcal{L}_{adv}$ | w/o $\mathcal{L}_{contra}$ | Full model |

Fig. 6. Results of ablation study in step 1.

Step 1. To verify the effectiveness of our framework in step 1, we conduct ablation experiments by removing the adversarial loss and contrastive loss, respectively. As depicted in Fig. 6, we train a network without a discriminator, resulting in obvious checkerboard effects and blurred images. It is difficult to learn the texture of the original style, so the generated results are far from the brushstrokes of the reference style image. In another experiment, we remove the entire contrastive loss, including content and style contrastive loss. It is apparent that the generated images in the first row suffer from poor content fidelity and exhibit gaps in color when compared with the style reference images. Without the contrastive constraints, it is difficult to learn the texture information of the style image. However, by incorporating the full set of losses, our method can better retain the content information of the original content image while faithfully transferring the texture and color of the style image. As shown in Table 3, without $\mathcal{L}_{adv}$ and $\mathcal{L}_{contra}$, the $\mathcal{L}_c$ increased by 0.323 and 0.225, while the $\mathcal{L}_s$ increased by 0.345 and 0.402. Additionally, the SSIM decreased by 0.097 and 0.075.

Table 3. Quantitative results of ablation study in step 1.

$\mathcal{L}_{adv}$	$\mathcal{L}_{contra}$	content loss($\mathcal{L}_c$)↓	style loss($\mathcal{L}_s$)↓	SSIM↑
✗	✓	2.561	2.443	0.501
✓	✗	2.336	2.502	0.523
✓	✓	2.238	2.098	0.598

Step 2. Moreover, to verify the effectiveness of our framework in step 2, we conduct an ablation study by removing the clip loss and token reconstruction loss, respectively. As depicted in Fig. 7, it is apparent that certain words are missing in the stylization results when the clip loss is excluded. For instance, the term "river" in the first line and "autumn" in the second line are not accurately reproduced.

Fig. 7. Results of ablation study in step 2.

4.5 Applications

Audio-Guided Image Stylization. In addition to image and text-guided stylization, our approach can also leverage the aligned image, text, and audio clip space [20] to encode audio. Figure 8 shows the synesthetic effect of audio as style guidance. For instance, the sound of fire leads to a predominantly red image, while the sound of wind produces a hazy effect. Our method can also reflect the mood of the music into the style of the image. Please refer to the supplementary material for more examples.

Mask-Guided Stylized Inpainting. As shown in Fig. 9(a), we can redraw some uninteresting areas by removing objects of the input image by mask and achieving stylization with free-form guidance simultaneously.

Text-Driven Stylized Image Editing. As shown in Fig. 9(b), we can achieve semantic editing by assigning new text caption to specific area and stylization with free-form guidance at the same time.

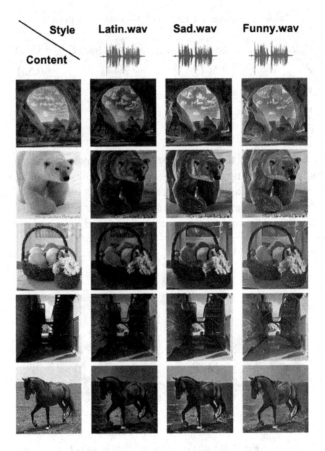

Fig. 8. Results of music-guided image stylization. The mood of different music show various visual effects.

Fig. 9. Results of different novel applications.

5 Limitations and Future Work

Although our method achieves high-quality results on stylization task for multi-modalities input as content or style, there are still several technical issues that need to be addressed. First of all, due to the limited number of tokens after quantization, it doesn't hold up very well for some painting styles or detailed strokes. However,we think it can be handled by extending the number of tokens. Secondly, our method will produce some failure cases for explicit text guided stylization generation due to some minor misalignment of content and style features in CLIP space. In the future, we will try to optimize our model to solve the problem by applying better encoder. At the same time, taking advantage of the quantization of features, there are many image editing operations that can be realized, e.g., inpainting or outpainting.

6 Conclusion

In this paper, we propose a unified image stylization framework which explicitly decouples the content and style branch, and supports various input forms, allowing image, text and audio as content and style information, respectively. The framework is built on a vector quantized style transfer approach, with a stylization transformer to fuse content and style information. Additionally, we incorporate a CLIP-based conditional transformer to align the discrete representation of image, text, and audio modality. Pseudo-paired token predictor is introduced and trained by image and pesudo caption pair generated by BLIP to estimate the representation from multi-modalities. We believe that our framework, which relies on discrete representations of input modalities, has the potential to be applied to other image processing tasks, and is worth exploring in future research.

Funding Information. This work was supported in part by National Science and Technology Major Project under no. 2020AAA0106200, in part by Beijing Natural Science Foundation under no. L221013, and in part by National Natural Science Foundation of China under no. U20B2070.

References

1. An, J., Huang, S., Song, Y., Dou, D., Liu, W., Luo, J.: Artflow: unbiased image style transfer via reversible neural flows. In: Proceedings of the IEEE/CVF Conference on Computer Vision and Pattern Recognition, pp. 862–871 (2021)
2. Chen, H., et al.: Artistic style transfer with internal-external learning and contrastive learning. Adv. Neural. Inf. Process. Syst. **34**, 26561–26573 (2021)
3. Crowson, K., et al.: VQGAN-CLIP: open domain image generation and editing with natural language guidance. In: European Conference on Computer Vision (ECCV), pp. 88–105 (2022). https://doi.org/10.1007/978-3-031-19836-6_6
4. Deng, Y., Tang, F., Dong, W., Huang, H., Ma, C., Xu, C.: Arbitrary video style transfer via multi-channel correlation. In: Proceedings of the AAAI Conference on Artificial Intelligence, vol. 35, pp. 1210–1217 (2021)
5. Deng, Y., Tang, F., Dong, W., Ma, C., Pan, X., Wang, L., Xu, C.: StyTr^2: image style transfer with transformers. In: IEEE/CVF Conference on Computer Vision and Pattern Recognition (CVPR), pp. 11326–11336 (2022)

6. Dhariwal, P., Nichol, A.: Diffusion models beat gans on image synthesis. Adv. Neural. Inf. Process. Syst. **34**, 8780–8794 (2021)

7. Ding, M., et al.: Cogview: mastering text-to-image generation via transformers. Adv. Neural. Inf. Process. Syst. **34**, 19822–19835 (2021)

8. Ding, M., Zheng, W., Hong, W., Tang, J.: Cogview2: Faster and better text-to-image generation via hierarchical transformers. arXiv preprint arXiv:2204.14217 (2022)

9. Esser, P., Rombach, R., Ommer, B.: Taming transformers for high-resolution image synthesis. In: Proceedings of the IEEE/CVF Conference on Computer Vision and Pattern Recognition, pp. 12873–12883 (2021)

10. Fu, T.J., Wang, X.E., Wang, W.Y.: Language-driven artistic style transfer. In: European Conference on Computer Vision, pp. 717–734. Springer (2022). https://doi.org/10.1007/978-3-031-20059-5_41

11. Gatys, L.A., Ecker, A.S., Bethge, M.: Image style transfer using convolutional neural networks. In: Proceedings of the IEEE Conference on Computer Vision and Pattern Recognition, pp. 2414–2423 (2016)

12. Gu, S., et al.: Vector quantized diffusion model for text-to-image synthesis. In: Proceedings of the IEEE/CVF Conference on Computer Vision and Pattern Recognition, pp. 10696–10706 (2022)

13. Huang, S., An, J., Wei, D., Luo, J., Pfister, H.: Quantart: quantizing image style transfer towards high visual fidelity. In: Proceedings of the IEEE/CVF Conference on Computer Vision and Pattern Recognition, pp. 5947–5956 (2023)

14. Huang, X., Belongie, S.: Arbitrary style transfer in real-time with adaptive instance normalization. In: Proceedings of the IEEE International Conference on Computer Vision, pp. 1501–1510 (2017)

15. Johnson, J., Alahi, A., Fei-Fei, L.: Perceptual losses for real-time style transfer and super-resolution. In: Leibe, B., Matas, J., Sebe, N., Welling, M. (eds.) ECCV 2016. LNCS, vol. 9906, pp. 694–711. Springer, Cham (2016). https://doi.org/10.1007/978-3-319-46475-6_43

16. Kingma, D.P., Ba, J.: Adam: A method for stochastic optimization. arXiv preprint arXiv:1412.6980 (2014)

17. Kwon, G., Ye, J.C.: CLIPstyler: Image style transfer with a single text condition. In: Proceedings of the IEEE/CVF Conference on Computer Vision and Pattern Recognition, pp. 18062–18071 (2022)

18. Kwon, G., Ye, J.C.: Diffusion-based image translation using disentangled style and content representation. arXiv preprint arXiv:2209.15264 (2022)

19. Lee, S.H., Kim, C., Byeon, W., Yoon, S.H., Kim, J., Kim, S.: Lisa: localized image stylization with audio via implicit neural representation. arXiv preprint arXiv:2211.11381 (2022)

20. Lee, S.H., et al.: Sound-guided semantic image manipulation. In: Proceedings of the IEEE/CVF Conference on Computer Vision and Pattern Recognition, pp. 3377–3386 (2022)

21. Li, C., Wand, M.: Precomputed real-time texture synthesis with markovian generative adversarial networks. In: Leibe, B., Matas, J., Sebe, N., Welling, M. (eds.) ECCV 2016. LNCS, vol. 9907, pp. 702–716. Springer, Cham (2016). https://doi.org/10.1007/978-3-319-46487-9_43

22. Li, Y., Fang, C., Yang, J., Wang, Z., Lu, X., Yang, M.H.: Universal style transfer via feature transforms. Adv. Neural. Inf. Process. Syst. **30** (2017)

23. Li, Y., Liu, M.-Y., Li, X., Yang, M.-H., Kautz, J.: A closed-form solution to photorealistic image stylization. In: Ferrari, V., Hebert, M., Sminchisescu, C., Weiss, Y. (eds.) ECCV 2018. LNCS, vol. 11207, pp. 468–483. Springer, Cham (2018). https://doi.org/10.1007/978-3-030-01219-9_28

24. Lin, J., Pang, Y., Xia, Y., Chen, Z., Luo, J.: TuiGAN: learning versatile image-to-image translation with two unpaired images. In: Vedaldi, A., Bischof, H., Brox, T., Frahm, J.-M. (eds.) ECCV 2020. LNCS, vol. 12349, pp. 18–35. Springer, Cham (2020). https://doi.org/10.1007/978-3-030-58548-8_2

25. Lin, M., Tang, F., Dong, W., Li, X., Xu, C., Ma, C.: Distribution aligned multimodal and multi-domain image stylization. ACM Trans, Multimedia Comput. Commun. Appli. (TOMM) **17**(3), 1–17 (2021)

26. Tsung-Yi, L., et al.: Microsoft COCO: common objects in context. In: Fleet, D., Pajdla, T., Schiele, B., Tuytelaars, T. (eds.) ECCV 2014. LNCS, vol. 8693, pp. 740–755. Springer, Cham (2014). https://doi.org/10.1007/978-3-319-10602-1_48

27. Liu, A.H., Liu, Y.C., Yeh, Y.Y., Wang, Y.C.F.: A unified feature disentangler for multi-domain image translation and manipulation. Adv. Neural Inform. Process. Sys. **31** (2018)

28. Liu, S., et al.: Adaattn: revisit attention mechanism in arbitrary neural style transfer. In: Proceedings of the IEEE/CVF International Conference on Computer Vision, pp. 6649–6658 (2021)

29. Park, D.Y., Lee, K.H.: Arbitrary style transfer with style-attentional networks. In: proceedings of the IEEE/CVF Conference on Computer Vision and Pattern Recognition, pp. 5880–5888 (2019)

30. Phillips, F., Mackintosh, B.: Wiki art gallery, inc.: a case for critical thinking. Issues in Accounting Educ. **26**(3), 593–608 (2011)

31. Radford, A., et al.: Learning transferable visual models from natural language supervision. In: International Conference on Machine Learning, pp. 8748–8763. PMLR (2021)

32. Ramesh, A., Dhariwal, P., Nichol, A., Chu, C., Chen, M.: Hierarchical text-conditional image generation with clip latents. arXiv preprint arXiv:2204.06125 (2022)

33. Ramesh, A., et al.: Zero-shot text-to-image generation. In: International Conference on Machine Learning, pp. 8821–8831. PMLR (2021)

34. Razavi, A., Van den Oord, A., Vinyals, O.: Generating diverse high-fidelity images with vq-vae-2. Adv. Neural Inform. Process. Syst. **32** (2019)

35. Rombach, R., Blattmann, A., Lorenz, D., Esser, P., Ommer, B.: High-resolution image synthesis with latent diffusion models. In: Proceedings of the IEEE/CVF Conference on Computer Vision and Pattern Recognition, pp. 10684–10695 (2022)

36. Saharia, C., et al.: Photorealistic text-to-image diffusion models with deep language understanding. arXiv preprint arXiv:2205.11487 (2022)

37. Ulyanov, D., Vedaldi, A., Lempitsky, V.: Improved texture networks: maximizing quality and diversity in feed-forward stylization and texture synthesis. In: Proceedings of the IEEE Conference on Computer Vision and Pattern Recognition, pp. 6924–6932 (2017)

38. Van Den Oord, A., Vinyals, O., et al.: Neural discrete representation learning. Adv. Neural Inform. Process. Syst. **30** (2017)

39. Wang, Z., Liu, W., He, Q., Wu, X., Yi, Z.: Clip-gen: language-free training of a text-to-image generator with clip. arXiv preprint arXiv:2203.00386 (2022)

40. Wu, H.H., Seetharaman, P., Kumar, K., Bello, J.P.: Wav2clip: learning robust audio representations from clip. In: ICASSP 2022-2022 IEEE International Conference on Acoustics, Speech and Signal Processing (ICASSP), pp. 4563–4567. IEEE (2022)

41. Wu, X., Hu, Z., Sheng, L., Xu, D.: Styleformer: real-time arbitrary style transfer via parametric style composition. In: Proceedings of the IEEE/CVF International Conference on Computer Vision, pp. 14618–14627 (2021)

42. Yoo, J., Uh, Y., Chun, S., Kang, B., Ha, J.W.: Photorealistic style transfer via wavelet transforms. In: Proceedings of the IEEE/CVF International Conference on Computer Vision, pp. 9036–9045 (2019)

43. Zhang, C., Yang, J., Wang, L., Dai, Z.: S2wat: image style transfer via hierarchical vision transformer using strips window attention. arXiv preprint arXiv:2210.12381 (2022)

W. Liu et al.

44. Zhang, H., Goodfellow, I., Metaxas, D., Odena, A.: Self-attention generative adversarial networks. In: International Conference on Machine Learning, pp. 7354–7363. PMLR (2019)
45. Zhang, Y., et al.: Domain enhanced arbitrary image style transfer via contrastive learning. arXiv preprint arXiv:2205.09542 (2022)
46. Zhao, Y., Wu, R., Dong, H.: Correction to: unpaired image-to-image translation using adversarial consistency loss. In: Vedaldi, A., Bischof, H., Brox, T., Frahm, J.-M. (eds.) ECCV 2020. LNCS, vol. 12354, pp. C1–C1. Springer, Cham (2020). https://doi.org/10.1007/978-3-030-58545-7_47

Vision Meets Graphics

Denoised Dual-Level Contrastive Network for Weakly-Supervised Temporal Sentence Grounding

Yaru Zhang[1,2], Xiao-Yu Zhang[1(✉)], and Haichao Shi[1]

[1] Institute of Information Engineering, Chinese Academy of Sciences, Beijing, China
{zhangyaru,zhangxiaoyu,shihaichao}@iie.ac.cn
[2] School of Cyber Security, University of Chinese Academy of Sciences, Beijing, China

Abstract. The task of temporal sentence grounding aims to localize the target moment corresponding to a given natural language query. Due to the large burden of labeling the temporal boundaries, weakly-supervised methods have drawn increasing attention. Most of the weakly-supervised methods heavily rely on aligning the visual and textual modalities, ignoring modeling the confusing snippets within a video and non-discriminative snippets across different videos. Moreover, the error-prone caused by the sparsity of video-level labels is not well explored, which brings noisy activations and is not robust to real-world applications. In this paper, we present a novel Denoised Dual-level Contrastive Network, namely DDCNet, to overcome the above limitations. Particularly, DDCNet is equipped with a dual-level contrastive loss to explicitly address the incomplete predictions by simultaneously minimizing the intra-video and inter-video loss. Moreover, a ranking weight strategy is presented to select high-quality positive and negative pairs during training. Afterward, an effective pseudo-label denoised process is introduced to alleviate the noisy activations caused by the video-level annotations, thereby leading to more accurate predictions. Comprehensive experiments are conducted on two widely used benchmarks, i.e., Charades-STA and ActivityNet Captions, manifesting the superiority of our method in comparison to existing weakly-supervised methods.

Keywords: Temporal sentence grounding · Weakly-supervised learning · Contrastive learning · Video denoising

1 Introduction

Temporal sentence grounding aims to localize the temporal boundaries of the target moment that semantically corresponds to the given language query. As a fundamental vision-language problem, temporal sentence grounding has attracted extensive attention due to its broad applications, including surveillance [10], video summarization [25], and so forth. With the rapid development of deep learning technologies, fully-supervised methods [6] have made tremendous achievements in recent years, where precise temporal boundaries of each query are required for the model training. However, such manually eye-watching annotations are laborious and time-consuming, leading to expensive annotation costs. In addition, labeling temporal boundaries corresponding with the

F.-L. Zhang and A. Sharf (Eds.): CVM 2024, LNCS 14593, pp. 281–301, 2024.
https://doi.org/10.1007/978-981-97-2092-7_14

specific query is usually subjective and ambiguous, which narrows its scalability and practicability potential in real-world scenarios. Therefore, the weakly-supervised learning schemes, where only video-level natural language queries are needed, have rapidly attracted much more research interest due to the low annotation cost and time efficiency.

To identify the target moment that best matches the given query, it becomes crucial to improve the snippet-wise feature discrimination ability of various video snippets. Generally, the snippet-wise feature embedding space is expected to satisfy two properties: 1) the most relevant video snippet with the given query should be distinguished from the other snippets within a video, *i.e., intra-video separability*; 2) video snippets and queries with similar semantics should be closer than those of different semantics, *i.e., intra-semantic compactness & inter-semantic separability*. This has raised several studies exploring contrastive learning [5,21,23,48,49] to foster feature discrimination. Figure 1 shows different contrastive learning schemes and their distinction with our proposed method. As illustrated in Fig. 1 (a), their focus is mostly on intra-video separability. After performing query-guided attention, snippet-wise target moments are pushed away from their backgrounds within a video. They unfortunately fail to capture the inter-semantic separability and discard the useful "global" contrast across different videos. In Fig. 1 (b), another type of effort strived to consider the matched and mismatched video-language pairs and engage them in the feature contrastive training process. Due to the uncertainty of sampling quality, this method would inevitably give rise to suboptimal performance of sentence grounding.

Due to the lack of frame-level temporal boundaries, snippet-wise pseudo-labels are often used to provide fine-grained supervision. For example, WSLLN [15] designs a parallel network with an extra surrogate module to generate pseudo labels, which will further encourage competition among candidate proposals and foster the feature discrimination. This also led to several pioneer studies exploring self-supervised learning [23], temporal adjacent network [37], pseudo-query generation [27] to refine the predictions. In spite of promising performance, the paradigm is easy to generate noisy activations, i.e., false positives and false negatives in the learned feature space. Most of the existing weakly-supervised temporal sentence grounding methods rely heavily on the pseudo-label strategy to provide refined supervision but do not explicitly handle the label noise.

To address the aforementioned problems, we propose a novel weakly-supervised method namely Denoised Dual-level Contrastive Network (DDCNet), by incorporating the label denoising process into video-language alignment under the constraints of intra-video and inter-video contrastive losses. DDCNet is reconstruction-based, dual-level contrast, and noise-label robust. As illustrated in Fig. 1 (c), for each video-language pair, we force the network to disentangle the query-related snippets (foreground) and other irrelative snippets (background) within a video. To attain the discriminative proposals in each video, we devise a margin ranking based intra-video contrastive loss to distinguish the foregrounds from backgrounds from easy to hard. Then all foreground and background representations among different videos are collected to engage in inter-video contrastive learning. As the natural language description is diverse and subjective, only foregrounds with similar semantic information or backgrounds with similar contexts can make a positive effect. In this case, we propose a similarity-based rank

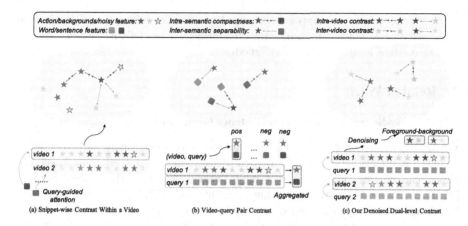

Fig. 1. Different contrastive learning schemes. (a) Exploiting *intra-video separability* to separate the target moments away from their backgrounds within a video. **(b)** Exploiting *intra-semantic compactness & inter-semantic separability* within minibatch to contrast the matched and mismatched video-language pairs. **(c)** Our denoised dual-level contrastive algorithm with 1) *intra-video contrast*, 2) *inter-video contrast* and 3) pseudo-label denoising module. The stars stand for the video features, and squares stand for the query features. Different colors indicate different videos or queries (better viewed in color). (Color figure online)

weighting module to reduce the impact of dissimilar positive pairs, and enhance the positive impact of similar pairs. Furthermore, to mitigate the negative influence of noisy pseudo-labels that are omnipresent in weakly-supervised methods, a determinant-based denoised loss is designed to generate reliable pseudo-labels and suppress the noisy activations. The denoised loss, on the other hand, is capable of encouraging a more robust joint feature space by enhancing the mutual information (MI) between query-related activations and pseudo-foreground within a video. To this end, the uncertainty of predictions is reduced, leading to more accurate predictions.

Our contributions are summarized as follows:

- We introduce a novel denoised dual-level contrastive network, named DDCNet, for the problem of weakly-supervised temporal sentence grounding. To the best of our knowledge, we are the first to explicitly address the pseudo-label noises that are omnipresent in weakly-supervised methods.
- We present a dual-level contrastive loss to enhance the discriminability and completeness of the target moment. By disentangling each untrimmed video into query-related foreground and irrelevant backgrounds, our proposed method achieves intra-video separability, intra-semantic compactness and inter-semantic separability simultaneously.
- We design a pseudo-label noise removal process to guarantee the robustness of temporal sentence grounding. In contrast to ignoring noisy activations in feature interaction, our method reduces the negative impact and achieves refined predictions.

– Comprehensive experiments are performed on Charades-STA and ActivityNet Captions datasets, which demonstrate the effectiveness of our DDCNet when compared with existing weakly-supervised methods.

2   Related Work

2.1   Weakly-Supervised Temporal Sentence Grounding

Weakly-supervised temporal sentence grounding is becoming more attractive due to its practical effects in reducing the burden of collecting frame-level annotations. Past efforts can be categorized as either multi-instance learning (MIL) based methods [15,24,26,37–39,47] or reconstruction-based methods [12,21,32,48,49]. The MIL-based methods treat an untrimmed video as a bag of instances with video-level query annotations, and typically learn to predict temporal boundaries with a triplet loss. Among them, TGA [26] first presents a text-guided attention to optimize the video-text alignment space. WSLLN [15] jointly learns the cross-modal alignment and discriminative proposal selection. Follow-up works expand the MIL-based framework by designing sophisticated cross-modal modules [33,37,38], proposing proposal selection strategies [24,47], or building effective objective functions [11,39,43]. However, these MIL-based methods heavily rely on the quality of randomly-selected negative pairs, and cannot provide enough strong supervision signal. In contrast, reconstruction-based methods aim to select moments that can reconstruct the given language query, and use the intermediate results for predicting temporal boundaries. Based on this concept, SCN [21], where masked words and predicted moments are fed to reconstruct the origin query, assuming localized moments should be able to accomplish those important words. Besides, CNM [48] and CPL [49] recently introduce a learnable Gaussian mask to generate high-quality positive and negative proposals, which highly improves the grounding performances due to the superiority of content-related proposal generation. Inspired by such advances, our approach takes a further step to explore the denoised contrastive learning from a large number of weakly annotated videos, which fosters the discrimination and robustness from both intra-video and inter-video aspects.

2.2   Contrastive Representation Learning

Contrastive learning presents a remarkable performance due to its great potential capability for un-/self-supervised representation learning [31,34,40]. These approaches seek to learn such an embedding feature space in which similar (or positive) sample pairs should be pulled together while dissimilar (or negative) ones are pushed apart. Some approaches even achieve favorable performance without engaging negative pairs [3,8,16]. Following the success of contrastive representation learning, some recent efforts are making an attempt to adapt such a paradigm into the video domain. For instance, VideoMoCo [28] employs the image-based MoCo method for video representation, which largely improves the temporal representation capability for video-related tasks. In video grounding task, AsyNCE [11] proposes to reduce the impact of the false positives by leveraging flexible AsyNCE loss, encouraging effective communication between cross-modal interaction for weakly-supervised grounding. To improve the training efficiency, CCL [47] develops a counterfactual contrastive framework, which verifies the effectiveness and robustness of vision-language grounding. However, these methods are mostly based on NCE loss and its variants, while other types of loss formulation have not been well explored. Different from these approaches, in this paper we perform contrastive learning on weakly-supervised temporal sentence grounding with both intra-video and inter-video contrast, and achieve compelling results both quantitatively and qualitatively.

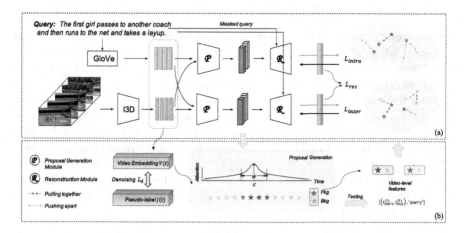

Fig. 2. The overall framework of our DDCNet. The focus of our method is to jointly enhance the discriminability and completeness of latent moment embeddings and addresses the pseudo-label noisy omnipresent in weakly-supervised learning. The upper stream (a) presents our method trained with dual-level contrastive loss, which consists of an intra-video and inter-video contrastive loss to optimize the proposal generation module $\mathcal{P}$. In the bottom stream (b), we propose a denoised algorithm aiming to reduce the impact of noisy activations in temporal sentence grounding. Besides query reconstruction loss $\mathcal{L}_{rec}$ in $\mathcal{R}$, the network is trained jointly using loss terms $\mathcal{L}_{intra}, \mathcal{L}_{inter}$ and $\mathcal{L}_d$.

3   The Proposed Method

3.1   Problem Formulation

Given a pair of untrimmed video and associated language query (V_i, Q_i), where V_i and Q_i separately represents a video and the corresponding language query. The goal of weakly-supervised temporal sentence grounding is to ascertain a moment τ that temporally matches the query Q_i with only the video-level annotation given. More specifically, we denote the input video as a frame sequence with l_V snippets, termed as $V_i = \{v_t\}_{t=1}^{l_V}$, where v_t represents the video snippet at timestamp t. Similarly, the associated language query can be represented as $Q_i = \{w_j\}_{j=1}^{l_S}$, where w_j and l_S represent the j-th single word in the language and the number of total words. Under this primary notation, our model is to learn a mapping function for predicting the moment boundary with parameter Θ, which can be formulated as follows:

$$f_\Theta : (V_i, Q_i) \rightarrow (\tau_s, \tau_e), \tau_s < \tau_e, \tag{1}$$

where τ_s and τ_e indicate the indices of the start and end timestamp of the predicted boundary, respectively.

3.2   Visual-Text Feature Extraction

Before generating more expressive representations, we first embed the given video and its corresponding language query into a continuous high-dimension feature space. For each video, we employ a pretrained feature extractor (e.g., C3D [35] or I3D [4]) to extract video representations V and then apply the temporal pooling operation on them to reduce the feature dimension. Here the extracted video features can be represented as $V = \{V_1, V_2, \ldots, V_{l_V}\} \in \mathbb{R}^{l_V \times d_V}$, where d_V stands for the video feature dimension. As for the language query, we employ the GloVe [29] model to obtain the query embedding with respect to each word. In this case, the query embedding can be naturally represented as $Q = \{W_i, W_2, \ldots, W_{l_s}\} \in \mathbb{R}^{l_s \times d_Q}$, where d_Q denotes the query embedding dimension. It's worth noting that we didn't finetune the pretrained feature extractor on the given untrimmed video datasets in order to guarantee a fair comparison with existing proposed methods.

3.3   Gaussian-Based Proposal Generation

Following the standard practice, we utilize a Gaussian-based mask generator $\mathcal{P}$ [48] to generate high-quality proposals with query-related semantics. Inspired by the recent success of Transformer [36], we first use the multi-head attention module to capture long-range semantic representations from the query, dubbed as $F = MHA(Q)$, and then arrive at fused hidden feature $\mathcal{H}$ that incorporate both video and query semantics, given by

$$\mathcal{H} = TransEncoder(V, F, V) \in \mathbb{R}^{l_V \times d_H}, \tag{2}$$

where $TransEncoder(\cdot)$ represents a Transformer-based encoder architecture, and d_H denotes the feature dimension. As $\mathcal{H}$ combines both semantic and vision information, we predict the center and width of our target proposal through a fully connected layer followed by a *Sigmoid* calculation, which can be denoted as G_c and G_w respectively. Afterwards, the Gaussian-based mask can be derived as

$$\varphi^p(i) = \exp\left(-\frac{\alpha(i/N - G_c)^2}{G_w^2}\right), i = 1, \ldots, N \tag{3}$$

where $\varphi^p(i)$ represents the probability of the i-th video snippet being the foreground proposal in the Gaussian mask, and α denotes a hyperparameter that controls the variance of the Gaussian curve.

To obtain more complete predictions, we encourage to produce K Gaussian masks through a multi-branch module. To avoid the branches lazily concentrating on the same video snippet, a diversity loss is imposed on them:

$$\mathcal{L}_{div} = \frac{1}{K} \sum_{k=1}^{K} \max \left(\left\| \varphi^p \varphi^{p\top} - \mathbf{I} \right\|_F^2 - b, 0 \right), \tag{4}$$

where K is the hyperparameter, b is a balance vector that controls the extent of overlap between different masks. After that, we average K Gaussian masks to obtain the final proposal:

$$\varphi^{avg} = \frac{1}{K} \sum \varphi_k^p(i). \tag{5}$$

In this case, the average mask captures and combines different action parts, effectively encode the entire action.

3.4 Intra-video Contrastive Learning

Although we have obtained a series of content-based proposals based on the Gaussian generation module, there still exist a few highly-confusing snippets inside the video that puzzle the generator, thereby leading to inaccurate boundary prediction. To enable the generator more distinguishable, we study the intra-video contrastive representation learning with both easy and hard negative snippets. Intuitively, we regard $\varphi^e = (1 - \varphi^p) \in \mathbb{R}^N$ as the easy negative sample, which corresponds to those video snippets that mostly do not match the given query. As for the hard negative sample, we refer to the entire video as it contains overlapping snippets with both foregrounds and semantically related backgrounds, given by

$$\varphi^h = [1, 1, \ldots, 1] \in \mathbb{R}^N. \tag{6}$$

Training the generator with both easy and hard negative samples can help the model to locate more accurate predictions and prevent the model from outputting longer boundaries that include the ground truth.

As discussed earlier, our goal is to highlight the salient moment that best matches the language query. To measure the semantic relevance between the moment proposal and query, we introduce the semantic completion module $\mathcal{R}$ [21] to calculate reconstruction scores and regard them as feedback to refine previous proposals. Firstly, we mask 1/3 keywords of the original query and then attain the masked query embedding, dubbed as $\hat{Q}$, which is subsequently fed into the $\mathcal{R}$ together with original video features and foreground Gaussian mask. The specific process can be formulated as follows:

$$\mathcal{W}^p = TransDecoder \left(\hat{Q}, U, \varphi^p \right) \in \mathbb{R}^{l_s \times d_U}, \tag{7}$$

where $\hat{Q}$ represents the masked query embedding, $U = TransEncoder(\mathcal{V}, \mathcal{V}, \varphi^p)$ aiming to attain visual representations with respect to φ^p, and $TransDecoder(\cdot)$ denotes the completion module that can be used to achieve the reconstructed feature with respect to each word.

To predict the masked words, we apply a single fully connected layer on $\mathcal{W}^p$ and output the probability distribution $\mathcal{P}^p$ of total reconstructed query. Finally, we use the cross-entropy loss to measure the similarity distance between the reconstructed query and the original query, which is given by

$$\mathcal{D}_{ce}^p = -\sum_{i=1}^{l_S-1} \log \mathcal{P}^p\left(w_{i+1} \mid \mathcal{V}, \mathcal{Q}_{1:i}\right). \tag{8}$$

Similarly, we arrive at $\mathcal{D}_{ce}^e$ and $\mathcal{D}_{ce}^h$ by replacing φ^p with φ^e and φ^h. As only positive sample and hard negative sample contain video snippets corresponding to the query, the final reconstruction loss is defined as:

$$\mathcal{L}_{rec} = \mathcal{D}_{ce}^p + \mathcal{D}_{ce}^h. \tag{9}$$

To contrast positive and highly-confusing negative proposals, we utilize the ranking-motivated loss for intra-video contrastive learning, which can be formulated as:

$$\mathcal{L}_{intra} = \left[\mathcal{D}_{ce}^p + \lambda_1 - \mathcal{D}_{ce}^e\right]_+ + \left[\mathcal{D}_{ce}^p + \lambda_2 - \mathcal{D}_{ce}^h\right]_+, \tag{10}$$

where $[\cdot]_+$ is the hinge function, λ_1 and λ_2 are hyperparameters with a constraint $\lambda_1 < \lambda_2$.

3.5   Inter-video Contrastive Learning

While the intra-video contrastive learning gives us good representations for distinguishing highly-confusing snippets and the real proposals, it fails to address the incompleteness issue of proposals, especially when encountering condition variations with respect to complex semantics (e.g. various scales, viewpoints, or illumination conditions). In this case, it is natural to resort to exploring the correspondence and knowledge transfer across different videos, extending intra-video contrastive learning into inter-video contrastive learning. In this section, we embrace the fact that learning from cross-video foreground-background contrast produces more reliable foreground proposals, and design an inter-video contrastive loss from two aspects: 1) the representation of different video snippets of the same semantics should be close and 2) other representations of opposite semantics should be pushed apart.

Given n video sequences, we first compute a set of Gaussian mask corresponding to their queries based on the generation module $\mathcal{P}$. Then, φ^p and $(1 - \varphi^p)$ are multiplied by $\mathcal{V}$ to disentangle each video into a foreground f and a background b representation. To this end, we can collect n *negative* foreground-background pair $\{(f_i, b_j)\}_{i=1}^n$ for the total video set. In this case, the negative contrastive loss is designed as:

$$\mathcal{L}_{inter}^{Neg} = -\frac{1}{n^2}\sum_{i=1}^n\sum_{j=1}^n \log\left(1 - \Delta(f_i, b_j)\right), \tag{11}$$

where $\Delta(i, j)$ is the cosine similarity between f_i and b_j. The $\mathcal{L}_{inter}^{Neg}$ considers the semantic contrasts both within a single video $(i = j)$ and cross different videos $(i \neq j)$.

To boost the discrimination of activated foregrounds and suppress the co-occurring backgrounds, we consider the other two *positive pairs* (f_i, f_j), (b_i, b_j) from different videos and intend to pull these positive pairs together in the feature space. However, only *positive pairs* with similar semantics that really benefit the model training while those with large distances will degrade the training process. To cope with it, we design a distance-based rank weighting strategy to automatically learn the effect of different positive pairs. It can reduce the impact of those dissimilar pairs to some extent for better contrastive learning. Formally, the positive contrastive loss $\mathcal{L}_{inter}^{Pos}$ is defined as a combination of $\mathcal{L}_{f}^{Pos}$ and $\mathcal{L}_{b}^{Pos}$, which is represented as:

$$\mathcal{L}_{f}^{Pos} = -\frac{1}{n(n-1)} \sum_{i=1}^{n} \sum_{j=1}^{n} \mathbb{1}_{[i \neq j]} \left(w_{i,j}^{f} \cdot \log\left(\Delta(f_i, f_j)\right) \right) \tag{12}$$

$$\mathcal{L}_{b}^{Pos} = -\frac{1}{n(n-1)} \sum_{i=1}^{n} \sum_{j=1}^{n} \mathbb{1}_{[i \neq j]} \left(w_{i,j}^{b} \cdot \log\left(\Delta(b_i, b_j)\right) \right), \tag{13}$$

where $\mathbb{1}$ is an indicator function that equals 1 if $(i \neq j)$. To this end, the overall inter-video objective loss can be formulated as a combination of $\mathcal{L}_{inter}^{Neg}$ and $\mathcal{L}_{inter}^{Pos}$, which is defined as:

$$\mathcal{L}_{inter} = \mathcal{L}_{inter}^{Pos} + \mathcal{L}_{inter}^{Neg}. \tag{14}$$

When contrastive loss $\mathcal{L}_{inter}$ is applied, our proposed network will enhance more complete proposal predictions and simultaneously suppress the co-occurring query-related backgrounds in the training process.

3.6 Pseudo-Label Noise Removal

The aforementioned two loss functions, however, only ensure φ^p to be more discriminative and completely cover the target moment, without considering the noisy activation in multi-modal interaction process. To enhance the robustness of foreground snippets and further refine the predictions, we propose to denoise the snippet-wise pseudo-labels by capturing the mutual information between the temporal activation and their corresponding pseudo-labels. Unlike directly reducing the impact of noisy features, the pseudo-label denoising process can serve as initial fine-grained annotations and be more applicable to existing weakly-supervised methods.

Based on the above observations, we first generate snippet-wise pseudo-label $\mathcal{J}$ to refine foreground and background regions, then build a denoised loss $\mathcal{L}_d$ to improve the robustness of foreground activation with respect to the noisy activation. Intuitively, we calculate snippet-wise pseudo-labels by computing the similarity of each video snippet and the corresponding query. The specific process is formulated as:

$$\mathcal{J}(t) = \frac{1}{2}\left(1 + \Delta\left(\mathcal{V}(t), \mathcal{Q}_{ref}\right)\right), \quad t \in [1, l_V], \tag{15}$$

where $\mathcal{V}(t)$ is the video feature corresponding to the timestamp t, $\mathcal{Q}_{ref}$ denotes the mean of query features over m iterations.

Let $t_f = \{t : \mathcal{J}(t) > 0.5\}$ and $t_b = \{t : \mathcal{J}(t) < 0.5\}$ represent the time slots for selecting the foreground and background snippets with respect to $\mathcal{J}(t)$, we can estimate the snippet-wise label for both foreground and background snippets.

After generating snippet-wise pseudo-labels, we need to reduce the impact of label noise caused by the absence of ground truth, thereby improving the accuracy of the predicted moments. The denoised loss $\mathcal{L}_d$ is designed to assign a confidence score to each snippet that estimates the probability of its pseudo-label being a trustworthy true label, which exploits the mutual information between query-related activation and corresponding labels. Concretely, our denoised loss is inspired by the Determinant based Mutual Information (DMI) [42], which is proposed for multi-class classification tasks and robust to a variety of noise patterns. The original DMI is first defined to compute the determinant of a joint distribution matrix, i.e., $Determin(\mathcal{Z}, \mathcal{Y}) = |\det(\mathcal{C})|$. Here, $\mathcal{Z}$ and $\mathcal{Y}$ denote the predicted probabilities and the ground-truth labels. $\mathcal{C} = 1/n\mathcal{Z}\mathcal{Y}$ is the joint distribution over $\mathcal{Z}$ and $\mathcal{Y}$. Therefore, the denoised loss function is defined as:

$$\mathcal{L}_d = -\mathcal{E}[\log(Determin(\mathcal{C}))], \tag{16}$$

where $\mathcal{E}$ represents the *Expectation* function. Taking the set of snippet-wise pseudo-labels into account, we construct a prediction matrix that considers the set of pseudo-foreground/background temporal locations. Therefore, the final prediction matrix and pseudo-label matrix are given by

$$\hat{\mathcal{Z}} = \begin{bmatrix} \mathcal{J}_f & \mathcal{J}_b \\ 1 - \mathcal{J}_f & 1 - \mathcal{J}_b \end{bmatrix}, \quad \hat{\mathcal{Y}} = 1/z \begin{bmatrix} 1_{n_f} & 0_{n_f} \\ 0_{n_b} & 1_{n_b} \end{bmatrix}, \tag{17}$$

where $z = n_f + n_b$, $n_f = |t_f|$ and $n_b = |t_b|$ represent the width of constructed pseudo-foreground/background snippets. To avoid an explicit computation cost that caused by a large number of video snippets, we use an approximate formulation [17] to replace the original loss function. Finally, the denoised loss is defined as:

$$\mathcal{L}_d = -\mathcal{E}[\log(Determin(\hat{\mathcal{Z}}\hat{\mathcal{Y}}))] = \mathbb{E}[\log(\Gamma)], \tag{18}$$

where Γ is the condition number of $\hat{\mathcal{Z}}\hat{\mathcal{Y}}$.

3.7 Training and Inference

In this section, we elaborate on the details of network training and the inference.

Training. The total loss of our DCCNet comprises four parts: the reconstruction loss $\mathcal{L}_{rec}$ is in charge of optimizing the semantic completion module, which guarantees the network to predict the reconstructed query that is conditioned on the given mask; the dual-level loss $\mathcal{L}_{dual}$ is used to ensure the video feature more distinguishable and distinct from highly confusing backgrounds within and without a video; the diversity loss $\mathcal{L}_{div}$ is used to encourage the K proposals as different as possible (if added); the denoised loss $\mathcal{L}_d$ is adopted to reduce the noisy activation caused by the absence of frame-level annotations.

To encourage the candidate predictions to best reconstruct the given query, we optimize the whole framework by alternately executing the following two steps:

1. Update reconstructor parameter by $\mathcal{L}_{rec} + \mathcal{L}_d$ while freezing the mask generator:

$$\alpha_1^* = \arg \min_{\alpha_1} L_{rec}(\alpha_1, \alpha_2) + L_d(\alpha_1, \alpha_2). \tag{19}$$

2. Update the mask generator with optimal α_1^* by minimizing $\mathcal{L}_{dual} + \mathcal{L}_{div}$:

$$\alpha_2^* = \arg \min_{\alpha_2} L_{dual}(\alpha_1^*, \alpha_2) + L_{div}(\alpha_1^*, \alpha_2). \tag{20}$$

where $\mathcal{L}_{dual} = \mathcal{L}_{intra} + \mathcal{L}_{inter}$, α_1 and α_2 are the parameters of the reconstructor and mask generator, respectively.

Inference. During inference, we can obtain the temporal boundary $\tau = (\tau_s, \tau_e)$ of predicted Gaussian mask through Eqn. 3. The predicted start and end timestamps are calculated as follows:

$$\begin{aligned} \tau_s &= \max(G_c - G_w/2, 0) * T_v \\ \tau_e &= \min(G_c + G_w/2, 1) * T_v, \end{aligned} \tag{21}$$

where T_v represents the duration of the target video to be locate. Since we do not use multi-scale sliding windows to generate proposal candidates, it's noteworthy that we do not have to perform complex post-processing operations like Non-Maximum Suppression (NMS).

4   Experiments

4.1   Datasets

To validate the effectiveness of our proposed DDCNet, we perform experiments for weakly-supervised temporal sentence grounding on two prevailing and challenging datasets: Charades-STA [14] and ActivityNet Captions [20].

Charades-STA. The Charades-STA dataset is originally constructed from Charades [30] dataset which contains $9,848$ untrimmed videos about human daily indoor activities. Based on the Charades dataset, Gao *et al.* [14] develops a semi-automatic method to annotate each video with a moment-sentence pair. Concretely, the dataset consists of $12,408$ moment-sentence pairs for training and $3,720$ pairs for testing. The average duration, moment length, and query length are 29.8 seconds, 8.09 seconds and 7.22 words, respectively.

ActivityNet Captions. The ActivityNet Captions dataset is a large-scale dataset for temporal sentence grounding. It originally stems from ActivityNet dataset [2] for human activity understanding task, which comprises $14,926$ untrimmed videos and $71,953$ moment-sentence annotations. Following the standard experimental setting, we utilize val_1 as the validation set and val_2 as the testing set, which consists of $37,417$ pairs of video moments and descriptions for training, $17,505$ and $17,031$ pairs for validation and testing, respectively. Each video has an average of 4.82 temporal moments with their language descriptions. And the moment length and query length are about 37.14 seconds and 14.41 words on average.

4.2 Evaluation Metric

To evaluate the performance of our proposed method, we employ the commonly used $\langle R@n, IoU@m \rangle$ as our evaluation metric. Concretely, this metric is defined to compute the percentage of language queries whose predicted moments have at least one correct prediction in the top-n results. Specifically, a predicted moment is correct only if its IoU (i.e., Inter-section over Union) is larger than m in contrast with the ground truth. In our experimental setting, we report results for $n \in \{1, 5\}$ with $m \in \{0.3, 0.5, 0.7\}$ on Charades-STA, and $m \in \{0.1, 0.3, 0.5\}$ for ActivityNet Captions datasets.

Table 1. Performance comparison between the proposed model and the state-of-the-arts on Charades-STA dataset.

Method	Rank@1, IoU=			Rank@5, IoU=		
	0.3	0.5	0.7	0.3	0.5	0.7
CTRL [4]	–	23.63	8.89	–	58.92	29.52
QSPN [41]	54.70	35.60	15.80	95.60	71.80	38.87
MAN [1]	–	46.53	22.72	–	86.23	33.09
2D-TAN [45]	–	39.81	23.25	–	79.33	52.15
TGA [26]	32.14	19.94	8.84	86.58	65.52	33.51
WSRA [13]	50.13	31.20	11.01	86.75	70.50	39.02
WSTAN [37]	43.39	29.35	12.28	93.04	76.13	<u>41.53</u>
VLANet [24]	45.24	31.83	14.17	95.70	<u>82.85</u>	33.09
SCN [21]	42.96	23.58	9.97	95.56	71.80	38.87
MARN [32]	48.55	31.94	14.81	90.70	70.00	37.40
CNM [48]	60.39	35.43	15.45	–	–	–
WSTG [5]	43.31	31.02	<u>16.53</u>	95.54	77.53	41.91
RTBPN [46]	60.04	32.36	13.24	**97.48**	71.85	41.18
DDCNet (Ours)	**63.96**	<u>37.14</u>	16.05	–	–	–
DDCNet*(Ours)	<u>63.71</u>	**46.58**	**20.68**	<u>97.12</u>	**84.45**	**50.03**

4.3 Implementation Details

Data Preprocessing. For Charades-STA dataset, we utilize the publicly available I3D [4] network to extract visual features. For ActicvityNet Captions dataset, we employ the C3D [35] model pre-trained on Sport1M [18] dataset to obtain $4,096$ dimension features, which is subsequently reduced to 500 dimensions with the PCA algorithm. For a fair comparison, the feature extractor is not finetuned on both datasets. The input video is downsampled every 8 frame and the maximum length of frames is set to 200. For the sentence query, we adopt NLTK [22] to split each sentence into several words and employ the pre-trained GloVe [29] word2vec model to initialize the word embeddings.

The maximum length of words is set to 20. And the vocabulary size is set to $1,111$ and $8,000$ for Charades-STA and ActivityNet Captions, respectively.

Model Setting. To improve the training stability, we utilize the multi-head mechanism proposed in [36] for the mask generator and semantic completion module. Specifically, the encoder and decoder are both equipped with 3 layers and 4 multi-attention heads. And the dimension of the hidden state is set to 256. In the training phase, we employ Adam [19] as our optimizer without weight decay. The learning rate is set to $4e^{-4}$ for Charades-STA and ActivityNet Captions. Besides, the hyperparameters λ_1 and λ_2 are set to 0.1 and 0.15, respectively. K is set to 5. Following the standard practice, we mask $1/3$ important words in each sentence by replacing them with a special token when reconstructing the origin query, in which nouns and verbs are more likely to be selected to be the keywords. Moreover, the maximum width of the predicted moments is limited to shorter than 0.45 as the inherent property on the Charades-STA dataset.

4.4 Comparisons with State-of-the-Art Methods

We compare our proposed DDCNet with existing state-of-the-art approaches in recent years, including both fully-supervised and weakly-supervised methods.

Table 2. Performance comparison between the proposed model and the state-of-the-arts on ActivityNet Captions dataset.

Method	Rank@1, IoU=			Rank@5, IoU=		
	0.1	0.3	0.5	0.1	0.3	0.5
TGN [6]	–	43.81	27.93	–	54.56	44.20
CTRL [4]	49.10	28.70	14.00	–	58.92	29.52
ABLR [44]	73.30	55.67	36.79	–	–	–
2D-TAN [45]	–	59.45	44.51	–	85.53	77.13
WS-DEC [12]	62.71	41.98	23.34	–	–	–
VCA [39]	67.96	50.45	31.00	92.14	71.79	53.83
EC-SL [7]	68.48	44.29	24.16	–	–	–
MARN [32]	–	47.01	29.95	–	72.02	57.49
SCN [21]	71.48	47.23	29.22	90.88	71.56	55.69
CTF [9]	74.2	44.3	23.6	–	–	–
WSLLN [15]	75.4	42.8	22.7	–	–	–
CCL [47]	–	50.02	31.07	–	77.36	**61.29**
CNM [48]	78.13	55.68	**33.33**	–	–	–
DDCNet (Ours)	<u>79.36</u>	<u>56.53</u>	31.81	–	–	–
DDCNet*(Ours)	**79.51**	**57.57**	<u>32.29</u>	**92.65**	**77.96**	<u>60.54</u>

Results on Charades-STA. We compare our DDCNet with the state-of-the-art fully-supervised and weakly-supervised methods on the Charades-STA testing set. The best results are highlighted in **bold** and the second best results are underlined in tables. As shown in Table 1, our method achieves impressive performance on almost all metrics except a slightly worse one, which verifies the effectiveness of our proposed DDCNet. Specifically, it can be seen that our approach achieves 63.96% on "Rank@1, IoU=0.3" and 37.14% on "Rank@1, IoU=0.5", bringing the compelling result by a large margin. Notably, we can see that a variant version of our approach (DDCNet*) with a multiple proposal generation scheme (Eqn. 4 and 5) outperforms other previous weakly-supervised methods at most of the IoU thresholds, demonstrating the superiority of denoised contrastive learning criteria without the precise frame-level annotations. It can be noticed that our method also attains competitive results even compared with some fully-supervised counterparts (in upper parts of the tables).

Table 3. Ablation studies of the proposed model on Charads-STA dataset.

ID	$\mathcal{L}_{rec}$	$\mathcal{L}_{intra}$	$\mathcal{L}_{inter}$	$\mathcal{L}_d$	$\mathcal{L}_{div}$	IoU=0.1	IoU=0.3	IoU=0.5	mIoU
1	✓					76.85	53.74	29.20	53.26
2	✓	✓				76.79	60.54	35.59	57.64
3	✓	✓	✓			78.75	61.43	<u>37.21</u>	59.13
4	✓			✓		74.35	58.58	36.42	56.45
5	✓	✓	✓	✓		<u>79.89</u>	**63.96**	37.14	<u>60.33</u>
6	✓	✓	✓	✓	✓	**79.94**	<u>63.71</u>	**46.58**	**63.41**

Results on ActivityNet Captions. As shown in Table 2, we also give a thorough study of the ActivityNet Captions dataset and report the corresponding results. Similarly, we compare the overall performance with both fully-supervised and weakly-supervised methods, where DDCNet* indicates an advanced version of our method with multiple proposals generation. As can be seen, our method shows significant improvements over existing weakly-supervised methods while maintaining competitive results with other fully-supervised methods. Specifically, we observe that our DDCNet attains the highest performance except for the "Rank@1, IoU=0.5" metric. This may stem from the intrinsic characteristics of this dataset. Since the query characteristics in ActivityNet Captions are diverse and complicated, there is a high probability to make the training models confused and ineffective. Compared with other recently proposed methods, however, like CCL [47] and CNM [48], our DDCNet still outperforms the MIL-based and reconstruction-based methods to a large extent. This suggests that our method is robust and applicable to a large-scale dataset of various query semantics. By extending the framework to multiple proposal generation, our method nearly achieves consistent improvements among different IoU metrics beyond all doubt. Besides, our method achieves favorable performance even in contrast with existing fully-supervised methods, which reduces the performance gap by a large margin and benefits the practicability to real-world applications.

4.5 Ablation Study and Analysis

To investigate the effectiveness of our proposed DDCNet for weakly-supervised temporal sentence grounding, we conduct extensive ablation studies on both datasets. The results are summarized in Tables 3, 4, and 5.

Q1: How Does the Proposed Multi-task Loss Help? To evaluate the effectiveness of our carefully-designed multi-task loss, we conduct ablation studies with respect to different losses, i.e., $\mathcal{L}_{intra}$, $\mathcal{L}_{inter}$, $\mathcal{L}_d$ and $\mathcal{L}_{div}$. The results are summarized in Table 3. As we can see, introducing the intra-video contrastive learning loss $\mathcal{L}_{intra}$ improves the Rank@1 mIoU from 53.26% to 57.64%, demonstrating that snippet-wise variances within the same video are essential for capturing discriminative representations. Furthermore, our method, which adds $\mathcal{L}_{inter}$ to perform inter-video contrastive learning, boosts the Rank@1 mIoU to 59.13%. This suggests $\mathcal{L}_{inter}$ effectively guides the network to produce more complete predictions by exploring cross-video relations. In addition, we also find that adding the denoised loss $\mathcal{L}_d$ achieves an absolute 1.2% improvement. And the modified version DDCNet* with $\mathcal{L}_{div}$ achieves the best average performance on Charades-STA dataset. This shows that each component provides an indispensable contribution to the learning model.

Table 4. Ablation studies of on $\mathcal{L}_{inter}$ terms on Charads-STA dataset.

Setting	Loss	IoU=0.5 ($\triangle$)
DDCNet (Ours)	$\mathcal{L}_{rec} + \mathcal{L}_{inter}$	**37.14%**
baseline	$\mathcal{L}_{rec}$	29.20% (−7.49%)
DDCNet w/o HN trm.	$\mathcal{L}_{rec} + \mathcal{L}_{inter}^{Pos}$	36.11% (−1.03%)
DDCNet w/o HP trm.	$\mathcal{L}_{rec} + \mathcal{L}_{inter}^{Neg}$	36.38% (−0.76%)

Table 5. The effectiveness of training strategy.

Setting	Rank@1			
	IoU=0.1	IoU=0.3	IoU=0.5	mIoU
$\min_{\alpha_1, \alpha_2} (\mathcal{L}_{recon} + \mathcal{L}_{gen})$	67.38	54.28	23.05	48.57
$\min_{\alpha_1} \mathcal{L}_{recon} + \min_{\alpha_2} \mathcal{L}_{gen}$	**79.89**	**63.96**	**37.14**	**60.33**

Q2: Is it Necessary to Consider both HP and HN Terms in $\mathcal{L}_{Inter}$ Loss? While we have validated that our inter-video loss helps the training model achieve better performance, it should also be considered whether both HP and HN terms are essential components. To explore this, we conduct experiments that use two variants of the $\mathcal{L}_{inter}$ loss, each of which contains one kind of the loss term in Eqn. 14, i.e., $\mathcal{L}_{inter}^{Pos}$ and $\mathcal{L}_{inter}^{Neg}$, respectively. We summarize the corresponding results in Table 4. As we can see, the performance drops largely when either type of sub-loss is removed, demonstrating that both loss terms contribute to the improved prediction. Compared with the baseline, our DDCNet is beneficial to make representations of similar snippets closer and helps to transfer informative knowledge. Overall, the above analyses strongly justify the significance of the two items in our proposed $\mathcal{L}_{inter}$ loss.

Q3: How Does Different Training Strategy Effect the Performance? As Table 5 shows, we conduct experiments to study how different training strategies influence the performance on the Charades-STA dataset. The first row indicates our DDCNet is trained by optimizing the mask generator and reconstruction module separately, where the weight of the generator is frozen when optimizing the query reconstruction module, and vice versa. In contrast, the second row demonstrates the entire model is optimized with $\mathcal{L}_{recon}$ and $\mathcal{L}_{gen}$ jointly. As we could see, the DDCNet performs better results when $\mathcal{L}_{recon}$ and $\mathcal{L}_{gen}$ work separately, with a consistent improvement in terms of Rank@1 metric at all IoU thresholds. This is because the iterative training manner can avoid a trivial solution that the reconstruction module always gives the predicted negative samples low scores at early training, thereby contributing to superior results.

4.6 Qualitative Results

Intuitively, we provide qualitative results from Charades-STA and ActivityNet Captions to further demonstrate the superiority of our DDCNet. As shown in Fig. 3, each video is presented with a human-annotated query description, along with the ground truth and predictions with different methods.

Specifically, Fig. 3 (a) displays two typical examples of the detected moments on the Charades-STA dataset. Compared with the ground truth, we can easily find that our method is capable of detecting more precise boundaries than CNM, especially when dealing with the easy-confusing backgrounds. In Fig. 3 (b), we visualize two qualitative examples on the large-scale ActivityNet Captions dataset. The first example demonstrates a set of consecutive scenes, where several firemen are washing windows while another man is speaking to the camera. As we can see, even though the backgrounds are diverse and the language description is complicated, our model successfully localizes the entire salient moment and suppress the false positive predictions. The second example demonstrates a *"play the instrument"* action observed with highly-confusing backgrounds, leading to inaccurate predictions with the CNM model. Our DDCNet, however, still performs well in this case except for a few failures in the end. In addition, we simultaneously present the reconstruction and prediction results to better reveal the rationale behind our DDCNet. We show two examples from both Charades-STA and ActivityNet Captions in Fig. 3 (c). As expected, we observe that our DDCNet achieves higher IoU results between the predicted moment and the ground truth, and the reconstructed query is also close to the original one. This demonstrates that our denoised dual-level contrastive framework captures more fine-grained semantic information inside and outside the video to reconstruct the query, leading to more complete and robust predictions.

Furthermore, we also visualize the frame-by-word attention to understand the cross-modal interaction process. As a fundamental component in temporal sentence grounding, this type of visualization also helps our model explain how frame-by-word attention

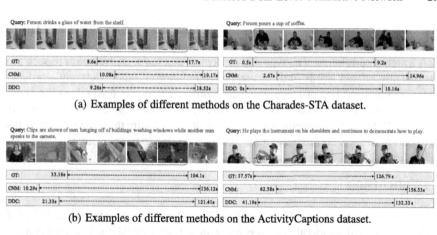

(a) Examples of different methods on the Charades-STA dataset.

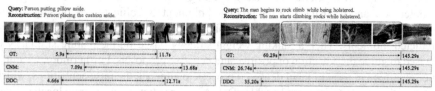

(b) Examples of different methods on the ActivityCaptions dataset.

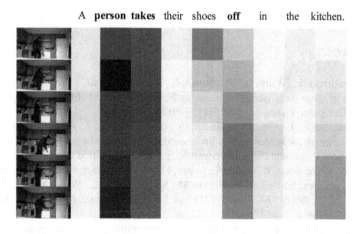

(c) Examples about query reconstruction and moment prediction on the Charades-STA and ActivityCaptions datasets.

Fig. 3. Qualitative visualization on both two datasets, i.e., Charades-STA and ActivityCaptions. The horizontal axis denotes the timestamps.

Fig. 4. Visualization results of the frame-by-word attention. The darker the color is, the larger the related attention value is. (Color figure online)

works when reconstructing the original sentence. As shown in Fig. 4, the correlation of the pair of frame and word representations is displayed, where the darker color represents a higher correlation. The typical case depicts that our DDCNet tends to seek more semantically related words in the sentence while ignoring other irrelevant words with subtle information. For instance, the 4-th positional frame is focused on the semantic correlated words "person", "takes off" and neglects the remote irrelative words like "their" and "the". This suggests our DDCNet is able to capture the semantic connections between visual and text representations, thereby leading to more accurate predictions.

5 Conclusion

In this paper, we propose a Denoised Dual-level Contrastive Network, DDCNet, for weakly-supervised temporal sentence grounding. Our method aims to encourage the completeness and robustness of the predicted moment. Specifically, we present a dual-level contrastive learning strategy to enable the completeness and robustness of the predicted moments. Then a ranking weight strategy based on the feature similarity is devised to guide the selection of positive and negative proposals. Furthermore, we introduce an effective pseudo-label denoised process to alleviate the false activations, which can ease the model training and enables DDCNet to predict more accurate localizations. The experiments are conducted on two publicly available datasets, namely Charades-STA and ActivityNet Captions, demonstrating the effectiveness and superiority of our DDCNet when compared with existing weakly-supervised methods.

Acknowledgement. This work was supported by the National Natural Science Foundation of China (NSFC) (Grant 62376265).

References

1. Anne Hendricks, L., Wang, O., Shechtman, E., Sivic, J., Darrell, T., Russell, B.: Localizing moments in video with natural language. In: Proceedings of the IEEE International Conference on Computer Vision, pp. 5803–5812 (2017)
2. Caba Heilbron, F., Escorcia, V., Ghanem, B., Carlos Niebles, J.: Activitynet: a large-scale video benchmark for human activity understanding. In: Proceedings of the IEEE Conference on Computer Vision and Pattern Recognition, pp. 961–970 (2015)
3. Caron, M., Bojanowski, P., Joulin, A., Douze, M.: Deep clustering for unsupervised learning of visual features. In: Ferrari, V., Hebert, M., Sminchisescu, C., Weiss, Y. (eds.) Computer Vision – ECCV 2018. LNCS, vol. 11218, pp. 139–156. Springer, Cham (2018). https://doi.org/10.1007/978-3-030-01264-9_9
4. Carreira, J., Zisserman, A.: Quo vadis, action recognition? a new model and the kinetics dataset. In: Proceedings of the IEEE Conference on Computer Vision and Pattern Recognition, pp. 6299–6308 (2017)
5. Chen, J., Luo, W., Zhang, W., Ma, L.: Explore inter-contrast between videos via composition for weakly supervised temporal sentence grounding **36**(01), 267–275 (2022)
6. Chen, J., Chen, X., Ma, L., Jie, Z., Chua, T.S.: Temporally grounding natural sentence in video. In: Proceedings of the 2018 Conference on Empirical Methods in Natural Language Processing, pp. 162–171 (2018)

7. Chen, S., Jiang, Y.G.: Towards bridging event captioner and sentence localizer for weakly supervised dense event captioning. In: Proceedings of the IEEE/CVF Conference on Computer Vision and Pattern Recognition, pp. 8425–8435 (2021)
8. Chen, X., He, K.: Exploring simple siamese representation learning. In: Proceedings of the IEEE/CVF Conference on Computer Vision and Pattern Recognition, pp. 15750–15758 (2021)
9. Chen, Z., Ma, L., Luo, W., Tang, P., Wong, K.Y.K.: Look closer to ground better: Weakly-supervised temporal grounding of sentence in video. arXiv preprint arXiv:2001.09308 (2020)
10. Collins, R.T., et al.: A system for video surveillance and monitoring. Vsam Final Report **2000**(1–68), 1 (2000)
11. Da, C., Zhang, Y., Zheng, Y., Pan, P., Xu, Y., Pan, C.: Asynce: disentangling false-positives for weakly-supervised video grounding. In: Proceedings of the 29th ACM International Conference on Multimedia, pp. 1129–1137 (2021)
12. Duan, X., et al.: Weakly supervised dense event captioning in videos. Adv. Neural. Inf. Process. Syst. **31** (2018)
13. Fang, Z., Kong, S., Wang, Z., Fowlkes, C., Yang, Y.: Weak supervision and referring attention for temporal-textual association learning. arXiv preprint arXiv:2006.11747 (2020)
14. Gao, J., Sun, C., Yang, Z., Nevatia, R.: Tall: temporal activity localization via language query. In: Proceedings of the IEEE International Conference on Computer Vision, pp. 5267–5275 (2017)
15. Gao, M., Davis, L.S., Socher, R., Xiong, C.: Wslln: weakly supervised natural language localization networks. arXiv preprint arXiv:1909.00239 (2019)
16. Grill, J.B., et al.: Bootstrap your own latent-a new approach to self-supervised learning. Adv. Neural. Inf. Process. Syst. **33**, 21271–21284 (2020)
17. Islam, A., Radke, R.: Weakly supervised temporal action localization using deep metric learning. In: Proceedings of the IEEE/CVF Winter Conference on Applications of Computer Vision, pp. 547–556 (2020)
18. Karpathy, A., Toderici, G., Shetty, S., Leung, T., Sukthankar, R., Fei-Fei, L.: Large-scale video classification with convolutional neural networks. In: Proceedings of the IEEE Conference on Computer Vision and Pattern Recognition, pp. 1725–1732 (2014)
19. Kingma, D.P., Ba, J.: Adam: A method for stochastic optimization. arXiv preprint arXiv:1412.6980 (2014)
20. Krishna, R., Hata, K., Ren, F., Fei-Fei, L., Carlos Niebles, J.: Dense-captioning events in videos. In: Proceedings of the IEEE International Conference on Computer Vision, pp. 706–715 (2017)
21. Lin, Z., Zhao, Z., Zhang, Z., Wang, Q., Liu, H.: Weakly-supervised video moment retrieval via semantic completion network. In: Proceedings of the AAAI Conference on Artificial Intelligence, vol. 34, pp. 11539–11546 (2020)
22. Loper, E., Bird, S.: Nltk: The natural language toolkit. arXiv preprint cs/0205028 (2002)
23. Luo, F., Chen, S., Chen, J., Wu, Z., Jiang, Y.G.: Self-supervised learning for semi-supervised temporal language grounding. arXiv preprint arXiv:2109.11475 (2021)
24. Ma, M., Yoon, S., Kim, J., Lee, Y., Kang, S., Yoo, C.D.: VLANet: video-language alignment network for weakly-supervised video moment retrieval. In: Vedaldi, A., Bischof, H., Brox, T., Frahm, J.-M. (eds.) ECCV 2020. LNCS, vol. 12373, pp. 156–171. Springer, Cham (2020). https://doi.org/10.1007/978-3-030-58604-1_10
25. Ma, Y.F., Lu, L., Zhang, H.J., Li, M.: A user attention model for video summarization. In: Proceedings of the Tenth ACM International Conference on Multimedia, pp. 533–542 (2002)
26. Mithun, N.C., Paul, S., Roy-Chowdhury, A.K.: Weakly supervised video moment retrieval from text queries. In: Proceedings of the IEEE/CVF Conference on Computer Vision and Pattern Recognition, pp. 11592–11601 (2019)

27. Nam, J., Ahn, D., Kang, D., Ha, S.J., Choi, J.: Zero-shot natural language video localization. In: Proceedings of the IEEE/CVF International Conference on Computer Vision, pp. 1470–1479 (2021)

28. Pan, T., Song, Y., Yang, T., Jiang, W., Liu, W.: Videomoco: contrastive video representation learning with temporally adversarial examples. In: Proceedings of the IEEE/CVF Conference on Computer Vision and Pattern Recognition, pp. 11205–11214 (2021)

29. Pennington, J., Socher, R., Manning, C.D.: Glove: global vectors for word representation. In: Proceedings of the 2014 Conference on Empirical Methods in Natural Language Processing (EMNLP). pp. 1532–1543 (2014)

30. Sigurdsson, G.A., Varol, G., Wang, X., Farhadi, A., Laptev, I., Gupta, A.: Hollywood in homes: crowdsourcing data collection for activity understanding. In: Leibe, B., Matas, J., Sebe, N., Welling, M. (eds.) ECCV 2016. LNCS, vol. 9905, pp. 510–526. Springer, Cham (2016). https://doi.org/10.1007/978-3-319-46448-0_31

31. Sohn, K.: Improved deep metric learning with multi-class n-pair loss objective. Adv. Neural Inform. Process. Syst. **29** (2016)

32. Song, Y., Wang, J., Ma, L., Yu, Z., Yu, J.: Weakly-supervised multi-level attentional reconstruction network for grounding textual queries in videos. arXiv preprint arXiv:2003.07048 (2020)

33. Tan, R., Xu, H., Saenko, K., Plummer, B.A.: Logan: latent graph co-attention network for weakly-supervised video moment retrieval. In: Proceedings of the IEEE/CVF Winter Conference on Applications of Computer Vision, pp. 2083–2092 (2021)

34. Tian, Y., Krishnan, D., Isola, P.: Contrastive multiview coding. In: Vedaldi, A., Bischof, H., Brox, T., Frahm, J.-M. (eds.) ECCV 2020. LNCS, vol. 12356, pp. 776–794. Springer, Cham (2020). https://doi.org/10.1007/978-3-030-58621-8_45

35. Tran, D., Bourdev, L., Fergus, R., Torresani, L., Paluri, M.: Learning spatiotemporal features with 3d convolutional networks. In: Proceedings of the IEEE International Conference on Computer Vision, pp. 4489–4497 (2015)

36. Vaswani, A., et al.: Attention is all you need. Adv. Neural Inform. Process. Syst. **30** (2017)

37. Wang, Y., Deng, J., Zhou, W., Li, H.: Weakly supervised temporal adjacent network for language grounding. IEEE Trans. Multimedia (2021)

38. Wang, Y., Zhou, W., Li, H.: Fine-grained semantic alignment network for weakly supervised temporal language grounding. arXiv preprint arXiv:2210.11933 (2022)

39. Wang, Z., Chen, J., Jiang, Y.G.: Visual co-occurrence alignment learning for weakly-supervised video moment retrieval. In: Proceedings of the 29th ACM International Conference on Multimedia, pp. 1459–1468 (2021)

40. Wu, Z., Xiong, Y., Yu, S.X., Lin, D.: Unsupervised feature learning via non-parametric instance discrimination. In: Proceedings of the IEEE Conference on Computer Vision and Pattern Recognition, pp. 3733–3742 (2018)

41. Xu, H., He, K., Plummer, B.A., Sigal, L., Sclaroff, S., Saenko, K.: Multilevel language and vision integration for text-to-clip retrieval. In: Proceedings of the AAAI Conference on Artificial Intelligence, vol. 33, pp. 9062–9069 (2019)

42. Xu, Y., Cao, P., Kong, Y., Wang, Y.: L_dmi: A novel information-theoretic loss function for training deep nets robust to label noise. Adv. Neural Inform. Process. Syst. **32** (2019)

43. Yang, W., Zhang, T., Zhang, Y., Wu, F.: Local correspondence network for weakly supervised temporal sentence grounding. IEEE Trans. Image Process. **30**, 3252–3262 (2021)

44. Yuan, Y., Mei, T., Zhu, W.: To find where you talk: temporal sentence localization in video with attention based location regression. In: Proceedings of the AAAI Conference on Artificial Intelligence, vol. 33, pp. 9159–9166 (2019)

45. Zhang, S., Peng, H., Fu, J., Luo, J.: Learning 2d temporal adjacent networks for moment localization with natural language. In: Proceedings of the AAAI Conference on Artificial Intelligence, vol. 34, pp. 12870–12877 (2020)

46. Zhang, Z., Lin, Z., Zhao, Z., Zhu, J., He, X.: Regularized two-branch proposal networks for weakly-supervised moment retrieval in videos. In: Proceedings of the 28th ACM International Conference on Multimedia, pp. 4098–4106 (2020)
47. Zhang, Z., Zhao, Z., Lin, Z., He, X., et al.: Counterfactual contrastive learning for weakly-supervised vision-language grounding. Adv. Neural. Inf. Process. Syst. **33**, 18123–18134 (2020)
48. Zheng, M., Huang, Y., Chen, Q., Liu, Y.: Weakly supervised video moment localization with contrastive negative sample mining. In: Proceedings of the AAAI Conference on Artificial Intelligence, vol. 1, p. 3 (2022)
49. Zheng, M., Huang, Y., Chen, Q., Peng, Y., Liu, Y.: Weakly supervised temporal sentence grounding with gaussian-based contrastive proposal learning. In: Proceedings of the IEEE/CVF Conference on Computer Vision and Pattern Recognition, pp. 15555–15564 (2022)

Isolation and Integration: A Strong Pre-trained Model-Based Paradigm for Class-Incremental Learning

Wei Zhang[ORCID], Yuan Xie[✉], Zhizhong Zhang, and Xin Tan

East China Normal University, Shanghai, China
weizhang_01@stu.ecnu.edu.cn, {yxie,zzzhang,xtan}@cs.ecnu.edu.cn

Abstract. Continual learning aims to effectively learn from streaming data, adapting to emerging new classes without forgetting old ones. Conventional models without pre-training are constructed from the ground up, suffering from severely catastrophic forgetting. In recent times, pre-training has made significant strides, opening the door to extensive pre-trained models for continual learning. To avoid obvious stage learning bottlenecks in traditional single-backbone networks, we propose a brand-new stage-isolation based class incremental learning framework, which leverages parameter-efficient tuning technique to finetune the pre-trained model for each task, thus mitigating information interference and conflicts among tasks. Simultaneously, it enables the effective utilization of the strong generalization capabilities inherent in pre-trained networks, which can be seamlessly adapted to new tasks. Then, we fuse the features acquired from the training of all backbone networks to construct a unified feature representation. This amalgamated representation retains the distinctive features of each task while incorporating the commonalities shared across all tasks. Finally, we use the selected exemplars to compute the prototype as the classifier weights to make final prediction. We conduct extensive experiments on different class incremental learning benchmarks and settings, results indicate that our method consistently outperforms other methods with a large margin.

Keywords: Continual Learning · Class-Incremental Learning · Pre-Trained Models · Parameter-Efficient Tuning

1 Introduction

Continual learning, also known as incremental learning or lifelong learning, aims to learn effectively from streaming data, that is adapt to emerging new class without forgetting old ones [19,38]. Current efforts are mainly based on the premise of learning from scratch. However, with the rapid development of pre-training techniques, recent advancements in pre-training have significantly facilitated the utilization of pre-trained models for downstream tasks [8]. These pre-trained models are typically trained with massive data, resulting in strong generalizability [18,41]. Therefore, continual learning with pre-trained models is emerging as a promising direction and is attracting increasing attention [22,29,31,32,36,41,42].

When confronted with a growing number of new tasks, conventional single-backbone models often encounter several significant challenges. Firstly, as new tasks are introduced, the existing model may grapple with knowledge conflicts stemming from disparities between the feature distributions of new and old tasks, resulting in a decline in the model's performance when handling novel tasks [11]. Secondly, upon learning a new task, the existing model might undergo catastrophic forgetting [7,16], wherein the feature representations of old tasks are overwritten by the newly acquired knowledge, causing performance degradation on the former tasks. Lastly, as the number of new tasks increases, the model may suffer from a decline in generalization performance, *i.e.*, its ability to generalize to new tasks deteriorates [37].

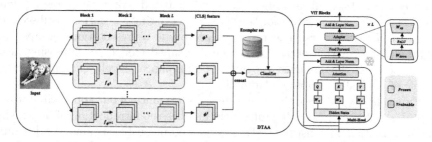

Fig. 1. Illustration of DTAA. **Left:** the architecture of DTAA. At each task, we dynamically tune the pre-trained model with adapter to learn new concepts and keep the pre-trained backbone frozen, then we fuse the features acquired from the training of all backbone networks to construct a unified feature representation and feed it to the prototype-based classifier. **Right:** the framework of ViT blocks with adapter. Red modules in the figure are trainable, while blue ones are frozen (Color figure online).

To tackle these challenges, drawing inspiration from techniques like DER [35], we employ a novel approach, Dynamically Tuning pre-trained model to Adapt and Aggregate new concepts (DTAA), as shown in Fig. 1. Specifically, we introduce an additional pre-trained backbone network, equipped with adapters [10], for each new task. Each of these backbone networks is tasked with fine-tuning the feature representation specific to its associated task. This approach offers distinct advantages: it ensures that feature representations for different tasks are learned independently, thereby averting information interference and conflicts between tasks. Simultaneously, it enables the effective utilization of the strong generalization capabilities inherent in pre-trained networks, which can be seamlessly adapted to new tasks.

Subsequently, we fuse the features acquired from the training of all backbone networks to construct a unified feature representation. This amalgamated representation retains the distinctive features of each task while incorporating the commonalities shared across all tasks. Such a holistic feature representation not only preserves the task-specific characteristics but also assimilates the overarching patterns common to all tasks. This integration enhances the model's adaptability and generalization prowess.

During the classification phase, we employ a unified classifier that caters to all tasks. This classifier takes the concatenated feature representation generated by the multi-backbone network as its input and conducts classification on this comprehensive feature set. This approach offers the distinct advantage of enabling the classifier to learn from the features of all tasks, eliminating the need for a separate classifier for each task. Consequently, it enhances the model's scalability and reduces computational overhead.

Upon the completion of learning for each task, we curate a subset of 20 instances for each category within that task, selecting those instances that exhibit the greatest similarity to the task's prototype. Subsequently, we recompute the prototype representations for the known categories using the exemplar samples drawn from all categories. These recalculated prototype representations then serve as the parameters for the classifier's existing categories in subsequent task learning endeavors. The resultant prototype representations encapsulate additional information derived from the fine-tuned model, encompassing task-specific features that enhance recognition performance, thereby ensuring a higher degree of generalization and adaptability.

Experiments showcase the exceptional performance of our approach in incremental learning scenarios. It proficiently handles the introduction of new tasks, the preservation of existing tasks, and simultaneously sustains the learning progress of established tasks during the incorporation of new ones. This underscores our method as an efficient and reliable solution to the multi-task incremental learning challenge.

To sum up, the main contributions of this work can be summarized as follows:

(1) We propose DTAA, which dynamically expand and tune the pre-trained network backbone with adapter for each task to solve the continual learning problem.
(2) We conduct extensive experiments to show that, DTAA reaches a new state-of-the-art performance in the different class incremental learning benchmarks and settings.
(3) We also compare DTAA to a set of strong continual learning baseline methods in a fair way using the same pre-trained backbone for all methods.

2   Realeated Work

Class-Incremental Learning (CIL). Class-Incremental Learning, a paradigm focused on continuous learning of new classes while retaining knowledge of the old ones, has seen the development of various algorithms, broadly categorized into three groups. Regularization-based methods [1,4,26] devise strategies like knowledge distillation or parameter regularization terms to alleviate catastrophic forgetting. LwF [14] was a pioneering success in applying knowledge distillation to CIL by enforcing consistent predicted probabilities among old classes. EWC [11] maintains an importance matrix to assess parameter significance, keeping vital ones static to preserve prior knowledge. Rehearsal-based methods [2,17,28, 34] store and employ exemplars from old classes to recover previous knowledge, displaying remarkable versatility and resilience. iCaRL [19] extends LwF with exemplar sets, aiding in better recall of past knowledge during the learning process. Structure-based methods [20,21,27] maintain learned parameters while allocating new ones or introducing additional networks to grasp novel concepts. DER [35], a prime example of this approach, expands a new backbone upon the arrival of a new task and aggregates features using a larger classifier.

CIL with Pre-trained Model. The rapid evolution of pre-training techniques has significantly streamlined incremental learning by harnessing pre-trained models. DyTox [6] pioneered the exploration of pre-trained Vision Transformers (ViTs) [5] in CIL, expanding solely task tokens for each new task, thereby demanding considerably less memory compared to saving the entire backbone. L2P [32] and DualPrompt [31] also leverage pre-trained ViTs to progressively fine-tune models using adaptable parameters known as "prompts". In L2P, the pre-trained model remains fixed during the learning process, with the model solely optimizing prompts within the prompt pool to accommodate new concepts. DualPrompt extends this approach by incorporating complementary prompts into the pre-trained model, enabling the learning of both task-invariant and task-specific information. CODA-Prompt [22] further advances prompt search through the incorporation of attention mechanisms. Additionally, S-Prompts [30] capitalizes on the pre-trained language-vision model CLIP [18] for incremental learning, simultaneously mastering language and visual prompts.

Adapter Tuning for Pre-trained Model. Parameter-efficient tuning encompasses techniques and methodologies aimed at refining pre-trained models while conserving computational resources and minimizing the count of task-specific parameters. In [10], the concept of integrating an adapter layer into the Transformer architecture is introduced for the purpose of model fine-tuning. The adapter layer's design is uncomplicated, comprising a downward projection onto a reduced dimension, followed by a stratum of nonlinear activation, and subsequently an upward projection to restore the initial dimension. Furthermore, there is an intrinsic residual connection linking the input and output of the complete adapter layer. This adapter can be incorporated into diverse layers of a model, affording adaptability in tailoring the model for different tasks, as elucidated in [3].

3   Method

We begin by describing the problem setup and, along the way, introduce the notations in Sect. 3.1. Then we present a minimum feasible prototype-based framework which serves as our baseline model in Sect. 3.2. In Sect. 3.3, we introduce the proposed method, which builds upon the baseline model.

3.1 Problem Setting

Class-incremental learning aims to learn from an evolving data stream with new classes to build a unified classifier. There is a sequence of B training tasks $\{\mathcal{D}^1, \mathcal{D}^2, ..., \mathcal{D}^B\}$, where $\mathcal{D}^b = \{(x_i^b, y_i^b)\}_{i=1}^{n_b}$ is the b-th incremental step with n_b instances. Here, the training instance $x_i^b \in \mathbb{R}^{W \times H \times C}$ belongs to class $y_i \in Y_b$, where Y_b is the label space of task b. $Y_b \cap Y_{b'} = \varnothing$ for $b \neq b'$. During the b-th training stage, we can only access data from $\mathcal{D}^b$ for model updating. This paper focuses on the exemplar-based CIL setting, where little historical data can be fetched for rehearsal. For example, 20 instances each class. The goal of CIL is to incrementally build a unified model for all seen classes, i.e., acquiring knowledge from new classes and meanwhile preserving knowledge from former ones. The model's capability is evaluated over all seen classes $\mathcal{Y}_b = Y_1 \cup ...Y_b$ after each incremental task. In general, a neural network at session t can be decoupled into an embedding function $f_{\phi^t}(\cdot) : \mathbb{R}^{W \times H \times C} \to \mathbb{R}^d$ and a classifier $g_{\psi^t}(\cdot) : \mathbb{R}^d \to \mathbb{R}^k$ that are parameterized by ϕ^t and ψ^t, respectively. Thus, the target is to fit a model $F(x) : X \to \mathcal{Y}_b$ that minimizes the empirical risk across all testing datasets:

$$\sum_{(x_i, y_i) \in \mathcal{D}_t^1 \cup ... \mathcal{D}_t^b} l(g_{\psi^t}(f_{\phi^t}(x_j)), y_j) \tag{1}$$

where $l(\cdot, \cdot)$ measures the discrepancy between prediction and ground-truth label. $\mathcal{D}_t^b$ denotes the testing set of task b. A good CIL model satisfying Eq. 1 has discriminability among all classes, which strikes a balance between learning new classes and remembering old ones.

Same as [41], we use a pre-trained model (e.g., a ViT) on ImageNet as the initialization of $F(x)$. In a plain ViT, the input encoding layer transforms the image into a sequence-like output features $x_e \in \mathbb{R}^{L \times d}$, where L is the sequence length. We assume the first token in x_e as the [CLS] token to simplify notation. x_e is then fed into the subsequent layers (i.e., multi-head self-attention and feed forward layer) to produce the final embeddings. We treat the embedded [CLS] token as $\phi(x)$ for ViT.

3.2 A Simple Baseline

As indicated by [41], pre-trained models are born with generalizability, which can be transferred to downstream tasks. They define a simple baseline, SimpleCIL, to transfer pretrained models for incremental tasks. With the embedding function $f_\phi(x)$ *frozen* throughout the learning process, we extract average embedding (i.e., prototype) of each class:

$$p_i = \frac{1}{K} \sum_{j=1}^{|\mathcal{D}|} \mathbb{I}(y_j = i) f_\phi(x_j) \tag{2}$$

where $K = \sum_{j=1}^{|\mathcal{D}|} \mathbb{I}(y_j = i)$, $\mathbb{I}(\cdot)$ is the indicator function, $f_\phi(\cdot)$ is initialized by a pre-trained ViT. SimpleCIL sets the classifier weights to the average embeddings of each new class for classification, and outperforms many state-of-the-art methods even without any tuning on these downstream tasks. In this paper, we also adopt SimpleCIL as our baseline model.

3.3   Dynamically Adaption and Aggregation

In class-incremental learning, given the scarcity of data from previous tasks, it is challenging for single-models trained through gradient descent to maintain good feature representations for these tasks because the parameters of the previous task are overwritten by those learned by the new task, causing catastrophic forgetting. However, the forgetting of the previously learned feature representation is the core problem of CIL. Therefore, inspired by the model expansion approach, we fine-tune the pre-trained model with adapter and save a fine-tuned backbone network for each task. It ensures that feature representations for different tasks are learned independently, thereby averting information interference and conflicts between tasks. Simultaneously, it enables the effective utilization of the strong generalization capabilities inherent in pre-trained networks, which can be seamlessly adapted to new tasks. The overview of our proposed method DTAA is shown in Fig. 1.

Denote the input of the Feed Forward Layer (FFL) in ViT as x_l, the output of the adapted FFL is formatted as:

$$\text{FFL}(x_l) + \text{ReLU}(x_l W_{down}) W_{up} \tag{3}$$

where W_{down} is down-projection operation to reduce the feature dimension, W_{up} is up-projection operation which projects it back to the original dimension, $ReLU$ is non-linear activation function.

At time step $t+1$, the models fine-tuned in previous tasks, $f_{\phi^i}(x)$, $i \leq t$, are frozen and a new model, $f_{\phi^{t+1}}(x)$, is learned from $\mathcal{D}_{t+1}$. The input x is then processed by all models, to produce a sequence of feature vectors

$$\phi^i(x) \leftarrow f_{\phi^i}(x), \ i = 1, 2, ..., t+1 \tag{4}$$

where $\phi^i(x)$ is the feature representation (i.e., embedded [CLS] token) of x under model $f_{\phi^i}(x)$.

Since each model $f_{\phi^i}(x)$ is fine-tuned on a large dataset $\mathcal{D}_i$ of the i-th task and then fixed, input x from the classes of task i can still be well represented by feature vector $\phi^i(x)$, after step $t+1$. Hence by combining all $\phi^i(x)$, $i \leq t+1$, the CIL model can obtain all necessary information to represent any input. This combination is usually implemented with the feature concatenation operation:

$$\phi(x) = \phi^0(x) \oplus \phi^1(x) \oplus \phi^2(x) \oplus ... \oplus \phi^{t+1}(x) \tag{5}$$

where $\phi^0(\cdot)$ is the original pre-trained model.

Then, we use a unified classifier for all tasks. This classifier receives the concatenated feature representation (i.e., $\phi(x)$) of the multi-backbone network as input and performs classification on this unified feature representation. Similar to SimpleCIL, we also use class prototypes as parameters to the classifier. The difference is that after learning each task, we save 20 examplar samples from each class that are closest to the prototype using the rehearsal algorithm:

$$g_\psi \leftarrow p_i = \frac{1}{K} \sum_{j=1}^{|\widetilde{\mathcal{D}}|} \mathbb{I}(y_j = i) f_\phi(x_j) \tag{6}$$

where $K = \sum_{j=1}^{|\widetilde{\mathcal{D}}|} \mathbb{I}(y_j = i)$, $\widetilde{\mathcal{D}}$ is the examplar set.

After the model is fine-tuned on each task, the prototype representation of the class is re-computed on the examplar set as the current classifier parameter. The resultant prototype representations encapsulate additional information derived from the fine-tuned model, encompassing task-specific features that enhance recognition performance, thereby ensuring a higher degree of generalization and adaptability.Finally, we use the Eq. (1) to make the final prediction.

4 Experiments

In this section, we present a series of experiments to investigate the performence of DTAA under different CIL settings. First, we detail the benchmark used for the experiments and discuss our implementation. Second, we compare DTAA with state-of-the-art methods on benchmark datasets to show the superiority.

4.1 Experimental Setups

Benchmark: Similar to L2P [32] and DualPrompt [31] , we evaluate CIL methods on the CIFAR-100 [12], ImageNet-R [9] and CUB-200 [24] benchmarks. CIFAR-100 consists of 60k images with a size of 32×32 from 100 classes, each class consists of 500 training and 100 testing samples. ImageNet-R contains 200 classes that are hard examples from ImageNet [13] or newly collected data of different styles (e.g. cartoon, graffiti, origami), split into 24k and 6k images with size of 224×224 for training and testing (similar ratio for each class), respectively. CUB-200 dataset, the most widely used dataset for fine-grained visual categorization tasks, contains a total of 11,788 image samples from 200 different bird species, of which the training set contains about 5,994 images and the test set contains about 5,794 images.

Dataset Split: Adhering to the benchmark configuration outlined in [19,38], we also adopt two types of dataset splits, *i.e.*, training from half and training from scratch. We unify them as "Base/B m, Inc n", which means the first incremental session contains m classes, and each following session contains n classes. $m = 0$ means the total classes are equally divided into each task. All classes are randomly shuffled with the same random seed before splitting for fair comparison. The evaluation process employs the original testing set to provide a comprehensive assessment.

Comparison Methods: Following [23], we first compare to the current state-of-the-art pre-trained model based methods L2P [32], DualPrompt [31], CODA-Prompt [22], ADAM-Adapter [41]. Also, we conduct experiments on typical class-incremental learning algorithms, including DER [35], FOSTER [25], iCaRL [19], Coil [40] and MEMO [39], within the context of pre-trained models to make a comparison.

Training Details: We implement all methods in PyTorch with a single NVIDIA RTX 3090 GPU, and choose the same network backbone ViT-B/16-IN1K for all compared methods for fair comparison. The model is trained with a batch size of 48 for 20 epochs on CIFAR-100 and a batch size of 16 for 10 epochs on ImageNet-R, respectively. We use SGD with momentum for optimization, and the learning rate starts from 0.01 and decays with cosine annealing. For some rehearsal methods, we use the herding algorithm [33] to select 20 exemplars per class for rehearsal after each task training.

Evaluation Metric: Assuming there are T tasks in total, we report the accuracy from the end session as $Acc = A_T$, and report the average accuracy over all sessions as $Acc = \frac{1}{T}\sum_{i=1}^{T} A_i$ (Table 1).

4.2   Comparison with State of the Art

In this section, we conduct a comparative analysis of DTAA against state-of-the-art approaches compatible with the Transformer architecture on the CIFAR-100 and ImageNet-R datasets. As depicted in Table 2, our comparison is conducted under the training from half and training from scratch configuration for CIFAR-100 and ImageNet-R benchmarks, respectively. The second column in the table represent the methods with and without exemplars. In the case of "FineTune", this approach involves continual training of a pre-trained model on new tasks, necessitating updates to all parameters and rendering it susceptible to severe catastrophic forgetting, and we involve it to make a comparison.

Table 1. Comparison of the methods with different settings on CIFAR-100 and ImageNet-R benchmarks. Avg and Last denote the average and final performance, respectively. The second column represent the methods with and without exemplars. The best performance is shown in bold.

Method	Exemplar	CIFAR B0-Inc10		IN-R B0-Inc20		CIFAR B50-Inc10		IN-R B100-Inc20	
		Avg	Last	Avg	Last	Avg	Last	Avg	Last
Coil	✓	87.33	79.84	77.85	71.75	85.26	80.27	79.40	74.37
DER	✓	88.79	78.72	80.95	75.22	86.67	81.36	80.59	77.83
iCaRL	✓	89.58	78.33	72.33	60.93	87.84	80.30	70.83	63.28
MEMO	✓	86.74	76.89	74.80	66.10	86.60	81.30	73.85	68.30
FOSTER	✓	91.61	87.18	82.13	76.02	90.41	87.69	**80.47**	76.77
L2P	✗	89.32	84.61	77.81	71.45	86.84	80.52	73.18	66.63
FineTune	✗	80.11	69.09	72.23	60.83	80.81	72.45	72.58	62.15
SimpleCIL	✗	82.32	76.21	67.05	61.28	78.67	76.21	63.51	61.28
DualPrompt	✗	87.38	82.30	74.35	68.67	86.08	80.92	70.15	65.08
CODA-Prompt	✗	91.31	86.93	78.68	74.72	88.13	83.63	76.61	73.03
ADAM-Adapter	✗	90.92	85.81	79.12	72.88	91.44	89.14	78.58	76.08
Ours	✓	**93.24**	**89.28**	**82.69**	**77.52**	**92.01**	**89.85**	80.17	**78.33**

Notably, as shown in second row, even when replacing the backbone of the traditional method with an existing pre-trained model, it exhibits a performance gap compared to our approach. DTAA achieves better results under different settings, outperforming alternative methods with rehearsal by a substantial margin.

Table 2. Comparison of the methods on CUB-200 benchmarks. Avg and Last denote the average and final performance, respectively. The second column represent the methods with and without exemplars. The best performance is shown in bold.

Method	Exemplar	CUB-200	B0-Inc10
		Avg	Last
Coil	✓	32.79	14.33
DER	✓	89.89	84.52
iCaRL	✓	88.69	81.38
MEMO	✓	89.32	84.61
FOSTER	✓	85.21	81.26
L2P	✗	73.19	60.90
FineTune	✗	64.89	43.55
SimpleCIL	✗	90.95	85.16
DualPrompt	✗	78.93	67.13
CODA-Prompt	✗	74.32	65.99
ADAM-Adapter	✗	90.91	85.20
Ours	✓	**91.08**	**86.13**

To provide specific insights, DTAA surpasses the second-place method, FOSTER [25], by 1.63% and 0.56% in average accuracy on the CIFAR-100 and ImageNet-R datasets under the setting of training form scratch, respectively. On the other hand, it is only slightly lower than FOSTER [25] by about 0.3% average accuracy on the training from half setting of the Imagenet-R dataset and leads FOSTER [25] by 1.6% average accuracy on the CIFAR-100 dataset. It's worth noting that FOSTER [25], a powerful competitive method, dynamically expands new modules to adapt to the residuals between the target model and the original model's output, is similar to which our method is based. Furthermore, it's worth noting that approaches excelling on the CIFAR-100 dataset may not perform as effectively on the ImageNet-R dataset due to significant domain differences. However, structure-based methods (*e.g.*, DER [35], FOSTER [25] and ours) consistently delivers strong performance on the ImageNet-R dataset, maintaining its position as the top performer.

As shown in the third row, Our method also shows considerable advantages compared with some recent methods based on pre-trained models, which are based on prompt or adapter and do not require exemplars. For example, on the training from scratch setting, DTAA leads the CODA-Prompt [22] by about 1.93% average accuracy on the CIFAR-100 data set, and leads the ADAM-Adapter [41] by about 3.57% average accuracy on the ImageNet-R data set. Finally, we show incremental performance for each step of all the compared methods in Fig. 2. For more complex incremental tasks, *e.g.* 20-step on CUB-200 benchmarks, we can see a similar case, which further proves the validity of our approach.

We attribute this excellent performance to the design of the isolation and integration: isolation ensures that feature representations for different tasks are learned independently, thereby averting information interference and conflicts between tasks. Simultaneously, it enables the effective utilization of the strong generalization capabilities inherent in pre-trained networks, which can be seamlessly adapted to new tasks. On the other hand, integration fuses the features acquired from the training of all backbone networks to construct a unified feature representation. This amalgamated representation retains the distinctive features of each task while incorporating the commonalities shared across all tasks. Such a holistic feature representation not only preserves the task-specific characteristics but also assimilates the overarching patterns common to all tasks. This underscores the robustness and stability of our approach.

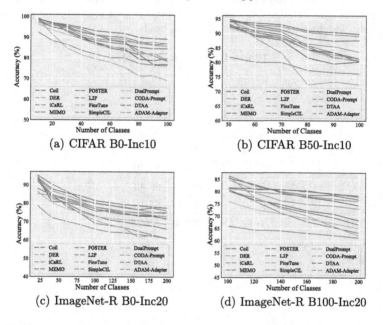

Fig. 2. The incremental performance for each step with ViT-B/16-IN1K as the backbone. (a) and (c) are under the setting of training from scratch, (b) and (d) are in the 5-step setting which half of the total classes are base classes.

4.3   Ablation Study

In this section, we conduct an ablation study to evaluate the contribution of our method.

The Effect of Adapter. Table 3 summarizes the results of our ablative experiments, which explore the impact of the location and number of adapters on experimental performance in the CIFAR-100 B0-Inc10 setting. Blocks-ID is "None" means that only the prototype classifier is used without using the adapter to fine-tune the network. Experimental results demonstrate that the performance of adapters in various locations (*i.e.*, front, middle, and rear) within the 12-blocks ViT network, or the adjustment of their numbers, remains largely consistent. However, the network performs best when each block is fine-tuned using an adapter. We believe that placing adapters near the input layer may enable the model to adapt to task-specific features in the early stages, while placing them in deeper positions may capture more abstract and general features. This is because when adapters are placed at every location, the network achieves the best performance.

Table 3. Comparison of how the location and number of adapters impact accuracy performance in the CIFAR-100 B0-Inc10 setting. "Blocks-ID" indicates which block uses the adapter for fine-tuning. Avg and Last denote the average and final performance, respectively. The best performance is shown in bold.

Blocks-ID	CIFAR	B0-Inc10
	Avg	Last
None	82.32	76.21
1–2	92.70	88.44
5–6	92.71	88.37
10–11	92.67	88.36
1–4	92.66	88.30
5–8	92.71	88.43
9–12	92.65	88.10
1–12	**93.24**	**89.28**

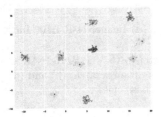 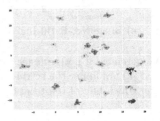

(a) 1st stage on CIFAR B0-Inc10   (b) 2nd stage on CIFAR B0-Inc10

Fig. 3. The visualization of the learned decision boundaries between two incremental sessions.

Visualization of Incremental Stages. We visualize the learned decision boundaries with t-SNE [15] on CIFAR-100 dataset between two incremental sessions, as shown in Fig. 3. The classes from the first and second incremental tasks are in colorful markers. Correspondingly, the class prototypes are represented by asterisks with black. Based on these visualizations, it is clear that models fine-tuned with adapters exhibit strong performance. They proficiently group instances into their respective classes. The central placement of class prototypes confirms their representativeness in the recognition process. Notably, when transitioning the model from the initial stage to the following stage, DTAA exhibits commendable performance across both previously learned and newly introduced classes. These visual representations offer compelling evidence of DTAA's robust generalization and adaptability capabilities.

5 Conclusion

In this paper, we propose a strong pre-trained model-based paradigm which dynamically tuning the pre-trained model with adapter to learn new concepts and keep the pre-trained backbone frozen to retain its good generalization ability, and then we introduce a prototype based classifier which receives the concatenated feature representation to make a final prediction. We conduct exhaustive experiments on the two major incremental classification benchmarks and compare traditional and recent state-of-the-art methods within the context of pre-trained models. The experimental results show that our method consistently performs better than other methods with a sizable margin.

Acknowledgments. This work was supported in part by the National Natural Science Foundation of China under Grants 62222602, 62302167, 62176224, 62106075, 61972157 and U23A20343, in part by Science and Technology Commission under Grant 21511100700, in part by CCF-Tencent Rhino-Bird Young Faculty Open Research Fund under Grant RAGR20230121.

References

1. Aljundi, R., Babiloni, F., Elhoseiny, M., Rohrbach, M., Tuytelaars, T.: Memory aware synapses: learning what (not) to forget. In: Proceedings of the European Conference on Computer Vision (ECCV), pp. 139–154 (2018)
2. Buzzega, P., Boschini, M., Porrello, A., Abati, D., Calderara, S.: Dark experience for general continual learning: a strong, simple baseline. Adv. Neural. Inf. Process. Syst. **33**, 15920–15930 (2020)
3. Chen, S., et al.: Adaptformer: adapting vision transformers for scalable visual recognition. Adv. Neural. Inf. Process. Syst. **35**, 16664–16678 (2022)
4. Dhar, P., Singh, R.V., Peng, K.C., Wu, Z., Chellappa, R.: Learning without memorizing. In: Proceedings of the IEEE/CVF Conference on Computer Vision and Pattern Recognition, pp. 5138–5146 (2019)
5. Dosovitskiy, A., et al.: An image is worth 16x16 words: transformers for image recognition at scale. arXiv preprint arXiv:2010.11929 (2020)
6. Douillard, A., Ramé, A., Couairon, G., Cord, M.: Dytox: transformers for continual learning with dynamic token expansion. In: Proceedings of the IEEE/CVF Conference on Computer Vision and Pattern Recognition, pp. 9285–9295 (2022)

7. French, R.M., Chater, N.: Using noise to compute error surfaces in connectionist networks: a novel means of reducing catastrophic forgetting. Neural Comput. **14**(7), 1755–1769 (2002)

8. Han, X., et al.: Pre-trained models: past, present and future. AI Open **2**, 225–250 (2021)

9. Hendrycks, D., et al.: The many faces of robustness: a critical analysis of out-of-distribution generalization. In: Proceedings of the IEEE/CVF International Conference on Computer Vision, pp. 8340–8349 (2021)

10. Houlsby, N., et al.: Parameter-efficient transfer learning for NLP. In: International Conference on Machine Learning, pp. 2790–2799. PMLR (2019)

11. Kirkpatrick, J., et al.: Overcoming catastrophic forgetting in neural networks. Proc. Natl. Acad. Sci. **114**(13), 3521–3526 (2017)

12. Krizhevsky, A., Hinton, G., et al.: Learning multiple layers of features from tiny images (2009)

13. Krizhevsky, A., Sutskever, I., Hinton, G.E.: Imagenet classification with deep convolutional neural networks. Adv. Neural Inf. Process. Syst. **25** (2012)

14. Li, Z., Hoiem, D.: Learning without forgetting. IEEE Trans. Pattern Anal. Mach. Intell. **40**(12), 2935–2947 (2017)

15. Van der Maaten, L., Hinton, G.: Visualizing data using t-sne. J. Mach. Learn. Res. **9**(11) (2008)

16. Nguyen, C.V., Achille, A., Lam, M., Hassner, T., Mahadevan, V., Soatto, S.: Toward understanding catastrophic forgetting in continual learning. arXiv preprint arXiv:1908.01091 (2019)

17. Prabhu, A., Torr, P.H.S., Dokania, P.K.: GDumb: a simple approach that questions our progress in continual learning. In: Vedaldi, A., Bischof, H., Brox, T., Frahm, J.-M. (eds.) Computer Vision – ECCV 2020. LNCS, vol. 12347, pp. 524–540. Springer, Cham (2020). https://doi.org/10.1007/978-3-030-58536-5_31

18. Radford, A., et al.: Learning transferable visual models from natural language supervision. In: International Conference on Machine Learning, pp. 8748–8763. PMLR (2021)

19. Rebuffi, S.A., Kolesnikov, A., Sperl, G., Lampert, C.H.: icarl: Incremental classifier and representation learning. In: Proceedings of the IEEE Conference on Computer Vision and Pattern Recognition, pp. 2001–2010 (2017)

20. Rusu, A.A., et al.: Progressive neural networks. arXiv preprint arXiv:1606.04671 (2016)

21. Serra, J., Suris, D., Miron, M., Karatzoglou, A.: Overcoming catastrophic forgetting with hard attention to the task. In: International Conference on Machine Learning, pp. 4548–4557. PMLR (2018)

22. Smith, J.S., et al.: Coda-prompt: continual decomposed attention-based prompting for rehearsal-free continual learning. In: Proceedings of the IEEE/CVF Conference on Computer Vision and Pattern Recognition, pp. 11909–11919 (2023)

23. Sun, H.L., Zhou, D.W., Ye, H.J., Zhan, D.C.: Pilot: a pre-trained model-based continual learning toolbox. arXiv preprint arXiv:2309.07117 (2023)

24. Wah, C., Branson, S., Welinder, P., Perona, P., Belongie, S.: The caltech-UCSD birds-200-2011 dataset (2011)

25. Wang, F.Y., Zhou, D.W., Ye, H.J., Zhan, D.C.: FOSTER: feature boosting and compression for class-incremental learning. In: Avidan, S., Brostow, G., Cisse, M., Farinella, G.M., Hassner, T. (eds.) Computer Vision, ECCV 2022. LNCS, vol. 13685, pp. 398–414. Springer, Cham (2022). https://doi.org/10.1007/978-3-031-19806-9_23

26. Wang, L., et al.: Afec: active forgetting of negative transfer in continual learning. Adv. Neural. Inf. Process. Syst. **34**, 22379–22391 (2021)
27. Wang, L., Zhang, X., Li, Q., Zhu, J., Zhong, Y.: CoSCL: cooperation of small continual learners is stronger than a big one. In: Avidan, S., Brostow, G., Cissé, M., Farinella, G.M., Hassner, T. (eds.) Computer Vision, ECCV 2022. LNCS, vol. 13686, pp. 254–271. Springer, Cham (2022). https://doi.org/10.1007/978-3-031-19809-0_15
28. Wang, L., et al.: Memory replay with data compression for continual learning. arXiv preprint arXiv:2202.06592 (2022)
29. Wang, R., et al.: Attriclip: a non-incremental learner for incremental knowledge learning. In: Proceedings of the IEEE/CVF Conference on Computer Vision and Pattern Recognition, pp. 3654–3663 (2023)
30. Wang, Y., Huang, Z., Hong, X.: S-prompts learning with pre-trained transformers: an Occam's razor for domain incremental learning. Adv. Neural. Inf. Process. Syst. **35**, 5682–5695 (2022)
31. Wang, Z., et al.: DualPrompt: complementary prompting for rehearsal-free continual learning. In: Avidan, S., Brostow, G., Cissé, M., Farinella, G.M., Hassner, T. (eds.) Computer Vision, ECCV 2022. LNCS, vol. 13686, pp. 631–648. Springer, Cham (2022). https://doi.org/10.1007/978-3-031-19809-0_36
32. Wang, Z., et al.: Learning to prompt for continual learning. In: Proceedings of the IEEE/CVF Conference on Computer Vision and Pattern Recognition, pp. 139–149 (2022)
33. Welling, M.: Herding dynamical weights to learn. In: Proceedings of the 26th Annual International Conference on Machine Learning, pp. 1121–1128 (2009)
34. Wu, Y., et al.: Large scale incremental learning. In: Proceedings of the IEEE/CVF Conference on Computer Vision and Pattern Recognition, pp. 374–382 (2019)
35. Yan, S., Xie, J., He, X.: Der: dynamically expandable representation for class incremental learning. In: Proceedings of the IEEE/CVF Conference on Computer Vision and Pattern Recognition, pp. 3014–3023 (2021)
36. Zhang, G., Wang, L., Kang, G., Chen, L., Wei, Y.: SLCA: slow learner with classifier alignment for continual learning on a pre-trained model. arXiv preprint arXiv:2303.05118 (2023)
37. Zheng, Z., Ma, M., Wang, K., Qin, Z., Yue, X., You, Y.: Preventing zero-shot transfer degradation in continual learning of vision-language models. arXiv preprint arXiv:2303.06628 (2023)
38. Zhou, D.W., Wang, Q.W., Qi, Z.H., Ye, H.J., Zhan, D.C., Liu, Z.: Deep class-incremental learning: a survey. arXiv preprint arXiv:2302.03648 (2023)
39. Zhou, D.W., Wang, Q.W., Ye, H.J., Zhan, D.C.: A model or 603 exemplars: towards memory-efficient class-incremental learning. arXiv preprint arXiv:2205.13218 (2022)
40. Zhou, D.W., Ye, H.J., Zhan, D.C.: Co-transport for class-incremental learning. In: Proceedings of the 29th ACM International Conference on Multimedia, pp. 1645–1654 (2021)
41. Zhou, D.W., Ye, H.J., Zhan, D.C., Liu, Z.: Revisiting class-incremental learning with pre-trained models: generalizability and adaptivity are all you need. arXiv preprint arXiv:2303.07338 (2023)
42. Zhou, D.W., Zhang, Y., Ning, J., Ye, H.J., Zhan, D.C., Liu, Z.: Learning without forgetting for vision-language models. arXiv preprint arXiv:2305.19270 (2023)

Object Category-Based Visual Dialog for Effective Question Generation

Feifei Xu, Yingchen Zhou[✉], Zheng Zhong, and Guangzhen Li

School of Computer Science and Technology, Shanghai University of Electric Power, Shanghai, China
xufeifei@shiep.edu.cn, {zhouyingchen,liguangzhen}@mail.shiep.edu.cn

Abstract. GuessWhat?! is a visual dialog dataset that consists of a series of goal-oriented questions and answers between a questioner and an answerer. The purpose of the task is to enable the questioner to identify the target object in an image based on the dialogue history. A key challenge for the questioner model is to generate informative and strategic questions that can narrow down the search space effectively. However, previous models lack questioning strategies and rely only on the visual features of the objects without considering their category information, which leads to uninformative, redundant or irrelevant questions. To overcome this limitation, we propose an Object-Category based Visual Dialogue (OCVD) model that leverages the category information of objects to generate more diverse and instructive questions. Our model incorporates a category selection module that dynamically updates the category information according to the answers and adopts a linear category-based search strategy. We evaluate our model on the GuessWhat?! dataset and demonstrate its superiority over previous methods in terms of generation quality and dialogue effectiveness.

Keywords: Visual dialog · Question generation · Category information · Questioning strategy

1 Introduction

In recent years, the domains of vision and language, especially image captioning [31,33,36], vision-and-language navigation [4,8,18], and visual dialog [9,13,32], have attracted increasing attention and research due to the continuous development of artificial intelligence technology and deep learning algorithms. In particular, visual dialog researchers have proposed several different visual dialog tasks, such as VisDial [3,7,9], GuessWhat?! [11,24,29], and GuessWhich [6,20,39], etc. Among these, GuessWhat?! is a goal-oriented visual dialog dataset that involves two players engaged in a question-and-answer session on a single image. Specifically, the Oracle randomly selects a target object from the image, and the Questioner agent asks a series of questions to identify that object while receiving binary answers (i.e., Yes or No) from the Oracle. An example of GuessWhat?! is shown in Fig. 1. Generating more efficient questions is what we

F.-L. Zhang and A. Sharf (Eds.): CVM 2024, LNCS 14593, pp. 316–331, 2024.
https://doi.org/10.1007/978-981-97-2092-7_16

are aiming for to help the model guess the target object faster. Researchers have divided the questioner agent task into two subtasks, namely the Guesser and the Question Generation (QGen). The Guesser deduces the target object based on dialog history, while the QGen generates relevant questions to aid the Guesser's inference. Independent training of the subtasks allows them to focus on their specific goals, resulting in improved performance. Modeling QGen is crucial for the success of the game, as high-quality questions yield more information about the target object. Furthermore, research on the QGen model facilitates the creation of inferential questions. Most importantly, the QGen model influences the selection of subsequent questions by leveraging previous questions and answers, thereby enhancing the system's conversational reasoning and decision-making capabilities. In this paper, we mainly focus on QGen.

Questioner(QGen)	Oracle
Is it a vase?	yes
Is it partially visible?	no
Is it in the left corner?	no
Is it the turquoise and purple one?	yes
Questioner(Guesser)	

Fig. 1. An Example of GuessWhat?! dataset

The previous QGen models suffer from two major limitations. First, most existing work concerns multimodal fusion [10,17,23] and model learning [2,11,23, 27,37], while neglecting effective question generation strategies. Consequently, repetitive and meaningless questions are always generated. To address this problem, researchers employ various strategies to minimize the number of questions. For instance, Testoni et al. [28] propose a visual dialogue strategy that generates more human-like questions, while Shi et al. [35] introduce a sentence-level questioning strategy that generates different types of questions. Notably, [11] indicates that object categories can help humans use linear search strategies to promptly guess the target object. Guiding the question generation under category information can narrow down the search space, allowing Guesser to guess the target object as early as possible. Nonetheless, to the best of our knowledge, no work has been mentioned using category information to guide question generation.

Second, image information is not fully utilized. Existing work encodes either a whole image [11,15,22,25,27,28,38] or the extracted object [5,20,24,29]. If the object's category information is introduced, QGen can generate further fine-grained questions guided by object categories, reducing the occurrence of repeated questions. Faster R-CNN has been shown to be able to detect object category information in images [19]. We can obtain the category information of each object with the help of Faster R-CNN for better question generation.

In this paper, we propose a novel question generation model, Object Category based Visual Dialogue (OCVD). An Object Information Extraction Module is employed to extract the feature and category information of the object. A Category Selection Module is put forward to select the appropriate category in the current round, based on the historical responses. We compute object-category similarity to acquire category-level attention distribution. Together with object-level attention distribution from the Object-Level Attention Update Module, the object features can be updated. Finally, the Object-Self Difference Attention Module is exploited to attain the final visual representation. To make better use of the category information, we connect the final visual representation to the category information to generate the new question. Experimental results demonstrate that our proposed model achieves state-of-the-art performance in the GuessWhat?! task. Additionally, the model introduces new information into the question generation model that helps to generate more informative and strategic questions, thus reducing the search space more efficiently.

Our contributions can be summarized as follows.

- First, we propose a novel question generation model OCVD based on an object category mechanism.
- Second, to simulate human thinking process, a linear search strategy is improved by adjusting the category priority in order to have a higher probability of guessing the target object.
- Third, to enable the model to better obtain useful information from object categories, we design a category selection module that guides the model to generate more informative and valuable questions. For all we know, it is the first time to consider object categories in QGen.
- Finally, we conduct supervised learning and reinforcement learning to train our model and achieve state-of-the-art results in the QGen task.

2   Related Work

Visual dialog is considered as one of the significant research tasks in the domain of vision and language. VisDial [9] and GuessWhat?! [11] are the most common datasets for visual dialog tasks. These datasets involve several rounds of question-answer sessions between two participants, which are based on a single image. Nevertheless, a crucial difference exists between these datasets. In VisDial, the questioner is unable to perceive the image, while the answerer can see the image and answer questions about it. Hence, VisDial models have generally focused on the role of the answerer. Conversely, in GuessWhat?!, both the questioner and the answerer have the same access to the image. The answerer must select an object in the image as a target object and respond to the questioner's inquiry. The questioner's task is to ask questions to identify the object chosen by the answerer. The questioner's role is more intricate than that of the answerer, which involves complex interactions between visual, language, and guessing behaviors, with a higher emphasis on generating goal-oriented questions in visual dialogue tasks.

The QGen model is first introduced by De Vries et al. [11]. It employs an encoder-decoder architecture that encodes the previous round's dialogue using the HRED [21] model's encoder. The result of encoder is connected with the image's VGG features, and both of them are fed into the LSTM [12] to generate questions. Supervised learning is used to train the model by maximizing the conditional log-likelihood. However, the supervised learning framework does not consider the dialogue strategy. To address this issue, Strub et al. [27] proposes a reinforcement learning approach using a policy gradient algorithm to optimize supervised models. The QGen model is optimized by using the supervised trained Oracle and Guesser model to build environment. It uses the final goal as a reward to optimize the question sequence and find the correct object. Zhang et al. [37] proposes a reinforcement learning model that assigns different intermediate rewards to each question to improve the quality of the question and generates concise and informative questions that aid in achieving the final goal. Abbasnejad et al. [2] employs a Bayesian deep learning approach to quantify uncertainty in the internal representation of reinforcement learning models and introduces an information search decoder that accounts for the environment's uncertainty and dialogue history, enabling a more accurate selection of words in each question. Zhao et al. [38] designs a QGen model based on Seq2Seq and introduces the Tempered Policy Gradients method to train the model. They dynamically adjust the temperature of each operation according to the operation frequency of each time step, resulting in better training effect and stability. The questioner task relies on two separate models: QGen and Guesser. However, Shekhar et al. [24] introduces a shared dialogue state encoder that integrates both models, resulting in improved performance and efficiency. This is achieved through a cooperative learning training approach, which tightly combines the two tasks and enables information sharing and interaction. The advantage of this approach is the ability to enhance the interdependence between the models, resulting in more accurate and meaningful questions being generated. Lee et al. [15] proposes an information theoretic algorithm, AQM, grounded in the theory of mind. This approach replaces the training task of question generation with training a neural network to infer answer probabilities. Shukla et al. [25] combines reinforcement learning with regularized information gain to construct a reward function that trains QGen model. This approach is based on the ideology that humans attempt to maximize the expected regularized information gain when asking questions. Shekhar et al. [22] adds a dialogue manager component to the QGen model to determine whether the question generator should continue asking questions or whether the Guesser should guess the target object after each Q&A pair. Pang et al. [17] proposes a Visual Dialogue State Tracking (VDST) approach for question generation. This model tracks the process state of the dialogue, updates the distribution of objects in the image, and adjusts the representation at the end of each round of dialogue, thus guiding the QGen model to ask different meaningful questions. Tu et al. [30] contends that previous models lack shared and a priori knowledge of visual language representation. To overcome this limitation, they leverage the pre-trained visual language model

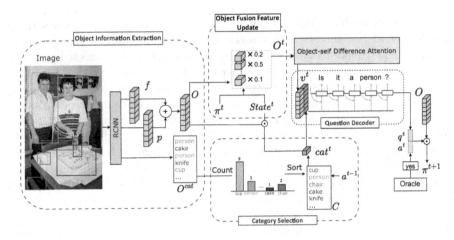

Fig. 2. Overall structure of OCVD model. p is the object position feature. f is the object feature. O is the initial object fusion feature. O^{cat} is the category information. COUNT and SORT are the aggregation and sort operations, respectively. cat^t is the object category to be focused on by the model in round t. O^t is the object fusion feature in round t. π^t and $State^t$ are the object-level attention distribution and category-level attention distribution in round t, respectively. v^t is the final visual representation. a^{t-1} and a^t are the answers of the previous and current rounds, respectively.

VilBERT to provide improved visual and language representation for dialogue agents. To this end, they propose new Oracle, Guesser, and Questioner models employing the pre-trained models. Testoni et al. [28] proposes a beam search re-ranking strategy called confirm-it, which seeks confirmation information during a dialogue. This approach mirrors human behavior in everyday dialogue, resulting in more natural and human-like questions generated by the model. Shi et al. [35] suggests a questioning strategy based on question categories, where questions are classified into four categories: object, color, location, and other. By analyzing the dialogue history and image features, appropriate question categories are selected to generate targeted questions.

The above methods still generate repetitive or nonsensical questions. In this paper, we use the category information of the object to simulate the way humans ask questions, thus facilitating the QGen model to generate more effective questions.

3   Model

In this section, we will introduce our question generation model OCVD in detail. The dialogue history is represented as $H_{t-1} = \{q^0, a^0, q^1, a^1, \ldots, q^{t-1}, a^{t-1}\}$, while the current question $q^t = \{w_1^t, w_2^t, \ldots, w_S^t\}$ is a sequence of words with a length of S in round t. The answer $a^t \in \{< \text{Yes} >, < \text{No} >, < \text{NA} >\}$ is restricted to one of three options: yes, no, or not applicable. Additionally, $I \in \mathbb{R}^{H \times W}$ represents the image with a given height H and width W. The model generates the current round question q^t by considering the previous question q^{t-1} and the provided image I. Figure 2 depicts the general structure of the model.

3.1 Object Information Extraction

we apply the Faster-RCNN [19] algorithm to extract an 8-dimensional object position feature p and a d_0-dimensional object feature f from the provided image. Rather than directly concatenating these two vectors, we leverage two fully connected layers to perform projection and normalization on them, respectively. Next, we employ summation and averaging operations to integrate these two features, which yields the object fusion feature O corresponding to the provided image I.

$$y = LayerNorm(W_1 f + b_1), \tag{1}$$
$$x = LayerNorm(W_2 p + b_2), \tag{2}$$
$$O = (x + y)/2. \tag{3}$$

where $W_1 \in \mathbb{R}^{d_0 \times d}$, $W_2 \in \mathbb{R}^{8 \times d}$, $O \in \mathbb{R}^{k \times d}$ including k objects $o \in \mathbb{R}^d$. This treatment aims to balance the incorporation of two distinct types of features and achieve a more integrated feature representation.

Our proposed model departs from the baseline model developed by Pang et al. in which we not only utilize objects and bounding boxes representation vectors but also employ object category information $O^{cat} = [o_1^{cat}, o_2^{cat}, \ldots, o_k^{cat}]$ extracted by the Faster-RCNN object detection model. O^{cat} provides category information for k objects, enabling us to obtain a more comprehensive understanding of the objects in the input image.

3.2 Category Selection

To effectively use this category information, we can analyze the distribution of various object categories in the image. This analysis helps us identify which category is more critical for recognizing the target object. In short, if a category appears more often in an image, then it is more likely to be the category of the target object. Therefore, we process the category information by defining an equation that incorporates it into our model.

$$C = \text{Sort}\left(\text{Counter}\left(\left[o_1^{cat}, o_2^{cat}, \ldots, o_k^{cat}\right]\right)\right), \tag{4}$$

where Counter is the aggregation function used to determine the number of objects in each category, and Sort is the process of arranging the categories in descending order based on their object counts, ultimately generating a list of candidate categories C. Suppose there are m different categories in the O^{cat}. The set of candidate categories is represented as $C = [c_1, c_2, \ldots, c_m]$.

People often quickly exclude or identify objects based on different object categories. Similar to human thinking, we design a category selection module. This module is designed to select the most relevant category for the question and guide the model's search process accordingly. To achieve this, we begin by setting a Boolean variable called *nofind* to True, which serves as a flag to determine whether there are any candidate categories left to explore. Then, a recursive selection mechanism is employed to update the variables *index* and *nofind* based on the answer from the previous round.

$$\begin{cases} index = index, nofind = \text{False} & \text{if } a^{t-1} = yes \\ index = index + 1 & \text{if } a^{t-1} = no \ \& \ nofind = \text{True}, \end{cases} \tag{5}$$

where *index* represents the index of the candidate category list, which is used to update the object category selected in each round of dialogue. The initial value of *index* is set to 0, indicating that the first element c_1 of the candidate category list is used as the initial category in the first round of dialogue. cat^t denotes the category selected in the tth round of dialogue, and its update is defined by the equation:

$$cat^t = C[index]. \tag{6}$$

3.3 Object Fusion Feature Update

In order to encourage the model to focus more on the object features that are consistent with the selected category cat^t, we compute the similarity score between the object fusion features O and cat^t. Specifically, the similarity score is computed using a similarity function that measures the similarity between the fused feature representation of an object and the feature representation of the selected category.

$$Score^t \left(O, cat^t \right) = \text{softmax} \left(\frac{O cat^t}{\sqrt{d}} \right), \tag{7}$$

where $O \in \mathbb{R}^{k \times d}$, $cat^t \in \mathbb{R}^{d \times 1}$, and $Sorce^t \in \mathbb{R}^{k \times 1}$. In the VDST model, the cumulative attention distribution on the kth object of the tth round is denoted as $\pi^{(t)} \in \mathbb{R}^{k \times 1}$, and it is updated in each round of the dialogue. To combine the object-level attention distribution $\pi^{(t)}$ with the category-level attention distribution $Score^t$, we introduce the concept of $State^t$. We update the object fusion feature O using $State^t$ and the formula for updating the object representation is as follows:

$$State^t = \text{softmax} \left(\left(\pi^t + Score^t \right) / 2 \right), \tag{8}$$

$$O^t = \left(State^t \right)^T O. \tag{9}$$

3.4 Object-Self Difference Attention Module

To obtain the final visual representation, the VDST model uses Object-self Difference Attention to capture the visual differences between objects, the result of which is used as the visual context. Object-self Difference Attention is defined by the following equation:

$$v^t = \text{softmax} \left(\left[o_i^t \odot \left(o_i^t - o_k^t \right) \right] W \right)^T O^t, \tag{10}$$

where $o_i^t, o_k^t \in O^t$. Attention towards objects may change in different rounds, and thus the visual representation v^t in each round can dynamically change under the influence of $State^t$.

3.5   Question Decoder

We choose to use LSTM as the question decoder since it possesses the memory property that can better generate complex natural language questions. To guide the model to generate dialogues related to the selected object category cat^t, we additionally incorporate cat^t into the input of the LSTM.

$$w_{i+1}^t = \text{LSTM}\left(\left[v^t; cat^t; w_i^t\right]\right), \tag{11}$$

where w_i^t denotes the ith word in the question q^t, while $[;]$ indicates concatenation. The final hidden state of the LSTM decoder serves as the representation of the question q^t.

3.6   Object-Level Attention Update

After obtaining the answer a^t from the Oracle, we concatenate the embedding of a^t with the representation of q^t, resulting in $h^t = [q^t; a^t]$. Based on the question-answer pair and object representation, we update π^t.

$$\pi^{t+1} = \text{Norm}\left(\text{softmax}\left(\frac{\tanh\left(O^t U^T \odot V^T h^t\right)}{\sqrt{d}}\right)\pi^t\right). \tag{12}$$

4   Experiments

4.1   Dataset

To evaluate our model, we use the GuessWhat?! dataset, which consists of 66k images and 821k question-answer pairs in 155k dialogues (Each image may correspond to multiple dialogues). The dialogues are about a target object in the image that Guesser tries to guess by asking yes/no questions to Oracle. The task is considered successful if the guesser correctly identifies the object. Following previous work, we split the dataset into training, validation, and test sets with a ratio of 70%, 15%, and 15%, respectively. We only include the dialogues that are successful (84.6% of the total) for training and evaluation, and exclude those that are unsuccessful (8.4%) or incomplete (7.0%).

4.2   Evaluation Metrics

Task Success Rate: The QGen model's performance is measured by the probability that the Questioner in a game can successfully identify the target object within a certain number of rounds. This means that the Questioner has to use relevant questions to achieve this objective. Nonetheless, the QGen model is constrained by the Guesser and Oracle models, so it can only be evaluated by associating with Guesser and Oracle models. A game example of the Qgen, Oracle, and Guesser models is shown in Fig. 3.

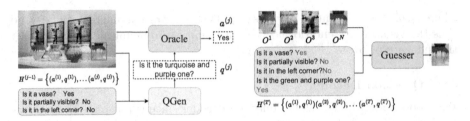

Fig. 3. An Example of Qgen, Oracle, and Guesser. On the left side, Oracle and QGen generate questions and answers through interaction. On the right side, Guesser makes a guess based on the complete dialogue history when a pre-defined number of rounds T is reached.

Rate of Games with Repeated Questions: Repeated questions are undesirable in a dialog, as they can reduce the task success rate. A question is considered repetitive if it has already been asked in the history of a dialogue. Rate of Games with Repeated Questions is the ratio of the number of games containing repeated questions to the total number of games. This metric reflects the validity and diversity of the questions generated by the model.

4.3   Experiment Settings

We use Faster-RCNN to extract a feature vector of dimension 1024 for each image region. We select $k = 36$ objects from each image based on object detection. Both historical questions and answers are embedded in 512 dimensions each, and the dimension of category information embedding is also 512. Therefore, the LSTM hidden unit number is 512.

We implement our model using PyTorch and train it in two stages: supervised learning (SL) and reinforcement learning (RL). In the SL stage, we use the Adam [14] optimizer with a learning rate of 1e-4 and a batch size of 64. We train the Guesser and Oracle models for 30 epochs each and train the QGen model for 50 epochs. In the RL stage, we follow the same setup as de Vries et al. [27] and train the QGen model for 100 epochs using stochastic gradient descent (SGD) with a learning rate of 1e-4 and a batch size of 64.

4.4   Results

Game Success Rate: We evaluate our model on the game success rate and compare it with several recent state-of-the-art models in this field: SL [11], GDSE [24], RL [31], TPG [38], VQG [37], ISM [1], Bayesian [2], RIG [25], VDST [17], CSQG [35], VilBert-Questioner [30], ISM [1], and ADVSE-QGen [34]. Table 1 and Table 2 show the results of the comparison under two settings: New Object, where we use images from the training set but change the target object; and New Game, where we use data from the test set with both images and targets being new. We conduct the experiments with 5 and 8 rounds of dialogues based on beam search or greedy search, respectively.

Table 1. Task success rate for SL models. The results of the baseline models are from its original paper.

NewObject			
	Max turn	Greedy	BSearch
SL [11]	5	43.5	47.1
VDST-SL [17]	5	49.49	–
	8	48.01	–
ADVSE-QGen [34]	5	50.66	47.47
TPG-SL [38]	8	48.77	–
CSQG [35]	5	53.2	52.4
	8	54.4	53.9
ours	5	**55.3**	**53.7**
	8	**55.9**	**54.8**
NewGame			
SL [11]	5	40.8	44.6
	8	40.7	–
VDST-SL [17]	5	45.94	–
	8	45.03	–
ADVSE-QGen [34]	5	47.03	44.7
CSQG [35]	5	49.9	48.1
	8	51.7	49.7
GDSE-SL [24]	5	47.8	–
	8	49.7	–
VilBert-Questioner [30]	–	52.5	–
ours	5	**52.6**	**50.1**
	8	**53.3**	**51.5**

Table 2. Task success rate for RL models. The results of the baseline models are from its original paper.

New Object			
	Max turn	Greedy	BSearch
RL [31]	5	60.3	60.2
	8	58.2	53.9
VQG [37]	5	63.6	63.9
ISM [1]	–	64.2	–
Bayesian [2]	5	62.1	63.6
RIG as rewards [25]	8	63	63.08
RIG(0-1 rewards) [25]	8	63.19	62.57
VDST [17]	5	67.07	67.81
	8	70.55	71.03
ours	5	**69.3**	**68.9**
	8	**71.8**	**72.1**
New Game			
RL [31]	5	40.8	44.6
	8	40.7	–
VQG [37]	5	60.7	60.8
ISM [1]	–	62.1	–
RIG as rewards [25]	5	59.8	60.6
	8	59	60.21
RIG(0-1 rewards) [25]	8	61.18	59.79
VDST [17]	5	64.36	64.44
	8	67.73	67.52
GDSE-CL [24]	5	53.7	–
	8	58.4	–
ours	5	**66.4**	**65.9**
	8	**67.9**	66.7

It is important to note that the focus of recent research has shifted to building Guesser vs. Oracle models rather than QGen model improvements. Due to this trend, no newer QGen models are available for comparison. Nevertheless, our work is dedicated to improving and optimizing the performance of QGen models and demonstrating the effectiveness of our proposed approach by comparing it with classical methods.

We compare our model with several existing models and report the results in Table 1 and Table 2. We categorize the models into SL models and RL models. Table 1 shows that our model achieves the highest success rate among the SL models. It can be seen that our model not only outperforms the other supervised learning models but also outperforms the QGen model that uses a pre-trained visual language encoder (VilBert-Questioner). Our model reaches a success rate of 55.9% on New Object and 53.3% on New Game, establishing new state-of-the-art results with SL. Table 2 shows that our model also exceeds the RL models, achieving a 72.1% success rate on New Object and a 67.9% success rate on New Game, which indicates the effectiveness of OCVD.

Table 3. Rate of games with repeated questions of different questioner models. OCVD-SL refers to OCVD models trained using supervised learning only.

% Games with Repeated Q's	
SL [11]	93.5
RL [31]	96.47
GDSE-SL [24]	55.8
GDSE-CL [24]	52.19
VDST-SL [17]	40.05
VilBERT-Questioner [34]	32.56
OCVD-SL	**31.85**
VDST [17]	21.9
ours	**18.73**
Human	N/A

Table 4. Experimental results of ablation studies.

Model	New game
OCVD(full model)	66.4
w/o Similarity score	66.0
w/o Category selection module	64.9
w/o Category information	64.36

Repeated Questions: Besides the task success rate, another important aspect of evaluating QGen model is the quality of the generated question, such as its relevance and informativeness and the avoidance of redundancy. To measure the quality of questions, we use the rate of games with repeated questions. Table 3 shows the rate of games with repeated questions for different models. From the results, it can be easily found that our OCVD has the lowest rate of games with repeated questions.

Qualitative Results: Figure 4 shows some dialogue samples generated by our OCVD model and a baseline VDST model. We can see that our model can effectively generate relevant questions based on the object categories in the image. Furthermore, the object categories can be dynamically updated according to the answers. For instance, in the first example, the image contains three possible object categories: "people, car, skateboard". The model first asks if the target object is a person. When the answer is "no", it switches to another object category until the answer is "yes". After determining the target object category, it will ask more specific questions to identify which car it is. In comparison, under the same training settings, the VDST model fails to learn this questioning strategy and generates unnatural dialogues. As illustrated in Fig. 5, we visualize the learned attention graph. The regions enclosed in red boxes signify higher attention weights, and we depict the bounding boxes corresponding to the first five highest scores.

Ablation Studies: To verify the effectiveness of our proposed Object Category based Visual Dialogue (OCVD) model, we conduct a series of ablation experiments on the GuessWhat?! dataset. We use the greedy search and maximum

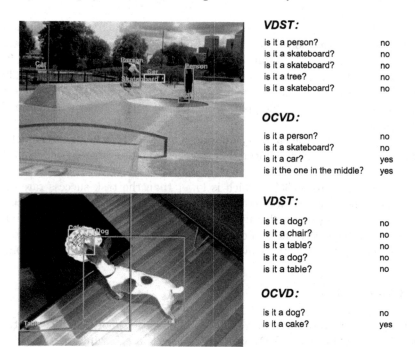

Fig. 4. Game examples of guessing the target object. The target object is highlighted in the green box. (Color figure online)

Fig. 5. Learned Attention Visualization with Top Five Highest Scores

of 5 questions on the test set and separately investigate different components of our model. The ablation experiment result shows in Table 4.

First, the component that calculates the similarity score between visual features and the selected category is removed. This component guides the model to concentrate on object features of the same category. The results show that without this component, the task success rate of our model decreases by 0.4% without the similarity score calculation. This indicates that this component is effective in guiding the model to generate category-related questions by focusing on the relevant object features.

Second, the category selection module is omitted, which dynamically adjusts the category information based on the answers to implement a linear search questioning strategy. The results show that randomly selecting category information instead of dynamically adjusting it according to the answers results in a 1.1% decrease in our model's task success rate. Therefore, we conclude that the category selection module plays an important role in improving the model's performance.

Finally, we delete the category information part, which helps the model with additional object category information to generate more targeted questions. The results show that removing the category information decreases the task success rate of the model to 64.36%, which is lower than the task success rate of the full model. Therefore, we argue that the consideration of category information is valid for generating more effective questions. Overall, the ablation experiments demonstrate the effectiveness of our proposed OCVD model in generating more diverse and effective questions by utilizing the object category information.

5   Conclusions

In this paper, we propose a novel question generation model, Object Category based Visual Dialogue (OCVD), which uses object category information as a clue for generating valid questions. This approach aims to help the model identify the target object by its category. We train the OCVD model on the Guess-What?! dataset and the results show that it can implement an effective linear search strategy based on object categories. In addition, the model performs well on the GuessWhat?! task, which indicates that using object category information is effective for question generation. Ablation experiments further confirm that object category information plays a vital role in enhancing the OCVD model performance. Specifically, when object category information is removed, the performance of the model significantly decreases, and the quality of the generated dialogues is substantially reduced. The OCVD model exhibits promise for extensibility across diverse visual language tasks. Specifically, within educational contexts, the OCVD model can enhance learning by generating image-related questions. These questions serve to assess students' understanding of visual content and encourage in-depth exploration of educational material. We argue that the OCVD model's utility extends beyond the GuessWhat?! visual dialog task, making it applicable to a broader range of visual dialog tasks, including generating datasets for conversations about images, highlighting the model's potential in supporting various aspects of visual learning. Nevertheless, it should be noted that this study only considers the category information of objects in images and does not incorporate other important attribute information such as color, shape, and location. Thus, in the future, we will incorporate multiple attribute information to generate more effective and natural questions. Furthermore, we will explore optimization methods for question generation strategies to enhance the performance of the model. Furthermore, we will explore ways to optimize the GuessWhat?! dataset [16,26] to improve the performance of the model.

References

1. Abbasnejad, E., Wu, Q., Abbasnejad, I., Shi, J.Q., van den Hengel, A.: An active information seeking model for goal-oriented vision-and-language tasks. ArXiv **abs/1812.06398** (2018)
2. Abbasnejad, E., Wu, Q., Shi, J.Q., van den Hengel, A.: What's to know? Uncertainty as a guide to asking goal-oriented questions. In: 2019 IEEE/CVF Conference on Computer Vision and Pattern Recognition (CVPR), pp. 4150–4159 (2018)
3. Agarwal, S., Bui, T., Lee, J.Y., Konstas, I., Rieser, V.: History for visual dialog: do we really need it? In: Proceedings of the 58th Annual Meeting of the Association for Computational Linguistics, pp. 8182–8197 (2020)
4. Anderson, P., et al.: Vision-and-language navigation: interpreting visually-grounded navigation instructions in real environments. In: Proceedings of the IEEE conference on computer vision and pattern recognition, pp. 3674–3683 (2018)
5. Bani, G., et al.: Adding object detection skills to visual dialogue agents. In: ECCV Workshops (2018)
6. Chattopadhyay, P., et al.: Evaluating visual conversational agents via cooperative human-AI games. In: Proceedings of the AAAI Conference on Human Computation and Crowdsourcing, vol. 5, pp. 2–10 (2017)
7. Chen, C., Tan, Z., Cheng, Q., Jiang, X., Liu, Q., Zhu, Y., Gu, X.: UTC: a unified transformer with inter-task contrastive learning for visual dialog. In: Proceedings of the IEEE/CVF Conference on computer vision and pattern recognition, pp. 18103–18112 (2022)
8. Chen, S., Guhur, P.L., Tapaswi, M., Schmid, C., Laptev, I.: Think global, act local: dual-scale graph transformer for vision-and-language navigation. In: Proceedings of the IEEE/CVF Conference on Computer Vision and Pattern Recognition, pp. 16537–16547 (2022)
9. Das, A., et al.: Visual dialog. In: Proceedings of the IEEE Conference on Computer Vision and Pattern Recognition, pp. 326–335 (2017)
10. Das, A., Kottur, S., Moura, J.M.F., Lee, S., Batra, D.: Learning cooperative visual dialog agents with deep reinforcement learning. In: 2017 IEEE International Conference on Computer Vision (ICCV), pp. 2970–2979 (2017)
11. De Vries, H., Strub, F., Chandar, S., Pietquin, O., Larochelle, H., Courville, A.: Guesswhat?! visual object discovery through multi-modal dialogue. In: Proceedings of the IEEE Conference on Computer Vision and Pattern Recognition, pp. 5503–5512 (2017)
12. Gers, F.A., Schmidhuber, J., Cummins, F.: Learning to forget: continual prediction with LSTM. Neural Comput. **12**, 2451–2471 (2000)
13. Guo, D., Wang, H., Zhang, H., Zha, Z.J., Wang, M.: Iterative context-aware graph inference for visual dialog. In: Proceedings of the IEEE/CVF Conference on Computer Vision and Pattern Recognition, pp. 10055–10064 (2020)
14. Kingma, D.P., Ba, J.: Adam: a method for stochastic optimization. CoRR **abs/1412.6980** (2014)
15. Lee, S.W., Heo, Y.J., Zhang, B.T.: Answerer in questioner's mind: information theoretic approach to goal-oriented visual dialog. In: Neural Information Processing Systems (2018)
16. Oshima, R., Shinagawa, S., Tsunashima, H., Feng, Q., Morishima, S.: Pointing out human answer mistakes in a goal-oriented visual dialogue. arXiv preprint arXiv:2309.10375 (2023)

17. Pang, W., Wang, X.: Visual dialogue state tracking for question generation. In: Proceedings of the AAAI Conference on Artificial Intelligence, vol. 34, pp. 11831–11838 (2020)
18. Pashevich, A., Schmid, C., Sun, C.: Episodic transformer for vision-and-language navigation. In: Proceedings of the IEEE/CVF International Conference on Computer Vision, pp. 15942–15952 (2021)
19. Ren, S., He, K., Girshick, R., Sun, J.: Faster R-CNN: towards real-time object detection with region proposal networks. In: Advances in Neural Information Processing Systems, vol. 28 (2015)
20. Sang-Woo, L., Tong, G., Sohee, Y., Jaejun, Y., Jung-Woo, H.: Large-scale answerer in questioner's mind for visual dialog question generation. In: Proceedings of International Conference on Learning Representations. ICLR (2019)
21. Serban, I., Sordoni, A., Bengio, Y., Courville, A.C., Pineau, J.: Hierarchical neural network generative models for movie dialogues. ArXiv **abs/1507.04808** (2015)
22. Shekhar, R., Baumgärtner, T., Venkatesh, A., Bruni, E., Bernardi, R., Fernández, R.: Ask no more: deciding when to guess in referential visual dialogue. In: Proceedings of the 27th International Conference on Computational Linguistics, pp. 1218–1233 (2019)
23. Shekhar, R., et al.: Beyond task success: a closer look at jointly learning to see, ask, and guessWhat. In: North American Chapter of the Association for Computational Linguistics (2018)
24. Shekhar, R., et al.: Beyond task success: a closer look at jointly learning to see, ask, and guessWhat. In: Proceedings of NAACL-HLT, pp. 2578–2587 (2019)
25. Shukla, P., Elmadjian, C., Sharan, R., Kulkarni, V., Turk, M., Wang, W.Y.: What should i ask? Using conversationally informative rewards for goal-oriented visual dialog. In: Proceedings of the 57th Annual Meeting of the Association for Computational Linguistics, pp. 6442–6451 (2020)
26. Sicilia, A., Alikhani, M.: Learning to generate equitable text in dialogue from biased training data. arXiv preprint arXiv:2307.04303 (2023)
27. Strub, F., de Vries, H., Mary, J., Piot, B., Courville, A., Pietquin, O.: End-to-end optimization of goal-driven and visually grounded dialogue systems. In: International Joint Conference on Artificial Intelligence (2017)
28. Testoni, A., Bernardi, R.: Looking for confirmations: an effective and human-like visual dialogue strategy. In: Conference on Empirical Methods in Natural Language Processing (2021)
29. Testoni, A., Bernardi, R.: Garbage in, flowers out: noisy training data help generative models at test time. IJCoL. Italian J. Comput. Linguist. **8**, 8–1 (2022)
30. Tu, T., Ping, Q., Thattai, G., Tur, G., Natarajan, P.: Learning better visual dialog agents with pretrained visual-linguistic representation. In: 2021 IEEE/CVF Conference on Computer Vision and Pattern Recognition (CVPR), pp. 5618–5627 (2021)
31. Wang, Y., Xu, J., Sun, Y.: End-to-end transformer based model for image captioning. In: Proceedings of the AAAI Conference on Artificial Intelligence, vol. 36, pp. 2585–2594 (2022)
32. Wang, Y., Joty, S., Lyu, M., King, I., Xiong, C., Hoi, S.C.: VD-BERT: A unified vision and dialog transformer with BERT. In: Proceedings of the 2020 Conference on Empirical Methods in Natural Language Processing (EMNLP), pp. 3325–3338 (2020)
33. Xu, K., et al.: Show, attend and tell: neural image caption generation with visual attention. In: International Conference on Machine Learning, pp. 2048–2057. PMLR (2015)

34. Xu, Z., Feng, F., Wang, X., Yang, Y., Jiang, H., Ouyang, Z.: Answer-driven visual state estimator for goal-oriented visual dialogue. In: Proceedings of the 28th ACM International Conference on Multimedia (2020)
35. Yanan, S., Yanxin, T., Fangxiang, F., Chunping, Z., Xiaojie, W.: Category-based strategy-driven question generator for visual dialogue. In: Proceedings of the 20th Chinese National Conference on Computational Linguistics, pp. 1000–1011 (2022)
36. Yuan, Z., et al.: X-trans2cap: cross-modal knowledge transfer using transformer for 3D dense captioning. In: Proceedings of the IEEE/CVF Conference on Computer Vision and Pattern Recognition, pp. 8563–8573 (2022)
37. Zhang, J., Wu, Q., Shen, C., Zhang, J., Lu, J., van den Hengel, A.: Asking the difficult questions: goal-oriented visual question generation via intermediate rewards. In: European Conference on Computer Vision (2017)
38. Zhao, R., Tresp, V.: Improving goal-oriented visual dialog agents via advanced recurrent nets with tempered policy gradient. In: LaCATODA@ IJCAI, pp. 1–7 (2018)
39. Zheng, D., Xu, Z., Meng, F., Wang, X., Wang, J., Zhou, J.: Enhancing visual dialog questioner with entity-based strategy learning and augmented guesser. In: Findings of the Association for Computational Linguistics: EMNLP 2021, pp. 1839–1851 (2021)

AST: An Attention-Guided Segment Transformer for Drone-Based Cross-View Geo-Localization

Zichuan Zhao, Tianhang Tang, Jie Chen, Xuelei Shi, and Yiguang Liu[✉]

Sichuan University, No.24 South Section 1, Yihuan Road, Chengdu, China
liuyg@scu.edu.cn

Abstract. To tackle the problem of drone-based cross-view geo-localization, we address how to match drone-view images and satellite-view images, which is extremely challenging due to the variability of view angles and view distances. Inspired by how humans recognize aerial images, we propose an effective Attention-guided Segment Transformer (AST) structure: a novel segmentation strategy is introduced to cope with the huge variations between aerial views, and this segmentation is adaptive and non-uniform, allowing it to segment regions with corresponding relationships even after significant changes in viewpoint; furthermore, a new segment token module is designed to generate segment tokens that are concatenated with the original class token to supplement the local information. Compared to CNN-based methods, AST fully utilizes the self-attention mechanism to establish global context correlations; and the newly introduced segment token module allows AST to effectively extract local features as well—a capability not present in the vanilla vision transformer. Remarkably, AST demonstrates good robustness to viewpoint changes, even when there are overlapping regions, and this good treat is confirmed by the experimental results on the University-1652 dataset, which also show competitive performance for both tasks of drone-view target localization and drone navigation.

Keywords: Geo-localization · Image retrieval · Drone-based cross-view

1 Introduction

Image-based cross-view geo-localization involves matching images that depict the same geospatial location but are captured from different views or platforms. This can be considered an image retrieval task. As the automation industry develops and satellite imaging technology matures, image-based cross-view geo-localization has become increasingly important. For example, in situations where

This work is supported by NSFC under grants U19A2071 and 61860206007, Sichuan Science and Technology Program under grant 2023YFG0334, as well as the funding from Sichuan University under grant 2020SCUNG205.

GPS signals are weakened or lost due to interference, unmanned devices require an alternative independent positioning method, such as matching images of the surrounding environment with geo-tagged images to determine their locations. Image-based geo-localization has been applied to various real-world fields such as autonomous driving, robot positioning, drone navigation, and precision delivery. Compared to sensor-based positioning methods, image-based methods have several advantages, including lower cost, stronger resistance to electromagnetic interference, and better environmental adaptability.

In recent years, research on image-based cross-view geo-localization has mainly focused on matching images between ground-level and satellite-level. And ground-to-aerial datasets such as CVUSA [37] and CVACT [21] have emerged. However, matching images between drone-view images and satellite-view images has received less attention. University-1652 [38] is the first drone-based geo-localization dataset that expands cross-view geo-localization from ground-satellite imagery to drone-satellite imagery and brings two new tasks: drone-view target localization and drone navigation. This expansion facilitates deep learning research on image-based cross-view geo-localization.

Researchers typically use a Siamese-like network architecture to tackle cross-view geo-localization tasks [8, 21, 28, 29, 33, 36, 40]. Identifying similarities between images from different views or platforms is the key to solving this problem. Humans tend to prioritize landmark buildings or patterns in aerial images and then analyze surrounding areas before making judgments based on global information. Inspired by this, we believe that image-based cross-view geo-localization should fully extract global image information and establish global context correlations. While CNN-based approaches often focus on small discriminative regions since the effective receptive field size of deep convolutional neural networks is Gaussian distributed [24], they ignore global context correlations, which can be detrimental for cross-view geo-localization. Therefore, we have chosen to use the Vision Transformer (ViT) [12] as our backbone.

In this paper, we introduce an Attention-guided Segment Transformer (AST) structure to address two tasks in the University-1652 dataset, i.e., drone-view target localization and drone navigation. To enhance the network's robustness to viewpoint changes, we propose an adaptive segmentation strategy. Utilizing the self-attention mechanism of the transformer, patches of similar importance are grouped together to form multiple non-uniform regions of decreasing significance. These regions can effectively adapt to variations in targets' position and size across different views—a crucial feature for aerial images. This process mirrors how humans match cross-view images, where attention is first directed towards key regions before expanding to surrounding regions. To enhance the extraction of local features, we design a new segment token module that generates segment tokens carrying additional local information for each region. These segment tokens are concatenated with the class token to form the final embedding features for matching. The segment tokens also enable spatial alignment between corresponding regions. Compared to CNN-based methods, AST establishes global context correlations while also focusing on local information. In contrast, the vanilla vision transformer mainly focuses on global features.

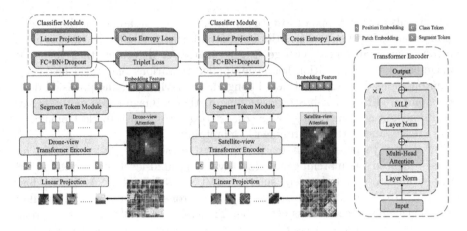

Fig. 1. An overview of our proposed AST framework. While training, the output of the class token and those segment tokens are fed into classifier modules that do not share parameters, and all the tokens are trained, respectively. While testing, the class token and segment tokens before linear projection layers are concatenated as the embedding feature for cross-view geo-localization tasks.

In summary, the main contributions of this paper are as follows:

1) A novel attention-guided segmentation strategy. The segmentation is adaptive, the regions are non-uniform, and no human intervention is required, so it can flexibly respond to changes in viewpoint.
2) A new segment token module. It enhances local information and achieves spatial alignment between cross-view images. Besides, it is easy to implement and has the potential to be fused with other backbones as long as the attention mechanism is available.
3) An effective Attention-guided Segment Transformer (AST) structure. AST outperforms the baseline model of University-1652 by a large margin on both benchmarks and achieves competitive results compared to existing methods. Astonishingly, experiments show that AST has good robustness to changes in viewpoint, even when there are overlapping regions.

The remainder of the paper is structured as follows: We briefly introduce several pertinent work in Sect. 2. Section 3 details our designed AST. Section 4 presents the experimental results, while Sect. 5 offers the conclusion.

2   Related Work

2.1   Image-Based Cross-View Geo-Localization

In recent years, image-based cross-view geo-localization has attracted a lot of attention due to its huge application potential. The large changes in viewpoint and the differences between imaging platforms make cross-view image matching more difficult. Inspired by Siamese Network [6], Lin et al. [20] apply it to image-based cross-view geo-localization, and many of the subsequent methods also adopt Siamese-like architecture. Our proposed AST has a Siamese-like architecture, too.

In order to deal with the large changes in viewpoint in cross-view geo-localization, a lot of methods have been proposed. Zhai et al. [37] use a VGG network to generate semantic segmentation and then apply an adaptive transformation to map aerial semantic segmentation into the ground-level perspective. Furthermore, Toker et al. [30] synthesize street views from satellite images, and Tian et al. [29] use a CGAN to conduct drone-satellite view synthesis. Besides, Hu et al. [17] combine the feature extractor with the NetVLAD, creating a model called CVM-Net, and introduce an effective weighted soft-margin ranking loss function, which speeds up its training convergence and improves its performance. Recently, Wang et al. [33] propose a square-ring partition strategy to take contextual patterns into consideration, which can be fused with existing methods to further boost performance. Lin et al. [19] combine representation learning and keypoint detection, which enhances the model's capability against large changes in viewpoint. With the rise of ViT, Yang et al. [36] propose a Layer-to-Layer Transformer (L2LTR) to model global dependencies, which decreases visual ambiguities. Zhu et al. [40] propose an "attend and zoom-in" strategy by taking advantage of ViT. And these two methods mainly focus on matching images between ground-level and satellite-level. Previous research has shown that researchers are attempting to determine the transformational relationship between different views. However, fixed transformations lack flexibility and hinder the creation of a robust feature space. Our adaptive segmentation strategy significantly alleviates this issue.

2.2 Vision Transformer

Transformer [31] was first proposed for large-scale pre-training in natural language processing (NLP) tasks and demonstrated its excellent performance and great potential [2,9]. ViT [12] is the first pure transformer-based architecture applied to classify the full images and achieves excellent performance with substantially fewer computational resources to train compared to other CNN-based methods.

With the proposal of ViT, a series of variants have come up to improve the performance of transformer in vision tasks. As ViT simply projects an image patch into a vector (patch token) through linear mapping, the extraction of local features is ignored. Han et al. [13] design a new architecture termed Transformer-iN-Transformer (TNT). It further divides patches into smaller patches (sub-patches) and applies an inner transformer block to excavate finer features and details. Similarly, Swin [22], Cswin [11], and Twins [7] are also working in this direction. In addition, improving the calculation of self-attention is another noteworthy direction. DeepViT [39] introduces a re-attention mechanism that enhances information exchange among attention heads. Similarly, there are KVT [32] and XCiT [1]. Moreover, many researchers try to improve vision transform architecture.

Learning from CNN, many new architectures are proposed. For example, the pyramid-like architecture is adapted in PVT [34], HVT [25], PiT [15], and so on. Some other architectures are also applied, e.g., two-stream architecture [5] and U-net architecture [4,35]. Researchers have made important contributions to the improvement of ViT by enhancing locality, improving self-attention, and designing new architectures. However, we discover that the majority of these improvements concentrate on getting a better global class token while disregarding patch tokens, whereas our suggested segment token module can utilize patch tokens more effectively.

3   Proposed Method

3.1   Problem Formulation

In the University-1652 [38] dataset, each satellite-view image has 54 corresponding drone-view images, and there are two tasks that we need to do:

Drone-View Target Localization (Drone → Satellite). Given one query drone-view image, the task aims to find the most similar geo-tagged satellite-view image so that the target building can be located. This is a many-to-one match task in the University-1652 dataset.

Drone Navigation (Satellite → Drone). Given one query satellite-view image, the drone aims to find the most relevant place (drone-view images) according to its flight history so that it can be navigated back to the target place. Also, a set of satellite images can be given to guide the drone step by step. This is a one-to-many match task in the University-1652 dataset.

In brief, we aim to output the ranking of the gallery images that are most similar to the query image. Therefore, we regard the two tasks as cross-view image retrieval problems. In the training set, we have a set of drone-view images $\{I_d\}$, a set of satellite-view images $\{I_s\}$, and class labels $\{y\}$ corresponding to all the images. Images are classified by geo-tags or target buildings. We aim to train a neural network to identify a mapping function $F(.)$ that could project drone-view images and satellite-view images to a shared feature space. In this space, the feature vectors with the same label are close together, while those with different labels are separated. When given a query image, we can extract its feature vector, which can subsequently be used to search for the closest gallery images' feature vectors in the shared feature space. We use $D(F(x_d), F(x_s)), x_d \in \{I_d\}, x_s \in \{I_s\}$ to measure the distance between feature vectors and apply the superscript y to represent images' corresponding labels. The optimal situation in the shared feature space can be expressed as follows:

$$\forall x_d^y \in \{I_d\}, \forall x_s^{y'} \in \{I_s\}, y \neq y',$$
$$D(F(x_d^y), F(x_s^y)) < D(F(x_d^y), F(x_s^{y'})) \tag{1}$$

where the positions of subscripts d and s can be switched. Usually, it doesn't matter whether the feature vectors with the same label are close if they are from the same view, as it doesn't affect the matching result directly.

3.2   Vision Transformer for Cross-View Geo-Localization

We briefly introduce the transformer structure adapted in AST, including patch embedding, class token, position embedding, and transform encoder.

Patch Embedding: Different from CNN, we need to convert an image into some tokens as the input of transformer encoder. Given the input images $x \in \mathbb{R}^{H \times W \times C}$, where H, W, C are respectively the height, width, and channel numbers of x. Firstly, the input images are divided into N patches with the same size $P \times P$ (usually $P = 16$), therefore $N = HW/P^2$. Then all the patches are reshaped into a 2D matrix $x_p \in \mathbb{R}^{N \times P^2 C}$. By adopting a trainable linear projection layer, we will get N tokens $x_t \in \mathbb{R}^{N \times D}$, where D is a hyperparameter representing the feature dimension of transformer encoder.

Class Token: Referring to ViT [12] and BERT [9], our vision transformer also has an extra learnable class token with the same dimension D in front of the N tokens, which is used to integrate the features of each patch as the global feature, and we get $x_t \in \mathbb{R}^{(N+1) \times D}$. After passing through the last transformer encoder, the output class token will become an important reference for subsequent cross-view geo-localization tasks, as will the segment token, which we propose and will introduce later.

Position Embedding: As images are divided into patches, the relative position relationships between patches are ignored. Referring to ViT [12], to make up for the information loss, learnable position embedding is adopted in our vision transformer. It is a learnable matrix $x_{pos} \in \mathbb{R}^{(N+1) \times D}$. Now we get the input of transformer encoder $x_{in} = x_t + x_{pos}$. The explicit position embedding of each patch enables the model to better learn the geometric correspondence between different views. Besides, it makes us able to improve the model's performance by flexibly aligning patches.

Transformer Encoder: As shown in Fig. 1, each transformer encoder has multiple cascaded transformer block layers. Each block consists of layer norm (LN), multi-head self-attention (MSA), and multi-layer perceptron (MLP), where MSA plays a key role. It converts the input matrix into three matrices Q, K, V through a learnable linear projection layer. They represent the query, key, and value of all the tokens, respectively. Then we can obtain the attention map of the input image by the following computation:

$$z = LN(x_{in}) \tag{2}$$

$$Q = zW^q, K = zW^k, V = zW^v \tag{3}$$

$$A = softmax\left(\frac{QK^T}{\sqrt{D}}\right) V \tag{4}$$

where W^q, W^k, W^v are linear projection matrices, K^T means the transpose of K and D is feature dimension. An h-head attention module performs linear projection with h different heads and conducts subsequent self-attention computations

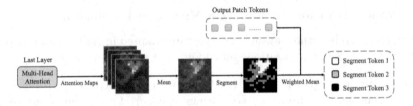

Fig. 2. Pipeline for generating segment tokens. The h-head attention module generates h different attention maps that represent different points of the input images. The lighter the pixel is, the more important the patch is. Then, with the guide of segmentation information, we can figure out the corresponding segment tokens for each group.

in parallel. For each token, the h outputs are concatenated and projected back to a vector with dimension D. The generated global attention map can distinguish the importance of different patches. However, it is important to note that in the vanilla vision transformer, only the output class token is considered at the end, while the rest of the tokens are ignored. We believe that these discarded patch tokens contain valuable information that can be leveraged to enhance the model's understanding of images. Our ablation studies (1) and (2) confirm this idea.

3.3   Attention-Guided Segment Tokens

In this subsection, we will introduce the pipeline for generating segment tokens, which includes our segmentation strategy and the segment token module.

The global attention map highlights the importance of different patches in a manner similar to how humans recognize aerial images. On this basis, we propose an attention-guided segment token that simulates the human process of matching cross-view images. Segment tokens are calculated in the last transformer block layer, as shown in Fig. 2. In the last MSA, we can get h attention maps of different heads $\{A_i | i \in \{1, 2, ..., h\}, A_i \in \mathbb{R}^{(N+1) \times (N+1)}\}$. Then we obtain the integrated attention map by doing an average operation. The computation is formulated as follows:

$$A_i = \frac{Q_i K_i^T}{\sqrt{D}} \qquad i \in \{1, 2, ..., h\} \qquad (5)$$

$$A = \sum_{i=1}^{h} A_i \qquad (6)$$

Based on the attention map, we can segment output tokens into groups, excluding the class token. These tokens are segmented into three groups according to their corresponding values in the attention map: most important, less important, and least important. It is important to note that we only consider the row corresponding to the class token in matrix A and reshape the row to its original grid size as the attention map. Then we use the following formula to calculate the proportion of tokens in each group:

$$softmax([1, 2, ..., N_{group}]) \qquad (7)$$

where N_{group} is the number of groups and $[1, 2, ..., N_{group}]$ is a vector that increases from 1 to N_{group}. The smaller the number in the vector is, the smaller the percentage is, and the more important the group is. We then perform *softmax* operations on the attention values of each group separately to obtain token weights within each group. During grouping, we do not interfere with the original computation of the last MSA. Instead, we obtain additional grouping and weight information based on the global attention map. After the last transformer block layer, we compute a weighted mean of tokens within each group as segment tokens using the following formula:

$$x_{seg_i} = \sum_{j=1}^{N_i} w_{ij} x_{ij} \qquad i \in \{1, 2, ..., N_{group}\} \tag{8}$$

where x_{seg_i} is the segment token of group i, N_i is the number of tokens in group i, w_{ij} is the weight of the j-th patch token x_{ij} in group i. Compared to the vanilla vision transformer, we take into consideration $[x_{cls}, x_{seg_1}, x_{seg_2}, ...]$.

3.4   Loss Function and Training Strategy

In the vanilla vision transformer, the output class token is then fed into an MLP or a classifier module to generate the final embedding feature. We feed $[x_{cls}, x_{seg_1}, x_{seg_2}, ...]$ into classifier modules that do not share parameters to generate multiple embedding features for different parts. The classifier module consists of a fully connected layer (FC), a batch normalization layer (BN), a dropout layer (Dropout), and a linear projection layer. During training, the classifier module is used to predict the class of each part. We can simply minimize the sum of the cross-entropy losses over all parts to optimize the network. To further optimize the distribution of embedding features of different parts in the shared feature space, we train the embedding features with weighted soft-margin triplet loss [17,40], respectively. The weighted soft-margin triplet loss function can be formulated as follows:

$$T(d_{pos}, d_{neg}) = log \left(1 + e^{\alpha(d_{pos} - d_{neg})} \right) \tag{9}$$

where d_{pos} and d_{neg} denote the squared l_2 distance of embedding features of the positive and negative pairs in a mini-batch, and α is a coefficient.

For each class, we sample one satellite-view image and N_{sample} drone-view images to form N_{sample} image pairs (images are from different views) in an epoch. While calculating triplet loss, we have B drone-view images and B satellite-view images after augmentation. B is the mini-batch size. We suppose one of these images is the query image, and each query image has B image pairs. Image pairs with the same label are positive pairs; otherwise, they are negative pairs. We can calculate the triplet loss of one part for the query image using the following formula:

$$\mathcal{L}_{tri} = \frac{1}{n_{pos} n_{neg}} \sum_{i=1}^{n_{pos}} \sum_{j=1}^{n_{neg}} T(d_{pos}^i, d_{neg}^j) \tag{10}$$

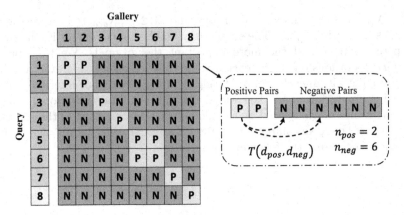

Fig. 3. Different colors stand for different labels. Image pairs with the same label are positive pairs (P); otherwise, they are negative pairs (N). Each query image has n_{pos} positive pairs and n_{neg} negative pairs in a mini-batch. d_{pos} and d_{neg} denote the squared l_2 distance of embedding features of the positive and negative pairs. We calculate $T(d_{pos}, d_{neg})$ for each possible combination and do an average to get the final triplet loss of this query image.

where n_{pos} and n_{neg} are numbers of positive and negative pairs for this query image, as shown in Fig. 3. Finally, we minimize the sum of the cross-entropy losses and the triplet losses over all parts to optimize the network. While testing, we obtain the embedding features of different parts before the linear projection layer, and they are concatenated as the final embedding feature of an input image for matching.

4   Experiment

4.1   Datasets and Evaluation Metrics

We train our model and conduct experiments on the University-1652 [38] dataset. It is a large-scale multi-view, multi-source dataset used for two drone-based geo-localization tasks. It selects 1,652 architectures from 72 universities around the world as target locations. For each target location, there are multiple synthetic drone-view images, which are generated from different angles, different heights, and different distances by Google Earth. According to University-1652 [38], the model trained on this dataset also has good generalization ability and still works on the real-world drone-view images. Following the University-1652, we use Recall@K (**R@K**) and Average Precision (**AP**) to evaluate the performance of our proposed method. More details are shown in Table 1.

Table 1. The detailed statistics of University-1652 training and test sets.

Split	Views	Images	Classes	Universities
Train	Drone	37,854	701	33
	Satellite	701		
Query	Drone	37,855	701	39
	Satellite	701		
Gallery	Drone	51,355	951	
	Satellite	951		

4.2 Implementation Details

We implement our method using Pytorch [26]. Both the drone-view images and the satellite-view images are resized to 256 × 256. For each class, we sample $N_{sample} = 8$ image pairs in one epoch. We adopt a small-size Vision Transformer (ViT-S) [12] as our backbone. We set $N_{group} = 3$, which means there is 1 class token and 3 segment tokens, and the final concatenated feature dimension is 2048. The transformer backbones of two branches share the same parameters. We adopt a stochastic gradient descent (SGD) optimizer. Our model is trained for 20 epochs in total with a mini-batch size 8. While training and testing, we use cosine similarity to measure two feature vectors, which is equivalent to measuring distance. All the experiments were performed on the Nvidia RTX 3090 GPU.

4.3 Comparison with Existing Methods

Table 2. Comparison with existing methods in terms of R@1 and AP on University-1652. The first two methods serve as baseline models and are distinguished by their use of different loss functions.

Methods	Drone→Satellite		Satellite→Drone	
	R@1	AP	R@1	AP
Contrastive Loss [38]	52.39	57.44	63.91	52.24
Weighted Soft Margin Triplet Loss [38]	53.21	58.03	65.62	54.47
Instance Loss + GeM Pooling [27]	65.32	69.61	79.03	65.35
LCM (ResNet-50) [10]	66.65	70.82	79.89	65.38
LPN [33]	75.93	79.14	86.45	74.79
LPN + CA-HRS [23]	76.67	79.77	86.88	74.84
Instance Loss + USAM + LPN [19]	77.60	80.55	86.59	75.96
LDRVSD [19]	78.66	81.55	89.30	79.17
PCL [29]	79.47	83.63	87.69	78.51
FSRA [8]	84.51	86.71	88.45	83.37
PAAN [3]	84.51	86.78	**91.01**	82.28
AST + Contrast Loss	85.45	87.52	90.44	84.81
AST + Weighted Soft-margin Triplet Loss	**86.29**	**88.20**	89.59	**85.06**

We evaluate our proposed AST on the University-1652 dataset and compare its performance with existing methods, as shown in Table 2. The first two methods serve as baseline models and are distinguished by their use of different loss functions. LPN (CNN-based) adopts a similar training strategy, and it segments the image into fixed square-ring blocks. FSRA optimizes LPN by using ViT to replace the backbone and segments the image into several regions of the same area. PAAN also optimizes LPN by combining the SE-block [16] and ResNet-50 [14] to replace the backbone, but still segments images into square-ring blocks. And we make full use of the self-attention mechanism, making the segmentation more flexible and reasonable, and assigning different weights to each patch, thus having better robustness to the change of viewpoint. PCL uses CGAN to perform perspective transformation to reduce the differences between cross-view images, but the information loss caused by occlusion is still difficult to make up for. Therefore, we not only pay attention to the overall information of the image, but also pay more attention to the key regions, and combine the surrounding regions to generate a discriminative feature vector. These improvements all lead to better performance of AST. When it comes to PAAN, we believe it might be more applicable at certain shooting angles and distances and thus achieve a higher R@1 value but a lower AP value. AST has better robustness to changes in viewpoint, so it achieves a higher AP value. Moreover, our segment token module is easy to implement and has the potential to be fused with other backbones as long as the attention mechanism is available.

4.4   Ablation Study

1) Effect of the Segment Token Module: We conduct experiments on the effect of our segment token module. We remove the segment token module and train the class token like the vanilla vision transformer does. As shown in Table 3, we list the values of R@5, and R@1% for further reference. In the drone→satellite task, the R@1 value improves by 15.15% and the AP value improves by 13.17%. In the satellite→drone task, the R@1 value improves by 5.00% and the AP value improves by 13.96%. Compared to the vanilla vision transformer, our model considers both global and local information. Local information helps extract global information, which in turn guides the extraction of local information. This positive feedback process effectively promotes the model's understanding of aerial images. In addition, the R@1 value is relatively little boosted in the satellite→drone task. When adopting the vanilla vision transformer, we find that the R@1 value in the satellite→drone task is significantly higher than the other three metric values (R@1 and AP). This is because the satellite→drone task is a one-to-many match, where each satellite-view query image has 54 corresponding drone-view images. This means it has a higher hit probability for R@1.

2) Effect of the Number of Segment Tokens: We conduct experiments to figure out how many groups we should segment so that our model has the best performance. As shown in Fig. 4, the horizontal colored dotted lines stand for the vanilla method's R@1 and AP values in both tasks. When $N_{group} = 3$,

Table 3. Ablation study on the segment token module.

Ablation	R@1	R@5	R@1%	AP
Drone→Satellite				
Vanilla	71.14	88.55	99.95	75.03
Ours	86.29	94.72	99.99	88.20
Satellite→Drone				
Vanilla	84.59	90.44	91.16	71.10
Ours	89.59	92.58	93.30	85.06

all the metrics have the highest values. We believe that at this point there is better discrimination between groups and better similarity within groups, with less variance in the attention values of the patches within groups. In addition, we visualize the attention maps generated in AST, as shown in Fig. 6. When $N_{group} = 4$ or $N_{group} = 6$, most of the attention is wrongly attracted by the surrounding buildings, resulting in a significant drop in performance. On the other hand, we concatenate the output segment tokens in order of importance (i.e., attention values), which achieves spatial alignment between cross-view images to some extent.

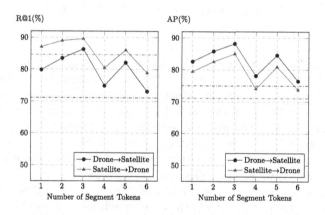

Fig. 4. Ablation study on the effect of number of segment tokens. The horizontal colored dotted lines stand for the vanilla method's R@1 and AP values in both tasks.

3) Effect of Grouping Strategy: Specifically, we conduct experiments on the effect of the number of tokens in each group. We consider three grouping strategies: the decreasing strategy, the averaging strategy, and the increasing strategy. They indicate the trend in the number of patches in the group as the attention value decreases. As shown in Table 4, we evaluate the different grouping strategies in detail. In the drone→satellite task, the increasing strategy achieves the best performance. In the satellite→drone task, the averaging strategy having the highest R@1 value, 0.16% higher than the increasing strategy, while the increasing strategy has the highest AP value, 0.74% higher than the averaging strategy. Regions with high recognition in aerial images generally have a small area percentage, and attention values are mainly concentrated in a few patches. Therefore, when patches are sorted by attention value, their values drop rapidly and then level off. The increasing strategy can make the attention values of patches in the same group relatively close to each other, resulting in better similarity within groups. It is worth noting that the increasing strategy with fixed proportions is applicable in most cases, but not all.

Table 4. Ablation study on grouping strategy.

Ablation	R@1	R@5	R@1%	AP
Drone→Satellite				
Decreasing	83.51	93.70	99.95	85.80
Averaging	85.19	94.32	99.98	87.27
Increasing	86.29	94.72	99.99	88.20
Satellite→Drone				
Decreasing	88.30	92.01	92.30	83.20
Averaging	89.73	93.44	93.58	84.32
Increasing	89.59	92.58	93.30	85.06

4) Effect of Fusion Strategy: We consider two strategies for fusing patch tokens to generate segment tokens. In addition to fusing patch tokens according to the weights generated by the attention map, we further try to average the patch tokens directly. As shown in Table 5, the weighted mean strategy is our default fusion strategy. In the drone→satellite task, the weighted mean strategy performs better than the mean strategy. In the satellite→drone task, the mean strategy has a 0.28% higher R@1 value, while the weighted mean strategy has a 0.86% higher AP value. We believe that the weighted mean strategy has better robustness to changes in viewpoint and thus achieves higher AP values in both tasks. The mean strategy, on the other hand, might be more applicable at certain shooting angles and distances and thus achieve a higher R@1 value in the satellite→drone task. And the data show that this advantage of the mean strategy is also weak.

5) Effect of Sample Size: In the University-1652 training dataset, each target has 54 drone-view images but only 1 satellite-view image because drones have a variety of viewpoints while satellites usually have a vertical view. This is realistic but not good for the training of neural networks. Therefore, we sample N_{sample} image pairs for each class, each image pair containing one drone-view image and one satellite-view image. There are two advantages: 1) We have the same number of drone-view images and satellite-view images after image augmentation, which

Table 5. Ablation study on fusion strategy.

Ablation	R@1	R@5	R@1%	AP
Drone→Satellite				
Mean	84.91	94.13	99.98	86.99
Weighted Mean	86.29	94.72	99.99	88.20
Satellite→Drone				
Mean	89.87	92.58	93.01	84.20
Weighted Mean	89.59	92.58	93.30	85.06

can alleviate the problem of data imbalance to some extent. 2) The paired format is more beneficial to the metric learning of cross-view images. As shown in Fig. 5, when $N_{sample} = 8$, the model achieves the best performance. We believe that data overfitting may occur when N_{sample} is too large. On the other hand, image augmentation cannot fundamentally solve the problem that the number of satellite-view images is much less than that of drone-view images. As for metric learning, an appropriate value of N_{sample} can increase the probability of images of the same class appearing in a mini-batch, which is beneficial for the model to mine the commonality among different perspectives of images. But it is bad for the model to learn inter-class differences when the probability is too high.

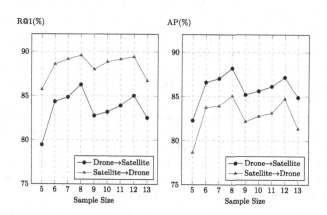

Fig. 5. Ablation study on the effect of sample size.

6) Effect of Triplet Loss: We obtain the embedding features before the linear projection layer, and these features can be used directly for image matching without optimization using triplet loss. We conduct several experiments to verify the effect of the additional triplet loss. As shown in Table 6, we try to remove the triplet loss and also try to adopt other loss functions. In both tasks, the values of each metric improve to different degrees after adopting the additional loss function. These loss functions are widely used in metric learning tasks. And they can be used to adjust the distance between the feature vectors of samples in the shared feature space, narrowing the distance between samples of the same class and expanding the distance between samples of different classes. This is beneficial for image matching.

Table 6. Ablation study on loss function. CE means Cross-Entropy loss, Contrast means Contrast loss, MT means Max-margin Triplet loss, WST means Weighted Soft-margin Triplet loss.

Ablation	R@1	R@5	R@1%	AP
Drone→Satellite				
CE	84.90	94.28	99.98	87.04
CE + Contrast	85.45	94.54	99.98	87.52
CE + MT	85.64	94.90	99.97	87.73
CE + WST	86.29	94.72	99.99	88.20
Satellite→Drone				
CE	89.02	92.44	92.87	84.40
CE + Contrast	90.44	92.72	92.87	84.81
CE + MT	89.16	93.30	94.01	84.96
CE + WST	89.59	92.58	93.30	85.06

7) Effect of Changes in Viewpoint: In the drone-view images, the regions with high recognition vary with the viewpoints. We divide the query drone-view images into 3 groups based on the distance to explore the effect of the drone distance to the target. In addition, we divide the images into 18 groups according to the shooting angle to verify the effect of view angle. As shown in Table 7, we obtain the best performance when the distance is middle, followed by the short distance, and finally the long distance, and they have close performances. As shown in Table 8, all the view angles also have close performance. Our grouping strategy and fusion strategy can guarantee discriminative patches' role in segment tokens when the area of highly discriminative regions changes. Experimental results indicate that our model has good robustness to changes in viewpoint.

Table 7. Ablation study on the effect of the drone distance to the target.

Drone→Satellite				
Distance	R@1	R@5	R@1%	AP
ALL	86.29	94.72	99.99	88.20
Short	86.16	94.27	99.48	88.01
Middle	87.30	95.14	99.66	89.07
Long	85.40	94.76	99.59	87.51

Table 8. Ablation study on the effect of view angle.

Drone→Satellite					
Angle	R@1	AP	Angle	R@1	AP
0°	87.69	89.36	180°	85.21	87.27
20°	87.26	89.04	200°	84.40	86.61
40°	87.35	89.11	220°	84.83	86.93
60°	87.26	89.19	240°	85.02	86.99
80°	87.97	89.64	260°	85.92	87.74
100°	87.02	88.88	280°	86.45	88.17
120°	86.21	88.24	300°	86.16	88.13
140°	86.07	88.05	320°	86.12	88.05
160°	85.54	87.60	340°	86.69	88.56

8) Effect of Sharing Weights: As we introduced before, our transformers of two branches share the same weights because both satellite-view and drone-view images are captured from an aerial view and have some similar patterns. Also, we test the model, which does not share weights during the training, as shown in Table 9. The R@1 value and the AP value drop rapidly when the weights are not shared. We believe that there are two main reasons: 1) The lack of satellite-view images. The single branch is liable to overfit since there is only one satellite-view image per location. 2) A decrease in the number of input images. When weights are not shared, the number of input images per branch is reduced by half. However, training a transformer requires sufficient data to achieve satisfactory performance. By sharing weights, more drone-view images can be input into the transformer to adjust the model. This helps address the above two issues and achieve better performance.

Table 9. Ablation study on sharing weights.

Ablation	R@1	R@5	R@1%	AP
Drone→Satellite				
W/o Sharing	23.27	47.70	98.03	29.20
Sharing	86.29	94.72	99.99	88.20
Satellite→Drone				
W/o Sharing	26.53	35.38	36.80	23.08
Sharing	89.59	92.58	93.30	85.06

4.5 Visualization

In Fig. 6, we present visualization of attention maps. Comparing the attention maps generated by the two models introduced in our first ablation experiment,

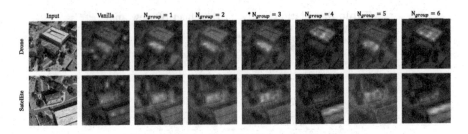

Fig. 6. Visualization of attention maps. We show attention maps generated by vanilla vision transformer and our AST using different numbers of segment tokens. Highlights represent the distribution of attention in the model.

we observe that while the vanilla model primarily focuses on the target building, it also exhibits unexpected interference spots around it. This can negatively impact cross-view image matching. In contrast, our model ($N_{group} = 3$) correctly focuses on the top of the target building before expanding its attention to surrounding buildings, roads, and finally indistinguishable trees. This allows for accurate matching between drone and satellite-view images. These results demonstrate that our proposed segmentation token module effectively enhances the vision transformer's ability to correctly interpret aerial images and improves drone-based cross-view image matching performance.

In Fig. 7 and Fig. 8, we present cross-view matching results in both drone-view target localization and drone navigation tasks. In the drone-view target localization task, we randomly select 3 drone-view images from and retrieve the top 5 satellite-view matches. For each query image, only the first-ranked satellite-view image corresponds to it. Notably, our model successfully distinguishes between satellite-view images with different centers despite overlapping areas, which situation appears in the first and third rows. In the drone navigation task, we follow a similar process and retrieve the top 5 drone-view matches. All retrieved drone-view images indicate the same location as their corresponding input satellite-view images. In summary, our method achieves completely accurate results in both tasks shown in the figures.

We further conduct some experiments to test the generalization ability of our method to real-world case. As shown in Fig. 9, we present two retrieval results: Real Drone → Synthetic Drone and Real Drone → Satellite. The former evaluates how well the synthetic data mimics the real drone camera images. We display the top-5 most similar images in the test set retrieved by our model. The results suggest that the synthetic drone-view images have similar visual features to the real drone-view query. The latter tests the generalization performance of our model on the real drone-view data. The result demonstrates that our model can also handle the real drone-view images for drone-view target localization. These results demonstrate that our model has good generalization ability to real-world case.

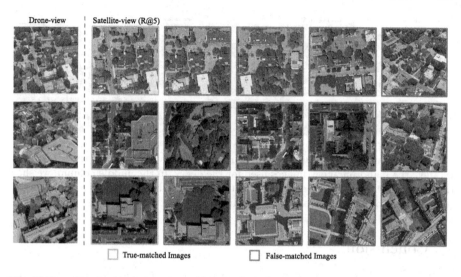

Fig. 7. Visualization of drone-view target localization. Inputting the drone-view images as the query images, we show the top 5 satellite-view images in the ranking of the matching results in the drone→satellite task.

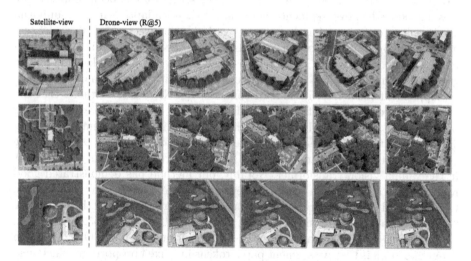

Fig. 8. Visualization of drone navigation. Inputting the satellite-view images as the query images, we show the top 5 drone-view images in the ranking of the matching results in the satellite→drone task.

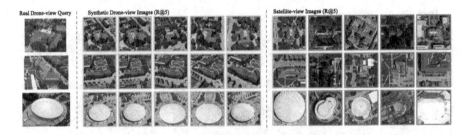

Fig. 9. Qualitative image search results using real drone-view query. In the left column, we show the real drone-view images used for the query. In the middle column, we show the top-5 most similar images in the test set retrieved by our model. In the right column, we show the retrieval results for drone-view target localization.

5   Conclusion

In this paper, we have addressed how to match drone-view images with satellite-view images to tackle the problem of drone-based cross-view geo-localization. To overcome the challenges posed by the variability of aerial views, an effective Attention-guided Segment Transformer (AST) structure has been proposed: we have introduced a novel segmentation strategy that is adaptive and non-uniform, allowing it to effectively handle the huge variations between aerial views by segmenting regions with corresponding relationships even after significant changes in viewpoint; furthermore, we have designed a new segment token module to generates segment tokens that are concatenated with the original class token to supplement local information. In contrast to CNN-based methods that are inclined to extract more fine-grained features but underestimate neighboring patches, AST takes full advantage of the self-attention mechanism to establish global context correlations; and the newly introduced segment token module enables AST to effectively extract local features as well, a capability not present in the vanilla vision transformer. Notably, our method has demonstrated good robustness to variations in viewpoint, even when there are overlapping regions. Our proposed AST has achieved competitive performance in both drone-view target localization and drone navigation tasks in the University-1652 benchmark.

Nonetheless, there remains potential for further improvement. One limitation of our approach is that we segment patch tokens in a fixed proportion, which may not be suitable in all situations. In future work, we plan to explore adaptive proportions or even an adaptive number of groups to improve model performance. Besides, it might be a good idea to improve our segmentation strategy by using advanced segmentation models, such as SAM [18].

References

1. Ali, A., et al.: XCIT: cross-covariance image transformers. Adv. Neural Inf. Process. Syst. **34**, 20014–20027 (2021)
2. Brown, T., et al.: Language models are few-shot learners. Adv. Neural Inf. Process. Syst. **33**, 1877–1901 (2020)
3. Bui, D.V., Kubo, M., Sato, H.: A part-aware attention neural network for cross-view geo-localization between UAV and satellite. J. Rob. Network. Artif. Life **9**(3), 275–284 (2022)
4. Cao, H., et al.: Swin-unet: Unet-like pure transformer for medical image segmentation. arXiv:2105.05537 (2021)
5. Chen, C.F.R., Fan, Q., Panda, R.: Crossvit: cross-attention multi-scale vision transformer for image classification. In: Proceedings of IEEE/CVF International Conference on Computer Vision, pp. 357–366 (2021)
6. Chopra, S., Hadsell, R., LeCun, Y.: Learning a similarity metric discriminatively, with application to face verification. In: IEEE Computer Society Conference on Computer Vision Pattern Recognition, vol. 1, pp. 539–546. IEEE (2005)
7. Chu, X., et al.: Twins: revisiting the design of spatial attention in vision transformers. Adv. Neural Inf. Process. Syst. **34**, 9355–9366 (2021)
8. Dai, M., Hu, J., Zhuang, J., Zheng, E.: A transformer-based feature segmentation and region alignment method for UAV-view geo-localization. IEEE Trans. Circ. Syst. Video Technol. **32**(7), 4376–4389 (2021)
9. Devlin, J., Chang, M.W., Lee, K., Toutanova, K.: Bert: pre-training of deep bidirectional transformers for language understanding. arXiv:1810.04805 (2018)
10. Ding, L., Zhou, J., Meng, L., Long, Z.: A practical cross-view image matching method between UAV and satellite for UAV-based geo-localization. Remote Sens. **13**(1), 47 (2020)
11. Dong, X., et al.: Cswin transformer: a general vision transformer backbone with cross-shaped windows. In: Proceedings of IEEE/CVF Conference on Computer Vision Pattern Recognition, pp. 12124–12134 (2022)
12. Dosovitskiy, A., et al.: An image is worth 16×16 words: transformers for image recognition at scale. arXiv:2010.11929 (2020)
13. Han, K., Xiao, A., Wu, E., Guo, J., Xu, C., Wang, Y.: Transformer in transformer. Adv. Neural Inf. Process. Syst. **34**, 15908–15919 (2021)
14. He, K., Zhang, X., Ren, S., Sun, J.: Deep residual learning for image recognition. In: Proceedings of the IEEE Conference on Computer Vision and Pattern Recognition, pp. 770–778 (2016)
15. Heo, B., Yun, S., Han, D., Chun, S., Choe, J., Oh, S.J.: Rethinking spatial dimensions of vision transformers. In: Proceedings of IEEE/CVF International Conference on Computer Vision, pp. 11936–11945 (2021)
16. Hu, J., Shen, L., Sun, G.: Squeeze-and-excitation networks. In: Proceedings of the IEEE Conference on Computer Vision and Pattern Recognition, pp. 7132–7141 (2018)
17. Hu, S., Feng, M., Nguyen, R.M., Lee, G.H.: Cvm-net: cross-view matching network for image-based ground-to-aerial geo-localization. In: Proceedings of IEEE Conference on Computer Vision Pattern Recognition, pp. 7258–7267 (2018)
18. Kirillov, A., et al.: Segment anything. arXiv:2304.02643 (2023)
19. Lin, J., et al.: Joint representation learning and keypoint detection for cross-view geo-localization. IEEE Trans. Image Process. **31**, 3780–3792 (2022)

20. Lin, T.Y., Cui, Y., Belongie, S., Hays, J.: Learning deep representations for ground-to-aerial geolocalization. In: Proceedings of IEEE Conference on Computer Vision Pattern Recognition, pp. 5007–5015 (2015)
21. Liu, L., Li, H.: Lending orientation to neural networks for cross-view geo-localization. In: Proceedings of IEEE/CVF Conference on Computer Vision Pattern Recognition, pp. 5624–5633 (2019)
22. Liu, Z., et al.: Swin transformer: hierarchical vision transformer using shifted windows. In: Proceedings of IEEE/CVF Conference on Computer Vision Pattern Recognition, pp. 10012–10022 (2021)
23. Lu, Z., Pu, T., Chen, T., Lin, L.: Content-aware hierarchical representation selection for cross-view geo-localization. In: Proceedings of Asian Conference on Computer Vision, pp. 4211–4224 (2022)
24. Luo, W., Li, Y., Urtasun, R., Zemel, R.: Understanding the effective receptive field in deep convolutional neural networks. Adv. Neural Inf. Process. Syst. **29** (2016)
25. Pan, Z., Zhuang, B., Liu, J., He, H., Cai, J.: Scalable vision transformers with hierarchical pooling. In: Proceedings of IEEE/CVF Conference on Computer Vision Pattern Recognition, pp. 377–386 (2021)
26. Paszke, A., et al.: Pytorch: an imperative style, high-performance deep learning library. Adv. Neural Inf. Process. Syst. **32** (2019)
27. Radenović, F., Tolias, G., Chum, O.: Fine-tuning CNN image retrieval with no human annotation. IEEE Trans. Pattern Anal. Mach. Intell. **41**(7), 1655–1668 (2018)
28. Shi, Y., Liu, L., Yu, X., Li, H.: Spatial-aware feature aggregation for image based cross-view geo-localization. Adv. Neural Inf. Process. Syst. **32** (2019)
29. Tian, X., Shao, J., Ouyang, D., Shen, H.T.: UAV-satellite view synthesis for cross-view geo-localization. IEEE Trans. Circuits Syst. Video Technol. **32**(7), 4804–4815 (2021)
30. Toker, A., Zhou, Q., Maximov, M., Leal-Taixé, L.: Coming down to earth: satellite-to-street view synthesis for geo-localization. In: Proceedings of IEEE/CVF Conference on Computer Vision Pattern Recognition, pp. 6488–6497 (2021)
31. Vaswani, A., et al.: Attention is all you need. Adv. Neural Inf. Process. Syst. **30** (2017)
32. Wang, P., et al.: KVT: k-nn attention for boosting vision transformers. In: Avidan, S., Brostow, G., Cisse, M., Farinella, G.M., Hassner, T. (eds.) ECCV 2022, vol. 13684, pp. 285–302. Springer, Heidelberg (2022). https://doi.org/10.1007/978-3-031-20053-3_17
33. Wang, T., et al.: Each part matters: local patterns facilitate cross-view geo-localization. IEEE Trans. Circuits Syst. Video Technol. **32**(2), 867–879 (2021)
34. Wang, W., et al.: Pyramid vision transformer: a versatile backbone for dense prediction without convolutions. In: Proceedings of IEEE/CVF International Conference on Computer Vision, pp. 568–578 (2021)
35. Wang, Z., Cun, X., Bao, J., Zhou, W., Liu, J., Li, H.: Uformer: a general u-shaped transformer for image restoration. In: Proceedings of IEEE/CVF International Conference on Computer Vision, pp. 17683–17693 (2022)
36. Yang, H., Lu, X., Zhu, Y.: Cross-view geo-localization with layer-to-layer transformer. Adv. Neural Inf. Process. Syst. **34**, 29009–29020 (2021)
37. Zhai, M., Bessinger, Z., Workman, S., Jacobs, N.: Predicting ground-level scene layout from aerial imagery. In: Proceedings of IEEE Conference on Computer Vision Pattern Recognition, pp. 867–875 (2017)

38. Zheng, Z., Wei, Y., Yang, Y.: University-1652: a multi-view multi-source benchmark for drone-based geo-localization. In: Proceedings of 28th ACM International Conference on Multimedia, pp. 1395–1403 (2020)
39. Zhou, D., et al.: Deepvit: towards deeper vision transformer. arXiv:2103.11886 (2021)
40. Zhu, S., Shah, M., Chen, C.: Transgeo: transformer is all you need for cross-view image geo-localization. In: Proceedings of IEEE/CVF Conference on Computer Vision Pattern Recognition, pp. 1162–1171 (2022)

Improved YOLOv5 Algorithm for Small Object Detection in Drone Images

Yitong Lin and Yiguang Liu[✉]

Vision and Image Processing Lab, College of Computer Science, Sichuan University, Chengdu 610065, China
liuyg@scu.edu.cn

Abstract. The object detection in the context of drone is a hot topic in the field of computer vision in recent years. In response to the challenge of limited image feature information and the presence of numerous small and densely packed objects in drone-captured images, this paper proposes a novel feature fusion detection model, HTH-YOLOv5, based on YOLOv5. Firstly, we enhance the detection capability of small objects by adding a detection channel from high-resolution feature maps and propose a Hybrid Transformer Head (HTH) that incorporates a hybrid Transformer module, aiming to improve the network's focus on small objects by fusing global and local feature information. Secondly, we introduce a Convolutional Attention Feature Fusion module (CA-FF) based on CBAM. This module dynamically adjusts attention weights for the allocation of original feature maps in both channel and spatial dimensions, aiming to enhance the feature extraction capability for small objects. Finally, to better capture global and contextual information, we introduce the Hybrid Transformer module into the backbone and enhance its original feature fusion method using the CA-FF module. Experiments on the Vis-Drone 2021 dataset demonstrate that, compared to the baseline YOLOv5s model, the improved model shows an increase of 7.2% in mAP_{50} and 6.3% in mAP_{75}. The model trained with an input resolution of 1540×1540 achieves an mAP_{50} of 57.1%, marking a 12.4% improvement over YOLOv5. The improved HTH-YOLOv5 achieves increased accuracy while maintaining a detection speed of 45 FPS, making it more suitable for small object detection in drone scenarios.

Keywords: Drone · Small object detection · Attention mechanism · Feature fusion

1 Introduction

In recent years, with extensive research into artificial intelligence technology, object detection technology in drone captured scenes has found widespread applications in various fields such as transportation, defense, wildlife conservation, and plant protection. In this article, we focus on improving the performance of small object detection in drone-captured images.

© The Author(s), under exclusive license to Springer Nature Singapore Pte Ltd. 2024
F.-L. Zhang and A. Sharf (Eds.): CVM 2024, LNCS 14593, pp. 354–373, 2024.
https://doi.org/10.1007/978-981-97-2092-7_18

Fig. 1. The distribution of objects in images captured by drones. The first, second, and third columns examples respectively illustrate the dense distribution of objects, significant variations in object sizes, and complex backgrounds captured on drone-captured images.

Since the integration of Convolutional Neural Networks (CNN) into object detection in 2014, there has been remarkable progress in this field. Nevertheless, the majority of preceding deep convolutional neural networks were tailored for natural scene images. The detection of small objects is an inevitable challenge in drone scene detection tasks and has consistently posed a difficulty in object detection missions. This is primarily due to the fact that small objects suffer from (1) insufficient image resolution, (2) limited feature information, and (3) a small proportion of the overall image, making their detection more challenging compared to conventional objects. Furthermore, the close clustering and considerable size variations of small objects when viewed from a high altitude, combined with a wide field of vision and intricate geographical factors, lead to the loss of detailed information and insufficient feature extraction. Consequently, this lowers the accuracy of detection, placing greater demands on object detection technology. Some examples in Fig. 1 also intuitively illustrate this issue: the first column displays densely distributed crowds and vehicles in street scenes; the second column shows significant variations in object sizes, even within the same image, with instances of objects appearing larger or smaller depending on their distance from the viewer; the third column demonstrates the wide aerial perspective of the drone, capturing backgrounds that include lakes, roads, houses, and more.

Addressing the aforementioned issues, this paper introduces an improved small object detection model, HTH-YOLOv5, based on YOLOv5 for drone scenarios. In the head section, we first propose a Hybrid Transformer Head (HTH) as the detection module to enhance attention on small object regions, achieving more efficient and accurate prediction capabilities. HTH-YOLOv5 comprises four detection heads designed for detecting micro, small, medium, and large objects, respectively. Subsequently, we incorporate the Convolutional Block Attention

Module (CBAM [26]) into YOLOv5, embedding the CBAM module after each convolutional feature extraction in the backbone network and within the feature pyramid network [15]. Leveraging CBAM, we devise CA-FF to enhance the feature pyramid structure, improving its adaptability to small objects. Furthermore, we propose CAH-Transformer to enhance the feature fusion capability at the end of the backbone network. Compared to YOLOv5s, our improved HTH-YOLOv5 demonstrates superior performance in handling images captured by drones.

The main contributions of this paper are as follows:

1) We propose a Hybrid Transformer Head (HTH) and integrate it into YOLOv5 to capture global and local information.
2) We integrate CBAM into YOLOv5, which is a lightweight and efficient module that can generate attention graphs sequentially along channel and spatial directions.
3) We propose a Convolutional Attention Feature Fusion (CA-FF) module, which can improve the ability of the model to extract features from small objects.
4) We propose the CAH-Transformer module to help further focus the effective feature areas.

The structure of the remaining sections of this paper is as follows: In Sect. 2, we briefly introduce several related works. The Sect. 3 provides a detailed description of our designed HTH-YOLOv5. The Sect. 4 presents the experimental results, and the Sect. 5 concludes the paper.

2   Related Work

2.1   Object Detection

The current mainstream object detection algorithms can be divided into two types: one-stage detector and two-stage detector. The two-stage algorithm requires initially proposing regions of interest (ROI [9]) through selective search method or RPN (Region Proposal Network [9]). These regions represent coarse estimations of where objects might be located, and then a CNN is employed for classification and fine-grained boundary regression. Representative algorithms include: R-CNN [9], SPP-Net [11], Fast R-CNN [8], Faster R-CNN [21], feature pyramid networks (FPN) [15], and Mask R-CNN [10]. The development of two-stage object detection algorithms has been rapid, and detection accuracy continues to improve. However, the inherent architectural limitations pose constraints on detection speed, preventing it from meeting the real-time detection requirements in drone scenarios.

The main difference between one-stage object detection algorithms and two-stage object detection algorithms lies in the fact that the former lacks a candidate region proposal stage, making the training process relatively simpler. One-stage algorithms treat classification and localization as regression problems, generating detection results directly through a single network. This end-to-end detection approach achieves high accuracy and a detection speed of up to 45 frames per second (FPS), meeting the basic requirements for drone scene detection. Representative algorithms include YOLO (You Only Look Once) [18], SSD (Single Shot MultiBox Detector) [25], and RetinaNet [16].

2.2 Small Object Detection

In the context of small object detection research, literature [29] proposed a cascaded sparse query structure to accelerate small object detection in high-resolution images, achieving a 1.0 increase in mAP on the COCO dataset, with an average improvement in high-resolution inference speed by a factor of 3.0. The literature [34] builds upon YOLOv5 by introducing the Transformer Prediction Head (TPH) to replace the original prediction head, proposing the TPH-YOLO model. Additionally, a self-trained classifier is employed to enhance the classification capability for certain confusing categories. The literature [24] conducts pruning experiments on the basis of SSD for model compression, while simultaneously improving feature fusion methods to obtain more beneficial information for detecting small objects. The literature [12] developed a novel lightweight small object segmentation network by integrating various convolutional modules. This approach, combined with clustering algorithms and object feature adjustment strategies, achieved a reduction in parameter count and an improvement in detection accuracy.

Based on the characteristics of drone images and the research difficulties at this stage, literature [33] proposes a Dense Cropping and Local Attention Object Detector Network (DCLANet) specifically designed for small objects in drone scenarios. This approach enhances the network's focus on small objects by incorporating dense cropping and local attention mechanisms. The literature [14] introduced a bidirectional feature pyramid (BiFPN) to enhance the feature extraction ability of small targets in the image, by adding a small target detection layer based on YOLOv5 and fusing feature information from different scales. In order to address the issue of semantic loss during the detection of small targets, literature [7] incorporated the convolutional block attention module (CBAM) into YOLOv5 and also introduced a small target detection layer. To retain more feature information of small targets, literature [17] incorporated the efficient channel attention (ECA) module into the backbone network of YOLOv5l and replaced the sampling method with transposed convolution. However, the enhanced model based on YOLOv5l possesses a considerable number of parameters, which poses challenges for deploying it on edge devices like UAVs. Literature [28] proposes the magnifying glass method for image preprocessing to increase the feature information that can be used for learning. Literature [30] proposes a fast and accurate real-time small target detection system based on a two-stage architecture, which combines traditional algorithms and deep learning algorithms. Literature [22] proposes a new method based on graph neural network (GNN) to refine the detection results generated by the target detector. However, due to the low confidence score, some real predictions are easy to be selected as negative samples. In the literature [3], based on YOLOv7, a large convolutional kernel architecture is used to design the backbone network of the model in order to expand the effective sensitivity field of the convolutional model, but the additional computation caused by the large kernel architecture still needs to be further reduced.

From the above studies, it can be observed that deep learning holds significant research value in small object detection and has achieved notable results. However, further research is warranted to address small object detection in the context of drone scenarios, adapting solutions for more practical application scenarios.

2.3   YOLOv5

The YOLO series, representing a typical example of single-stage object detection algorithms, includes YOLOv1 through YOLOv8. YOLOv3 [20], an improvement upon YOLOv1 [18] and YOLOv2 [19], replaced the base classification network with Darknet-53, leading to a significant improvement in inference speed compared to R-CNN [9] and Fast R-CNN [8].

Combining various improvements, Bochkovskiy et al. proposed YOLOv4 [1], which can be trained on a regular GPU (1080Ti), meeting real-time requirements and deployable in production environments. YOLOv5 incorporates the advantages and addresses the drawbacks of previous versions, further enhancing both detection accuracy and speed. Meituan's Visual AI Department introduced YOLOv6 [5], a detector without anchor points. Wang et al. introduced YOLOv7 [4], featuring the E-ELAN and MPConv structures, achieving speeds and accuracy surpassing all known object detectors within the range of 5 FPS to 160 FPS. Subsequently, Alibaba Group released DAMO-YOLO [27], with the best model achieving 50.0% AP at 233 FPS on NVIDIA V100. This year, Ultralytics released YOLOv8, an anchor-free model that accelerates the speed of Non-Maximum Suppression (NMS).

YOLOv5 comprises three parts: the backbone, neck, and head, as illustrated in Fig. 2. The backbone is primarily responsible for extracting features from input images, the neck handles multi-scale feature fusion on the feature maps, and transmits these feature details to the head. The head receives features from the neck and performs regression predictions. YOLOv5 has four versions: YOLOv5s, YOLOv5m, YOLOv5l, and YOLOv5x. These versions share a consistent structure but correspond to different network widths and depths. Among them, YOLOv5s has the smallest network parameters, the fastest speed, and the lowest AP accuracy.

To validate the effectiveness of the algorithm in terms of both speed and accuracy and to meet the requirements for real-time detection on drone and deployment on mobile devices, YOLOv5s was chosen as the baseline model for improvement in this paper.

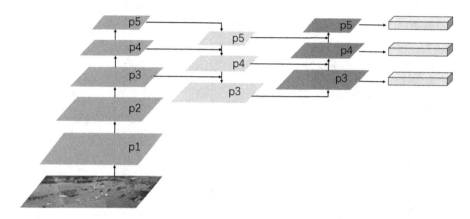

Fig. 2. The YOLOv5 architecture consists of three components: the backbone, neck, and head.

3   HTH-YOLOv5

The structure diagram of the improved model HTH-YOLOv5 proposed in this paper is shown in Fig. 3, and the improvement measures of specific modules are introduced in the following sections to make the model more suitable for small objects and drone scenarios.

3.1   Hybrid Transformer Head

In the small object detection task of drone scenarios, the complex background is easy to block the small object, which interferes with the model's understanding of effective object and background. In recent years, models based on Self-Attention structures have gained quite good performance in the field of computer vision. The Self-Attention structure adopts the weighted average operation based on the input feature context, and the similarity function is used to dynamically calculate the attention weight between the relevant pixel pairs, so that the attention module can self-adapt to pay attention to different regions in the global and capture more effective features. This weight distribution allows the model to focus more on the effective object rather than the irrelevant background, so it is suitable for capturing the features of the effective object in the complex background. The Self-Attention structure calculates the self-attention weight as follows:

$$Z = Attention(Q, K, V) = softmax(\frac{QK^T}{\sqrt{d_K}})V \tag{1}$$

Where, Z denotes the self-attention weight, QK^T describes the calculation of the correlation degree between each image block and other image blocks, $\sqrt{d_K}$ describes the scaling factor, the weight coefficient is normalized by softmax, and finally the weight coefficient and V are weighted and summed to obtain the self-attention weight matrix of each image block.

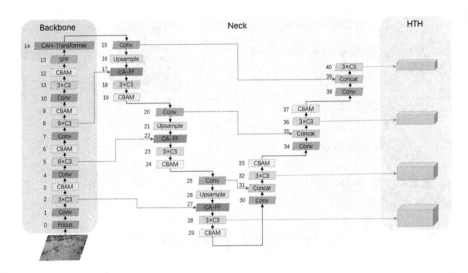

Fig. 3. The architecture of the HTH-YOLOv5. The number of each block is marked with a number on the left side of the block.

In addition, Q, K and V are three matrices with dimensions d_Q, d_K and d_V respectively (generally set $d_Q = d_K = d_V$), which can be calculated by multiplying the input sequence X by three random initialization matrices W^Q, W^K and W^V respectively:

$$Q = XW^Q, K = XW^K, V = XW^V \tag{2}$$

Inspired by high efficiency hybrid transformers [23], this paper proposes a Hybrid Transformer Head (HTH) based on Self-Attention for detection. The Hybrid Transformer module is divided into two sub-layers. The first layer captures the global context with multi-head attention block, introduces the convolutional layer to extract the local context, and then aggregates the global and local context to obtain a stronger feature representation. The second layer is a feedforward neural network, which is mainly composed of a multi-layer perceptron (MLP). LayerNorm is applied before each sublayer and DropPath is applied after each sublayer. The comparison of the structure of the standard Transformer module and the Hybrid Transformer module is shown in Fig. 4.

The main module of the hybrid Transformer module is the global-local attention structure, which is a hybrid structure that uses linear multi-head self-attention to capture the global context and convolutional layers to extract the local context. Finally, an addition operation is applied to the global context and local context to extract the global-local context. The details are shown in Fig. 5.

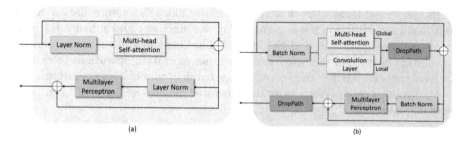

Fig. 4. (a) Standard Transformer module and (b) Hybrid Transformer module

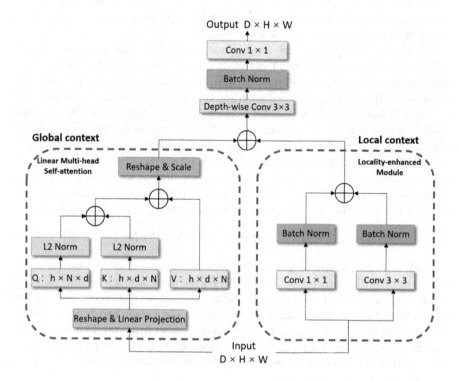

Fig. 5. Global-local attention structure of the Hybrid Transformer module

Where, H and W represent the resolution of the feature map, D and h represent the number of channels and the number of heads, respectively.

$$N = H \times W \tag{3}$$

$$d = D/h \tag{4}$$

In the global-local attention structure, the global structure uses a linear multi-head self-attention mechanism to improve efficiency and enhance the ability of sequence modeling, and the local enhancement module uses two parallel convolution layers and then performs batch normalization operations to extract the local context. Further deep convolution, batch normalization operations, and 1×1 convolution are performed on the generated global-local context to enhance generalization.

3.2   Convolutional Attention Feature Fusion Module

In order to extract and fuse the features of small projects effectively, a Convolutional Attention Feature Fusion (CA-FF) module based on CBAM [26] is designed from the perspective of feature fusion.

CBAM is a simple and effective attention module that is trained end-to-end and can be integrated into most CNN architectures. CBAM consists of two main modules: the Channel Attention Module (CAM) and the Spatial Attention Module (SAM). CAM pays more attention to semantic features. For feature map Y, whose input size is $H \times W \times C$, CAM will use average pooling to aggregate spatial information and maximum pooling to obtain more detailed object feature information. By combining these two pooling methods, CAM can reduce the computation of feature maps and improve the expression of the network. The two one-dimensional vectors obtained after pooling are calculated at the fully connected layer, and 1×1 convolution kernel is used when the weights are shared between the eigenvectors. The process of generating channel attention Z_c is:

$$Z_c = sigmoid(MLP(AvgPool(Y)) + MLP(MaxPool(Y))) \qquad (5)$$

SAM pays more attention to the location of features in the feature map, that is, the region with many effective features. By means of average pooling and maximum pooling, SAM compresses the feature map Y_c in channel dimension, and then obtains two two-dimensional feature maps. Then these two two-dimensional feature maps are concat together to get a feature map with two channels. Finally, a hidden layer containing a single convolution kernel is used to convolve the feature graph, and the process of generating the spatial attention weight Z_s through sigmoid operation is as follows:

$$Z_s = sigmoid(conv(AvgPool(Y), MaxPool(Y))) \qquad (6)$$

When given a feature map, CBAM can independently infer attention maps along both channel and spatial dimensions. Subsequently, it refines features adaptively by multiplying the attention map with the input feature map. According to experiments in the paper [26], integrating CBAM into various models on different classification and detection datasets significantly improves the performance, demonstrating the effectiveness of this module.

The core idea of the CA-FF module proposed in this paper is to add attention mechanism on the basis of the feature fusion structure, and carry out feature refinement from the two dimensions of channel and space, so as to improve the feature extraction ability of the model. The structure diagram of CA-FF module is shown in Fig. 6, and the contents in the dotted box are the original feature fusion structure. The feature fusion process of CA-FF module for feature maps of different scales can be expressed as:

$$Z = CBAM(X \oplus Y) \otimes X + (1 - CBAM(X \oplus Y)) \otimes Y \qquad (7)$$

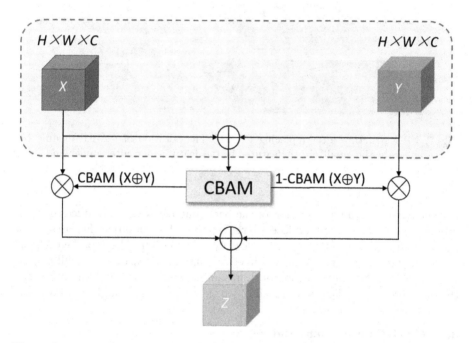

Fig. 6. Structure of the CA-FF module. X and Y are the feature maps before processing. Z is the feature map after processing.

Where, Z denotes the feature map after feature fusion processing; X denotes the low-level high-resolution feature map in the feature pyramid; Y denotes the feature map that is obtained by up-sampling the high-level, high-semantic feature map; $CBAM(X \oplus Y)$ represents the attention weight matrix obtained from the CBAM module after performing an element-wise sum of X and Y.

In this paper, CA-FF module is used to replace Concat module in YOLOv5 feature pyramid network, and the replaced structure diagram is shown in Fig. 7.

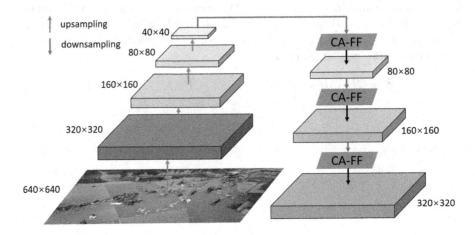

Fig. 7. FPN structure after replacing CA-FF. The addition of CA-FF module can better integrate the small object features in the feature map after upper and lower sampling.

The down-sampling operation of the backbone network will reduce the resolution of the feature map and lose a large number of small object features, while the upsampling can not bring more feature information. The modified feature fusion module is designed to more effectively integrate features of small objects within the feature map following both upsampling and downsampling processes, thereby minimizing the loss of small object features during the fusion process.

3.3   CAH-Transformer Module

This paper introduces further improvements to the Hybrid Transformer module by replacing the Hybrid Transformer's residual connection feature fusion module with a CA-FF module. Figure 8 illustrates the structure of the proposed CAH-Transformer module. By inserting the CAH-Transformer module at the end of the YOLOv5 backbone network, it further enhances the network's feature fusion capabilities across both channel and spatial dimensions.

4   Experiment

4.1   Data Sets and Evaluation Metrics

The model proposed in this paper is implemented in Pytorch 1.8.1, and the epoch is trained 300 times on NVIDIA RTX 3080Ti GPU with an initial learning rate

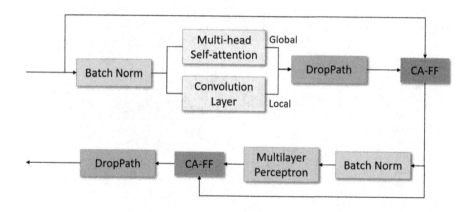

Fig. 8. Structure of the CAH-Transformer module. Compared with the Hybrid Transformer module, two feature fusion modules are replaced with CA-FF.

of 0.01. The experiment was conducted on the VisDrone2021 dataset and COCO dataset.

VisDrone2021 dataset was collected by the AISKYEYE team at the Machine Learning and Data Mining Laboratory of Tianjin University, and the baseline dataset included 288 video clips consisting of 261,908 frames and 10,209 still images. The dataset was collected using different drones in different scenarios, weather and lighting conditions, and included 10 types of images including pedestrian, people, bicycle, car, van, truck, tricycle, awning-tricycle, bus and motor. Figure 9(a) shows the number of labels for each category. The horizontal and vertical coordinates in Fig. 9(a) represent the number of label instances and label categories, respectively. The horizontal and vertical coordinates in Fig. 9(b) respectively represent the width and height of the label box. The lower left corner of the figure has a high aggregation degree, indicating that the data set contains a high content of small objects, which can fully represent the general situation of object size in the drone capture scene.

MS COCO (Microsoft common objects in context) is one of the most authoritative and high-profile competitions in the field of machine vision. The dataset, which is mostly taken from complex everyday scenes, contains more than 330,000 images covering 80 different target categories, including people, animals, vehicles, food, furniture and more. COCO datasets are widely used in computer vision research and algorithm evaluation, providing an important benchmark for tasks such as object detection, segmentation, and key point detection.

To validate the performance of the proposed improved algorithm, this study employs mAP_{50}, mAP_{75}, $mAP_{50:95}$, Params, GFLOPs and Frames Per Second (FPS) as evaluation metrics for model performance. mAP_{50} and mAP_{75} represent the average detection accuracy of all object categories at IoU thresholds of 0.5 and 0.75, respectively. mAP_{50} reflects the algorithm's comprehensive detection capability for different object categories, while mAP_{75} demonstrates the

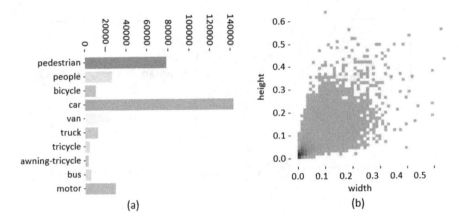

Fig. 9. VisDrone2021 data set (a) distribution of the number of labels in different categories (b) distribution of label sizes

algorithm's ability in bounding box regression. $mAP_{50:95}$ calculates the average accuracy for all IoU thresholds from 0.5 to 0.95 with a step size of 0.05. FPS stands for Frames Per Second, representing the number of frames that the algorithm can detect per second. It reflects the detection speed or real-time capability of the algorithm. Since the images captured in drone scenarios often have high resolutions, and the detection speed decreases with higher resolutions, the FPS measurements in this paper are conducted at a high resolution of 1504×1504.

4.2   Comparison with Existing Methods

To validate the superiority of the improved object detection algorithm proposed in this paper compared to other algorithms, we conducted comparative experiments with various advanced object detection algorithms, and the specific results are presented in Table 1. First, we compare with some classical object detection algorithms, then with YOLOv3, YOLOv4 and YOLOv5 models, and finally with the latest small object detection models to verify the progressiveness of our proposed method. Conclusions drawn from the data in Table 1 indicate that our proposed algorithm exhibits excellent performance in object detection accuracy, with mAP50 surpassing YOLOv4 by 14.1%, reaching 57.1%, and surpassing YOLOv5 by 12.4%. Moreover, our accuracy surpasses that of the most recent papers [17] and [6]. Furthermore, in terms of detection speed, our algorithm achieves an FPS_{1504} of 45, which is twice that of Faster-RCNN, 45.2% higher than YOLOv3, and 28.6% higher than both YOLOv4 and YOLOv5, only slightly lower than the performance reported in paper [6]. This suggests that the algorithm proposed in this paper not only demonstrates a significant improvement in detection accuracy but also has a good performance in real-time, making it more suitable for object detection tasks in drone capture scenarios.

Table 1. Comparison experiments of different object detection algorithms.

Methods	mAP_{50} (%)	mAP_{75} (%)	$mAP_{50:95}$ (%)	FPS_{1504}
RetinaNet	28.7	11.6	11.8	–
RetfineDet [32]	28.8	14.1	14.9	–
Cascade-RCNN [2]	31.9	15.6	16.1	–
FPN	32.2	14.9	16.5	–
Light-RCNN [31]	32.8	15.1	16.5	–
Faster-RCNN	33.2	15.2	17.0	15
CornerNet [13]	34.1	15.9	17.4	33
YOLOv3	41.7	22.9	24.5	31
YOLOv4	43.0	25.2	24.9	35
YOLOv5	44.7	26.8	26.4	35
paper [17]	52.2	–	32.4	–
paper [6]	54.5	33.1	32.0	46
HTH-YOLOv5	**57.1**	**35.3**	**34.7**	45

4.3 Ablation Experiment

In order to verify the effectiveness of HTH, CA-FF and CAH-Transformer modules proposed in this paper, ablation experiments are conducted to evaluate the influence of different modules on the performance of object detection algorithms under the same experimental conditions. The results of ablation experiments are shown in Table 2.

Table 2. The ablation experiments of HTH, CA-FF and CAH-Transformer modules proposed in this paper are carried out, and the original Transformer, CBAM and $CBAM(X \oplus Y)$ are also included.

Model	Methods						mAP_{50} (%)	mAP_{75} (%)	$mAP_{50:95}$ (%)	Params(M)	GFLOPs
	HTH	CA-FF	CAH-Transformer	CBAM	Transformer	$CBAM(X \oplus Y)$					
A							33.0	14.8	16.5	7.0371	15.9
B	✓						36.6	17.4	18.4	8.4112	19.0
C		✓					34.5	16.2	17.7	7.4098	17.0
D			✓				36.1	17.1	18.2	8.4464	19.1
E				✓			35.6	16.8	17.9	8.3998	19.2
F						✓	33.7	15.8	17.3	7.2230	16.4
G	✓	✓					38.3	18.6	19.5	8.7831	19.8
H		✓	✓				37.7	18.2	19.4	8.8184	20.0
I	✓		✓				39.8	19.6	20.7	9.8205	21.4
J	✓	✓	✓				41.7	20.3	21.4	10.1925	22.2
K	✓	✓	✓	✓			42.3	20.7	21.7	10.7502	23.3

In the ablation experiment, Ultralytics 5.0 version of YOLOv5s was selected as the benchmark model. The input image resolution was 640×640. After training for 300 epochs, the results were shown in model A. Model B uses the HTH module in the detection head, which introduces some computation, but the mAP_{50},

mAP_{75} and $mAP_{50:95}$ are respectively 3.6%, 2.6% and 1.9% higher than the baseline of YOLOv5s, indicating that the HTH proposed in this paper can be used as the detection head to better improve the detection effect. The CA-FF module proposed in this paper is added to the neck network in model C. Compared with model A, mAP_{50}, mAP_{75} and $mAP_{50:95}$ are 1.5%, 1.4% and 1.2% higher than the baseline of YOLOv5s, respectively, reflecting the superiority of CA-FF module in feature fusion. After introducing the CAH-Transformer module into the model D backbone, the detection accuracy significantly improved, showing a 3.1% increase compared to YOLOv5s, which demonstrates the effectiveness of the CAH-Transformer. However, the parameter count increased by 1.4093 million and GFLOPs increased by 3.2. The analysis indicates that the CAH-Transformer itself requires a large amount of computing resources to calculate the correlation weights among each pixel in every feature map. Additionally, the detection speed exhibits a clear negative correlation with the number of parameters and the computational complexity. Therefore, considering the practical application scenario, this paper focuses on reducing computational costs, improving training efficiency, and enhancing the accuracy and speed of the model detection. To achieve these goals, the proposed approach only integrates the module at the end of the backbone network. To demonstrate the superiority of our proposed CAH-Transformer, we designed the model E. Model E differs from model D only in that the attention module at the end of the trunk uses the original Transformer. It can be seen from the data that the mAP_{50} of model D is 36.1%, 0.5% higher than the 35.6% of model E, which can prove that our proposed CAH-Transformer is more helpful to model detection effect in context acquisition ability. Compared to model C, the feature fusion module in model F is simply replaced by $CBAM(X \oplus Y)$, resulting in a significant decrease in accuracy. This further demonstrates the excellent feature fusion capability of the CA-FF module proposed in this paper. We combine the proposed modules with each other to test the effectiveness of the modules proposed in this paper. Model G uses HTH and CA-FF. Compared to models B and C, which solely utilize individual modules, model G exhibits significant improvements in mAP_{50}, mAP_{75} and $mAP_{50:95}$. This enhancement more effectively demonstrates the efficacy of embedding HTH and CA-FF modules within the overall network. Model H is embedded with CA-FF and CAH-Transformer in the network, and the effect is further improved compared with models C and D, indicating that the fusion of these two modules is better than the single use. Model I uses both HTH module and CAH-Transformer and obtains 39.8% mAP_{50}, which proves the excellent effect of the combination of the two modules. Then, we tested the model with simultaneous use of the three modules, and the results, as demonstrated by model J, surpassed those of all previously mentioned models. This suggests that integrating the three modules proposed in this paper yields superior detection performance. Finally, we added some CBAM modules to the backbone and neck networks. As a lightweight and effective attention module, after embedding CBAM, the effect of the model was further improved. In the final model K, the mAP_{50}, mAP_{75} and $mAP_{50:95}$ of the network size s were 42.3%, 20.7% and 21.7%, respectively. Improvements over YOLOv5s baseline were 9.3%, 5.9% and 5.2%, respectively.

4.4 Experimental Analysis of COCO Dataset

In order to further verify the performance of the model proposed in this paper, we conducted experiments on the COCO dataset, and compared the experimental results with those of YOLOv5s, SSD, YOLOv4-Tiny, YOLOX-Tiny, YOLOv6-N, and YOLOv7-Tiny. Detailed results are shown in Table 3. Although our algorithm introduces a certain amount of parameters and computation, it still enables it to meet most lightweight target detection tasks and mobile deployment requirements. The experimental results show that at $mAP_{50:95}$, our algorithm is obviously superior to other target detection algorithms, which indicates that our method has certain advantages in performance.

Table 3. Experimental analysis of COCO dataset.

Methods	Params (M)	GFLOPs	$mAP_{50:95}$ (%)
YOLOv5s (2020)	7.2	16.5	37.2
SSD	36.1	–	25.1
YOLOv4-Tiny (2022)	6.1	–	21.7
YOLOX-Tiny (2021)	6.5	5.1	32.8
YOLOv6-N (2022)	4.3	11.7	35.9
YOLOv7-Tiny (2022)	6.2	13.7	37.4
HTH-YOLOv5	10.8	23.3	**37.5**

4.5 Algorithm Effectiveness Analysis

In order to directly reflect the detection effect of the improved algorithm in the actual scene, this paper uses four representative pictures in the VisDrone2021 test set for testing, and makes visual comparison with the test results of YOLOv5. As shown in Fig. 10, the first row is the test result of HTH-YOLOv5 in this paper, and the second row is the test result of YOLOv5. These four pictures correspond to different detection difficulties. The first column shows the scene with large changes in light. There are a large number of pedestrians in both bright and dim areas, accompanied by partial occlusion. In this figure, (a1) shows that the algorithm in this paper is less affected by light and can accurately identify pedestrians and some bicycles in distant dim areas, while (a2) has many defects in the detection of pedestrians in the upper part and many missed detection of pedestrians in the right side. The second column shows the overhead shooting perspective. There are some vehicles and many pedestrians on the way, and the pixels occupied by pedestrians are very small. It can be seen from (b1) that for pedestrians, the algorithm in this paper can almost recognize them, which shows that the algorithm in this paper has outstanding detection ability for small objects. Compared with (b1), (b2) has lost many detection boxes for pedestrians. The third column is a high-altitude image of the street scene, with a large number of vehicles of different models distributed on the street and a large number of trees to shield it. Compared with (c2), (c1) has better anti-occlusion ability and can accurately identify pedestrians riding in the middle and rear, indicating that the algorithm in this paper can better handle occlusion and small object scenes. The fourth column is a blurry and distorted image, possibly caused by the shaking of the drone. For this graph, (d1) can still perform well on fuzzy objects in the graph, indicating that the algorithm in this paper has certain robustness and can better cope with actual scenes. In general, although the algorithm introduced a certain amount of computation, FPS can be maintained at 45 to meet the real-time needs. In addition, it can be seen from the detection effect diagram that the proposed algorithm has a good performance in the drone capture scenario, and the increased calculation amount is also worthwhile. Therefore, the algorithm in this paper is more suitable for the application and deployment of drones in practical scenarios.

Fig. 10. Comparison of detection results of HTH-YOLOv5 and YOLOv5 on Vis-Drone2021.

5   Conclusion

This paper presents an enhanced approach based on YOLOv5 to boost the accuracy of detecting small objects within drone-captured scenarios. We propose the HTH detection head in YOLOv5 based on a Hybrid Transformer to enhance focus on small objects. Subsequently, we introduce the CBAM module and propose the Convolutional Attention Feature Fusion module (CA-FF) based on it to further improve feature fusion efficiency. Finally, we use CA-FF to enhance the structure of the Hybrid Transformer in the backbone, enabling better capture of global and contextual information. The effectiveness and real-time performance of these improvements are validated on the VisDrone2021 dataset. Experimental results demonstrate that HTH-YOLOv5, along with its modules, achieves a higher mAP for object detection in drone scenarios compared to the original YOLOv5s. The algorithm in this paper introduces a certain amount of computation, which can continue to carry out the research on the lightweight of the improved YOLOv5 network.

Acknowledgments. This work is supported by NSFC under grants 61860206007 and U19A2071, as well as the funding from Sichuan University under grant 2020SCUNG205.

References

1. Bochkovskiy, A., Wang, C.Y., Liao, H.Y.M.: YOLOv4: optimal speed and accuracy of object detection. arXiv arXiv:2004.10934 (2020). https://doi.org/10.48550/arxiv.2004.10934
2. Cai, Z., Vasconcelos, N.: Cascade R-CNN: delving into high quality object detection. In: 2018 IEEE/CVF Conference on Computer Vision and Pattern Recognition, pp. 6154–6162 (2018). https://doi.org/10.1109/CVPR.2018.00644
3. Chen, H., Wang, J., Li, J., Qiu, Y., Zhang, D.: Small object detection for drone image based on advanced YOLOv7. In: 2023 42nd Chinese Control Conference (CCC), pp. 7453–7458 (2023). https://doi.org/10.23919/CCC58697.2023.10239784
4. Wang, C.Y., Bochkovskiy, A., Liao, H.Y.M. : YOLOv: trainable bag-of-freebies sets new state-of-the-art for real-time object detectors. arXiv arXiv:2207.02696 (2022). https://doi.org/10.48550/arxiv.2207.02696
5. Li, C., et al.: YOLOv6: a single-stage object detection framework for industrial applications. arXiv arXiv:2209.02976 (2022). https://doi.org/10.48550/arxiv.2209.02976
6. Feng, Z., Xie, Z., Bao, Z., Chen, K.: Real-time dense small object detection algorithm for UAV based on improved YOLOv5. Acta Aeronauticaet Astronautica Sinica **44**(7), 327106 (2023)
7. Gao, T., Wushouer, M., Tuerhong, G.: Small object detection method based on improved YOLOv5. In: 2022 International Conference on Virtual Reality, Human-Computer Interaction and Artificial Intelligence (VRHCIAI), pp. 144–149 (2022). https://doi.org/10.1109/VRHCIAI57205.2022.00032
8. Girshick, R.: Fast R-CNN. In: International Conference on Computer Vision (2015). https://doi.org/10.1109/ICCV.2015.169
9. Girshick, R., Donahue, J., Darrell, T., Malik, J.: Rich feature hierarchies for accurate object detection and semantic segmentation. IEEE Computer Society (2014). https://doi.org/10.48550/arxiv.1311.2524
10. He, K., Gkioxari, G., Dollár, P., Girshick, R.: Mask R-CNN. IEEE Trans. Pattern Anal. Mach. Intell. (2017). https://doi.org/10.1109/ICCV.2017.322
11. He, K., Zhang, X., Ren, S., Sun, J.: Spatial pyramid pooling in deep convolutional networks for visual recognition. IEEE Trans. Pattern Anal. Mach. Intell. **37**, 1904–1916 (2015). https://doi.org/10.1109/TPAMI.2015.2389824
12. Kou, R., et al.: LW-IRSTNet: lightweight infrared small target segmentation network and application deployment. IEEE Trans. Geosci. Remote Sens. **61**, 1–13 (2023). https://doi.org/10.1109/TGRS.2023.3314586
13. Law, H., Deng, J.: CornerNet: detecting objects as paired keypoints. Int. J. Comput. Vis. **128**(3), 642–656 (2020). https://doi.org/10.1007/s11263-019-01204-1
14. Li, S., Yang, X., Lin, X., Zhang, Y., Wu, J.: Real-time vehicle detection from UAV aerial images based on improved YOLOv5. Sensors **23**(12) (2023). https://doi.org/10.3390/s23125634. https://www.mdpi.com/1424-8220/23/12/5634

15. Lin, T.Y., Dollár, P., Girshick, R., He, K., Hariharan, B., Belongie, S.: Feature pyramid networks for object detection. arXiv e-prints (2016). https://doi.org/10.1109/CVPR.2017.106

16. Lin, T.Y., Goyal, P., Girshick, R., He, K., Dollár, P.: Focal loss for dense object detection. In: 2017 IEEE International Conference on Computer Vision (ICCV), pp. 2999–3007 (2017). https://doi.org/10.1109/ICCV.2017.324

17. Liu, S., Liang, P., Duan, Y., Zhang, Y., Feng, J.: Small target detection for unmanned aerial vehicle images based on YOLOv5l. In: 2022 10th International Conference on Information Systems and Computing Technology (ISCTech), pp. 210–214 (2022). https://doi.org/10.1109/ISCTech58360.2022.00042

18. Redmon, J., Divvala, S., Girshick, R., Farhadi, A.: You only look once: Unified, real-time object detection. In: Computer Vision & Pattern Recognition (2016). https://doi.org/10.1109/cvpr.2016.91

19. Redmon, J., Farhadi, A.: YOLO9000: better, faster, stronger. In: 2017 IEEE Conference on Computer Vision and Pattern Recognition (CVPR), pp. 6517–6525 (2017). https://doi.org/10.1109/CVPR.2017.690

20. Redmon, J., Farhadi, A.: YOLOv3: an incremental improvement. arXiv e-prints (2018). https://doi.org/10.48550/arxiv.1804.02767

21. Ren, S., He, K., Girshick, R., Sun, J.: Faster R-CNN: towards real-time object detection with region proposal networks. IEEE Trans. Pattern Anal. Mach. Intell. **39**(6), 1137–1149 (2017). https://doi.org/10.1109/TPAMI.2016.2577031

22. Tang, Z., Liu, Y., Shang, Y.: A new GNN-based object detection method for multiple small objects in aerial images. In: 2023 IEEE/ACIS 23rd International Conference on Computer and Information Science (ICIS), pp. 14–19 (2023). https://doi.org/10.1109/ICIS57766.2023.10210246

23. Wang, L., Fang, S., Zhang, C., Li, R., Duan, C.: Efficient hybrid transformer: learning global-local context for urban scence segmentation. arXiv arXiv:2109.08937 (2021). https://doi.org/10.48550/arXiv.2109.08937

24. Wang, Q., Zhang, H., Hong, X., Zhou, Q.: Small object detection based on modified FSSD and model compression. In: 2021 IEEE 6th International Conference on Signal and Image Processing (ICSIP), pp. 88–92 (2021). https://doi.org/10.1109/ICSIP52628.2021.9688896

25. Liu, W., et al.: SSD: single shot multibox detector. In: Leibe, B., Matas, J., Sebe, N., Welling, M. (eds.) ECCV 2016. LNCS, vol. 9905, pp. 21–37. Springer, Cham (2016). https://doi.org/10.1007/978-3-319-46448-0_2

26. Woo, S., Park, J., Lee, J.-Y., Kweon, I.S.: CBAM: convolutional block attention module. In: Ferrari, V., Hebert, M., Sminchisescu, C., Weiss, Y. (eds.) ECCV 2018. LNCS, vol. 11211, pp. 3–19. Springer, Cham (2018). https://doi.org/10.1007/978-3-030-01234-2_1

27. Xu, X., Jiang, Y., Chen, W., Huang, Y., Zhang, Y., Sun, X.: DAMO-YOLO: a report on real-time object detection design. arXiv arXiv:2211.15444 (2023). https://doi.org/10.48550/arxiv.2211.15444

28. Yan, X., Shen, B., Li, H.: Small objects detection method for UAVs aerial image based on YOLOv5s. In: 2023 IEEE 6th International Conference on Electronic Information and Communication Technology (ICEICT), pp. 61–66 (2023). https://doi.org/10.1109/ICEICT57916.2023.10245156

29. Yang, C., Huang, Z., Wang, N.: QueryDet: cascaded sparse query for accelerating high-resolution small object detection. In: 2022 IEEE/CVF Conference on Computer Vision and Pattern Recognition (CVPR), pp. 13658–13667 (2022). https://doi.org/10.1109/CVPR52688.2022.01330

30. Yu, M., Leung, H.: Small-object detection for UAV-based images. In: 2023 IEEE International Systems Conference (SysCon), pp. 1–6 (2023). https://doi.org/10.1109/SysCon53073.2023.10131084

31. Li, Z., Peng, C., Yu, G., Zhang, X., Deng, Y., Sun, J.: Light-head R-CNN: in defense of two-stage object detector. arXiv arXiv:1711.07264 (2017). https://doi.org/10.48550/arxiv.1711.07264

32. Zhang, S., Wen, L., Bian, X., Lei, Z., Li, S.Z.: Single-shot refinement neural network for object detection. In: 2018 IEEE/CVF Conference on Computer Vision and Pattern Recognition (2018). https://doi.org/10.1109/CVPR.2018.00442

33. Zhang, X., Feng, Y., Zhang, S., Wang, N., Mei, S.: Finding nonrigid tiny person with densely cropped and local attention object detector networks in low-altitude aerial images. IEEE J. Sel. Top. Appl. Earth Observ. Remote Sens. **15**, 4371–4385 (2022). https://doi.org/10.1109/JSTARS.2022.3175498

34. Zhu, X., Lyu, S., Wang, X., Zhao, Q.: TPH-YOLOv5: improved YOLOv5 based on transformer prediction head for object detection on drone-captured scenarios. In: 2021 IEEE/CVF International Conference on Computer Vision Workshops (ICCVW), pp. 2778–2788 (2021). https://doi.org/10.1109/ICCVW54120.2021.00312

Author Index

Printed in the United States
by Baker & Taylor Publisher Services